I0109994

"Rockhill's illuminating and original work offers a crucial historical understanding of twentieth-century critical thought."
—SUCHETANA CHATTOPADHYAY, AUTHOR, *VOICES OF KOMAGATA MARU*

"Rockhill's book meticulously deconstructs the age-old myth that Western Marxism represents a radical departure from capitalism and imperialism. Instead, we are compelled to reckon with the painful reality that opportunistic Marxist academics are servants of Western imperialism posing no threat to the bourgeois order, but are cyphers of repression operating in the guise of scholarly respectability. Rockhill's detailed account compels us to revisit more than 50 years of twisted Marxist prattle purveying unscientific stupor upon generations of sincere students who reproduce and sustain imperialism and capitalist exploitation under the pretense of Marxism."
—IMMANUEL NESS, AUTHOR, *MIGRATION AS ECONOMIC IMPERIALISM*

"From a farm in Kansas, Rockhill went seeking enlightenment in Paris, becoming an acolyte of empire, until discovering it to be an imaginary la-la land, paralyzing explanation of actual historical events. From there, he set out to map the maze of knowledge production in which the military-industrial-academic complex has adopted a two-pronged strategy in relation to Marxism. Its preferred line of attack was to discredit it altogether. However, recognizing its attraction, it also promoted an anticommunist version of Marxism to reintegrate potentially insurgent elements. Seeing this as a conflict that forces us to take sides, Rockhill is a frontline warrior in this intellectual world war. He marshals both philosophical argument and empirical archival research to make his case, revealing the extent to which such radical recuperators as the Frankfurt School have been directly funded and promoted by the capitalist state and its cultural apparatus. This, along with two further books in a trilogy, is essential reading for anyone serious about the historiography of Marxism within the political economy of knowledge of our times."
—HELENA SHEEHAN, AUTHOR, *UNTIL WE FALL*

Who Paid the Pipers of Western Marxism?

THE INTELLECTUAL WORLD WAR
MARXISM VERSUS THE IMPERIAL THEORY INDUSTRY
VOLUME I

by GABRIEL ROCKHILL

FORTHCOMING VOLUMES
Volume II: *French Theory Made in USA*
Volume III: *Radical Theory's Infantile Disorder*

MR

MONTHLY REVIEW PRESS
New York

Library of Congress Cataloging-in-Publication data
available from the publisher.

ISBN 978-1-68590-134-9 paper
ISBN 978-1-68590-135-6 cloth

MONTHLY REVIEW PRESS | NEW YORK
www.monthlyreview.org

Typeset in Minion Pro

5 4 3 2

Contents

Psychological Warfare is a weapon. As the airplane, the 155 millimeter gun, the Patton Tank, and the bazooka are weapons, so also is psychological warfare.

—STUDY FOR THE PSYCHOLOGICAL STRATEGY BOARD OF
THE U.S. GOVERNMENT[1]

Psychological strategy is not . . . a separate course of action, but . . . an integral component of all our policies and programs, economic, military, and political.

—PANEL REPORT FOR THE U.S. PSYCHOLOGICAL STRATEGY
BOARD PREPARED BY C.D. JACKSON (*TIME*),
HENRY KISSINGER (HARVARD), PHILIP MOSELY
(COLUMBIA), MAX MILLIKAN (MIT) ET AL.[2]

1. Anonymous study attached to S. Everett Gleason, Memorandum for General Robert Cutler, February 13, 1953, Dwight D. Eisenhower: Records as President, White House Central Files (Confidential File), 1953–1961, Subject Series, Box 61, Folder Psychological Strategy Board, Dwight D. Eisenhower Library.
2. Psychological Aspects of United States Strategy: Panel Report, November 1955, Dwight D. Eisenhower: Records as President, White House Central Files (Confidential File), 1953–1961, Subject Series, Box 61, Folder Nelson Rockefeller (4), Dwight D. Eisenhower Library.

Acknowledgments

I would like to express my deep gratitude, first and foremost, to Monthly Review Press for supporting this project and assisting me in its completion. *Monthly Review*'s long-standing dedication to rigorous scholarly work in the Marxist tradition that challenges dominant dogmas has made it materially possible to bring this book into the world. I am particularly grateful to Martin Paddio and Michael Yates for working with me on the project and helping me find ways of improving it.

Many friends, colleagues, and students have provided support and feedback over the years. I would like to thank, to begin with, those who provided research and editorial assistance, as well as important suggestions, including Vishnu Bachani, Jared Bly, Helmut-Harry Löwen, Jaden Oates, Luke Ohr, Jennifer Ponce de León, and Hope Wilson. I would also like to express my gratitude to those who read drafts of the book or provided suggestions based on oral presentations of its findings (or earlier publications rooted in the same research agenda): Colin Bodayle, Brett Clark, John Bellamy Foster, John Harfouch, Ali Kadri, Nazia Kazi, Aymeric Monville, Immanuel Ness, Julian Sempill, Ádám Takács, and Randall Williams, among others. Many scholars have reached out to me over the years, sharing their insights and advice. Although I could not possibly provide an exhaustive list, I greatly appreciate their input.

This book has benefited from numerous opportunities to present my findings at conferences and via various media outlets and public educational platforms. I would therefore like to thank those responsible for engaging with my research and asking probing questions that have helped ameliorate the current manuscript. Special recognition is due to all the participants in the activities of the Critical Theory Workshop/Atelier de

Théorie Critique, where I have often had the opportunity to share my scholarship and receive critical feedback. I am also deeply grateful to my students at Villanova University, who have been exposed in various ways to some of the ideas in this book, and whose questions and comments have helped refine them. In particular, I greatly appreciate the insightful contributions of my doctoral students and undergraduates in the philosophy department, who have provided me with a vital community of scholarly exchange.

I would like to thank Villanova University for providing the material conditions necessary to complete this manuscript. This includes, in addition to my position as a professor of philosophy and global interdisciplinary studies, a Research Semester, a University Summer Grant, a University Travel Grant, a sabbatical, and a CLAS Faculty Research and Development Grant to visit numerous archives.

I am grateful to the librarians and archival research assistants who have helped me over the years. Nik Fogle at Villanova University's Falvey Library deserves particular mention for his ability to track down obscure resources. I am equally grateful to the research assistants at the National Archives, the Dwight D. Eisenhower Presidential Library, the Rockefeller Archive Center, the Hanna Holborn Gray Special Collections Research Center at the University of Chicago, and the Tamiment Library at New York University.

Last, but certainly not least, I would like to thank Jennifer Ponce de León and my sons, Marlow and Finley, for the daily pleasures of sharing life together, bringing so much joy, wit, and insight to my years of research. Jennifer is deserving of the greatest recognition for having commented on multiple drafts of my work and discussed every detail with me in long and extremely productive conversations. Her insights and recommendations have been invaluable.

Nota Bene: Unless otherwise noted, all translations in the book are my own.

ABBREVIATIONS

AAU	American Association of Universities
ACCF	American Committee for Cultural Freedom
ACLB	American Committee for Liberation from Bolshevism
ADEX	Administrative Index (FBI)
AEA	American Economic Association
AHA	American Historical Association
APSA	American Political Science Association
BASR	Bureau of Applied Social Research (Columbia University)
BBC	British Broadcasting Corporation
BPP	Black Panther Party
CBS	Columbia Broadcasting System
CCF	Congress for Cultural Freedom
CENIS	Center for International Studies (MIT)
CFR	Council on Foreign Relations
CIA	Central Intelligence Agency
CIAA	Office of the Coordinator of Inter-American Affairs
CIC	Counterintelligence Corps
COI	Office of the Coordinator of Information
COINTELPRO	Counter Intelligence Program (FBI)
CWC	Committee on World Communism (U.S. State Department)
DCI	Director of Central Intelligence
DGI	Directorio General de Inteligencia (Cuba)
DHM	Dialectical and Historical Materialism
DOD	Department of Defense
DOJ	Department of Justice
ECA	Economic Cooperation Administration
FBI	Federal Bureau of Investigation
FEP	Free Europe Press
FO	Foreign Office (UK)
FOIA	Freedom of Information Act
FRG	Federal Republic of Germany
FTUC	Free Trade Union Committee
FYSA	Foundation for Youth and Student Affairs
GDR	German Democratic Republic
GM	General Motors
HICOG	High Commission for Occupied Germany
IACF	International Association for Cultural Freedom
INR	Bureau of Intelligence and Research (U.S. State Department)

IOD	International Organizations Division
IRD	Information Research Department (British Foreign Office)
IRIS	Interim Research and Intelligence Service (U.S. State Department)
ISC	Institute for the Study of Conflict (UK)
JLC	Jewish Labor Committee
LAIIR	Latin American Institute of International Relations
LSE	London School of Economics
MI5	Military Intelligence, Section 5, or the domestic Security Service (UK)
MI6	Military Intelligence, Section 6, or the foreign intelligence agency, also known as the Secret Intelligence Service or SIS (UK)
MOI	Ministry of Information (UK)
MoMA	Museum of Modern Art
NATO	North Atlantic Treaty Organization
NED	National Endowment for Democracy
NEP	New Economic Policy (USSR)
NGO	Non-Governmental Organization
NIE	National Intelligence Estimate
NSA	National Security Agency
NSC	National Security Council
NYU	New York University
OCI	Office of Current Intelligence (CIA)
OCL	Office of Intelligence Coordination and Liaison (U.S. State Department)
OIR	Office of Intelligence Research (U.S. State Department)
OMGUS	Office of Military Government, United States
ONE	Office of National Estimates
OPC	Office of Policy Coordination
ORI	Office of Research and Intelligence (U.S. State Department)
ORR	Office of Radio Research (Columbia University)
OSS	Office of Strategic Services
OTE	Office of Training and Education (CIA)
OWI	Office of War Information
PAO	Public Affairs Office (CIA)
PQLI	Physical Quality of Life Index
Prela	Prensa Latina
PRRP	Princeton Radio Research Project
PSB	Psychological Strategy Board

PWE	Political Warfare Executive (UK)
R&A	Research and Analysis Branch
RI	Russian Institute (Columbia University)
RIT	Rochester Institute of Technology
RRC	Russian Research Center (Harvard University)
SI	Secret Intelligence
SIS	Secret Intelligence Service, also known as MI6
SOE	Special Operations Executive (UK)
USIA	United States Information Agency
USIS	United States Information Service
USSR	Union of Soviet Socialist Republics
VOA	Voice of America
WAY	World Assembly of Youth
WFDY	World Federation of Democratic Youth

Opening Salvo of *The Intellectual World War*

Ideas are not only an instrument to create consciousness so that people fight, but ideas have become the main instrument of struggle; not an inspiration, not a guide, not an orientation, but the main instrument of struggle.

—FIDEL CASTRO, QUOTATION IN THE CENTRO
FIDEL CASTRO RUZ[1]

CHE'S HEAD

The bullets were aimed much more at Che's spirit [*esprit*].

—THOMAS SANKARA, "YOU CANNOT KILL IDEAS"[2]

They wanted his head. A worldwide manhunt, sparing no cost, was launched to track him down. The masters of empire and their minions needed the head of the man who was outsmarting them, and who openly stated his ambition to spark "two, three or many Vietnams."[3] Too much

---

1. This citation, presented in the Centro Fidel Castro Ruz in Havana, Cuba, was adapted from Fidel Castro, "Discurso pronunciado en la Clausura del VII Congreso de la Unión de Jóvenes Comunistas," Palacio de las Convenciones, December 10, 1998, http://www.fidelcastro.cu/es/discursos/discurso-pronunciado-en-la-clausura-del-vii-congreso-de-la-union-de-jovenes-comunistas.
2. Thomas Sankara, *Thomas Sankara Speaks: The Burkina Faso Revolution 1983–87* (New York: Pathfinder Press, 2007), 456.
3. Ernesto Che Guevara, *Che Guevara Reader: Writings on Politics & Revolution*, ed.

damage had already been done in the Caribbean, as well as in Africa, and South America was next. They did not understand this task in metaphorical terms. Apparently, they literally wanted him decapitated so that his head could be placed in a jar and expedited to Washington as a war trophy.[4]

They wanted the head of the rebel who had seen through the psychological warfare undertaken by the U.S. empire in the coup d'état that would serve as one of its models for overthrowing foreign governments around the world. This was in Guatemala, in the early 1950s, when President Jacobo Árbenz decided to pursue a path of national development rather than have his country remain a woefully underdeveloped banana republic. Such a stance set him on a collision course with the United Fruit Company, which controlled the country as a neocolony.[5] He had to go, and the empire's other enemy, known as Ernesto Guevara at the time, was there to see it unfold.

In the United States' long history of toppling governments, which includes more than fifty since the Second World War, it has consistently combined militant actions with psychological warfare in what we might call the one-two punch of empire.[6] The war for hearts and minds, as innumerable internal documents attest, is a foundational aspect of U.S. empire building.

In the case of Guatemala, one of the dons of modern propaganda, who was none other than Freud's double nephew, oversaw the entire operation for United Fruit. Serving as its "counsel on public relations" since the early 1940s, Edward Bernays opportunistically drew on his uncle's theories to engage in well-paid mass mind manipulation.[7] United Fruit also

---

David Deutschmann and María del Carmen Ariet (Havana: Ocean Press, 2013), 361.

4. See Joel Whitney, *Finks: How the C.I.A. Tricked the World's Best Writers* (New York: OR Books, 2016), 249, and Jon Lee Anderson, *Che Guevara: A Revolutionary Life* (New York: Grove Press, 1997), 742.

5. See Stephen Schlesinger and Stephen Kinzer, *Bitter Fruit: The Story of the American Coup in Guatemala* (Cambridge, MA: Harvard University Press, 1999).

6. See William Blum, *Rogue State: A Guide to the World's Only Superpower* (London: Zed Books, 2014), x, as well as the author's online inventory titled "Overthrowing Other People's Government: The Master List," https://williamblum.org/essays/read/overthrowing-other-peoples-governments-the-master-list.

7. Edward L. Bernays, *Biography of an Idea: The Founding Principles of Public Relations Counsel Edward L. Bernays* (New York: Simon & Schuster, 1965), 744. Also see Robert Skvarla, "Edward Bernays: Propaganda and the U.S.-Backed 1954 Guatemalan Coup," *Covert Action Magazine* (December 10, 2021) and Adam Curtis, *The Century of the Self*, BBC, 2002, film.

retained an inside lobbyist in Washington, Thomas G. Corcoran, who had close friends in the Central Intelligence Agency (CIA) and was involved in a CIA plot to arm Árbenz's opponents, known as Operation Fortune.[8] Soon, multiple agencies of the U.S. government were engaged in what would become known as Operation PBSuccess, whose objective was to overthrow the Guatemalan government. This is unsurprising given the intimate relationship between the bourgeoisie and the bourgeois state:

> [Secretary of State John Foster] Dulles had, for decades, been one of [United Fruit's] principal legal counselors. His brother, Allen, the CIA director, had also done legal work for the company and owned a substantial block of its stock. John Moors Cabot, the assistant secretary of state for inter-American affairs, was a large shareholder. So was his brother, Thomas Dudley Cabot, the director of international security affairs in the State Department, who had been United Fruit's president.[9]

Dulles's CIA thus undertook a major psychological warfare operation that cross-pollinated with the campaign undertaken by Bernays, who collaborated with the Agency, and the U.S. mainstream press marched in lockstep to the tune they called.[10] Disingenuously depicting Árbenz as a staunch communist with links to the Soviet Union, they stoked the ire of

---

8. See Schlesinger and Kinzer, *Bitter Fruit*.

9. Stephen Kinzer, *Overthrow: America's Century of Regime Change from Hawaii to Iraq* (New York: Times Books, 2007), 129–30. Kinzer adds: "General Robert Cutler, head of the National Security Council, was its [United Fruit's] former chairman of the board. John J. McCloy, the president of the International Bank for Reconstruction and Development, was a former board member [of United Fruit]. Both Undersecretary of State Walter Bedell Smith and Robert Hill, the American ambassador to Costa Rica, would join the board after leaving government service" (130). On the numerous connections between the U.S. capitalist ruling class, the bourgeois state, and the coup d'état in Guatemala, also see Stephen Kinzer, *The Brothers: John Foster Dulles, Allen Dulles, and Their Secret World War* (New York: Times Books, 2013).

10. Internal documents that have been released reveal that, at least in 1958 and 1959, Bernays corresponded and shared information with the CIA. See "Letter to Mr. Edward L. Bernays from (Sanitized)," April 4, 1958, the CIA FOIA Electronic Reading Room, https://www.cia.gov/readingroom/document/cia-rdp80b01676r003800020083-0; "Letter to Mr. Edward L. Bernays from (Sanitized)," June 30, 1958, the CIA FOIA Electronic Reading Room, https://www.cia.gov/readingroom/document/cia-rdp80b01676r003800020084-9; "Letter to Mr. & Mrs. Edward L. Bernays from (Sanitized)," April 20, 1959, the CIA FOIA Electronic Reading Room, https://www.cia.gov/readingroom/document/cia-rdp80r01731r000200050163-9.

the U.S. public, already broadly inculcated with anticommunist propaganda.[11] The war for hearts and minds laid the ideological groundwork for the CIA's 1954 coup d'état, which put in power the brutal dictator Carlos Castillo Armas, "initiating 40 years of military-government, death squads, torture, disappearances, mass executions, and unimaginable cruelty, totaling more than 200,000 victims—indisputably one of the most inhumane chapters of the 20th century."[12]

Guevara was radicalized watching the coup unfold, and he joined a medical brigade to support the anti-imperialist resistance. He also learned important lessons, such as the need to arm a liberated people for their own self-defense, and he understood that war is played out on two fronts at once. The psychological battle lays the groundwork for imperialist warfare, preparing for military assaults that would otherwise be unthinkable. It also provides cover during and after the fact, psywar accompanying military war like its shadow.

When the man who became known around the world as Che waged his own war, he also did it on two fronts. Having successfully organized with the Cuban people to overthrow another U.S.-backed dictator, Fulgencio Batista, he engaged in an international intellectual war of liberation. He helped found, among other things, Prensa Latina (Prela), a news outlet that broke the chains of information imperialism. Two young journalists working for Prela, Gabriel García Márquez and Rodolfo Walsh, discovered and deciphered a CIA telex discussing the planned Bay of Pigs invasion to depose the Cuban government.[13] They shared the information with the leaders of the country, who were already aware of it through other channels, and the Cuban people were thereby prepared for the attack and successfully routed the Agency's invasion. They outsmarted empire and embarrassed a powerful state agency intent on projecting its omnipotence.

Unable to kill him in Cuba, and incapable of defeating him in Africa,

---

11. It is important to note that the U.S. government knew full well that Moscow was not conspiring to spread the so-called virus of communism to the doorstep of the United States, even though this is what the propaganda campaign claimed. "The Soviets had no military, economic, or even diplomatic relations with Guatemala," and "a study by the State Department itself had found the few Guatemala Communists to be 'indigenous to the area.'" Kinzer, *Overthrow*, 136.

12. William Blum, *Rogue State: A Guide to the World's Only Superpower* (London: Zed Books, 2014), 168. See Allan Francovich's documentary film *The Houses Are Full of Smoke* (1987), the first part of which focuses on Guatemala.

13. See Whitney, *Finks*, 185–86, and Joel Whitney, *Flights: Radicals on the Run* (New York: OR Books, 2024), 78.

they tracked him down in Bolivia, where he was training guerrillas to overthrow yet another U.S.-backed dictatorship. Having financed, armed, and trained counter-revolutionary battalions in the country, injecting $15 million between 1962 and 1968, the U.S. war machine, led by CIA officers, pursued its manhunt by any means necessary.[14] When they finally caught up with him, they captured him alive. Fearful of how powerful he had become, as a symbol and rallying point for the international anti-imperialist movement, they ignominiously murdered him. The movement was thereby decapitated, or so they hoped.

THEY DID NOT ONLY WANT to kill the man, however; they wanted to kill the ideas and values he embodied. They therefore undertook a battle to take control of his literary estate by overseeing the publication of his Bolivian diary. It had fallen into the hands of the United States' local strongman, Bolivian dictator René Barrientos, "who immediately sent copies to the CIA, the Pentagon, and the U.S. government."[15] The Barrientos regime eventually sought to auction off its publication rights to the highest bidder.

Two intelligence assets vied for the rights. Andrew Saint George, who had worked for the U.S. Army's intelligence service and was suspected of having links to espionage agencies, negotiated for Magnum Publishing.[16] Then Sol Stein stepped in with his own publishing house. Stein was an across-the-board anticommunist propagandist who had been on the CIA's payroll at least twice, served as the executive director of the Agency-supported American Committee for Cultural Freedom (ACCF), ran the ACCF's *The New Leader*, collaborated with the Psychological Strategy Board (PSB), and worked for the U.S. propaganda agency Voice of America (alongside the Frankfurt School scholar Leo Löwenthal).[17]

---

14. See Michèle Ray, "The Execution of Che by the CIA," *Ramparts*, March 1968, 37.

15. Fidel Castro, "A Necessary Introduction," in Ernesto Che Guevara, *The Bolivian Diary: Authorized Edition* (New York: Seven Stories Press, 2006), 13. Castro added that "journalists with links to the CIA [also] had access to the document inside Bolivia."

16. See Whitney, *Finks*, 245. Carlos Soria Galvarro T. describes St. George as "linked to the CIA" and says that he was given privileged access to review the original diary, along with another CIA-connected journalist, Juan de Onis. See "La odisea del Diario del Che en Bolivia," in Carlos Soria Galvarro T., *El Che en Bolivia: Documentos y testimonios* (La Paz: La Razón, 2005), 7-8.

17. See Whitney, *Finks*, 245–46 and Henry Butterfield Ryan, "Introduction" in Daniel James, *Ché Guevara: A Biography* (New York: Cooper Square Press, 2001), x. Regarding

Henry Butterfield Ryan maintains that it was the Company—as the CIA is known in internal parlance—that "almost certainly" secured the Bolivian diaries for Stein's publishing house.[18]

The left organized a counterattack. Journalist Michèle Ray negotiated on behalf of French publisher Jean-Jacques Pauvert. The *yanquis* were shadowing her, sharing intelligence reports with the Bolivian generals, and her financial ceiling—despite her bluffs—was far lower than Agency collaborators could muster. Barney Rosset of Grove Press also tried his luck and was able to publish six pages of Che's diary in his *Evergreen Review*. Reactionary Cuban exiles responded by bombing the Grove Press offices in downtown New York. And this time, they did not miss their target, as they had in 1964, when they turned a bazooka on the United Nations during Che's speech. Grove Press filed a lawsuit accusing the CIA of being behind the bombing, as well as engaging in surveillance, infiltration, and economic sabotage by covertly financing Grove competitors like Praeger, Inc. and Fodor, Inc.[19] Castro, for his part, published what he could as quickly as possible, and he signed an agreement with *Ramparts* to serialize English translations.[20]

It was a veritable war of ideas, and it knew no limits. The Agency responsible for assassinating Che was not satisfied with his murder; it sought to kill his revolutionary legacy and the ideas he incarnated. Its agents were committed to taking ownership over the past and present by rewriting history to fit their narrative, and then flooding the market with their imperialist propaganda, which they fabricated with the assistance of collaborationist academics, journalists, publishers, and public relations experts.

The publisher, Stein, who worked for the same agency that had

---

his collaboration with the PSB, see Memorandum for the Record re Luncheon with Mr. Sol Stein, January 19, 1955, Edward P. Lilly: Papers, 1928–1992, Box 55, Folder Freedom Academy (4), Dwight D. Eisenhower Library.

18. Ryan, "Introduction," xi.

19. See United Press International, "Grove Press Sues CIA in Bombing," *San Francisco Examiner,* July 18, 1975; "Grove Press Sues CIA; Asks $10-Million Damages," *Publisher's Weekly,* July 28, 1975; Anna Marcum, "Grove Press: Cuba Libre, Che, and the CIA," July 26, 2022, https://www.villagepreservation.org/2022/07/26/grove-press-cuba-libre-che-and-the-cia-southofunionsquare/; "Court Bars a Move to Seize C.I.A. Files," *New York Times,* August 21, 1975, https://www.nytimes.com/1975/08/21/archives/court-bars-a-move-to-seize-cia-files.html.

20. For information regarding how Fidel obtained Che's diary, see Soria Galvarro T., "La odisea del Diario del Che en Bolivia."

assassinated the iconic revolutionary thereby collaborated with an editor who showed numerous signs of being an agent of the CIA, Daniel James, to publish their own version of Che's Bolivian diary, without of course mentioning that this was a Company product (an agent, in CIA lingo, is generally anyone mobilized by the Agency for its agenda, though it is sometimes used to refer to a paid operative, whereas an officer is a full-time employee).[21] According to their account of history, the aim of Che's intervention in Bolivia was not liberation from dictatorship; it was rather to "create enough trouble for the Bolivian government that it would be forced to ask for major American intervention."[22] However, as the CIA-connected writer claimed in his nearly 60-page introduction, "Ché [sic] lacked the ability to plan a military campaign" and "returning to guerrilla life at 39 after seven years of chauffeur-driven limousines and comparatively rich living cannot have been easy."[23] In spite of his purported inabilities and bourgeois softening, though, Che was apparently driven to try and fail because otherwise he would have fallen "by the wayside and become lost to history": "He needed a revolution far more than the revolution needed him."[24] His final, quixotic quest for fame and glory led nowhere, however, other than to the definitive "destruction of the myth of Ché [sic] Guevara as a great guerrilla technician."[25]

The author of these lines, Daniel James, likely began a relationship with the CIA when he worked as a journalist for one of the magazines it funded, *The New Leader*, which was in the network of the ACCF and had actively participated in the propaganda blitz against Guatemala mentioned above (Bernays had a close relationship with the magazine and was a friend of the executive editor, Sol Levitas).[26] In fact, James made a major contribution to this anticommunist campaign by penning a book that alleged that Guatemala's land reform was part of a sinister Soviet plot.

---

21. Since the expression "CIA agent" is widely used to refer to an employee of the Agency, including in a lot of the secondary literature, "agent" is sometimes used in this more expansive sense in this book. The context should clarify how the term is to be understood.

22. Daniel James, "Preface," in *The Complete Bolivian Diaries of Ché Guevara and Other Captured Documents*, ed. Daniel James (New York: Stein and Day 1968), 7.

23. Daniel James, "Introduction" in *The Complete Bolivian Diaries of Ché Guevara and Other Captured Documents*, ed. Daniel James, 68, 69.

24. Ibid., 69, 68.

25. Ibid., 67. For James, Che and Fidel were so lost in theory and the overemphasis of their Cuban experience that they could not see "Bolivia in realistic terms" (ibid.).

26. See Ryan, "Introduction," xi; Whitney, *Finks*, 43, and 155–56; Schlesinger and Kinzer, *Bitter Fruit*, 80, 89, 107.

"He never mentions the CIA" in the book, "even as a suspected patron of the insurgents."[27] However, it showed "definite signs of CIA collaboration" and was published by a Company conduit.[28] James's *Red Design for the Americas: Guatemalan Prelude* was so beloved by United Fruit that the company behind the 1954 coup bought up copies and distributed them to the media. The same CIA-aligned writer was thus involved in the psywar to overthrow Guatemala, as well as the fight to take ownership over Che's legacy.

Although the imperialist propagandists lost this battle, thanks to Castro, Ray, *Ramparts*, and many others, they certainly did not give up on the war of ideas. The professional propagandist Daniel James began working on a biography of Che, which was published in 1969 by Stein's CIA-linked publishing house. Hackneyed anticommunism was its hallmark, and it depicted Che "as more of the apostle of violence than the maker of revolution."[29] Its conclusion—which was that the slogan "Ché [*sic*] lives" resonates "almost exclusively" within a small, pathological minority in the West—gives a clear sense of its overall tenor:

> Even in the West, where he has wider appeal, Ché [*sic*] "lives" principally for small minority groups: the extremist students, the New Left and some Old Left retreads, the incurably romantic liberals who cannot live without *caudillo*-type symbols, the rebellious adolescents and the frustrated middle-aged who are as much fans of Bonnie and Clyde, the Boston Strangler, and any antihero whose trademark is violence as they are of Ché [*sic*].[30]

"THE CURE FOR PROPAGANDA," Edward Bernays maintained, fondly quoting a magazine writer and editor, "is more propaganda."[31] This is certainly true for the ongoing war over Che's life and legacy, including the incessant attempts to exonerate the U.S. government for his murder. Michael Ratner and Michael Steven Smith have provided an overview of some of these endeavors, while also laying out extensive documentary

---

27. Ryan, "Introduction," xi.
28. Ibid. The book was published by John Day, "one of those myriad CIA conduits who ran 'black' printing operations for the CIA's propaganda needs." Whitney, *Finks*, 156.
29. James, *Ché Guevara*, 346.
30. Ibid., 304–5.
31. Bernays, *Biography of an Idea*, 384. The writer is Bruce Bliven, editor of *The New Republic*.

evidence to the contrary, reminding their readers that the accused is a well-known serial killer (the United States was involved in the assassination of at least eighteen other prominent leaders between 1948 and 1967):

> It was in the U.S. government's interest to have Che killed. The CIA and U.S. Special Forces trained the Bolivian Ranger Battalion that captured Che; CIA agents disguised as Bolivian officers accompanied the Rangers into the field; the U.S. supplied the weapons and provided the intelligence; and a CIA agent apparently was present at the time of his murder.[32]

One of the most interesting cases is Henry Butterfield Ryan's *The Fall of Che Guevara*, which Oxford University Press published in 1998. Ratner and Smith describe Ryan's book as "the best-researched account of Che's murder," and Ryan does come closer to "pinning the responsibility on the United States" than other publications.[33] Yet he ultimately contends that "the U.S. government exerted a moderating influence on its Bolivian allies in dealing with Guevara, [and] it neither killed him nor ordered him to be killed."[34] To understand such a conclusion, it is helpful to know that Ryan, very much like Daniel James, has a series of connections that allow us to contextualize his work within the larger war of ideas. Although his byline for the book refers to him simply as "a retired United States Foreign Service officer and professional historian," he spent twenty-five years working in the United States Information Agency (USIA).[35] Here is how former USIA director Alvin Snyder candidly described its role:

---

32. Michael Ratner and Michael Steven Smith, *Who Killed Che? How the CIA Got Away with Murder* (New York: OR Books, 2011), 30 (also see 31). In addition to the documents published in this book, there are at least two online repositories of the National Security Archive with documentation regarding Che's assassination: https://nsarchive2.gwu.edu/NSAEBB/NSAEBB5/ and https://archive.org/details/the-death-of-che-guevara-declassified/CIA%2C%20Foreign%20Broadcast%20Information%20Service%2C%20Fidel%20Castro%20Delivers%20Eulogy%20on%20Che%20Guevara%2C%20October%2019%2C%201967/.

33. Ratner and Smith, *Who Killed Che?*, 29.

34. Henry Butterfield Ryan, *The Fall of Che Guevara: A Story of Soldiers, Spies, and Diplomats* (Oxford: Oxford University Press 1998), 3–4.

35. This information is available via online biographies like https://prabook.com/web/henry.ryan/146836 and https://www.encyclopedia.com/arts/educational-magazines/ryan-henry-butterfield-1931.

The U.S. government ran a full-service public relations organization, the largest in the world, about the size of the twenty biggest U.S. commercial PR firms combined. Its full-time professional staff of more than 10,000, spread out among some 150 countries, burnished America's image and trashed the Soviet Union 2,500 hours a week with a "tower of babble" comprised of more than 70 languages, to the tune of over $2 billion per year. The biggest branch of this propaganda machine is called the United States Information Agency.[36]

Reed Harris laid out the objectives of the USIA's book program in the following terms: "we have books written to our own stipulations, books that would not otherwise be put out, especially those books that are strongly anti-Communist. . . . We control the book from its conception down to the final edited manuscript."[37]

Ryan spent his career working for this propaganda agency. His book on Che's murder was written at the Institute for the Study of Diplomacy at Georgetown University, which is stocked with national security state operatives and even served as the publisher for a 1993 USIA report that Ryan helped oversee.[38] He acknowledged, moreover, that his book was reviewed by U.S. officials and a CIA officer (but not by Castro or his supporters).[39] This lifelong propagandist was clearly part of the historical clean-up crew, and he endeavored, once again, to whitewash the crimes of empire by academically laundering state disinformation. The intellectual world war is incessant.

TO RETURN TO THE MAN a CIA writer compared to the Boston Strangler, they literally wanted Che's head. His assassins wanted to cut it off and send it to Washington, via La Paz. Such a war trophy deserved to be admired by the masters of the game who had ordered and commissioned it but did not want blood on their hands, always preferring

---

36. Alvin A. Snyder, *Warriors of Disinformation: American Propaganda, Soviet Lies, and the Winning of the Cold War* (New York: Arcade Publishing, 1995), xi.
37. Cited in Claude Julien, *America's Empire*, trans. Renaud Bruce (New York: Pantheon Books, 1971), 313, translation slightly modified.
38. See Hans Binnendijk, Henry Butterfield Ryan, and Robert R. Gosende, eds., *USIA: New Directions for a New Era* (Washington D.C.: Institute for the Study of Diplomacy, Georgetown University, March 1993).
39. Ryan, *The Fall of Che Guevara*, x.

plausible deniability. The idea was apparently deemed "too barbaric," in the telling words of on-site CIA operative, Félix Rodríguez, who proposed cutting off a finger instead.[40] The compromise reached was equally significant: his murderers decided to sever the revolutionary's hands. Since the oligarchs of imperialism generally do not want to look their victims in the eye, they prefer beheading without a barbaric face. They would have it their way, thanks to the hands of their assassins. In the end, they ultimately preferred to have his head in the figurative sense: they wanted him dead, and they wanted to kill the idea that he embodied by taking over his legacy, thereby decapitating the global anti-imperialist movement.

It is often said, when you lose an ally on the left, that you can kill a person, but you cannot kill an idea. This trilogy is an extended study of the forces in the world that have sought to put a much more radical thesis to the test, namely, that by killing an idea—that of communism—you can destroy a lot more people, as well as the planet. Their failure is a testament to humanity.

---

40. Anderson, *Che Guevara*, 742. Also see Soria Galvarro T., "La odisea del Diario del Che en Bolivia," and Jorge I. Pérez, "'Lo único llevado a Cuba son las manos' del Che, afirma quien lo capturó," *SWI swissinfo.ch*, July 6, 2022, https://www.swissinfo.ch/spa/lo-único-llevado-a-cuba-son-las-manos-del-che-afirma-quien-lo-capturó/47732964.

EMPIRE OF IDEAS

Ideas as Weapons

The most potent weapon in the hands of the oppressor is the mind of the oppressed.

—STEVE BIKO[1]

Ideas are not separate from reality, hovering above it in a pristine realm of conceptual purity. They are developed within particular, concrete circumstances, and they result from specific theoretical practices, which themselves are an outgrowth of society's overall organization of intellectual production, as well as production more generally. In class societies, ideas are therefore situated, inevitably, in class struggle. This takes myriad and sundry forms, as we shall see, but the fundamental polarization of class society is a result of ownership. Those who possess and control the means of production also own and oversee the means of intellectual production. This gives them an incredible advantage in the battle of ideas since they are the proprietors of the very system that manages the mindscape of the masses.

Capitalism has led to a greater concentration of wealth in the hands of an increasingly small minority, and this resulting polarization has only intensified in the monopoly and imperialist phase of capitalism. This socioeconomic reality makes actually existing capitalism, objectively speaking, more difficult to maintain, since it obviously does not and cannot serve the material interests of the overwhelming majority of the population (and the planet). Hence the importance of exercising, as much as possible, monopoly control over the world of ideas, in the broadest sense of the term. Since the objective situation tilts in the direction of system change, at least in the big picture and without considering some of the countervailing tendencies, this can be corrected by creating subjective conditions, via ideology, that lean in the opposite direction.

Ideology is thus a crucial aspect of class struggle. Due to the degree of development of the imperialist system of ideological production and dissemination, which far surpasses anything seen before, ideology arguably exercises greater dominion over broader swaths of the population,

---

1. Steve Biko, *I Write What I Like: Selected Writings* (Chicago: University of Chicago Press, 1996), 92.

imposes itself in massive quantities, abides by an accelerated rhythm of renewal, has been developed into ever more complex and sophisticated forms, is more centrally controlled, and increasingly reaches people in their intimate lives through the digital penetration of the private sphere. The battle against the dominant ideology is thus extremely difficult to wage, and the anti-imperialist forces have been obliged to fight like scrappy underdogs to get their message across wherever and however they can.

Che famously set up Radio Rebelde in 1958 in the jungle of the Sierra Maestra in order to broadcast the aims of the July 26th movement. It went up against the juggernaut of an international system of cultural imperialism symbolized by Hollywood. This confrontation, between the David of Radio Rebelde and the Goliath of Hollywood, is precisely how the intellectual world war has been fought out in reality. Those who own the means of production have used their stolen wealth to exercise near monopoly control over the means of communication, whereas the dispossessed of the world have had to fight tooth and nail to develop their own systems of communication to help spread their ideas and defend a fundamental proposition: a better world is possible.

Contemporary Cuban intellectuals like Antonio Ramón Barreiro Vázquez and Raúl Antonio Capote have demonstrated how this battle is ultimately an all-encompassing cultural war.[2] Drawing on government documents and personal experience (Capote worked for the CIA for eight years while undercover for Cuban intelligence), they have brought into relief the totalizing nature of this war for hearts and minds, highlighting how central it has been to the U.S.'s specific version of empire building, particularly since the mid-twentieth century.[3] In the words of Barreiro Vázquez:

> Cultural war is a system that encompasses all levels of consciousness and activity of a given society. It mobilizes instruments and resources from any

---

2. See, for instance, the Critical Theory Workshop's interviews: Raúl Antonio Capote, "La guerra cultural," February 18, 2025, https://www.youtube.com/watch?v=gO9Ikpr0ZLg and Antonio Ramón Barreiro Vázquez, "La cultura en la estrategia de la guerra imperialista," February 20, 2025, https://youtu.be/Udnyvsxzd1Y.

3. See Barreiro Vázquez's insightful discussion of the "Dulles Doctrine" and the "Santa Fe Programs" in "La cultura en la estrategia de guerra imperialista," *Revista Cubana de Ciencias Sociales*, No. 55 (July-December 2021): 48–72, https://rccs.edicionescervantes.com/index.php/RCCS/article/view/27/23, as well as Capote's *Enemigo* (Madrid: Ediciones Akal, 2015) and *Guarimbas: Los gestores del caos* (Caracas: La Iguana Ediciones, 2024).

of the spheres of social life: political, moral, economic, juridical, scientific, artistic, aesthetic and others. It carries out public actions and of course maintains covert operations. They try, by all means, to exercise control over information, public opinion, tastes, preferences, feelings; to extend their power over education, promotion, and diffusion, to favor behaviors of submission, passivity, and demobilization; or of indiscipline and aggressiveness, which together with the replacement and substitution of values, with the creation of other false ones, guarantee to secure domination and imperial hegemony.[4]

As diverse and totalizing as it is, the cultural war is nonetheless organized around a fundamental objective, namely, to achieve the political goal of advancing imperialism and destroying its principal impediment: socialism.

Invisible Empire

In 1964, the U.S. journalist Lisa Howard did an interview with Ernesto Che Guevara for a major outlet of imperial disinformation (ABC News). She asked him: "It has appeared to us, viewing the Cuban scene, that two of your chief problems are: this difficulty disciplining the people to a Communist state, and a kind of strangling bureaucracy. Do you feel these are two great problems?"[5] After confirming that she was asking about Cuba's problems, he replied, with a serious demeanor: "Our two main problems are . . ." Che's face suddenly lit up with a broad smile, as he counted on his fingers for emphasis: "imperialism and imperialism."[6]

THE UNITED STATES IS, AND always has been, an empire. From its very beginning as a settler colony on the Eastern seaboard until today, it has been constantly expanding. As historian Daniel Immerwahr

---

4. Barreiro Vázquez, "La cultura en la estrategia de guerra imperialista." Also see Barreiro Vázquez, "La guerra cultural y la subversión político ideológica en tiempos de guerra no convencional" (unpublished paper) and "La guerra cultural," in Juan Carlos Garnier Galán, Leyla Carrillo Ramírez, et al., *Los problemas de seguridad del mundo* (La Habana: Casa Editorial Verde Olivo, 2022), 262–302.
5. Ernesto Che Guevara, interview by Lisa Howard, ABC News, February 12, 1964, https://lapupilainsomne.wordpress.com/2017/06/29/dialogo-del-che-con-lisa-howard-transcripcion-y-video/.
6. Ibid.

demonstrated in *How to Hide an Empire*, the "logo map" image of forty-eight contiguous states, which most people have in mind when they think of the United States, was only a reality for three years of its existence.[7] It continued to acquire overseas territories and has, today, ringed the globe with some 800 military bases, which is likely more "than any other people, nation, or empire in history."[8] This, of course, is only the geographic and military footprint of empire, but much the same could be said of its economic, political, social, cultural, and intellectual dominion.

The United States is an empire, however, of a peculiar sort: it has a unique tradition of denying its own existence. This custom is certainly not the only one since there is also a lineage of explicit imperialists, but it has deep historical roots.[9] These are visible, for instance, in its self-description as a democracy and a land of the free, liberated from the stranglehold of the British empire, when it was actually established as an antidemocratic republic—meaning oligarchy—founded on a violent war of aggression and dispossession against the working class, characterized by colonization, Indigenous genocide, chattel slavery, indentured servitude, and domestic slavery.[10]

What is remarkable, though, about this U.S. tradition of empire denial is that it has tended to become predominant in precisely the time period when the United States came to assert itself as the world's leading imperialist power. This occurred in the wake of what Domenico Losurdo calls the second "Thirty Years' War," meaning the conflagration of inter-imperialist rivalry that lasted from roughly the early to the mid-twentieth century. As the United States emerged from this extended conflict as the primary empire in the world, it emphatically denied its imperial status,

---

7. See Daniel Immerwahr, *How to Hide an Empire: A History of the Greater United States* (New York: Picador, 2020).

8. David Vine, "The United States Probably Has More Foreign Military Bases Than Any Other People, Nation, or Empire in History," *The Nation*, September 14, 2015, https://www.thenation.com/article/archive/the-united-states-probably-has-more-foreign-military-bases-than-any-other-people-nation-or-empire-in-history/.

9. Stephen Kinzer provides some insight into the debates at the end of the nineteenth century, when the United States accelerated its acquisition of overseas territories, in *The True Flag: Theodore Roosevelt, Mark Twain, and the Birth of American Empire* (New York: St. Martin's Griffin, 2018).

10. Although lacking a proper Marxist framing, I provided a materialist analysis of the United States' undemocratic history in *Counter-History of the Present: Untimely Interrogations into Globalization, Technology, and Democracy* (Durham, N.C.: Duke University Press, 2017).

and it relied heavily on neocolonialism and clandestine operations to do so. One of the principal reasons for this is that its imperial expansion was held in check by the USSR, which not only supported anti-imperialist struggles but also engaged in the war of information to reveal the truth behind U.S. machinations around the world.[11] Another important reason is that the United States, in wresting lands from the former imperialist powers, often presented itself as a liberator from empire rather than a new imperial overlord, which proved useful for mobilizing certain segments of the local population on its behalf, as well as garnering support for imperialism on the home front. The preferred solution has thus been to have imperial expansion go hand in hand with imperial denial, while propagandistically depicting the USSR as the real empire that, coincidentally, needed to be overthrown.[12] Under the banner of democracy, freedom, and human rights, the United States has thereby extended its dominion over large swaths of the world, presenting itself as a benevolent benefactor rather than a domineering despot. It has, in this way, perfected the use of empire denial as the best cover for the construction of its imperium.

In order to do this, it has developed the most powerful, far-reaching, and centrally controlled cultural apparatus in the history of humanity, which it has imposed, as much as possible, on the entire world through cultural imperialism. This apparatus is composed of an expansive system of cultural production, circulation, and consumption, and it forms a key component of the superstructure. It not only encompasses culture in the restricted sense of the arts and entertainment, but it also includes so-called news and information, the world of the professional intelligentsia, sports, digital culture, social media, and the entire realm of industrially produced or mediated culture (in the broadest sense of the term). U.S. imperial expansion has thus been accompanied, every step of the way, by the construction of a cultural empire, whose power and reach far outstrips such earlier endeavors due to the level of development of its ideological system. It is capable of magically transforming imperial vices into democratic virtues, at least in the hearts and minds of some of its consumers. These must be trained, however, not to perceive the entire

---

11. Although biased against the USSR, Stephen Kinzer makes this point in *Overthrow*.

12. Soon after the CIA orchestrated coup d'état in Guatemala, Secretary of State Dulles asserted in a radio address: "the Guatemalan government and Communist agents throughout the world have persistently attempted to obscure the real issue— that of Communist imperialism—by claiming that the U.S. is only interested in protecting American business" (Kinzer, *Overthrow*, 147).

process. One of the most important psychological wars is thus the battle to hide propaganda itself by passing it off as something else, such as journalism, academic scholarship, culture, art, or simply entertainment.[13]

This process of dissimulation also applies to cultural imperialism itself, which the U.S. cultural apparatus generally describes as freedom of the press and media, as well as artistic, cultural, and intellectual liberty. What this so-called freedom actually means is that those who own the cultural apparatus are free to impose it everywhere in the world, and those who do not are free to consume it as much as possible. The U.S. imperium can thereby also fight wars for people's freedom to be systematically indoctrinated by its cultural empire, as it has regularly done against Cuba and, more generally, against any country that lays claim to its own cultural sovereignty, meaning its right not to be the victim of imperial propaganda.

An Actually Existing Impediment to Empire

The national liberation of a people is the regaining of the historical personality of that people, its return to history through the destruction of the imperialist domination to which it was subjected.

—AMÍLCAR CABRAL[14]

The greatest obstacle to imperial expansion has been actually existing socialism, which breaks the chains of empire in the name of defending the right of the peoples of this world to self-determination. Although the United States' imperial dream machine is deeply invested in power projection, and many assume that the leading imperialist country has been the undisputed world leader for quite some time, it is crucially important to recognize, as analysts like Radhika Desai have emphasized, that it has never truly exercised global dominion.[15] As a matter of fact, the

---

13. Elmer Davis, the Director of the Office of War Information (OWI), where a number of Frankfurt School scholars worked, explained in 1942: "The easiest way to inject a propaganda idea into most people's minds is to let it go through the medium of an entertainment picture when they do not realize that they are being propagandized." Cited in Matthew Alford and Tom Secker, *National Security Cinema: The Shocking New Evidence of Government Control in Hollywood* (n.p.: CreateSpace Independent Publishing Platform, 2017), 22. The same, however, is true, as we shall see, for scholarly publications.

14. Amílcar Cabral, "The Weapon of Theory," address delivered to the first Tricontinental Conference of the Peoples of Asia, Africa and Latin America held in Havana in January, 1966, https://www.marxists.org/subject/africa/cabral/1966/weapon-theory.htm.

15. This is a theme throughout Radhika Desai's work. It is central to *Geopolitical Economy:*

United States took over the helm of imperialism at a moment of major losses and retreats. By imperialism, in this context, I mean what Amílcar Cabral referred to as "a worldwide expression of the search for profits and the ever-increasing accumulation of *surplus value* by monopoly financial capital, centered in two parts of the world; first in Europe, and then in North America."[16] At the close of the Second World War, imperialism faced a powerful adversary that had just done what many in the imperial core considered to be impossible: it routed the Nazi war machine and was the principal force responsible for liberating Europe from fascism. The Soviet Union helped break, moreover, many of the chains of imperialism and expand the socialist world. Between the official end of the Second World War and the early 1980s, the movements of anticolonial liberation spread socialism across many countries in the Global South, and numerous non-socialist or semi-socialist projects of national self-determination also blossomed. By 1950, around one-third of the global population was living under a self-declared socialist government. In 1959, with the Cuban Revolution, revolutionary socialism arrived in the Western Hemisphere, liberating an island that is literally on the doorstep of the U.S. empire. In the big picture, and despite endless wars to try to prove the contrary, imperialism was on the retreat during this first phase of U.S. leadership.

The neoliberal conjuncture of counter-revolution did turn the tide, and the destruction of the Warsaw Pact countries was a major setback for the socialist camp. However, the United States has still failed to definitively decapitate the many-headed hydra of anti-imperialist resistance, and the global socialist movement more specifically. In the current conjuncture, there are many signs that the counter-revolutionary wave is cresting, at least in the sense that the imperial power of the United States is not what it once was. The world is looking increasingly multipolar, and the rise of China, as a self-declared socialist country, is one sign among many that the imperial dominion of the United States is still held in check.

The war against communism has thus been coextensive with the fight for imperialism. While the waging of the first battle has sometimes been open, at least for a few of the fronts of struggle, the second has frequently been disguised, even though they are ultimately the same war. The empire of ideas has been tasked with providing cover for the brutality of imperial warfare, while denigrating its enemies—the anti-imperialists—as the true monsters seeking global domination. The battle to turn the world upside

---

After US Hegemony, Globalization and Empire (London: New York: Pluto Press, 2013).
16. Cabral, "The Weapon of Theory."

down and capture hearts and minds for the imperial project thus constitutes one of the most fundamental features of the U.S. imperium.

To bring this clearly into view, consider a fact highlighted by William Blum, namely that only one country in the world has since the Second World War:

- Endeavored to overthrow more than fifty foreign governments, most of which were democratically elected;
- Grossly interfered in democratic elections in at least thirty countries;
- Attempted to assassinate more than fifty foreign leaders [some, such as Fidel Castro, multiple times];
- Dropped bombs on the people of more than thirty countries;
- Attempted to suppress a populist or nationalist movement in twenty countries.[17]

David Michael Smith calculated that this same country has been responsible or shared responsibility for the death of some 54 million people in its wars abroad between 1945 and 2020.[18] If we add domestic social murder to the equation and open up the time scale to include the entire history of what Smith calls the *Endless Holocausts* of the U.S. empire, the number is "close to 300 million deaths."[19] Based on these brute facts (Blum's are ten years old and would need to be updated), most people would easily recognize this country for what it is: "the greatest purveyor of violence in the world today" (in the words of Martin Luther King Jr.).[20] Many, however, do not share this view, and for one principal reason: this same country— the United States—has developed an incredibly powerful empire of ideas to hide, obscure, or deny these facts. In other words, it is also the greatest purveyor of intellectual war in the contemporary world.

What Che and his comrades represented was an actually existing impediment to empire. They leveraged one of its prize colonial possessions—which had served as a center for gambling, prostitution, the drug

---

17. William Blum, *America's Deadliest Export: Democracy and the Truth about US Foreign Policy and Everything Else* (London: Zed Books, 2013), 1.

18. See David Michael Smith, *Endless Holocausts: Mass Death in the History of the United States Empire* (New York: Monthly Review Press, 2023), 209, 256.

19. Ibid., 15.

20. Martin Luther King, Jr., "Beyond Vietnam: A Time to Break Silence," speech delivered at Riverside Church in New York City on April 4, 1967, https://www.commondreams.org/views/2018/01/15/beyond-vietnam-time-break-silence.

trade, agricultural extractivism, and tourism—away from the *yanquis*, and they put it back in the hands of the Cubans. This is why they needed to be destroyed, and this is why the U.S. war on Cuba and its crippling, illegal blockade have continued unabated. Whatever problems might occur within socialist countries, it should never be forgotten that they emerged out of, and within, a capitalist world intent on crushing them by any means necessary because of what they represent: an alternative to imperialism.

War of Ideas

The conscious and intelligent manipulation of the organized habits and opinions of the masses is an important element in democratic society. Those who manipulate this unseen mechanism of society constitute an invisible government which is the true ruling power of our country.

—EDWARD BERNAYS[21]

This book, like the two volumes that will follow it, focuses on a specific aspect of the war of ideas by concentrating on the capitalist ruling class's failed attempt to destroy its nemesis: communism. The story of Che's head recounted above provides, in microcosm, an overview of the fundamental issues at play in the macrocosm of this international class struggle in theory. It thereby provides a concise summary of some of the key themes of the analysis that follows:

- Imperial war goes hand in hand with ideological warfare.
- The battle for hearts and minds has multiple facets. It can serve to prepare for imperialist expansion, provide cover for repressive violence, manage the historical narrative, and much more.
- The intelligentsia—including journalists, writers, artists, pundits, and professors—plays a major role in psychological warfare, and thus class struggle in theory.
- The ideas that have been the most denigrated by empire—particularly communism—are those that are the most dangerous to it, whereas the ideas that have been the most promoted are those that serve imperial interests in various ways (sometimes indirectly).
- Bourgeois culture seeks to domesticate, and use for its own purposes, whatever dangerous ideas it cannot destroy or control outright.

---

21. Edward Bernays, *Propaganda* (New York: Ig Publishing, 2005), 37.

- The bourgeois democratic state, though it seeks to project an image of itself as a neutral guarantor of individual rights, works in the service of the bourgeoisie, whose bidding it does through both overt (government) and covert means (intelligence services). The relationship between a major corporation like United Fruit and a state agency like the CIA reveals a fundamental pattern regarding how the capitalist ruling class relates to its state, captured by the corrected acronym *Capitalism's Imperial Agency* (CIA).
- The war of anti-imperialist liberation is very much a material struggle, but it is also an ideological one.
- Theory, at some level, is engaged in class struggle, but ideas take on real transformative power when they grip the masses and are acted upon through organized politics.
- Anti-imperialist state building projects that develop socialism in the real world are the principal means of fighting imperialism.

This study focuses on a specific aspect of the psywar on communism by concentrating on the intellectual world war fought out among the professional intelligentsia. As witnessed in the case of Che, this battle is multifaceted, and it is by no means the product of mechanical causes. The approach in this investigation is dialectical, in the sense that it analyzes the nuances and complexities of this conflict as a many-sided phenomenon, emphasizing all of the different forms of agency at work. This includes, crucially, the political economy of knowledge, but not in a crassly reductivist sense. Rather than hypostasizing a superstructure and correlating it rather abstractly to an equally reified infrastructure, it examines the complex and fine-grained relationship between socioeconomic forces, on the one hand, and ideological production and dissemination on the other, while elucidating how dialectically enmeshed they are. This is not done, however, to shore up the Western Marxist thesis regarding the primacy of the ideological, but rather to demonstrate that socioeconomic conditions—in the macroscopic sense—are ultimately the primary driving forces, but they do not mechanically determine ideology.

It is therefore important to be attuned, from the outset, to the complex nature of the activities undertaken in the intellectual world war within the professional intelligentsia. These range from the practice of academically laundering state propaganda to the funding of publications and conferences, the establishment of research institutions and international knowledge networks, providing grants for particular projects, hiring theoreticians—wittingly or unwittingly—for certain tasks, promoting and translating the work of collaborationist intellectuals, and much more. It is essential to recognize, in this regard, how deeply Western intelligence services are involved in psychological warfare, which goes a long way to explaining why so many intellectuals have ties to them.

The thinkers who have participated in these psywar projects have played many different roles, and they have exercised their agency rather than somehow being rigorously determined in their thoughts and actions. Some of them have worked for the U.S. national security state, such as Sidney Hook and James Burnham, who were both prominent philosophy professors at New York University employed by the CIA.[22] The same is true for most of the members of the Frankfurt School hired in Washington, who worked for the Office of Strategic Services (the CIA's predecessor organization), the State Department, and propaganda agencies like the Office of War Information (OWI) and Voice of America.

Let us consider a few other examples, which illustrate one of the important but under-analyzed features of intellectual life in the imperial core, namely the sheer number of major figures who collaborated—in various and sundry ways—with imperial intelligence services (and whose careers certainly benefited from this). The liberal feminist icon Gloria Steinem worked as an agent of the CIA for at least four years. When this was revealed by *Ramparts*, she defended herself by claiming that the Agency's

---

22. Burnham moonlighted for the Office of Policy Coordination (OPC), the clandestine operations agency linked to the CIA, and he was apparently brought into the Agency "to help plan the CIA coup against Mossadegh in Iran." Richard Harris Smith, *OSS: The Secret History of America's First Central Intelligence Agency* (Berkeley, CA: University of California Press, 1972), 367. Hook served as a consultant to the Director of Central Intelligence and to the Psychological Strategy Board (PSB). He also "negotiated directly with CIA director Allen Dulles for committee funding [for the CIA-supported American Committee for Cultural Freedom]." Peter Finn and Petra Couvée, *The Zhivago Affair: The Kremlin, the CIA, and the Battle Over a Forbidden Book* (New York: Pantheon Books, 2014), 132. Hook's philosophy student at New York University (NYU), Felix Morrow, also had multiple CIA connections and was involved in publishing Agency propaganda (see ibid.). Burnham and Hook were major operators, moreover, in the CIA's Congress for Cultural Freedom (CCF) and, more generally, the intellectual world war on communism. For some of the details regarding both NYU professors, see Frances Stonor Saunders, *The Cultural Cold War: The CIA and the World of Arts and Letters* (New York: The New Press, 2000); Hugh Wilford, *The New York Intellectuals: From Vanguard to Institution* (Manchester: Manchester University Press, 1995); and Hugh Wilford, *The Mighty Wurlitzer: How the CIA Played America* (Cambridge, Massachusetts: Harvard University Press, 2008).

people "were enlightened, liberal, non-partisan activists."[23] "If I had the choice," she added, "I would do it again."[24] She had found in the CIA powerful allies for promoting "the diversity of our government's ideas" over and against communism.[25] Steinem's close collaboration with "psywar supremo" and Time, Inc. executive C. D. Jackson, who worked closely with the CIA, surely helped bolster her career as the face of U.S. feminism, thereby shoring up liberal and corporate approaches to gender and sexual relations over and against socialist feminism.[26]

The well-known anarchist political scientist James C. Scott also frankly admitted that he was recruited to the CIA when he went to Burma on a Rotary Fellowship, where he wrote reports for the Agency on the local political situation.[27] The anti-state radical then continued his sub rosa work for the deep state when his CIA contacts "arranged through the National Student Association [which they controlled] to have [him] go to Paris for a year and be an overseas representative."[28] As the International Vice President of the National Student Association, he was, in his own words, "a CIA agent."[29] Although he boldly claimed, in strict anarchist

23. The interview where Steinem made this claim is available here: https://www.youtube. com/watch?v=aoukTBdTio0. For more information on Steinem's work for the CIA, see Hugh Wilford, *The Mighty Wurlitzer*, 141–148; Joël Kotek, *Students and the Cold War*, trans. Ralph Blumenau (Basingstoke: Macmillan Press Ltd, 1996), 210–11, 220; Karen M. Paget, *Patriotic Betrayal: The Inside Story of the CIA's Secret Campaign to Enroll American Students in the Crusade Against Communism* (New Haven: Yale University Press, 2015); Markos Kounalakis, "The Feminist Was a Spook," *Chicago Daily Tribune*, October 25, 2015.

24. Quoted in Aryeh Neier, "When the Student Movement Was a CIA Front," *The American Prospect*, April 14, 2015, https://prospect.org/api/content/0d6b5f38-4c8f-5b07-b598-cd02524b6e5f/.

25. Cited in ibid.

26. Wilford, *The Mighty Wurlitzer*, 143.

27. See James C. Scott and Todd Holmes (interviewer), "James C. Scott: Agrarian Studies and Over 50 Years of Pioneering Work in the Social Sciences," The Yale Agrarian Studies Oral History Project, 2020, https://digicoll.lib.berkeley.edu/record/219393?v=pdf.

28. Ibid., 9. For more information on the CIA's control of the NSA, see "A Short Account of International Student Politics & the Cold War with Particular Reference to the NSA, CIA, Etc.," *Ramparts Magazine*, March 1967, http://archive.org/details/ramparts-magazine-march-1967-nsa-and-the-cia, and Wilford, *The Mighty Wurlitzer*, 123-48.

29. James C. Scott, Interview by Alan Macfarlane, March 26, 2009, https://www. youtube.com/watch?v=MP5bvOx4pyM (a rough transcript is available here: https:// api.repository.cam.ac.uk/server/api/core/bitstreams/523a2aab-8e5d-4fb8-b2c5-c47f8a0b34a7/content). This is his longer explanation of the situation: "when I worked for the National Students Association it turned out, after I was elected to be International

fashion, that "when the revolution becomes the State, it becomes my enemy again," Scott neglected to add that the most powerful state, which was an enemy of all revolutions, also happened to be his secret friend.[30]

To take a final example, one of the leading intellectuals affiliated with world-systems analysis, Immanuel Wallerstein, served in the U.S. Army during the Korean War from 1951 to 1953 and then began working in non-Communist international student organizations. He even became Vice President of the World Assembly of Youth (WAY), "a confederation of 51 youth groups from Western and non-Communist countries" that served to counter the World Federation of Democratic Youth (WFDY), headquartered in Warsaw.[31] WAY was financially precarious until the Foundation for Youth and Student Affairs (FYSA) became a major contributor. Bernice Bridges wrote to Wallerstein to express her concern about FYSA's outsized contributions and that the WFDY could now "prove their charges about American control."[32] It is not clear what Wallerstein responded. However, about a decade later the real source behind this foundation was revealed: the CIA.[33] In fact, in 1967 former CIA officer Thomas

---

Vice-President, I was delivering some resolutions we had passed at our annual student meeting on Haiti and other places, in Washington; I was asked to go to a meeting with someone who turned out to be a CIA agent, who wanted me to write reports for them; at the time I don't think I was ideologically opposed to that but I refused; it turned out that during my period working for the National Student Association, all my reports were sent by the president, who had been recruited by the CIA, to them; I wasn't paid, but I was in effect a CIA agent" (ibid.). For more information on Scott's CIA connections, see Paget, *Patriotic Betrayal*.

30. Benjamin Ferron, Claire Oger, and James C. Scott, "'When the Revolution Becomes the State It Becomes My Enemy Again': An Interview with James C. Scott," *The Conversation* (June 20, 2018), http://theconversation.com/when-the-revolution-becomes-the-state-it-becomes-my-enemy-again-an-interview-with-james-c-scott-98488. "The one thing I did learn," Scott explained in the video recording of this interview, "is that centralized revolutionary movements have almost always resulted in a state that was more oppressive than the state that they replaced. We think of Leninism and so on" (ibid.).

31. Neil Sheehan, "Foundations Linked to C.I.A. Are Found to Subsidize 4 Other Youth Organizations," *New York Times*, February 16, 1967, 26.

32. David Maunders, "Controlling Youth for Democracy: The United States Youth Council and the World Assembly of Youth 1946–1986," *Commonwealth Youth and Development* 1:2 (September 2003), 36.

33. See Rene Wadlow, "In Memory of Immanuel Wallerstein: Ah, We Were Once Young and Hopeful!" *Toward Freedom*, September 6, 2019, https://towardfreedom.org/story/in-memory-of-immanuel-wallerstein-ah-we-were-once-young-and-hopeful/. I would like to thank Franciszek Krawczyk for drawing my attention to this article and sharing with me a few insightful paragraphs of his dissertation that deal with Wallerstein.

W. Braden disclosed that the Agency had placed one of its men in the organization, which was also deeply penetrated by French intelligence.[34] It is interesting to note that Wallerstein avoided any direct mention of this in his autobiographical introduction to *The Essential Wallerstein*, and I am not aware of any public statement he made about serving as one of the leaders of an anticommunist student organization funded by the CIA and penetrated by Western intelligence services.[35] However, as his fellow student activist Rene Wadlow pointed out, Wallerstein maintained connections with members of these organizations, such as André Schiffrin, who later established The New Press and published many of Wallerstein's books.[36] There was "a real consensus between the American executive and the youth leaders of the time," according to Jöel Kotek, and many of them later pursued academic careers—like Wallerstein—or "chose to work for the CIA or one of its subsidiaries."[37] The famous Columbia and Yale professor, for his part, made an international career in knowledge networks bound up with the intellectual world war on communism.[38]

Many other such cases could be cited.[39] Collaboration with power-

---

34. See Thomas W. Braden, "I'm Glad the CIA Is 'Immoral,'" *Saturday Evening Post*, May 20, 1967, 13.

35. See Immanuel Wallerstein, *The Essential Wallerstein* (New York: The New Press, 2000), xvi. Wallerstein also received "a Ford Foundation African Fellowship to study in Africa and write a dissertation on the Gold Coast (Ghana) and the Ivory Coast in terms of the role voluntary associations played in the rise of the nationalist movements in the two countries" (ibid.).

36. See Wadlow, "In Memory of Immanuel Wallerstein."

37. Kotek, *Students and the Cold War*, 220-21.

38. For instance, in addition to obtaining a Ford Foundation African Fellowship to write his dissertation in Africa, Wallerstein served intermittently as a Directeur d'études associé at the École des Hautes Études en Sciences Sociales (EHESS) in Paris (and also founded the Fernand Braudel Center). Braudel and the EHESS, as we shall see, played important roles in the psywar on communism and tended to be recognized as allies by the Ford and Rockefeller interests, as well as the CIA.

39. Documentary and testimonial evidence has been brought forth to demonstrate that Julia Kristeva, in the early 1970s, secretly collaborated with the foreign-intelligence arm of Bulgarian State Security. This seems to have been primarily for opportunistic reasons, and she increasingly took her distance as her fame grew in the West and her politics turned sharply against the East (twin phenomena that tend to accompany one another). Kristeva, ostensibly to preserve her status as an icon of the imperial theory industry, has vigorously rejected the copious evidence as fiction, in what appears to be an opportunistic attempt to mobilize postmodern irrationalism for the purposes of self-aggrandizing exoneration. Much has been written on the topic, but *Le Nouvel Observateur* published a number of articles on the topic in March and April 2018, including this reply by Kristeva:

ful state agencies often accompanies, like a shadow, intellectual fame in the capitalist world. This is not only the case for right-wing thinkers but also, as we have just seen, for leftists subservient to anticommunist dogma such as the liberal, the anarchist, and the eclectic Western Marxist just mentioned.[40] These are all positions that the CIA identified as part of the compatible or respectable left, meaning the left that was compatible with capitalism and respectable because it condemned communism. The Agency promoted this non-communist left, from behind the scenes, precisely because it was one of the best ways of fragmenting the left and, most importantly, waging an all-out war on the incompatible left of the communists. To be clear, connections to this project do not, in and of themselves, invalidate the entirety of a scholar's contributions. These need to be assessed dialectically through a nuanced process of interpretation that distinguishes useful developments from ideologically compromised positions. Wallerstein, for instance, has done some important work, which will be referenced in the pages that follow.

In undertaking a dialectical analysis of intellectual collaboration, it is essential to avoid focusing narrowly on particular agencies, such as the CIA, and instead construct a comprehensive understanding of the social totality, encompassing various state agencies, non-governmental organizations, and corporate soft power initiatives. An intellectual did not have to collaborate directly with the CIA to play a role in the intellectual world war on communism. The world-famous anthropologist Margaret Mead, for instance, served as a State Department consultant and "secured funding from the Air Force's new think tank, the Rand Corporation, to set up a Studies in Soviet Culture project."[41] Ernesto Laclau, a towering figure

Julia Kristeva, "Droit de réponse à 'L'Obs,'" *Le Nouvel Observateur*, April 11, 2018, https://www.nouvelobs.com/actualites/20180411.OBS4959/droit-de-reponse-a-l-obs-par-julia-kristeva.html. In English, although it suffers from rank anticommunism, this article provides a helpful overview, including some of the testimonial evidence by the agents who worked with Kristeva: Dimiter Kenarov, "Was the Philosopher Julia Kristeva a Cold War Collaborator?" *The New Yorker*, September 5, 2018.

40. Wallerstein eclectically drew on Marxism and many other traditions, particularly Fernand Braudel's version of Annales School historiography, and he did not understand his research agenda as part of the collective tradition of dialectical and historical materialism. See, for instance, Immanuel Wallerstein, Carlos Aguirre Rojas, and Charles C. Lemert, *Uncertain Worlds: World-Systems Analysis in Changing Times* (London and New York: Routledge, 2012), 18–21.

41. Thomas Meaney, review of *The Swaddling Thesis*, by Peter Mandler, *London Review of Books*, March 6, 2014, https://www.lrb.co.uk/the-paper/v36/n05/thomas-meaney/the-

in post-Marxist critical theory, was employed as a researcher in the Ford Foundation's *Proyecto Marginalidad* (Marginality Project). According to Néstor Kohan's insightful analysis, which draws on Daniel Hopen's exacting scholarship, this 1960s project "sought to identify what would happen to the sectors of the working class that would become unemployed and marginalized."[42] The imperialists were thereby preparing for the neoliberal shock therapy that would begin in earnest in Chile after the CIA's 1973 coup d'état, and they wanted to understand possible reactions in order to develop counter-insurgency plans. Everyone knew, according to Kohan, that behind Ford stood "the world's leading counterinsurgency institution" (the CIA).[43]

Moreover, collaboration comes in many forms, and it is important to be attentive to what we might call the concentric circles of collaboration. If the inner circle consists in direct witting employment, followed by another tight ring of unwitting work serving the same purpose, there are many other orbits, which often interact with one another. Some intellectuals were directly involved in anticommunist subversion campaigns but were not, as far as we know, in the direct employ of intelligence services like the CIA. This was the case for major figures like Jacques Derrida, Michel Foucault, and Slavoj Žižek, who committed themselves, in very practical terms, to the overthrow of communism. Other professors collaborated with the knowledge networks supported by the ruling class and—sometimes clandestinely—government agencies, thereby owing a portion of their fame to promotion by the bourgeoisie and its men and women of the shadows (Theodor Adorno, Hannah Arendt, Raymond Aron, Max Horkheimer, and countless others, but of course to varying degrees). As Frances Stonor Saunders asserted in her pathbreaking study of the CIA's Congress for Cultural Freedom (CCF): "Whether they liked it or not, whether they knew it or not, there were few writers, poets, artists, historians, scientists or critics in post-war Europe whose names were not

---

swaddling-thesis. Mead's book, *Soviet Attitudes towards Authority* (1951), was prepared for the Rand Corporation. Mead was also involved in the intelligence-connected Salzburg Seminar. See Wilford, *The Mighty Wurlitzer*, 129, and Ioana Popa, "International Construction of Area Studies in France during the Cold War: Insights from the École Pratique des Hautes Études 6th Section," *History of the Human Sciences*, Vol. 29, No. 4–5 (2016), 131.

42. Néstor Kohan, *La brújula y el mapa: Cultura, crítica y ciencias sociales en la revolución cubana* (Cuba: Ocean Sur, 2022), 269. Also see Néstor Kohan, ed., *Ciencias sociales y marxismo latinoamericano* (Buenos Aires: Amauta Insurgente, 2015).

43. Kohan, *La brújula y el mapa*, 269-70.

in some way linked to this covert enterprise."[44] Many intellectuals have developed their work in what they consider to be an autonomous fashion and do not have clear connections to the networks just mentioned. However, they tend to ignore or downplay the fact that, materially speaking, they are working within systems of knowledge ultimately controlled by the bourgeoisie, so their advancement within them largely depends on how much their intellectual labor segues with the interests of the owners of the means of intellectual production (this is the real meritocracy).

These nuances will be spelled out through the course of this analysis, but it is important to insist at the outset on a dialectical approach to intellectual collaboration in order to preempt crude and reductivist interpretations of the study that follows. This book, like its companion volumes, is most definitively not advancing a simplistic and reductive argument that the intelligentsia has been remote-controlled by the CIA, or that there is a centralized theoretical conspiracy that explains every aspect of intellectual history. On the contrary, by examining the material reality of intellectual production dialectically, it brings to the fore the intricate complexities of social relations, with all of the various types of agency at work, which are never stagnant or isolated, but are rather interrelated as processes situated within the social totality.

Doctrinal Warfare

Doctrinal (ideological) warfare is, or should be, a central factor in our psychological warfare. It exposes the basic vulnerabilities of the hostile systems and exploits the beneficial or favorable aspects of one's own system to persuade people away from the former and to adopt rational solutions. It should provide the foundation on which effective propaganda could be based.

—MEMO FOR THE DOCTRINAL (IDEOLOGICAL) WARFARE PANEL OF THE PSYCHOLOGICAL STRATEGY BOARD (PSB)[45]

The war of ideas is not simply a battle over particular notions or specific issues. As clearly outlined in internal documents from the early Cold War,

---

44. Saunders, *The Cultural Cold War*, 2.
45. Memo on Tentative Terms of Reference for the Doctrinal (Ideological) Warfare Panel (PSB), November 14, 1952, Edward P. Lilly: Papers, Box 54, Folder Doctrinal Programs 1952, Dwight D. Eisenhower Library, 2.

it is, at the highest level, a question of doctrinal warfare.[46] This expression is used to refer to the fight to control people's overall ideological world-view or "doctrine," meaning the general framework within which specific ideas are situated. The psywarriors of the U.S. national security state recognized how important this is because if you are able to consolidate an ideological gestalt, then any particular experience will be mediated by it, including ones that appear to contradict it. In this way, apparent exceptions are interpreted via an all-encompassing ideological paradigm, which—if the doctrinal warfare is successful—remains unshakeable, in spite of potential countervailing evidence. This resilience stems from the role of ideological doctrine in interpreting the totality of experience, allowing anomalies to be rationalized or dismissed without undermining the core system of belief. Doctrinal warfare thereby serves to fortify a foundational ideological worldview that remains impervious to empirical contradictions.

This approach to the war of ideas was clearly outlined by the U.S. Psychological Strategy Board (PSB), which was established in 1951 and tasked with "the formulation and promulgation, as guidance to the departments and agencies responsible for psychological operations, of over-all national psychological objectives, policies and programs, and for the coordination and evaluation of the national psychological effort."[47] Composed of agency directors, the PSB reported to the National Security Council (NSC).[48] In its June 29, 1953, report on the U.S. doctrinal program it explained that the goal of the PSB was to provide "permanent literature" and foster "long-term intellectual movements, which will appeal to intellectuals, including scholars and opinion-forming groups."[49] It explicitly recognized that the target audience for doctrinal warfare is the professional intelligentsia. The logic is simple: because it manages the minds of

---

46. Among other sources, see the folders on the "Doctrinal Programs" in Edward P. Lilly: Papers, Boxes 54-55, Dwight D. Eisenhower Library.

47. Directive Establishing the Psychological Strategy Board, June 20, 1951, Harry S. Truman Library, https://www.trumanlibrary.gov/library/public-papers/128/directive-establishing-psychological-strategy-board.

48. The PSB included "the Undersecretary of State, the Deputy Secretary of Defense, and the Director of Central Intelligence, or, in their absence, their appropriate designees," as well as "an appropriate representative of the head of each such other department or agency of the Government as may, from time to time, be determined by the Board" (ibid.).

49. Psychological Strategy Board, Report on U.S. Doctrinal Program, June 29, 1953, Edward P. Lilly: Papers, Box 54, Folder Doctrinal Programs 1953 (3), Dwight D. Eisenhower Library, 1.

the masses through the media, education, religious organizations, civic associations, etc., the intelligentsia—if correctly trained—can establish and consolidate an ideological doctrine among the general population.

Part of this project was negative, and internal documents clearly spell out the importance of an intellectual world war on communism as the rival doctrine to be broken down and ideally eliminated. Indeed, there are long and detailed PSB documents that provide point by point refutations of major communist themes, which served as guidelines for the intelligentsia.[50] At the same time, the other principal objective of doctrinal warfare is to "foster a world-wide understanding and sympathetic acceptance of the traditions and viewpoints of America and the Free World."[51] In its studies, the PSB found that negative doctrinal warfare was much less effective if it was not combined with the positive battle for hearts and minds that sought to consolidate a belief in the superiority of "the Free World."

One of the most intriguing and strategically significant tactics that is encouraged, which is essential to understand for a complete picture of the history of Western Marxism, consists in a subtle, soft-sell campaign against communism. Rather than systematically attacking everything to do with Marxism and communism, the PSB recognized that it was preferrable, at least in certain cases, to foster the development of a form of Marxism that could serve as a tool for both criticizing communism and defending the so-called Free World. A PSB memorandum on ideological warfare therefore explicitly recommends two tasks that might sound surprising to those who assume that the U.S. government was crudely anticommunist across the board: "Attacks against Communist ideology developed in Marxist terms" and "defense of Western society in Marxist terms."[52] In both cases, the objective was to mobilize Marxism to assail communism and defend the capitalist world. By putting Marxism itself in the service of doctrinal warfare, intellectuals convinced by Marxist

---

50. See, for instance, the paper "dealing with current major Communist themes as well as some arguments refuting them," March 28, 1956, Edward P. Lilly: Papers, Box 55, Folder Doctrinal Programs 1956–1964, Dwight D. Eisenhower Library and Character and Content of the Ideological Attack, Edward P. Lilly: Papers, Box 55, Folder Doctrinal Programs—undated material, Dwight D. Eisenhower Library.

51. Psychological Strategy Board, Report on U.S. Doctrinal Program, June 29, 1953, Edward P. Lilly: Papers, Box 54, Folder Doctrinal Programs 1953 (3), Dwight D. Eisenhower Library, 1.

52. "Ideological Warfare," May 16, 1952, the CIA FOIA Electronic Reading Room, https://www.cia.gov/readingroom/document/cia-rdp80-01065a000100010006-0.

theory were thereby encouraged to hold on to a purportedly authentic version of Marxism while using it to vilify Marxism in practice and—at a minimum—accommodate capitalism.

It is revealing that both tasks were taken up in earnest by Western Marxists of various stripes. Some of them had direct ties to the U.S. national security state, and others simply operated within the imperial intellectual system of knowledge, generally receiving uplift for their ideological alignment on the dominant doctrine. Among those who worked for the bourgeois state, Herbert Marcuse stands out as a particularly revealing case, as we will see in detail, because he was not simply one of the Western Marxists who took up the torch of the anticommunist Marxism that was being covertly promoted by government agencies like the PSB. Rather than being a target of doctrinal warfare, he was one of its perpetrators: the PSB "used the memoranda of [Marcuse's] CWC [Committee on World Communism in the State Department] as one of its most important sources of information."[53]

Unlike short-term propaganda campaigns, then, doctrinal warfare is a long-term battle to shore up the ideology of the intelligentsia, thereby guaranteeing that the rest of the population will be constantly exposed to the same fundamental worldview. If all of the experts agree on the fundamentals, despite any minor disagreements, it sends the message that their consensus is based on objective reality rather than being driven by an ideological agenda. In order to be effective, doctrinal warfare cannot be intermittent but instead requires the development of three interlocking projects, according to the PSB:

1 Long-range plans for the production and distribution of intellectual materials and for the direction of activities aimed separately and concurrently at appealing to intellectuals, including scholars and opinion-forming groups.
2 Provocative and stimulating doctrinal materials which critically and effectively analyze Communist doctrines, as well as those objectively setting forth the viewpoints of America and the Free World.
3 Improve distribution mechanisms for permanent literature, not only American, but also foreign materials.[54]

---

53. Tim B. Müller, *Krieger und Gelehrte: Herbert Marcuse und die Denksysteme im Kalten Krieg* (Hamburg: Hamburger Edition, 2011), 145.
54. Psychological Strategy Board, Report on U.S. Doctrinal Program, June 29, 1953, 2. Also see Draft Summary Statement, Edward P. Lilly: Papers, Box 55, Folder Doctrinal

Successful doctrinal warfare therefore necessitates a powerful material system of ideological production, distribution, and consumption that constantly and consistently communicates the appeal of the dominant ideology, while criticizing its rival through "provocative and stimulating" materials. The massive industry of anti-Cuban ideological production and dissemination would be one example of how doctrinal warfare works, as long as it is understood as part of a much larger anticommunist psywar that seeks to shore up the doctrinal belief in the superiority of the supposed free world—that is, the one intent on destroying Cuba's freedom.

You Cannot Kill Ideas that Fight Back

The upside-down world teaches us to suffer reality instead of changing it, to forget the past instead of listening to it, and to accept the future instead of imagining it: that is how it practices crime, and that is how it recommends it. In its school, the school of crime, the classes of impotence, amnesia, and resignation are obligatory. But it is clear that there is no misfortune without fortune, nor a side that does not have its flip side, nor discouragement that does not seek its encouragement. Nor is there a school that does not encounter its counter-school.

—EDUARDO GALEANO[55]

The intellectual world war is an endeavor to turn the world upside down by presenting imperial expansion as democracy promotion and counter-revolutionary violence as the struggle for freedom, while simultaneously slandering anti-imperialist state building projects grounded in democratic self-determination as part of an evil empire. The imperial forces have the most powerful cultural apparatus in the history of the world on their side. Yet they have been incapable of killing an idea—in the broad sense of a general ideological worldview—that has meant so much

---

Programs—undated material, Dwight D. Eisenhower Library: "The Doctrinal Program seeks to utilize long-range and pervasive channels of international communication to convey to foreign audiences the 'case' for genuine democracy as opposed to Soviet communism. That 'case' embraces two emphases: the negative, or anti-communist, and the positive, or pro-free society."
55. Eduardo Galeano, *Upside Down: A Primer for the Looking-Glass World*, trans. Mark Fried (New York: Picador, 2000), 8, translation significantly modified based on Eduardo Galeano, *Patas arriba: La escuela del mundo al revés* (Madrid, 2019), 8.

to so many people around the world, who are struggling for liberation and to save the planet from capitalist liquidation. They have also failed to crush the autonomous systems of cultural production built up by the anti-imperialist camp—the counter-school mentioned by Galeano—in an effort to spread this idea and mobilize it for a material project of social transformation.

Thomas Sankara, sometimes referred to as the Che of Africa, gave a speech in 1987 at the inauguration of an exhibition honoring the life of the great revolutionary. Titled "You Cannot Kill Ideas," Sankara asserted that "for us Che Guevara is not dead."[56] He was alive in Burkina Faso, and Africa more generally, "because some of his ideas live in each of us in the daily struggle we wage."[57] Che's revolutionary conviction, his sense of humanity, and his demanding character that forced him to make common cause with the people, all of these were operative in the Burkinabé revolutionary project. The same was true, more generally, of his resolute anti-imperialism, his defense of self-determination, his dedication to building socialism, and his use of dialectical and historical materialism as the most powerful weapon of class struggle.

A week after this speech, Sankara's revolutionary government was overthrown and he was assassinated, revealing, once again, that the intellectual world war is not simply theoretical.[58] It is a fight for the kind of world that we want to live in, a battle over the very nature of reality and what we think is possible. It is a conflict that positions us all and forces us to take sides. Are we with the imperialists, reaping material rewards for trampling on others, or do we make common cause with the anti-imperialists, who seek to uplift the lives of all? Whose ideas do we want to carry forth in the world and embody in material reality through our struggles: those of the liberators who have strived, under dire circumstances and constant onslaught, to make the idea of a better world into a material reality, or those who have sought to stop the socialist project in its tracks by not only killing its leaders, but also attempting to destroy the very idea they embody?

---

56. Thomas Sankara, *Thomas Sankara Speaks: The Burkina Faso Revolution 1983–1987* (New York: Pathfinder Press, 2007), 453.

57. Ibid., 455.

58. Regarding Sankara's assassination, see Bruno Jaffré, "Les circonstances de l'assassinat de Thomas Sankara," *Thomas Sankara* (blog), February 26, 2021, https://www.thomassankara.net/who-killed-thomas-sankara-by-bruno-jaffre/.

Introduction to
The Intellectual World War

CLASS STRUGGLE IN THEORY

Prologue

Some books take a decade to write. This one took three. It even became three books in the process (or actually four, if one counts the French version I wrote before this trilogy, which the publisher pulled the plug on at the last second for political and economic reasons). It is the result of extensive research and a journey, with many unexpected twists and turns, through the heart of the imperial theory industry. Since it advances a counter-history of contemporary thought that not only challenges established interpretations and hallowed canons but proposes a historiographical paradigm shift, at least regarding the standard imperial narratives, it is essential that the reader be able to situate it within the material system of knowledge production out of which it emerged. This, after all, is what allowed me to develop my research agenda from subjective self-criticism, which was its starting point, to systemic ideology critique.

The autobiographical interlude that follows—the tone of which is markedly different than the rest of the book because it is narrated in the first person—provides an opportunity to dialectically situate the author within the broader material reality that is the project's focal point. This also serves to clarify the motivations behind this work, while detailing its basic orientation, method, and structure.

From Self-Criticism to Systemic Ideology Critique

> It's easier to fool someone than convince them that they've been
> fooled.
>
> —ATTRIBUTED TO MARK TWAIN[1]

In the fall of 2001, I was studying philosophy in Paris, France. I had completed a master's degree under the direction of Jacques Derrida, after
having worked with Luce Irigaray, and I was enrolled for my Ph.D. with
Alain Badiou. I thought I was on the top of the intellectual world, living
my American dream of studying with the leading luminaries of French
theory. When the attacks of September 11 happened, I was asked to make
sense of the events in a public lecture at one of the institutions where I
was teaching.

To say I was ill-equipped would be generous. What did I really have to
say about what had just happened? Given my training, perhaps I could
frame the events, which I scarcely understood at the time, in terms of
an irreconcilable differend between phrase regimens, or a confrontation
with the big Other? Maybe the planet was being deterritorialized under
our feet, or we had just entered the desert of the Lacanian Real? If all else
failed, I could fall back on references to the ever-nebulous *différance* as
the condition of possibility—and impossibility—of all thought and discourse, thereby making some ponderously abstract metaphysical claims
that could not possibly be beholden to reality.

As I tried to collect my thoughts and apply them to an actual historical
occurrence, I could not help but feel like all of this conceptual gibber-
ish sounded like I was saying we were living in la-la land, an imaginary
world of big Others, great mystical divides, shifting sands, and personified landscapes. Why not add cellophane flowers and marmalade skies
to this surreal conceptual scenery, which made the world seem like an
utterly meaningless plaything? I became nauseous thinking about it, and I
desperately wanted to go back through the looking glass to retrieve some
sense of reality, to have something concrete and meaningful to say. But
it was too late, and all I could do with my elite education in the imperial
core was cobble together an ill-fated attempt to explain reality through

---

1. Although this saying has been widely attributed to Twain, he did not actually write
it, according to the Center for Mark Twain Studies, which suggests that W. L. Baldridge
penned a statement closer to this formulation. See   https://marktwainstudies.com/
easiertocon/.

the lens of trend-setting critical theory. Fortunately, there was at least one important lesson. I was forced to see, reflected back at me, an image of what I had become: an utterly useless intellectual. Even worse, I had been trained to think of myself in opposite terms, namely as a participant in the theoretical avant-garde of humanity. The world was upside down.

This was one moment of crystallization, which I am intentionally simplifying, in a much more complex trajectory, but it forced me to do something that I was never taught to do: self-critically reflect on my own theoretical practice. Here I was, after years of vigorous study at premier institutions in Paris, and I was ignorant of imperialism and the geopolitical world in which I was living. I knew so much about things that mattered so incredibly little, and I knew nothing about what counted most in the world and was literally an issue of life or death for the majority of humanity and the biosphere. I had passed all of the exams with flying colors and received the highest possible academic distinctions, but what had I really learned? What I had been trained in, most fundamentally, was imperial ignorance.

How could I not be ashamed, given where I had come from, and what I had set out to do? After all, I had grown up on a farm in Kansas, working construction. What had first attracted me to the life of the mind was that I cherished the respite from grueling manual labor. My earliest intellectual ambitions were to try to understand why life was marred by such drudgery and figure out how it could be ended. What I had learned, instead, was that, in the words of my legendary *maître* (Derrida), it is impossible to formulate meaningful sentences with the term *social class*.[2] Apparently, if you are a renowned intellectual, you can simply will into nonexistence, through supercilious proclamation, the most fundamental structural aspect of life in class society. This, I later realized, is a flagrant performative contradiction: Derrida was signaling his class standing in the very act of making such a statement. It was a shibboleth, in the precise sense of this term.

When I went to college in Iowa in the early 1990s, I sought out the most radical forms of theory available because I wanted the tools necessary to understand and change a world characterized by exploitation and oppression. What was on offer was French theory, Frankfurt School

---

2. See Jacques Derrida, *Negotiations: Interventions and Interviews, 1971–2001*, trans. Elizabeth Rottenberg (Stanford, CA: Stanford University Press, 2002), 170: "I cannot construct finished or plausible sentences using the expression *social class*. I don't really know what *social class* means."

critical theory, as well as more recent trends in the Anglophone world inspired by these traditions. I therefore dedicated myself to learning all of the languages and histories necessary to understand them. Having found French theory, and in particular the work of Derrida, the most challenging and—at least in my young mind—the most radical, I decided that I wanted to try and study under him in Paris. I was able to obtain a scholarship from Rotary International, and I moved there in 1996.

My interests in radical theory were thereby canalized, through institutional mechanisms, in a very specific direction. When I arrived in Paris, I eagerly frequented all of the lectures and seminars by the thinkers who were the most renowned in the United States, as well as those who had potential to become so, including—in addition to those under whom I was studying—Étienne Balibar, Hélène Cixous, Julia Kristeva, François Laruelle, Jean-François Lyotard, Jean-Luc Marion, Jacques Rancière, and Paul Ricœur. I also shunned those doing work that sounded old school or unsophisticated.

As a sedulous student intimidated by being outclassed by my peers, I not only read the writings of these major theorists, but I also carefully studied the texts that they interpreted. I was surprised to discover so many discrepancies between the two. As I would later write in my first book, Derrida was so preoccupied, à la Martin Heidegger, with finding the specter of Western metaphysics haunting canonical texts that he discovered it wherever he wanted, independently of the empirical reality of the texts themselves (not to mention their material context, which he systematically ignored).[3] Although he presented himself as a serious student of history, unlike Derrida, Michel Foucault's work ended up revealing a strikingly similar pattern. For instance, he haughtily proclaimed that there was a crucial distinction between *Herkunft* and *Ursprung* (both translatable as "origin") in Friedrich Nietzsche's writings, but he referenced innumerable texts where these words either did not appear at all or were employed in ways that directly contradicted his interpretation.[4] If their writings did not hold up to a minimum of

---

3. See Gabriel Rockhill, *Logique de l'histoire: Pour une analytique des pratiques philosophiques* (Paris: Éditions Hermann, 2010). Some of my work from this period is also available in English in Gabriel Rockhill, *Interventions in Contemporary Thought: History, Politics, Aesthetics* (Edinburgh: Edinburgh University Press, 2016).
4. See Gabriel Rockhill, "Foucault, Genealogy, Counter-History," *Theory & Event* 23/1 (January 2020): 85–119, as well as Gabriel Rockhill, "Comment penser le temps présent? De l'ontologie de l'actualité à l'ontologie sans l'être," *Rue Descartes* 75 (2012/3): 114–26.

scholarly scrutiny, how could this work be celebrated as some of the most important in the world?

My reaction to these disappointments was to seek out more radical discourses that were directly engaged in elucidating the concrete, material world. I read broadly in Frankfurt School critical theory and Western Marxism. I also enrolled for a master's degree in the historical social sciences, writing a thesis under the guidance of Bourdieusian sociologists, and I later completed a postdoctoral degree in political theory. In a similar vein, I began a working group and pooled resources to organize an international lecture series and interviews with cutting-edge critical theorists like Seyla Benhabib, Judith Butler, Nancy Fraser, Chantal Mouffe, Immanuel Wallerstein, and Cornel West.[5] Here, I thought, were truly political thinkers engaged in understanding the real world and struggling to change it. Increasingly attracted to radical discourses, I dedicated myself to studying the most revolutionary theory I could find, which included the writings of Badiou and Rancière, as well as those of Giorgio Agamben, Michael Hardt, Antonio Negri, Slavoj Žižek, and many others.

I continued to have doubts and self-doubts, however. For all of these theorists' radical phraseology, the principal takeaways were usually less than satisfying. Some, for instance, flatly proclaimed that Gilles Deleuze's addled statements on control societies could better elucidate the world than the scientific approach of dialectical and historical materialism, but they could never clearly explain why or how. Others seemed to be formulating Marxist critiques, but they would frequently be interrupted by the need to proliferate pseudo-intellectual references or engage à la Žižek in navel-gazing reflections about their *jouissance* and what they saw online that day. They all agreed, including those in the Frankfurt School, that Marxism could only be of value if it was spruced up with the requisite dose of bourgeois culture. This ran the gamut from raucous Lacanian sex jokes on the ultraleft to pedantic Habermasian palaver further to the right, but the consensus was clear: they were all doing something innovative and much more sophisticated than what the old school Marxists had done.

It took more than a decade of studying and teaching in Paris, as well as nearly two decades of activism and doing my own research on the history of anti-imperialist Marxism and the global socialist movement, to finally start to see the system of knowledge production for what it was. Initially,

---

5. The interviews, which I conducted with my collaborator Alfredo Gomez-Muller, were published in *Politics of Culture and the Spirit of Critique: Dialogues* (New York: Columbia University Press, 2011).

I had only grasped it from the point of view of a rat in the maze, and I began by mapping out the parts that I knew well. Little by little, however, the map started to cohere into a systematic outline, and everything began to fall into place. It was this shift that was the most fundamental. When I was asked to give that ill-fated lecture on September 11, 2001, it led to an intensification of my subjective ideology critique, which consisted in an extremely painful but absolutely necessary process of calling into question my own indoctrination (which I had misinterpreted as education). However, once I was able, over the course of decades, to build up a materialist analysis of the system of knowledge production, circulation, and consumption within which I had been trained, I could map out the entire maze. It is this that allowed me to begin the deeper and much more important task of systemic ideological criticism. This consists in diagnosing and seeking to dismantle the system that forges individuals and composes them as ideological subjects.

If you demonstrate to someone that they've been ideologically inculcated, they may be able to overcome it. If you teach them how the system works that brainwashed them, they are given the tools necessary to liberate themselves and others because objective ideological criticism of this sort brings into relief the system that produces—and will continue to produce and reproduce—ideological subjects. This is one of the ultimate objectives of this book, as well as the rest of the trilogy, namely to provide an objective ideological critique of the material system of ideas that produced an ideological subject like me and, much more importantly, legions of others indoctrinated into the same brand of imperial ignorance. I was, after all, far from being the only one living in a conceptual la-la land where metaphorical thinking and superstitious free association are considered a sophisticated ersatz for rigorous, empirically grounded argumentation, as anyone who has been to a theory conference is—or should be—well aware. And I was certainly not unique in mistakenly assuming that Western or cultural Marxism was the most advanced form of Marxism.

The bourgeois knowledge regime is not only epistemological, however; it is a system of power and control. It is one thing to recognize how it works and study it systematically. It is something else entirely to be able to publish one's findings and have them be taken seriously. Attempting to do so sets one on a collision course with those who own the means of communication and their managers. I would be remiss, then, not to mention that this entire research project has been extremely difficult to bring into the world. Many platforms have refused to publish its findings, and an equal number have taken pot shots at it, usually with no engagement with the evidence. In the most extreme case, I was given a crash course in the real, material operations of the imperial theory industry and the awesome power of its gatekeepers by Éditions La Fabrique in Paris. As briefly mentioned, this trilogy began, years ago, as a book I finished for this publishing house, which is approximately the French equivalent of Verso Books. After a long process of constant interventions by editors who admitted that they knew little or nothing about the material but nonetheless insisted that I make changes, they pulled the plug on the entire project right before it was set to go to press. They claimed, in short, that I should have praised instead of criticized certain golden calves of the imperial theory industry, but the real reason for sinking the project was that it called into question La Fabrique's market niche. I was too naïve to understand this at the time, and I thought that self-declared radical publishers would support well-researched scholarship that was pushing the envelope, even if it was critical of some of their established values. La Fabrique provided me with a practical understanding of how the gatekeepers of the imperial theory industry will exclude any in-depth critique of their profit model. Fortunately, although I lost years of research time, this experience sharpened my analysis by offering an invaluable lesson in the political economy of knowledge production and the power dynamics of publishing.

Motive

> The truth is warlike, it does not only fight against untruthfulness, but also against certain people who spread untruth.
>
> —BERTOLT BRECHT[6]

Why put so much time and energy into engaging in a systemic ideology critique of the Western left intelligentsia?

The purpose of this critique is fourfold. First of all, it seeks to elucidate the fundamental driving forces behind ideological production and dissemination, while also detailing the precise mechanisms by which the entire system operates. It thereby provides people with an understanding of the social totality that situates ideas within the broader framework of material reality and class struggle. This aspect of ideology critique cultivates a scientific understanding of how the world of ideas operates,

---

6. Bertolt Brecht, *Brecht on Art and Politics*, ed. Tom Kuhn and Steve Giles (London: Methuen, 2003), 148.

shedding light on the ways in which the dominant ideology is produced and perpetuated, whose interests it serves, whom it targets, and how exactly it functions in specific situations. Ideological criticism of the left intelligentsia in the imperial core contributes, in this way, to a more scientific account of the production, circulation, and consumption of ideas.

The second purpose is to provide a more scientifically rigorous analysis of reality in general, above and beyond ideology. Science should not be understood in reductively positivist terms as the perfect apprehension of objective reality, but rather as a collective process of establishing the most coherent framework of explanation, testing it in practical reality, and continuing to perfect it based on new information. Science is thus a fallibilistic process of developing knowledge via the dialectical relationship between human beings and the larger material world. Engaging in systemic ideological criticism thereby not only allows us to properly diagnose and fully understand the disease of ideology, but it also helps to cultivate the cure by apprehending material reality in the most rigorous manner possible. The intellectual world war that is the focal point of this study is not only an ideological battle; it is a fight over the very nature of reality, as well as who has the right—and the power—to define it.

The third reason to undertake a systemic ideology critique is to provide the most coherent framework for practical action since the point is not only to understand reality, but to change it. One of the goals of this project is to rejuvenate class struggle in theory, as a contribution to an overall revitalization of class struggle. Much of what passes for intellectual debate in the imperial core takes place within the same fundamental ideological framework, and it is relatively rare to have this called into question. Anticommunism, for instance, remains largely hegemonic, even among those who are self-declared Marxists or even communists. One of the most pernicious effects of the dominant ideology has been a discrediting and perversion of dialectical and historical materialism (DHM), based on widespread misrepresentations and propagandistic versions of history. Given the proven ability of DHM to serve as a practical guide to action, with a proven record of success, one of the most pressing tasks of class struggle in theory is to shore up and further develop this tradition.

Last, but certainly not least, this critique of the Western left intelligentsia is part of a broader critical reflection on the history of the left in the imperial core and the need for a fundamental reorientation. Theory, Marx incisively explained, takes on real power in the world when it comes to grip the masses. The anticommunist, capitalist accommodationist theory of the Western left intelligentsia has seized the masses to the point of becoming hegemonic within the broader left. This is due in large part to the material position of the working class in the imperial core, which is situated as a labor aristocracy at the apex of the global division of labor, but it is also the result of the ideological power wielded by the imperial intelligentsia. In attacking the latter, the ultimate goal is to reorient the left in general, above and beyond the intelligentsia, toward an anti-imperialist politics that embraces, rather than rejects, projects of socialist sovereignty.

Why, though, be so critical of the Western left and its leading intellectuals? The short answer is because they have abandoned, sidelined, or modified beyond recognition the primary weapon of class struggle for the working and oppressed peoples of the world. This is partially a result of the global class standing of the Western left intelligentsia, or what would better be described as the intellectual labor aristocracy. As members of the imperial professional managerial class stratum, these intellectuals are perched comfortably atop a global system of intellectual production. They do not have any material incentive to change the system, since it supports and even promotes them, and they have therefore tended to accommodate capitalism, and even imperialism, by maintaining that there is no real-world alternative.

The Western left intelligentsia's general abandonment of revolutionary politics comes into sharp relief in a historical conjuncture where the stakes of international class struggle could not be higher. We have definitively entered the age of exterminism, according to Georges Gastaud, when it is code red for humanity and the entire planet.[7] Capitalist social murder is systematically destroying life, as Ali Kadri has powerfully argued, and global socioeconomic inequality has never been more extreme.[8]

---

7. See, for instance, John Bellamy Foster, *The Dialectics of Ecology: Socialism and Nature* (New York: Monthly Review Press, 2024), 199: "We are rapidly approaching a planetary tipping point in the form of a climate Armageddon, threatening to make the earth unlivable for the human species, as well as innumerable other species."

8. According to Oxfam, "the richest 1 percent of humanity in 2017 controlled more than half of the world's wealth; the top 30 percent of the population controlled more than 95 percent of global wealth, while the remaining 70 percent of the population had to make do with less than 5 percent of the world's resources." William I. Robinson, "Who Rules the World?," in Peter Phillips, *Giants: The Global Power Elite* (New York: Seven Stories Press, 2018), 15. To put this in perspective, this means that "80 percent of the world's people live on less than $10 per day, the poorest half of the global population lives on less

The Doomsday Clock that measures the risks of nuclear annihilation is closer to midnight than at any point in history. The destruction of the biosphere, already well underway, is advancing at the most alarming rate ever known.[9] Class struggle today is not only a question of life and death for certain individuals or even large groups; it is for the entire species and the planet. Given these material circumstances, more trenchant forms of criticism are clearly necessary to shake people out of the dominant ideology of anticommunism before it is too late.

Ideas do not change reality in and of themselves, unless they become a material force through coordinated mass action. This investigation is rather specialized because it drills down into the material history of the fetishized commodities of the imperial theory industry. Its target audience is the intelligentsia, in the broadest sense of this term. However, its fundamental message—that socialism is the solution—does not at all require specialized knowledge. This work thereby seeks to contribute to the all-important task of reorienting the left before it is too late.

Method

> Dialectics as *living*, many-sided knowledge (with the number of sides eternally increasing), with an infinite number of shades of every approach and approximation to reality (with a philosophical system growing into a whole out of each shade).
>
> —VLADIMIR LENIN[10]

One of the predominant accounts of at least some of the theoretical traditions examined in this trilogy, including by self-declared Marxists of

---

than $2.50 per day, and more than 1.3 billion people live on only $1.25 per day" (ibid., 30). Oxfam's 2024 report on inequality found that since 2020, "the five richest men in the world have seen their fortunes more than double, while almost five billion people have seen their wealth fall." Oxfam, "Inequality Inc.," Oxfam International, 2024, https://oi-files-d8-prod.s3.eu-west-2.amazonaws.com/s3fs-public/2024-01/Davos%202024%20Report-%20English.pdf, 9.

9. See all of John Bellamy Foster's excellent work on this topic, including, for instance, *The Dialectics of Ecology*; *Capitalism in the Anthropocene: Ecological Ruin or Ecological Revolution* (New York: Monthly Review Press, 2022); John Bellamy Foster, Richard York, and Brett Clark, *The Ecological Rift: Capitalism's War on the Earth* (New York: Monthly Review Press, 2010).

10. Vladimir Lenin, *Collected Works*, Vol. 38 (Moscow: Foreign Languages Publishing House, 1963), 362.

the Western persuasion, consists in framing them in terms of a relationship between so-called postmodernism—an extremely loose conceptual
category with questionable value—and neoliberalism. Since they both
emerged at about the same time, and the latter refers to the economic
base and the former the ideological superstructure, it is assumed that
there must be some kind of connection between the two. Both categories
are often reified in very abstract terms, and the accounts of their inter-
relationship generally tend to slip à la Fredric Jameson into idealist forms
of historiography by relying on vague appeals to the *Zeitgeist* or spirit of
the times.[11] Furthermore, class struggle often disappears into thin air, and
there is little to no account of imperialism and the anticolonial struggle
for socialism. Instead, we are simply told that there is a new era of capitalism that ushered in a novel way of thinking and producing culture.

In these accounts, there is rarely, if ever, a materialist analysis of the
political economy of knowledge and culture, the institutional matrices
of the superstructure, geopolitical class struggle, psychological warfare
operations, concrete theoretical and cultural practices, and all of the link-
ages between specific cultural networks and the material forces driving
and shaping them. In other words, what tends to be lacking is detailed
materialist analysis and dialectics in the precise sense defined by Lenin in
the epigraph. Dialectics, in addition to recognizing reality as composed
of inter-relational processes rather than reified entities, is a form of living knowledge that is multifaceted and fine-grained insofar as it seeks to
grasp the intricacies of material reality in an ongoing process of conceptual elucidation that strives to delineate the overall system of relations.

One of the methodological objectives of this book and its companion
volumes is to demonstrate the explanatory superiority of a dialectical and
historical materialist approach to knowledge (and, by extension, culture).
Far from postulating reified binary abstractions and arbitrarily linking
them via idealist historiography that occludes class struggle, it delves into
the minute details of the concrete points of connection between the economic forces driving society and the specific ways in which they shape
the production, circulation, and consumption of knowledge. It also situates class struggle at the center of its analysis and elucidates how the
radical theory industry in the imperial core is related to a broad series
of psychological warfare operations aimed at shoring up, at a minimum, anticommunism and capitalist accommodation. Furthermore, it

---

11. For an analysis of a number of these discourses, including Jameson's, see Rockhill,
Logique de l'histoire, 447–89.

simultaneously demonstrates how these operations have failed to contain the many-headed hydra they are trying to defeat, precisely due to ongoing class struggle, in both theory and practice.

Unlike the zeitgeist historiography of reified epochs characteristic of many Western Marxist accounts, this study advances on the basis of a dialectical historiography that is always attentive to three heuristically distinct dimensions of history: time, space, and class stratification. Historical reality does not march along, undialectically, as a unified entity with absolutely distinct stages. It is a highly differentiated reality based on the geographical location under discussion, as well as the specific class stratum, both of which are essential dimensions for bringing into relief the realities of class struggle (which has often taken the form of the struggle between nations). Moreover, change is always variably distributed across these three dimensions, meaning that there are no simple and clean breaks when a new era magically appears, such as that of neoliberalism or postmodernism.[12]

This book, as well as the others in the trilogy, provides a fine-grained analysis of the dialectical relationship between the general system of knowledge and individual subjects of knowledge production. Marxism has often been denigrated for purportedly privileging the system over and against the subject, so much so that Western Marxists have regularly claimed that it was necessary to supplement their analyses with subjectively oriented discourses like phenomenology, existentialism, and psychoanalysis. In general, the subjectivism and idealism that plagues these approaches have not, however, enhanced Marxism, but have rather served to dilute it with liberal ideology. Rigorous DHM analysis always accounts for the subject as well as the system, individuals along with collectivities, agency as well as forms of determination. However, it does not reify these as distinct and opposed poles but rather understands them as intertwined processes whose complexity far surpasses our simplistic concepts.

This investigation does not only include a materialist elucidation of the political economy of knowledge, the intellectual sector of the

---

12. Discussing an earlier phase of capitalism, Lenin similarly rejected epochal thinking: "Needless to say, all the boundaries in nature and in society are conditional and changeable, and, consequently, it would be absurd to discuss the exact year or the decade in which imperialism 'definitely' became established." Vladimir Lenin, *Essential Works of Lenin: "What Is to Be Done?" and Other Writings*, ed. Henry M. Christman (New York: Dover Publications, 1987), 238.

superstructure, and the imperial theory industry. It also goes to great lengths to analyze in detail the lives and works of the subjects in question, including many of the major figures in the Frankfurt School, French theory, and contemporary critical theory more generally. Instead of relying on an opposition between internal analysis (the preferred method of the bourgeois humanities) and external analysis (the dominant approach in the bourgeois social sciences), this study proposes a dialectical elucidation of the theoretical practices of subjects working within specific systems of knowledge. It thereby brings into relief how both of these reference points are actually processes that are so enmeshed in one another that separating them out through conceptual abstraction distorts their material reality. In other words, it makes little sense to act as if there were phenomena like "Adorno's philosophy" or "Derrida's thought" independently of the systems of knowledge—as well as the forces driving them—that gave birth to thinkers like these and played a major role in producing and disseminating their work. The same is true of these systems themselves, which could not function without the subjects operative within them, and that would not operate in the precise manner that they have without the specific contributions that particular subjects have made.

Much of what passes for ideology critique within the Western Marxist tradition amounts to a critical analysis of the ideology operative within a particular subject or a specific object such as a cultural product. Although this book, like its sister tomes, engages with this type of work, it is also dedicated to developing a level of ideology critique that focuses on the objective systems that produce particular ideologies. This is one of the reasons for examining such a broad swath of intellectual production across traditions that are often considered to be distinct or even openly opposed to one another (as German critical theory and French theory are often presented). It is precisely in order to demonstrate that there are objective socioeconomic forces undergirding these theoretical trends and contributing to their ideological alignment on the most fundamental issues.

From a dialectical and historical materialist perspective, it makes perfect sense that there would be so much ideological consistency. The subjects of knowledge production under scrutiny are all part of the same class formation and have been ideologically composed in a similar manner. They have been trained in elite educational institutions in the imperial core to participate in the same basic forms of exchange-value–driven theoretical practice. They have also generally operated within nearly identical international networks and participated in similar activities. In many cases, particularly with the later traditions of French theory and U.S.-driven radical theory, they have generally spent their lives reading and responding to one another. Most important, they have been working within a material system of knowledge production owned and controlled—directly or indirectly—by the same class, that sets the ultimate rules of the game. One thing they all share is that they have succeeded, albeit in different ways, in playing that game. There is thus a coherent relationship between their subjective ideologies and the objective systems that have produced them, which fosters a remarkable amount of ideological uniformity.

In an effort to give the best possible form to this dialectical approach to history and hermeneutics, this study mobilizes a constellational methodology. Rather than a linear narrative, a big picture overview, or snapshots of purported time periods or individual thinkers, it seeks to discursively perform what Lenin called "many-sided knowledge." Every subsection of each chapter provides a detailed analysis of one facet of the overall reality under examination. This allows us to descend to a level of microscopic scrutiny that brings out all of the various details that in a broader overview would need to be jettisoned. At the same time, each of these micro-studies fits into a coherent system that takes the shape of a constellation in which every subsection is a nodal point. This brings into view a telescopic apprehension of the totality of the system of knowledge under analysis. This constellational method thereby fosters a clear understanding of the total system, with all of its complexities and different dimensions, via a nuanced account of specific nodal points within it.

Finally, it bears recalling that dialectics is, as Lenin emphasized, a *living* knowledge, meaning that it is constantly expanding and refining itself in relationship to a reality whose complexity far surpasses our simple conceptual tools. There is, in this regard, much more work to be done, and these books do not presume to be exhaustive or definitive. They seek instead to make a contribution to a living knowledge in the material sense, meaning a knowledge of our lives that can serve as a vital force for practically reconfiguring them. The fundamental point, then, of the diagnosis that follows is not simply for us to increase our knowledge, it is for us to learn from the past and present so that we can transform our lived reality in the future.

The Road Ahead

This book opens with three chapters that serve as a discourse on Marxist method for the project as a whole. The first elucidates the dialectical and historical materialist approach to ideas, shedding light on the *modus operandi* of the imperial intellectual superstructure in general. The second chapter provides an overview of some of the material networks of the empire of ideas that have been built up by the leading imperialist powers over the last century or so, and which serve as the general backdrop for their intellectual world war. The third turns, more specifically, to the imperial theory industry as a major force for shoring up and promoting a form of compatible critical theory over and against the revolutionary tradition of DHM. All three of these chapters provide the methodological and conceptual framework necessary for understanding and correctly situating all of the more specific analyses that follow.

Part Two of this book focuses on the Frankfurt School, and it drills down into a tradition that has been one of the principal driving forces behind what is called Western or cultural Marxism. It begins with an analysis of the deep-seated and dogmatic anticommunism of Theodor Adorno and Max Horkheimer, which was appreciated and supported by powerful segments of the capitalist ruling class and sectors of the bourgeois state, including the CIA. It then examines the work of the seven Frankfurt scholars who were directly employed by the U.S. government in propaganda organizations like the Office of War Information (OWI) and Voice of America, intelligence agencies like the Office of Strategic Services (OSS), and the State Department. It also examines the complexities of these developments by unpacking the convoluted case of Frankfurt School research associates who were in contact with Soviet intelligence. The final chapter is a deep dive into the life and work of perhaps the most prominent figure in Western Marxism, the man the bourgeois press proclaimed to be the godfather of the New Left: Herbert Marcuse. Many questions have been raised about his work for the U.S. government, and some have accused him of being an agent of imperialism. Now that the archival record has finally come to light, it is possible to situate Marcuse much more precisely within the intellectual world war on communism, and his contributions are more far reaching and problematic than most would likely assume.

The title of this first volume, *Who Paid the Pipers of Western Marxism?*, echoes the pathbreaking work by Frances Stonor Saunders, *Who Paid the Piper? The CIA and the Cultural Cold War.*[13] Engaging in extensive

---

13. Saunders's book was published under a different title in the United States (*The Cultural Cold War*). The U.S. edition was almost scrapped because Free Press, which had published many of the authors critically analyzed by Saunders, tried to force her to add a disclaimer reversing the book's fundamental argument. She was asked to write that

archival research, Saunders demonstrated the role of the foundations of the ruling class and the intelligence services in funding and promoting anticommunist culture and the compatible left. The focus here is more specifically on the intelligentsia and the theory industry, but it shares with Saunders's book the fundamental question of the political economy of cultural production, distribution, and consumption. It is by answering the question of who paid the pipers that we can bring to light the material forces driving the promotion of the dominant ideology.

The Frankfurt School has commonly been interpreted, at least within the imperial core, as having contributed to a type of Marxism that is more sophisticated and culturally savvy than those forms of Marxism, many of them Eastern-oriented, that purportedly suffered from economism, reductive determinism, productivism, authoritarianism, totalitarianism, teleology, and so forth. This was one of the primary ideological objectives of the powerful forces in the capitalist class and the bourgeois state that supported Western Marxism as a weapon of ideological warfare against the revolutionary Marxism of the anti-imperialists. The position that is widely accepted today as common sense by the imperial intelligentsia, namely that Western Marxism is somehow more advanced, is thus a consequence of a semi-clandestine intellectual world war. This dogma will be called out for what it is, and the real specificity of Western Marxism will come clearly into view. It is an ideological construct aimed at transforming the greatest theoretical weapon of class struggle from below into an ineffectual philosophical position that is accommodationist toward capitalism, and even imperialism.

German-style critical theory has served as one of the two most important foundational reference points for the imperial theory industry. The other is French theory, and it is to this tradition that the forthcoming second volume turns. Whereas the Frankfurt School revised Marxism to such an extent that it became, in many important ways, anti-Marxism, French theory has largely been marketed as a more radical form of thinking that surpasses Marxism, or at least remakes it in highly original and idiosyncratic ways. One of its trademarks has been to question totalizing forms of explanation, identity thinking, the resolution of contradictions through dialectics, and so forth. What Deleuze referred to as French theory's "generalized

---

the CIA was "*on the side of the angels*" and that "America's was a good cause" (quoted in Whitney, *Flights*, 134). When she refused, Free Press dumped the project and sent her a bill for $15,000. Fortunately, New Press picked up the project and hired a lawyer to obtain the rights and save the book (ibid., 126–36).

anti-Hegelianism" is but thin cover for its generalized anti-Marxism, as
we will see, in spite of the fact that some French theorists have sought to
recuperate Marx as one philosopher among others within the bourgeois
canon (thereby using him to bolster their symbolic capital as radicals).[14] In
either case, one of the goals of the French theorists has been to bury anti-
imperialist Marxism as passé and promote themselves as the vanguard of
human thought. The world's leading imperialist power, the United States,
not only strongly supported them in this endeavor, but its global networks
of knowledge production were largely responsible for making this coterie
of anti-Marxist French intellectuals into global superstars. Following the
same basic pattern as the Frankfurt School, the capitalist ruling class was in
on the coup, as well as the state, and the CIA identified French theory as a
major ally in its intellectual world war on communism.

The final volume in the trilogy engages head-on with a question that
my previous publications on the Frankfurt School and French theory
have often generated: if there has been a confluence of interests between
the imperial ruling class and compatible critical theory—of the German
or French variety—are these patterns visible in the contemporary forms
of cutting-edge theory promoted in the imperial core? In particular,
many scholars and activists, including self-proclaimed Marxists, have
been impressed by a relatively novel brand of radical theory that has
been heavily marketed since the turn of the twenty-first century. Figures
like Agamben, Badiou, Balibar, Butler, Hardt, Laclau, Mouffe, Negri,
Rancière, and Žižek have, according to many, put forth more politically
trenchant forms of analysis, sometimes openly rejecting French theoretical developments affiliated with so-called postmodernism and a perceived turn away from the political. In addition to this band of radicals
in theory, some of whom are self-proclaimed communists, the third and
fourth generations of Frankfurt School critical theory have witnessed a
rejuvenation of interest in socialism (Axel Honneth) and overt criticisms
of capitalism (Nancy Fraser and Rahel Jaeggi). Finally, some of the most
cutting-edge forms of theory—including postcolonial theory, subaltern
studies, decolonial theory, Afro-pessimism, liberal queer theory, etc.—
have branded themselves, in an implicit teleology, as more profoundly
political or deeply critical than anything that has preceded them (a few
have even claimed à la Bruno Latour to surpass critique itself in their level
of sophistication). All of this suggests, at least to some, that the Western

---

14. Gilles Deleuze, *Difference and Repetition*, trans. Paul Patton (New York: Columbia
University Press, 1994), xix.

left intelligentsia's complicity with empire is a thing of the past. The dialectical and historical materialist analysis of these theoretical trends and
their knowledge networks demonstrates just the opposite: the patterns
analyzed in the first two volumes are alive and well. To perceive them,
we have to be able to see through the chameleonic nature of ideology
and identify the material relations of ideological production behind it.
Engaging in this political economy of knowledge and working through
the nuances of the philosophic positions taken by some of the theorists in
question will bring to light a lesson that equally applies to the Frankfurt
School and French theory: the empire does not promote work that is a
real threat to its existence.

Although these intellectual traditions have marketed themselves as distinct, and each thinker within them has promoted their own idiosyncratic
brand to seemingly no end, there is a remarkable degree of ideological consistency. What they all share in common, and what becomes visible via a
materialist analysis of the social totality, is their opposition to actually existing socialism, with only the rarest—and absolutely explainable—exceptions. They also generally reject Communist parties and anti-imperialist
state-building projects, and some of them even rebuff parties and disciplined political organizations in general, as well as any focus on state power.
Any political solutions they put forth for the problems they diagnose within
the capitalist world usually amount to jacqueries, anarchist islands of resistance, liberal political measures, or social-democratic reforms devoid of an
understanding that the welfare state in the imperial core was, among other
things, a class compromise—and ideological construct—necessitated by
the existence of the Soviet Union. Those that are self-declared communists
generally provide little more than idealist projections of a magical third way
beyond capitalism and socialism that only exists in their minds. Hence the
importance of systemic ideological criticism, which examines the complex
inner workings of the imperial intellectual superstructure and situates the
agency of individual knowledge producers within it. This sheds light on the
fact that the towering figures of the imperial theory industry are not working in a vacuum. On the contrary, they are producing ideas within a very
specific material system of knowledge production that has promoted them
precisely because they are doing the type of ideological work necessary to
police the left border of critique: they exclude, as beyond the pale, the very
idea that knowledge could have real use-value by being put in the service
of developing anti-imperialist, socialist state-building projects in the real
world of the here and now.

PART I

IMPERIAL KNOWLEDGE

CHAPTER 1

Breaking the Chains of Imperial Knowledge

How to Hide a Cultural Empire

In some departments of our daily life, in which we imagine ourselves
free agents, we are ruled by dictators exercising great power.
—EDWARD BERNAYS[1]

Bourgeois culture presents itself as a realm of freedom, just as bourgeois
knowledge prides itself on being based on open-ended, democratic, and
meritocratic forms of inquiry. This appearance of freedom, in both cases,
is belied by deeply determined structures that limit the purview and possibilities of bourgeois culture and knowledge. An analysis of the totality,
including the systemic material relations of socioeconomic production and
reproduction driving culture and knowledge, is generally foreclosed, further fostering the illusion that the cultural and intellectual products pitched
to the hearts and minds of the masses are autonomously produced, circulate meritocratically, and are consumed based on freedom of choice.

The deficiencies of bourgeois culture and knowledge are particularly
apparent in the standard accounts of the state and culture itself (in the
broad sense, including knowledge and the intellectual world). The state is
generally taken at face value, with little to no assessment of the large and
powerful sectors of the state apparatus engaged in clandestine activities
and not at all beholden to even the minimal forms of pseudo-democracy
inherent in bourgeois electoral politics. Culture tends to be understood as
a free realm of exploration rather than a highly regimented material system of production, circulation, and consumption that is intimately bound

---

1. Edward Bernays, *Propaganda* (New York: Ig Publishing, 2005), 61.

up with political imperatives. What is almost never perceived, then, is the connection between covert state operations, on the one hand, and the system of constraints that structures the broad cultural world, including academia, on the other. As we will see, however, the part of the bourgeois state sometimes referred to as the invisible government has a long and deep history of working behind the scenes to control culture, which includes promoting the illusion that it is a domain of freedom.

The bourgeois state and bourgeois culture are products of a particular socioeconomic system: capitalism. This is what is driving the contradiction between democratic appearance and authoritarian reality. The dominant class within this system faces a major problem: it endeavors to present itself as ruling in the interests of the hoi polloi when it systematically exploits the latter for its own benefit. One of the principal propaganda tools that it has developed to obscure this fundamental structural relationship is its use of foundations. These are front organizations, which declare themselves to be philanthropic, but are actually mechanisms for leveraging stolen wealth for soft power projects that serve the interests of the ruling class. They are thus a thinly veiled attempt to mask the influence of power and wealth on cultural production, circulation, and consumption. As we will see, the foundations of the capitalist ruling class work hand in glove with the invisible government to tightly control cultural and intellectual work from the shadows, while broadcasting the illusion that the bourgeois cultural and intellectual system is a realm of unalloyed freedom.

One example that clearly illustrates all of these points, which will be spelled out in much greater detail below, is the 1950 Manifesto issued by the Congress for Cultural Freedom (CCF), an international organization explicitly dedicated to promoting the cherished liberties of the West. "We hold it to be self-evident," the Manifesto begins, "that intellectual freedom is one of the inalienable rights of man."[2] A veritable panegyric on freedom, a term it uses no less than seventeen times, the document claims that "freedom and peace are inseparable."[3] It simultaneously condemns what it describes as the curtailments of freedom by "totalitarian states," even claiming that neutrality in the face of their challenge to liberty "amounts to a betrayal of mankind and to the abdication of the free mind."[4]

---

2. Peter Coleman, *The Liberal Conspiracy: The Congress for Cultural Freedom and the Struggle for the Mind of Postwar Europe* (New York: Free Press, 1989), 249.
3. Ibid., 249.
4. Ibid., 250–51.

Far from being a free organization celebrating intellectual and cultural liberty, however, the CCF was a CIA front, with funding from the capitalist ruling class through its foundations. This is the kind of freedom it represented: the freedom of the capitalist class and its bourgeois state operatives to intercede in culture and control it from behind the scenes, using front organizations to publicly promote the illusion of freedom in order to better control it, while waging an all-out war on those dedicated to freeing the world from capitalism.

It is telling that the celebrated intellectuals analyzed in this book and its companion volumes, who are often described as veritable masters of suspicion, have generally remained silent on the CIA's involvement in the CCF, even though they were either directly or indirectly implicated themselves, or they participated in parallel projects serving the same fundamental objectives. What better collaborators in enterprises of free thinking like this than those who willfully ignore—and thus accept—how conditioned their freedom actually is?

Confronting the Limits of the Bourgeois Knowledge Regime

"The only thing of interest in the personality of a philosopher is: he was born then and then, he worked and died."[5] This statement, made by Martin Heidegger at the opening of his 1924 lecture course on Aristotle, is a concise summary of intellectual commodity fetishism. The material circumstances of a philosopher's work, as well as the personal realities of their actual life, are generally judged to be irrelevant, except perhaps for peripheral information regarding their birth and death. The products of their intellect are all that really matter.

The strong position that Heidegger took on biography and historical contextualization would soon prove to be particularly useful. Having embraced National Socialism with the expectation of "a deliverance of western Dasein [existence] from the dangers of communism," he joined the Nazi Party and oversaw the Aryanization of his university as its rector.[6] Since the Nazis were eventually defeated, due first and foremost to

---

5. Martin Heidegger, *Grundbegriffe der aristotelischen Philosophie*, *Gesamtausgabe*, Vol. 18 (Frankfurt: Vittorio Klostermann, 2002), 5.

6. "Heidegger to Marcuse, January 20, 1948," in Herbert Marcuse, *Technology, War and Fascism*, Vol. 1 of *Collected Papers*, ed. Douglas Kellner (London: Routledge, 1998), 265. On Heidegger and Nazism, see, for instance, Victor Farías, *Heidegger and Nazism*, trans. Paul Burrell and Gabriel R. Ricci (Philadelphia: Temple University Press,

the monumental sacrifices of those communists he judged to be so dangerous, Heidegger clearly had a vested interest in maintaining the purity of his intellectual project, preferring to go down in bourgeois history as perhaps the greatest thinker of the twentieth century, instead of a resolute fascist philosopher.

Although he remained an unrepentant Nazi after the war, as his former students Herbert Marcuse and Jürgen Habermas helped demonstrate, the philosopher who presided over at least one public book burning of "Jewish-Marxist" literature, was not only rehabilitated, but his international fame grew precipitously in the imperial core.[7] He had a major and lasting impact on two traditions of thought that figure prominently in this study, as well as those theoretical trends that emerged out of them: German critical theory and French theory. As a matter of fact, Heidegger

---

1989); Adam Knowles, *Heidegger's Fascist Affinities: A Politics of Silence* (Stanford, CA: Stanford University Press, 2019); and Domenico Losurdo, *Heidegger and the Ideology of War: Community, Death, and the West* (Amherst, NY: Humanity Books, 2001); as well as the overview of some of the debate in David S. Luft, "Being and German History: Historiographical Notes on the Heidegger Controversy," *Central European History*, Vol. 27, No. 4 (1994): 479–501. Heidegger's famous address as rector, as well as his correspondence with Marcuse, are both worth consulting in this regard: Martin Heidegger, "The Self-Assertion of the German University and the Rectorate 1933/34: Facts and Thoughts," *Review of Metaphysics*, Vol. 38, No. 3 (March 1985): 467–502; Marcuse, *Technology, War and Fascism*, 261–67.

7. When asked if he had taken part in book burnings, Heidegger disingenuously depicted himself as against such practices by claiming that he forbade one of them. See Martin Heidegger, "Only a God Can Save Us," trans. William T. Richardson, in *Heidegger: The Man and the Thinker*, ed. Thomas Sheehan (New York: Routledge, 2017), 45–67. Archival research by Heiko Wegmann has since revealed that, as university rector, Heidegger presided over at least one book burning on June 24, 1933, where he made a speech invoking the "flame that shows us the path from which there is no return." See Heiko Wegmann, *Dunkle Wolken über Freiburg: Nationalsozialistische Bücherverbrennungen, "Säuberungen" und Enteignungen* (Ubstadt-Weiher, Germany: Verlag Regionalkultur, 2023) and the following video, in which an actor reads excerpts from Heidegger's speech: https://www.youtube.com/watch?v=AB9E53NbUPQ. The author of *Being and Time* may have participated in other book burnings organized in the same spirit, which was clearly articulated in the announcement for a book burning by the University of Freiburg Students' Union—meaning Heidegger's students—on May 8, 1933: "The German student body is determined to carry out the intellectual struggle against the Jewish-Marxist decomposition of the German people to the point of total annihilation." Wegmann, *Dunkle Wolken über Freiburg*, 72. I would like to express my gratitude to Helmut-Harry Löwen for drawing my attention to this and sharing all of these resources.

became so important in France, where existential phenomenologists began to celebrate his work early on, that he attained the status of the principal philosophic reference—along with the radical aristocrat Friedrich Nietzsche—for many of the leading luminaries of French theory. As early as September 1, 1945, Heidegger played the victim in his correspondence, grousing about how he was being mistreated in Germany, while gloating over his reception abroad: "I am valued in Paris and France, where my philosophy is in 'vogue.'"[8]

Many of the French theorists who bore Heidegger's torch not only agreed with the statement in his Aristotle lecture, but they attempted to elevate it to the level of an unquestionable principle. This served them well in their own context, if I can take the liberty of using a concept they despised, since it was quite the intellectual feat to festoon the work of a Nazi scholar and bureaucrat while maligning the Marxist tradition in a historical conjuncture where the latter had enormous public support for having soundly defeated the social and political philosophy embraced by the former. Jacques Derrida provided a concise synthesis of the view he shared with his closest collaborators, which helped him champion the work of figures like Heidegger and the ardent Zionist Emmanuel Levinas: "There is nothing outside the text [*il n'y a pas de hors-texte*]."[9] This philosophic fiat was also a particularly useful crutch when it was revealed that Derrida's close friend, who formed the other half of the dynamic duo of deconstruction, Paul de Man, had collaborated so closely with the Nazis that he had anticipated becoming a minister of culture in the postwar European Reich (though he had to settle, instead, with becoming the don of decon at Yale, where he regularly invited his French counterpart). To be sure, Derrida's quintessentially logocentric affirmation—in the precise sense of the Greek term *logos*, which means both word and reason, or discourse—needs to be understood in its full-blown metaphysical or Heideggerian sense: he postulated arche-writing as the process of spatial differing and temporal deferring (*différance*) that is the condition of possibility (and impossibility) of all language and thought, and ultimately of everything, meaning that he was not simply talking about empirical texts. Nevertheless, the same basic methodological orientation was at work: discourse in this absolutized sense à la Heideggerian Being is all that really matters, not its material conditions of production or a supposed reality outside the text.

---

8. Cited in Farías, *Heidegger and Nazism*, 281.
9. Jacques Derrida, *Of Grammatology*, trans. Gayatri Spivak (Baltimore: Johns Hopkins University Press, 1997), 158.

The views expressed by Heidegger and Derrida are common tropes within the bourgeois humanities, which tend to recount the history of ideas, and of philosophy more specifically, in terms of a largely immaterial trajectory of thought punctuated by individual discursive contributions. This logocentric understanding of intellectual history, which undergirds bourgeois canons, goes hand in hand with a homologous logic of circulation and consumption: the thoughts of these luminaries are disseminated via consumer products (texts), which are then analyzed in isolation through internal analysis. This practical logic of theoretical production, circulation, and consumption is imbibed with and fosters intellectual commodity fetishism: the specific theoretical product takes on the magical quality of a singular creation, and the material social relations of intellectual production disappear behind its enchanting aura. There is, just as Derrida insisted, nothing outside the text (for those under the spell of intellectual commodity fetishism).

IN CONTRAST TO THE HUMANITIES, the bourgeois social sciences have often attempted to flesh out particular facets of the concrete relations of intellectual production. While many of the social scientific criticisms of the philosophic fetishism just mentioned are welcome correctives, the social sciences nonetheless bear the traces of their own material history since they have also emerged, like philosophy and the humanities, within a unique ideological framework grounded in a specific material world. Although this history developed at diverse rates and varied considerably based on the precise time, place, and class strata, a brief and general overview allows us to clearly understand the contributions and significant limitations of the bourgeois social sciences, while also bringing to the fore the extent to which regimes of knowledge are the result of specific material social relations.[10]

As capitalism emerged and developed in its long and complex history, it brought with it profound transformations of a socioeconomic order that had been largely naturalized, leading in certain cases to major upheavals in the form of bourgeois revolutions. Within this general context, there was a need to forge new tools of analysis to understand and try to control a changing world. In order to fill this gap, the bourgeois

---

10. This section draws on much of my previous research, and in particular Gabriel Rockhill, *Logique de l'histoire: Pour une analytique des pratiques philosophiques* (Paris: Éditions Hermann, 2010).

social sciences began to emerge in the imperial core in a rather incho-
ate fashion through the course of the long eighteenth century, and they
were later consolidated and institutionalized between approximately
the mid-nineteenth century and the mid-twentieth century. They were
influenced, in part, by the earlier developments of the natural sciences,
which created forms of secular, verifiable, empirical analysis with concrete, practical applications. There were, and still are, some hermeneu-
tically oriented elements of the bourgeois social sciences, that remain
closer to philosophy. However, they generally distinguished themselves
from the humanities and encroached upon their institutional space,
forcing them to consolidate themselves around the *geistig*—meaning
both spiritual and intellectual—realm of culture. This social scientific
intrusion was, and still is, considered to be a threat by those invested,
like Heidegger and Derrida, in maintaining an idealist form of theologi-
cally infused speculation as the highest form of thought, thereby securing their social position as the specialists of generalities or, in more
extreme cases, the high priests of the unknowable.[11]

The overall framework of analysis for the bourgeois social sciences,
including their disciplinary divisions, is a direct outgrowth of the material social relations of modern capitalism. According to the dominant
ideology that developed, the world is composed of the separate spheres
of the market (economics), the state (political science), and civil society
(sociology), which each have their own *modi operandi*.[12] It thereby makes
sense, ideologically, to have distinct sciences for each of these realms, at
least when it comes to analyzing the present state of the developed societies of the capitalist core, which have been, at least historically, the primary
focal points of these social sciences. The study of the past of the developed capitalist world required its own discipline (history). In its modern

---

11. Although they are not Marxist, there have been some important sociological
critiques of this tradition by figures like Pierre Bourdieu, Jean-Louis Fabiani, and
Louis Pinto.

12. This paragraph and the next draw on the findings of the Gulbenkian Commission,
published in Immanuel Wallerstein, ed., *Open the Social Sciences: Report of the Gulbenkian
Commission on the Restructuring of the Social Sciences* (Stanford, CA: Stanford University
Press, 1996). Also see Immanuel Wallerstein, *World-Systems Analysis: An Introduction*
(Durham, NC: Duke University Press, 2007); Immanuel Wallerstein, *Unthinking Social
Science: The Limits of Nineteenth-Century Paradigms* (Philadelphia: Temple University
Press, 2001); and the interview with Wallerstein in Gabriel Rockhill and Alfredo Gomez-
Muller, eds., *Politics of Culture and the Spirit of Critique: Dialogues* (New York: Columbia
University Press, 2011), 98–112.

form, history tended to break with the naturalized, circular patterns of the chronicles of great men, in favor of a linear development where the past was recognized as an autonomous realm that needed to be studied empirically as it actually was (*"wie es eigentlich gewesen ist"*).[13] As capitalist societies grew and expanded through colonization, there was a need for another discipline (anthropology) focused specifically on studying the underdeveloped societies in the periphery that were subjected to colonialism.[14] Although this is no longer a common category, the countries of the capitalist core also established a discipline (Orientalism) focused on analyzing developed societies that did not follow the pattern of Western capitalist modernization like Persia, India, and China.

There are other disciplines, of course, and their precise configurations and interrelations have always depended on the specific sociohistorical conjuncture. Nevertheless, a basic pattern is visible: the bourgeois social sciences—like the humanities—are products of a particular material world, namely that of capitalist societies involved in colonial expansion. Far from being impartial, then, as their structure itself reveals, they have generally been oriented toward shoring up the dominant ideology within colonial capitalism, in spite of sometimes being mobilized by specific actors, at particular moments, for alternative ends.

Moreover, as Vladimir Lenin cogently explained: "In one way or another, *all* official and liberal science *defends* wage-slavery."[15] It has a normative orientation that is so deeply ingrained that it is often considered to be value neutral. Similarly, bourgeois social science does not provide people with an adequate account of the fundamental force of history, namely class struggle, which would allow them to understand how social reality has been formed, the mechanisms undergirding and driving it, as well as how best to intervene in order to transform it.

As Walter Rodney argued, the very division between the natural and social sciences is itself a product of a particular class dynamic. Scientific knowledge of the natural world is aggressively pursued, and not subjected

---

13. See Reinhart Koselleck, *Futures Past: On the Semantics of Historical Time* (Cambridge, MA: MIT Press, 1985); François Hartog, *Régimes d'historicité: Présentisme et expériences du temps* (Paris: Éditions du Seuil, 2003); and Hannah Arendt, *Between Past and Future: Eight Exercises in Political Thought* (New York: Penguin Books, 1968).

14. See Kathleen Gough, "Anthropology and Imperialism," *Monthly Review*, Vol. 19, No. 11 (April 1968), https://monthlyreviewarchives.org/index.php/mr/article/view/MR-019-11-1968-04_2, and Bernard McGrane, *Beyond Anthropology: Society and the Other* (New York: Columbia University Press, 1989).

15. Vladimir Lenin, *Collected Works*, Vol. 19 (Moscow: Progress Publishers, 1977), 23.

to deliberate mystification, insofar as this knowledge aids in production, and thus ultimately in capitalist accumulation. By contrast:

> The bourgeois class—the capitalist class—has an interest in specifically mystifying the application of scientific principles to society; because the same application of scientific principles to society would suggest that we must understand the changes—the transitions by which capitalism itself came into being, and by which the particular class in power will be removed from power.[16]

Echoing Friedrich Engels, Rodney maintained that the severing of the natural from the social world is the result of a "metaphysical assumption which makes a separation between the application of scientific principles to the society as distinct from the application of scientific principles to the real world—to the natural world."[17]

These are inordinately complex histories, and many nuances would need to be added to this account, including the fact that the disciplinary regime and intellectual Taylorism of bourgeois research have nonetheless made some major contributions, which should by no means be abandoned. Given the centuries-long domination of capitalism around the world, bourgeois knowledge is the most advanced form currently available, due to the fact that no other type of knowledge has had so much material support for its development. As Lenin argued, we need to learn from, and often draw on, all of the most developed forms of thought, but we also have to be very vigilant regarding their ideological orientation.

I am intentionally painting in broad strokes in order to bring an essential point into focus: the dominant system of knowledge is a product of the material relations operative in the history of capitalism. The bourgeois regime of knowledge has been based on a fundamental separation between nature and society, ensconced in the intellectual division of labor between the natural and the social sciences, and this separation has been seconded by a partition, within the social sciences, between a series of different disciplines rooted in liberal ideology and its colonialist worldview. The humanities have, over time, been whittled down to being the guardians of the *geistig*, and they tend to be a refuge for superstitious thinking, except for those sectors—like certain forms of analytic

---

16. Walter Rodney, *Decolonial Marxism: Essays from the Pan-African Revolution* (London: Verso, 2022), 60.
17. Ibid., 59.

philosophy—that have modeled themselves on techno-scientific social sciences. Just as Heidegger's and Derrida's approach to the history of ideas is largely a consequence of the material relations of their intellectual production, and more precisely their ideological conditioning within the modern institutionalized discipline of philosophy, the bourgeois social scientific accounts of knowledge are similarly undergirded by the dominant ideology that structures those disciplines. This means that they tend to be characterized by a fragmentary and non-holistic worldview, the social chauvinism of the imperial core, partiality to wage-slavery (under cover of neutrality), and the obfuscation of class struggle.

It is certainly true that efforts have been made, on the part of some intellectuals, to stitch the world back together again through interdisciplinary endeavors. However, these are reactions to the problems inherent in the ideological division between nature, society, and the individual (the privileged realm of the humanities and psychology, a discipline that has a more scientific wing and a wing methodologically oriented like the humanities). They are destined to remain feckless if they do not go to the root of the problem: an ideological and non-dialectical worldview, grounded in material social relations, that obscures the totality and the class struggle driving it.

Dialectical Materialist Epistemology

The Marxist doctrine is . . . comprehensive and harmonious, and provides men with an integral world outlook irreconcilable with any form of superstition, reaction, or defense of bourgeois oppression.

—VLADIMIR LENIN[18]

What is fundamentally lacking in the bourgeois humanities and social sciences is an analysis of the socio-natural totality and the systemic material relations of socioeconomic production and reproduction, as well as the forces driving them. Such an approach is capable of situating the specific relations of intellectual labor within this totality in order to elucidate the dialectical relationship between objective forces and subjective agency. Dialectical and historical materialism (DHM) provides this. Rather than beginning with abstract thoughts isolated in the work of an individual or one facet of a collective world, it situates intellectual labor within the general socioeconomic relations of production, which themselves are

---

18. Vladimir Lenin, *Collected Works*, Vol. 19 (Moscow: Progress Publishers, 1977), 23.

embedded in the natural world. It thereby starts out, as Marx and Engels wrote, from the "real premises" of human beings "in their actual, empirically perceptible process of development under definite conditions."[19] Humans, as material beings capable of thinking, are produced, and they participate in their own production and reproduction, within a larger system of relations: "What they are . . . coincides with their production, both with *what* they produce and with *how* they produce. Hence what individuals are depends on the material conditions of their production."[20]

Those operating within the ideological confines of the bourgeois humanities, like Heidegger and Derrida, often dismiss such an approach as reductivist or determinist. This is usually due to their deep-seated— though sometimes unacknowledged—investment in the bourgeois ideology of individual freedom, which excludes a dialectical understanding of the relationship between objective material conditions and subjective agency. They desperately aspire to put consciousness first and thus suffer from idealism, the dominant ideology of the humanities, "which always, in one way or another, amounts to the defense or support of religion."[21]

The bourgeois social sciences have also frequently criticized DHM for reductivism, albeit for different reasons, namely that there are specific logics of the social world that are not reducible to class dynamics (as if DHM, rather than capitalism, was intent on reducing the world to class warfare). This, for instance, was the argument made by one of Derrida's archenemies on the French theoretical scene, Pierre Bourdieu. He framed his entire book on Heidegger in terms of a double refusal that not only rejected the absolute autonomy of the philosophic text à la Derrida but also rebuffed, in an obvious attack on Marxism, the "direct reduction of the text to the most general conditions of its production."[22] Claiming that the philosophic field within which Heidegger operated followed its own autonomous logic, distinct from that of the political field, Bourdieu took what he described as a non-incriminating stance on Heidegger's Nazism, disparaging not only those who attribute too much autonomy to his philosophic discourse (since it is structured by "the field"), but also those who accord it too little autonomy (because they situate it, as well as

19. Karl Marx and Friedrich Engels, *Collected Works*, Vol. 5 (New York: International Publishers, 1976), 37.
20. Ibid., 31–2.
21. Lenin, *Collected Works*, Vol. 19, 24.
22. Pierre Bourdieu, *The Political Ontology of Martin Heidegger*, trans. Peter Collier (Stanford, CA: Stanford University Press, 1991), 2.

the academic marketplace of ideas in which he participated, within class struggle).[23]

One of the other criticisms commonly leveled against DHM by those ensconced in the bourgeois knowledge regime is that it is dogmatic and objectivist, or even that it purports to be totalizing in its knowledge claims. However, DHM understands itself to be a science in the broad sense of *Wissenschaft*—meaning a reliable method and form of knowledge in general—and makes a more minimal claim: it is possible to distinguish between more or less accurate accounts of reality.[24] This does not require omniscience or some form of total and absolute understanding of the real, including perhaps predicting the future. *Wissenschaft* is, instead, a historical process of collectively developing tools of analysis, testing them in reality, and modifying them based on experience. As a *Wissenschaft*, DHM is founded on the primacy of practice, not the dogmatic preeminence of theory or the rigid objectivism found in positivistic bourgeois sciences (let alone the God-like omniscience that anti-Marxists sometimes project on it). Unlike the extremes of idealism and empiricism, materialism draws on as much concrete data as possible to account for the socio-natural totality, but it concretely abstracts from the minutia of empirical details in order to integrate and synthesize them at a higher level by establishing the most coherent explanatory framework, which it continues to test and modify based on practical trials. It is important in this regard, and it needs to be emphasized, that DHM does not simply scrap all of the work done within the framework of bourgeois knowledge production. On the contrary, it draws on whatever aspects of it that can make valuable contributions, but it seeks to move knowledge to a higher level of synthesis, coherence, and practical relevance by developing a superior explanatory and transformative *Wissenschaft* of human life on planet Earth.[25]

Regarding intellectual production, DHM maintains that "the ideas of the ruling class are in every epoch the ruling ideas: i.e., the class which is the ruling *material* force of society is at the same time its ruling *intellectual*

---

23. See ibid., 103–5.

24. See, for instance, John Bellamy Foster, *The Dialectics of Ecology: Socialism and Nature* (New York: Monthly Review Press, 2024), 85.

25. See, in this regard, Foster's important argument that it is necessary, over and against the dominant tendency in Western Marxism, to develop "a unified praxis based on reason as science . . . by reunifying Marxism's *first foundation* in the critique of bourgeois political economy with its *second foundation* in the critique of mechanistic science." Foster, *The Dialectics of Ecology*, 96.

force. The class which has the means of material production at its disposal, consequently also controls the means of mental production."[26] In
the capitalist world, it is the bourgeoisie that, directly or indirectly, owns
and controls the schools and universities, think tanks, libraries, media,
publishing platforms, culture industries, the means of communication,
the digital world, and numerous other institutions of knowledge production, circulation, and consumption. It makes perfect sense, then, that the
dominant forms of knowledge—such as the bourgeois humanities and
social sciences—would reflect the material world that produced them.
Knowledge, in this regard, is a product of power, which is a consequence
of property in class societies. This does not mean, however, that everything is rigidly determined. There is instead a dialectical play of forces
between the extant system of theoretical production and the agents participating in it. Except as an abstract category, freedom does not disappear. Instead, it takes on a specific material form: the freedom to mobilize
one's agency within a defined field of action conditioned by a set of constraints, albeit an agency that can sometimes push against certain restrictions while nonetheless being formatted by them to varying degrees.

In one of Marx's most detailed descriptions of the relationship between
the systems of material and mental production, he wrote:

> In the social production of their existence, humans inevitably enter into
> definite relations, which are independent of their will, namely relations of
> production appropriate to a given stage in the development of their mate-
> rial forces of production. The totality of these relations of production con-
> stitutes the economic structure of society, the real foundation [*Basis*], on
> which arises a legal and political superstructure [*Überbau*] and to which
> correspond definite social forms of consciousness [*bestimmte gesellschaftli-
> che Bewusstseinsformen*]. The mode of production of material life condi-
> tions the general process of social, political and intellectual life. It is not
> the consciousness of men that determines their existence, but their social
> existence that determines their consciousness.[27]

The relationship between the socioeconomic infrastructure, on the
one hand, and the ideological superstructure on the other is dialectical

---

26. Marx and Engels, *Collected Works*, Vol. 5, 59.

27. Karl Marx and Friedrich Engels, *Collected Works*, Vol. 29 (New York: International
Publishers, 1987), 263, translation slightly modified.

through and through. Marx was not postulating a completely separate realm of economics that is not affected by the forms of social consciousness described above, nor was he claiming that ideology has no internal logic of its own. Engels had to insist on these points later in life, after Marx's death, in order to avoid any confusion. In a letter to Franz Mehring on July 14, 1893, he explained that ideology formally develops semi-autonomously and has a "historical efficacy" insofar as it "may exert a reciprocal influence on its environment and even upon its own causes."[28] It is imperative, therefore, to avoid hypostasizing the infrastructure and superstructure as two entities, approaching them from the point of view of what G. W. F. Hegel called the understanding or, more precisely, what Engels described as metaphysics. They are complex, intertwined processes, which are only really assumed to be distinct and somehow separate elements due to our impoverished conceptual vocabulary. If one of these processes is identified as more foundational, or what Engels referred to as the determinant in the last instance, this is because it serves as the fundamental organizational structure of production and reproduction— meaning the overall economic mode of production, such as feudalism or capitalism—that conditions the material lives of human beings and their ideological composition.

Returning to the quote from Marx, we can see that the ideological superstructure is composed of two heuristically distinct elements: the politico-legal apparatus and "forms of social consciousness" operative in the religion, culture, and philosophy of a particular society. This formulation, and others like it, has led to a rich debate regarding how exactly this process of ideological composition operates and is related to the infrastructure. This book, along with the rest of the trilogy, is in many ways a detailed investigation into this question, with the focal point being the superstructure of the most developed imperialist countries. It seeks to provide, among other things, a nuanced dialectical materialist account of the intricate relations and complex forms of mediation operative in the political economy of knowledge production, circulation, and consumption.

Nota Bene

Within the bourgeois knowledge regime, DHM is often reductively described with the label *Marxism*. Since under capitalism intellectual

---

28. Karl Marx and Friedrich Engels, *Collected Works*, Vol. 50 (New York: International Publishers, 2004), 165.

property law regulates theoretical production, establishing a correlation between ideas and their supposed progenitor for the purposes of commodification, this makes perfect sense. However, it occludes something fundamental: DHM is an ongoing, collective science—in the sense of *Wissenschaft*—that requires innovation and adaptation to changing circumstances. It is not a theory established once and for all in the sacred texts of a genius figure who transcends history. Marx was a man living in a specific material context, which inevitably conditioned his work, and he collaborated on a common project with Engels and many others, while also drawing on so much work that preceded them. He made extraordinary contributions, like a Charles Darwin or an Albert Einstein, but he did not work alone, nor did he establish biblical texts to be worshiped rather than tested. He contributed to the collective project of DHM, and the greatest homage we can pay him is by endeavoring to do the same, which includes materially situating him in his concrete context. It is the collective project of scientific elucidation and social transformation that is primary, not the individual, as Marx himself would have said, and did in fact say. When the term *Marxism* or *Marxist* is used in this study, then, this should not be interpreted as a tradition of thought governed by a patronym and abiding by the bourgeois laws of intellectual property. It is simply a convenient sobriquet, given its brevity, for a collective science to which Marx and Engels made foundational contributions: dialectical and historical materialism (DHM).

Sub-Rosa Politics and the Intellectual Apparatus

Marx and Engels understood that intellectual production functioned like an industry and that it was therefore necessary to analyze it from the point of view of the social relations of theoretical production. They opened *The German Ideology* with a brilliant description of the "industrialists of philosophy" who opportunistically contrived singular theoretical concoctions that they retailed, entering into competition with one another.[29] When they later encountered a glutted market, these manufacturers of ideas then engaged in "cheap and spurious production [*fabrikmässige und Scheinproduktion*]" in a bitter struggle to push their commodities.[30] Soundly criticizing those who naively interpreted the Young-Hegelian movement as an intellectual "upheaval of world significance," thereby

---

29. Marx and Engels, *Collected Works*, Vol. 5, 27.
30. Ibid., 28.

indulging in intellectual commodity fetishism, the authors of *The German Ideology* explained that their theoretical practice was ultimately anchored in socioeconomic relations and driven by opportunist careerism.[31]

Given the fact that Marx and Engels were writing in the nineteenth century, we have the advantage of historical perspective. In an effort to further develop DHM within the current conjuncture, I draw on this perspective in order to elucidate the evolution of the two intertwined components of the superstructures in the imperial core. Regarding the political-legal apparatus, to begin with, it has increasingly developed a division of labor between the visible form of legal government that administers the spectacle of public politics, on the one hand, and a largely invisible government that manages capitalist social relations, often through illegal means, on the other. As historian Annie Lacroix-Riz has explained, the increasing concentration of wealth under monopoly capitalism has required greater recourse to the men and women of the shadows.[32] The arrival of socialism on the world's historical stage, which poses an existential threat to capitalism, has exacerbated the need to rely on covert mechanisms of governance, particularly because the governments of the imperial core have attempted to maintain their hegemony by presenting themselves as democracies rather than plutocratic, oligarchic empires. The bourgeois state, under these conditions, has thus increasingly developed its somber underside. The fact that Vladimir Lenin and Leon Trotsky were both, for a few days in the spring of 1917, in the custody of the networks of the United Kingdom's recently minted (1909) Secret Intelligence Service (SIS, also known as MI6) provides insight into how important shadow government became in the monopoly imperialist phase of the war on communism.[33] MI6 then collaborated with U.S. and French intelligence, with the financial backing of both of these countries, in planning a failed anticommunist coup d'état against the Bolsheviks.[34]

Unfortunately, the bourgeois social sciences, and political science more specifically, focus almost exclusively on overt forms of governance, thereby foreclosing the possibility of analyzing the full spectrum of activities of the bourgeois state. Indeed, there is no extant discipline for

---

31. Ibid.
32. This is a theme across Lacroix-Riz's brilliant work, but she provides a concise summary of it in the interview titled "Les hommes de l'ombre" for *Une certaine idée de l'Histoire*, https://www.youtube.com/watch?v=7RUE6uMHTFY.
33. See Giles Milton, *Russian Roulette: How British Spies Thwarted Lenin's Plot for Global Revolution* (New York: Bloomsbury Press, 2014), 40–45.
34. See ibid., esp. 148–67.

studying the governmental agencies engaged in the dark arts of covert operations. Consider professor David N. Gibbs's findings:

> I surveyed the five top journals in political science that specialize in international relations during the period 1991–2000. I did not find a single article in any of these journals that focused on CIA covert operations. Mentions of these operations were very rare and, when they occurred at all, they were confined to a few sentences or a footnote. In effect, an entire category of international conduct has been expunged from the record, as if it never occurred.[35]

Elsewhere citing the additional fact that "a significant number of social scientists, especially political scientists, regularly work with the Central Intelligence Agency," Gibbs has been doing important work to bring to light the ways in which the bourgeois social sciences have served to whitewash the sordid history of U.S. foreign policy.[36] More generally, former CIA officer turned university professor Richard Smith aptly pointed out that "not a single university in the United States fosters a serious research effort into the organization and activities of the 'intelligence community,' that massive bureaucratic conglomerate that has played such a major role in our foreign policy."[37] Bourgeois knowledge production is thus complicit in covering up the crimes of the U.S. national security state, whose depth and breadth boggle the imagination. For instance, according to the meticulous calculations of fourteen former members of the CIA, the Agency they worked for was responsible for the death of at least six million people between 1947 and 1987 (if one assumes the same pace, these

---

35. David N. Gibbs, "The Question of Whitewashing in American History and Social Science," in *Unlearning the Language of Conquest: Scholars Expose Anti-Indianism in America*, ed. Four Arrows [Donald Trent Jacobs] (Austin: University of Texas Press, 2006), 214.

36. David N. Gibbs, "Academics and Spies: The Silence That Roars," *Los Angeles Times*, January 28, 2001, http://articles.latimes.com/2001/jan/28/opinion/op-18012. Also see David N. Gibbs, "The CIA Is Back on Campus," *CounterPunch*, April 7, 2003, https://www.counterpunch.org/2003/04/07/the-cia-is-back-on-campus/; *Democracy Now!*, November 13, 2002, https://www.democracynow.org/2002/11/13/cia_on_campus_the_intelligence_community. For more information on the CIA and the contemporary academic world, see the useful bibliography compiled by Gibbs: https://dgibbs.faculty.arizona.edu/debate_cia_and_academe.

37. Richard Harris Smith, *OSS: The Secret History of America's First Central Intelligence Agency* (Berkeley: University of California Press, 1972), xii.

numbers would have doubled by 2017).[38] This veritable Third World War, to use CIA officer John Stockwell's apt expression, is rarely, if ever, so much as registered within the realm of bourgeois knowledge.

This book, like the next two in the series, draws on extensive archival research and innumerable Freedom of Information Act (FOIA) requests, as well as a large body of scholarship based on archival research and first-person testimonies of those involved in covert operations. This research was undertaken in order to both overcome the limitations of bourgeois knowledge and demonstrate the superior explanatory power of DHM regarding how the bourgeois state functions, particularly in the monopoly and imperial phase of capitalism.[39] This is not to deny in the least that parallel structures have played a major role in the deeper history of capitalist governance, which they most certainly have. The argument is rather that they have been developed at an industrial scale in the contemporary world and become increasingly central to both the hegemonic and repressive modalities of political management.

The other focal point of this study is the sector of the superstructure that formats social consciousness, with particular attention paid to its industrial-scale development in the contemporary world. The superstructure, as the name suggests, is not simply the result of ideologies that are organically produced through class relations. While arising from class dynamics, these ideologies are structured and organized through a powerful institutionalized system that forges and formats subjects in every aspect of their being, including their consciousness, but also their values, affects, perceptions, practices, desires, and drives.[40] The superstructure thus includes all of the cultural, religious, educational, media, intellectual, and other institutions that compose people as ideological subjects and

---

38. John Stockwell mentions this in the lecture excerpted here under the title "CIA's War on Humans": https://www.youtube.com/watch?v=m3ioJGMCr-Y. Also see John Stockwell, *The Praetorian Guard: The U.S. Role in the New World Order* (Boston: South End Press, 1991).

39. In addition to consulting numerous digital archives and reading documents obtained through FOIA requests, I did research at the National Archives, the Dwight D. Eisenhower Presidential Library, the Rockefeller Archive Center, the Hanna Holborn Gray Special Collections Research Center at the University of Chicago (to study the records of the Congress for Cultural Freedom), and the Tamiment Library at New York University (to examine the records of the American Committee for Cultural Freedom).

40. See Jennifer Ponce de León and Gabriel Rockhill, "Toward a Compositional Model of Ideology: Materialism, Aesthetics, and Cultural Revolution," *Philosophy Today*, Vol. 64, No. 1 (January 2020): 95–116.

direct their activities, as well as the entire material system by which cultural productions—in the broadest sense of this term—circulate and are consumed. In the imperialist phase of monopoly capitalism, especially in its latest form, the superstructure is so highly industrialized and centralized that it arguably exercises an awesome degree of power never before seen in history.[41] To take but one telling example, journalist Alan Macleod claimed in 2019 that "five gigantic corporations control over 90 per cent of what America reads, watches or listens to."[42]

The dark underside of the politico-legal superstructure has been much more involved in consolidating the cultural and intellectual sector of the superstructure than most people are aware, and this clearly demonstrates the central importance of a dialectical approach that does not reify these two elements as separate components but rather conceptualizes them as interrelated forces. Cultural production under capitalism, like intellectual production more specifically, is characterized by a fundamental contradiction: it has to appear to be free and open to all, based on the principles of democratic meritocracy, while actually being tightly controlled from behind the scenes in order to enforce the dominant ideology. It is for this reason that capitalist states have developed powerful propaganda and disinformation agencies, which—through covert operations—have been deeply but discreetly involved in the system of intellectual and cultural production, distribution, and consumption. This is, indeed, one of the key functions of the intelligence agencies of imperialist states: they are engaged in an intellectual world war. As Ralph W. McGehee explained, based on his twenty-five years of experience as a CIA case officer: "The CIA is not an intelligence agency. In fact, it acts largely as an anti-intelligence agency, producing only that information wanted by policymakers to support their plans and suppressing information that does not support those plans. As the covert action arm of the President, the CIA uses disinformation, much of it aimed at the U.S. public, to mold opinion."[43] William Casey,

---

41. In addition to Lenin's foundational work, see John Bellamy Foster, "Late Imperialism," *Monthly Review*, Vol. 71, No. 3 (July 2019), https://monthlyreview.org/2019/07/01/late-imperialism/, and Cheng Enfu and Lu Baolin, "Five Characteristics of Neoimperialism: Building on Lenin's Theory of Imperialism in the Twenty-First Century," *Monthly Review*, Vol. 73, No. 1 (May 2021), https://monthlyreview.org/2021/05/01/five-characteristics-of-neoimperialism/.

42. Alan Macleod, *Propaganda in the Information Age: Still Manufacturing Consent* (New York: Routledge, 2019), 48.

43. Ralph W. McGehee, *Deadly Deceits: My 25 Years in the CIA* (New York: Open Road

CIA director from 1981 to 1987, explained what this meant in concrete terms during a meeting with newly elected President Ronald Reagan. When he was asked to explain the goal of his agency, he flatly stated: "We'll know our disinformation program is complete when everything the American public believes is false."[44]

In this regard, ideology, while arising out of class dynamics, is shaped, developed, and overseen by an ensemble of institutionalized forces that condition social life. Organic class ideologies, such as that of the imperial professional-managerial class stratum, are structured, enhanced, and incentivized by the cultural system within which members of this middle layer operate. It is essential to remember, in this regard, that Marx's metaphor of the base and the superstructure is precisely that: a metaphor. It is not intended to capture every aspect of the relationship between these two heuristically distinct components. It is instead focused on bringing into relief one key feature of the reality it indexes: the dependence of the ideological superstructure on the economic base that supports it. It thereby leaves aside, for purely pedagogical purposes, other important aspects, like the fact that these two elements are ultimately dialectically enmeshed. We must not, then, approach this metaphor as if it was a literal description, nor should we apprehend it—as mentioned above, but it bears repeating—from an undialectical point of view, assuming for instance that there are literally two fixed and clearly differentiated entities with one literally perched upon the other and having absolutely distinct parts. In order to materially demonstrate the dialectical relationship between the infrastructure and the superstructure, this study proposes a political economy of knowledge that details the intricate relationships between the capitalist base, the politico-legal superstructure, the cultural-intellectual sector of the superstructure, and the subjects of knowledge production and consumption. For the purposes of this work, the focal point is much more specifically the academic side of the intellectual apparatus, meaning the industrialized system of theoretical production, circulation, and consumption that governs the professional academic intelligentsia and forms a key component of the superstructure.

Media, 2015). This quote is from the introduction to the book, which is oddly lacking in page numbers.

44. "Source of CIA Director William J. Casey's Disinformation Program Quote," 1981, http://archive.org/details/cia-director-william-casey-disinformation-program-quote-soruce.

Political Economy of Knowledge: The Foundation-CIA-University Nexus

The political economy of knowledge, which is integral to the analysis that follows, allows us to track the impact of political and economic forces on the types of knowledge that are produced, widely circulated, and consumed. It also sheds light on which forms of knowledge are excluded from support, marginalized, and targeted for widespread discrediting or even elimination. As we shall see, multiple forces have been at work in the political economy driving the intellectual sector of the superstructures in the imperial core. Universities have, of course, been key since they are major corporations involved in the manufacturing and dissemination of knowledge. The same is true of think tanks, and various intellectual organizations and associations have also played supporting roles. The publishing industry has been central for its importance in the distribution and consumption of knowledge, as well as the mass media and culture industries more generally.

The capitalist ruling class, which controls and oversees the institutions just mentioned, has also interceded directly by using its foundations to exercise its dominion over intellectual life. In doing so, it has often worked hand-in-glove with state agencies. This intimate relationship between the bourgeoisie and the bourgeois state is important to understand for everything that follows because these are the two principal forces at work within the political economy of bourgeois knowledge. Although liberal ideology attempts to drive a wedge between the two by distinguishing between so-called private and public sectors, the materialist tradition of Marx and Engels has long understood that the state is not a neutral body independent of economic interests but rather an agent of class warfare.[45] Another powerful illusion pushed by liberal ideology is that there is a fundamental difference between corporations and their foundations. This distinction, however, is little more than a propagandistic stratagem. It allows companies to steal twice over: once from the worker via exploitation, and a second time by funneling money owed in taxes into foundations, thereby avoiding making payments to the government that could—at least in principle—indirectly redistribute wealth to the workers.[46] They then use their twice-stolen pelf for soft power initia-

---

45. "The state," Lenin wrote, "is a special organization of force; it is the organization of violence for the suppression of some class." Vladimir Lenin, *Collected Works*, Vol. 25 (Moscow: Progress Publishers, 1964), 402.
46. On foundations as "repositories of twice-stolen wealth—*profit* sheltered from *taxes*,"

tives marketed as philanthropic endeavors—in order to whitewash their reputations—whose fundamental purpose is to advance their interests and increase accumulation (that is, theft).

The "Big Three" foundations (Rockefeller, Ford, Carnegie) have historically played the leading roles in fashioning the intellectual world in their own image, but many smaller foundations have contributed as well. The bourgeois state has been very involved at multiple levels, especially through its national security state, which has played an important—though widely undertheorized—role in psychological warfare operations alongside the foundations. In 1975, the Church Committee, convened to investigate abuses committed by intelligence services and the Internal Revenue Service (IRS), helped shed light on the intimate relationship between the U.S. ruling class's foundations and its government:

> The CIA's intrusion into the foundation field in the 1960s can only be described as massive. Excluding grants from the "Big Three"—Ford, Rockefeller, and Carnegie—of the 700 grants over $10,000 given by 164 other foundations during the period 1963–1966, at least 108 involved partial or complete CIA funding. More importantly, CIA funding was involved in *nearly half* the grants the non-"Big Three" foundations made during this period in the field of international activities. In the same period more than one-third of the grants awarded by non-"Big Three" in the physical, life and social sciences also involved CIA funds.[47]

It is thus part of the public record that the CIA has worked closely with the foundations of the ruling class to advance their common agenda, and nothing has prohibited this tendency from continuing or even intensifying.

It is notable that the Church Committee intentionally excluded the Big Three in its analysis, although it did admit that they were considered "the best and most plausible kind of funding cover," and they allowed the CIA to finance "a seemingly limitless range of covert action programs affecting youth groups, labor unions, universities, publishing houses, and other

---

see Ruth Wilson Gilmore, *Abolition Geography: Essays Towards Liberation*, ed. Brenna Bhandar and Alberto Toscano (London: Verso, 2022), 233.

47. Senate Select Committee to Study Governmental Operations with Respect to Intelligence Activities, *Final Report*, Book I, *Foreign and Military Intelligence* (Washington, DC: U.S. Government Printing Office, 1976), https://www.intelligence.senate.gov/sites/default/files/94755_I.pdf, 182.

private institutions."[48] The illogical exclusion of the Big Three makes perfect sense if one is familiar with the modus operandi of faith-in-government campaigns like the Church Committee.

It is enlightening, in this regard, that the person put in charge of investigating the relationship between the CIA and the journalistic and academic world for the Church Committee was William B. Bader, a lifelong servant of the U.S. military and national security state, as well as governmental propaganda organizations like the United States Information Agency (USIA).[49] Bader was in fact a former member of the CIA, which is renowned for never having any retirees ("once a Company man, always a Company man" is the operational mantra of the Agency).[50] The multilayered hypocrisy of this endeavor should not be lost on us: in response to public outcry regarding major crimes committed by the bourgeois state, the latter convened a committee to investigate itself, and its examination of the relationship between its most notorious agency (the CIA) and the intelligentsia was overseen by an Agency man.

Nevertheless, the bourgeois state is a site of struggle, and some important evidence did come to light through this process. In spite of the reticence of his former colleagues to turn over the most damning information, Bader was able to discover an enormous operation that far surpassed even his own expectations. His findings were never discussed by the Church Committee, however, and they were not integrated into its final report, whose account clearly minimizes the CIA's penetration into the media and the university. It did nonetheless report that the Agency was in contact with "many thousands" of academics in "hundreds" of institutions.

William Corson, who served as an intelligence officer in the U.S. Marines and worked very closely with the CIA in this capacity, was an unofficial adviser to Frank Church and his investigative committee.[51] In preparing his 1977 book *Armies of Ignorance*, he had "extended discussions" with William Bader, as well as Bill Miller and Fritz Schwarz of the Church Committee.[52] If their private knowledge of the depth and breadth

---

48. Cited in Frances Stonor Saunders, *The Cultural Cold War: The CIA and the World of Arts and Letters* (New York: New Press, 2000), 135.

49. See Bader's brief biography on the State Department's website: https://1997-2001. state.gov/www/about_state/biography/bader.html.

50. See Matt Schudel, "William B. Bader, Official Who Helped Uncover CIA, Defense Abuses Dies at 84," *Washington Post*, March 19, 2016.

51. See "William R. Corson," *Spartacus Educational*, https://spartacus-educational.com/ JFKcorsonW.htm.

52. William R. Corson, *The Armies of Ignorance: The Rise of the American Intelligence*

of CIA penetration into the academy leaked into the public, Corson's book would have likely been one of its main sources. Here is what he said:

> Today, the original band of OSS academics has been expanded tenfold, producing a situation in which some 5,000 American academics are doing the bidding of the CIA: not only identifying and recruiting American students to its service, but providing screening committees designed to select 200–300 future agents in place from among the 250,000 foreign students who come to the United States each year. Of these 5,000 "professors, administrators, and researchers" approximately 60 percent are fully aware of what they are doing and either receive compensation directly from the CIA as contract employees, or indirectly in the form of research grants or subsidies to carry out intelligence-related tasks. The other 40 percent appear to believe that they are assisting the career development of their foreign student charges by identifying those with a potential for employment by one of the United States multinational firms. Rarely, if ever, does the unwitting academic relate to the fact that the recruiter from corporation X is other than he represents himself.[53]

The CIA's collaborations with the academy are too extensive to summarize, but a wealth of internal documents testify to the fact that the university serves as its principal site of recruitment, a major research partner, a training and experimentation center for Agency operatives and their collaborators, a consultancy hub, a residency refuge for its officers, and much more.[54] The CIA has collaborated, for instance, on a Summer

---

Empire (New York: Dial Press, 1977), v.

53. Ibid., 312.

54. Among other documents, see "Agency-Academic Relations," February 25, 1969, the CIA FOIA Electronic Reading Room, https://www.cia.gov/readingroom/document/cia-rdp86b00985r000300070016-5; "Activities in Academic Relations," November 3, 1977, the CIA FOIA Electronic Reading Room, https://www.cia.gov/readingroom/document/cia-rdp86b00985r000300010001-8; "Academic Relations," October 14, 1981, the CIA FOIA Electronic Reading Room, https://www.cia.gov/readingroom/document/cia-rdp85m00364r002003810016-4; "Proposed Consolidation of Cultural Assets," January 29, 1985, the CIA FOIA Electronic Reading Room, https://www.cia.gov/readingroom/document/cia-rdp87m00539r002103300001-9; "DCI's Program for Deans, Memo for ADCI," May 6, 1987, the CIA FOIA Electronic Reading Room, https://www.cia.gov/readingroom/document/cia-rdp90g00152r001001990006-4; and "NFAC Notice: Academic Relations," no date (released July 7, 2004), the CIA FOIA Electronic Reading Room, https://www.cia.gov/readingroom/document/cia-

Intern Program with students, Agency-Academic Seminars, a program that hosts college deans and other administrators at the Agency, and regular briefings with students and faculty. It has also provided CIA speakers to address academic groups, hosted scholars at the Agency, coordinated publication and teaching opportunities for its officers, and run public relations campaigns in order to improve the image of the CIA on university campuses. By 1976, the collaborations between the Company (as the CIA is known) and the academy were so extensive that the Agency assigned two full-time officers as Academic Coordinators.[55] When the National Foreign Assessments Center was established in 1977, the academic relations program "was additionally upgraded" and these two officers "formed the core of the new Academic Relations staff."[56]

In the wake of the Church Committee hearings in 1975, no reform prevented the CIA from continuing or expanding its practices in the university. As a matter of fact, Admiral Stansfield Turner, CIA director from 1977 to 1981, openly rejected the Committee's recommendations about transparency and related guidelines put forth by Harvard (which only ten schools adopted in diluted form). He made it clear that "the agency had no intention of following them."[57]

This is borne out by later examples of ongoing collaboration. Robert Gates served for twenty-six years in the CIA, including working as its director, before becoming president of Texas A&M University.[58] In a 1986 lecture at Harvard titled "CIA and the University," he explained that the Agency's involvement in the academic world includes consulting work by

rdp81m00980r001200090014-5. Also see Ami Chen Mills, *CIA Off Campus: Building the Movement against Agency Recruitment and Research* (Boston: South End Press, 1991); Robert Witanek, "The CIA on Campus," *CovertAction Information Bulletin*, No. 31 (Winter 1988); John Hollister Hedley, "Twenty Years of Officers in Residence: CIA in the Classroom," *Studies in Intelligence*, Vol. 49, No. 4 (December 2005); and Narda Sacchimo and Robert Scheer, "Longtime CIA Links with UC Disclosed," *Los Angeles Times*, February 20, 1978.

55. See "Activities in Academic Relations," November 3, 1977, the CIA FOIA Electronic Reading Room, https://www.cia.gov/readingroom/document/cia-rdp86b00985r000300010001-8.

56. Ibid.

57. Daniel Golden, *Spy Schools: How the CIA, FBI, and Foreign Intelligence Secretly Exploit America's Universities* (New York: Picador, 2017), 173.

58. The same year as Gates's appointment, Arizona State University chose as its president Michael Crow, "vice chairman of In-Q-Tel Inc., the nonprofit venture-capital arm of the CIA that funds companies developing spy technology." Daniel Golden, "After Sept. 11, the CIA Becomes a Force on Campus—The Agency Needs Experts from Academia," *Wall Street Journal*, October 4, 2002.

academics, sponsorship of conferences, the funding of research, scholars in residence programs that cycle academics through the CIA with full security clearances, and general information sharing.[59] According to the 1991 Gates memo on greater CIA openness, "the Agency has a wide range of contacts with academics through recruiting, professional societies, contractual arrangements and OTE [Office of Training and Education]."[60] The Agency's Public Affairs Office (PAO) "maintains a mailing list of 700 academicians who receive unclassified Agency publications four times a year."[61] The PAO also sponsors the Director of Central Intelligence (DCI) Program for Deans that exposes "administrators of academic institutions to senior Agency officials."[62]

The same year as Gates's memo, a scandal rocked the Rochester Institute of Technology (RIT) when it was revealed that its president was clandestinely working for the CIA.[63] He had signed a memorandum of agreement with the Company that converted RIT "into a virtual subsidiary of the CIA," with the president giving "the CIA a say in faculty appointments and curriculum."[64] This scandal did not, however, alter the fundamental architecture of the CIA-academic complex, due in part to the public relations efforts of the Agency. For instance, "a 1996 Directorate of Intelligence memo calls 'public outreach' a top priority and targets academia in particular."[65] According to Chris Mooney, who cites intelligence experts to support his claim, this strategy has worked: "Since the end of the Cold War, spies and scholars have grown more cozy than at any time since Vietnam drove a wedge between professors and the government."[66]

Daniel Golden has provided one of the most recent overviews of these relationships in his 2017 book *Spy Schools*. Citing numerous examples, he draws the following conclusion: "Invited or not, openly or not, U.S.

---

59. "Letter to B.R. Inman from Robert M. Gates," January 22, 1986, the CIA FOIA Electronic Reading Room, https://www.cia.gov/readingroom/document/cia-rdp90g01359r 000200070018-2.

60. Task Force on Greater CIA Openness, "Memorandum for Director of Public Affairs," November 18, 1991, http://www.takeoverworld.info/cia-openness.html.

61. Ibid.

62. Ibid.

63. See Golden, "After Sept. 11, the CIA Becomes a Force on Campus."

64. Philip Agee, "CIA Off Campus Movement," discussion at Carnegie Mellon University, 1992, https://www.youtube.com/watch?v=HMI_h3LDrAI.

65. Chris Mooney, "For Your Eyes Only: The CIA Will Let You See Classified Documents— But At What Price?," *Lingua Franca* (November 2000).

66. Ibid.

intelligence today touches virtually every facet of academic life. Its influence likely equals or surpasses its previous peak in the 1950s."[67] The intelligence agencies are involved in a very wide array of activities. Universities remain, to begin with, primary recruitment sites, as well as being important for intelligence gathering and threat assessments. Second, they provide training and education for current or future officers, with universities routinely offering "degrees in homeland security and courses in espionage and cyber-hacking."[68] Third, university administrators, as well as national associations of higher education trustees and attorneys, are provided with trainings from the intelligence community, such as the FBI-sponsored seminars that have taken place at MIT, Michigan State, Stanford, and other colleges. Fourth, universities do research for intelligence agencies as well as their cut-outs like Centra Inc., "a leading independent provider of high-end intelligence support" and "one of the government's elite pre-approved contractors."[69] They vie for lucrative governmental grants and for "federal designation as Intelligence Community Centers for Academic Excellence and National Centers of Academic Excellence in Cyber Operations."[70] Obscure federal agencies like the Intelligence Advanced Research Projects Activity, which sponsors "high-risk/high pay-off research that has the potential to provide our nation with an overwhelming intelligence advantage," have funded researchers representing more than 175 academic institutions.[71] Fifth, the intelligence agencies sponsor and monitor conferences worldwide, often paying professors handsome honoraria for participating, plus expenses. Finally—though this list is not exhaustive—agencies like the CIA are involved in exchange and residency programs such as the following:

> In 1982, it brought fourteen college presidents to its Langley headquarters to meet the director and other top officials. In 1977, it started a "scholars-in-residence" program in which professors on sabbatical from their universities were given contracts to advise CIA analysts and made "privy to

---

67. Golden, *Spy Schools*, 265.

68. Ibid., 164.

69. Loren Blinde, "PAW to Acquire CENTRA Technology," *Intelligence Community News,* October 26, 2020, https://intelligencecommunitynews.com/pae-to-acquire-centra-technology/; Jason Leopold, "The CIA Paid This Contractor $40 Million to Review Torture Documents," *Vice News,* July 27, 2015, https://www.vice.com/en/article/the-cia-paid-this-contractor-40-million-to-review-torture-documents/.

70. Golden, *Spy Schools*, 164.

71. Cited in ibid.

information that would never be available to them on campus." In 1985, the agency added an "officers-in-residence" component, which placed intelligence officers nearing retirement at universities at CIA expense.[72]

RETURNING TO THE RULING-CLASS foundations, multiple sources testify to the intimate working relationship between the U.S. government, particularly intelligence services like the CIA, and the Big Three in the field of psychological warfare. CIA director Allen Dulles explained in his correspondence with Shepard Stone in 1956 that he was able to use secret Company funds from time to time for cultural projects, but then had the idea of encouraging large foundations to fill the gaps left by the government.[73] This also had the great advantage, considered entirely necessary by Dulles's colleague Frank Wisner, of creating the illusion that the cultural projects of the Agency were not linked to the imperialist ambitions of the U.S. government. Stone himself had worked in the intelligence service of the U.S. Army, then as a journalist at the *New York Times*, and he helped CIA agent Melvin Lasky launch the Ford-funded magazine *Der Monat* (Ford even paid Lasky's salary at the time).[74] In 1952, Stone became the Director of International Affairs at the Ford Foundation. This was by far the largest U.S. foundation, and one of the first to embark on an international cultural program. No other foundation had carried out a global mission of such magnitude or had comparable resources. It became the most powerful philanthropic organization in the world and influenced the cultural and intellectual production of the planet like no other. Its assets in 1960 were $3.316 billion (the equivalent of $35 billion in 2024), while the Rockefeller Foundation was in second place with $648 million. Even before Stone arrived at Ford, there were talks between the automobile company and the CIA. Wisner had reportedly asked if the

---

72. Ibid., 178.
73. See Saunders, *The Cultural Cold War*.
74. In addition to the discussions in Saunders, *The Cultural Cold War* and Hugh Wilford, *The Mighty Wurlitzer: How the CIA Played America* (Cambridge, MA: Harvard University Press, 2008), see Francis X. Sutton, "The Ford Foundation and Europe: Ambitions and Ambivalences," in *The Ford Foundation and Europe (1950's–1970's): Cross-Fertilization of Learning in Social Science and Management*, ed. Giuliana Gemelli (Brussels: European Interuniversity Press, 1998), 31–3. Lasky was a "'witting' CIA agent" according to Hugh Wilford, *The CIA, the British Left and the Cold War* (New York: Routledge, 2014), 275. Indeed, Lasky admitted to this, as was reported in the media. See the press clippings in the International Association for Cultural Freedom Records, Box 319, Folder 2, Hanna Holborn Gray Special Collections Research Center at the University of Chicago.

foundation could serve as a conduit for government funding, but Ford preferred to directly finance the same operations as the infamous Agency (such as the Congress for Cultural Freedom). Stone regularly visited his many contacts at the CIA, including Dulles and Cord Meyer, and "many believed he was an Agency man."[75]

It is revealing that David Rockefeller had suggested to Allen Dulles that he could become president of the Ford Foundation if he wanted, but he was named head of the CIA two days later.[76] Stone's colleagues at Ford, John McCloy and Henry Heald (the former president of New York University), as well as at least one board member, Charles Wyzanski, were aware of the collaboration with the Agency. After participating in the formation of the OSS, McCloy spent his life between Washington and Wall Street, becoming known as "the Chairman of the American Establishment."[77] He went from his post as Assistant Secretary of War to head of the World Bank, then U.S. High Commissioner for Germany (where he "had agreed to provide cover for scores of CIA agents"), before becoming Chairman of the Ford Foundation, and so on.[78] At Ford, he established an administrative unit responsible for managing the relationship between the foundation and the CIA, which met whenever the latter wanted to use the former. With this arrangement, they collaborated on innumerable projects together, including, for instance, Ford's channeling of $523,000 into Chekhov Publishing House for "the purchase of proscribed Russian works, and translations into Russian of Western classics."[79] James Petras, drawing out the ultimate consequences from Frances Stonor Saunders's groundbreaking archival research, explained the situation with the hallmark clarity of historical materialist analysis:

---

75. Saunders, *The Cultural Cold War*, 143.

76. See ibid., 140–41.

77. Sutton, "The Ford Foundation and Europe," 25.

78. Saunders, *The Cultural Cold War*, 141. Also see Inderjeet Parmar, *Foundations of the American Century: The Ford, Carnegie, and Rockefeller Foundations in the Rise of American Power* (New York: Columbia University Press, 2012), 54, and Paul Labarique, "La Fondation Ford, Paravent Philanthropique de La CIA," *Réseau Voltaire,* April 5, 2004, https://www.voltairenet.org/article13171.html.

79. Saunders, *The Cultural Cold War*, 142. Philip Mosely, a top-level CIA consultant and a close personal friend of Herbert Marcuse, was at least partially involved in the machinations surrounding the Chekhov Publishing House. See "Letter to Miss Nancy Hanks, Assistant to Mr. Rockefeller," May 19, 1955, Dwight D. Eisenhower: Records as President, White House Central Files (Confidential File), 1953–1961, Subject Series, Box 14, Folder Chekhov Publishing House, Dwight D. Eisenhower Library.

From its very origins there was a close structural relation and interchange of personnel at the highest levels between the CIA and the Ford Foundation. This structural tie was based on the common imperial interests which they shared . . . The Ford Foundation funding of . . . anti-Marxist organizations and intellectuals provided a legal cover for their claims of being "independent" of government funding (CIA).[80]

The relationship between the intelligence services and the Rockefeller Foundation followed the same pattern. Nelson Rockefeller "had regional jurisdiction over Latin America in the intelligence field."[81] He ran his own intelligence and propaganda agency, the Office of the Coordinator of Inter-American Affairs (CIAA), which worked so closely with the OSS (the CIA's predecessor organization) that there was talk of it absorbing the CIAA.[82] A personal friend of longtime CIA director Allen Dulles, Rockefeller was chosen by Eisenhower to serve on the National Security Council in the mid-1950s, where he gave the green light to clandestine operations. Rockefeller would also become the vice president of the United States from 1974 to 1977. John Foster Dulles, Allen's brother, served as president of the Rockefeller Foundation, as did Dean Rusk. They both subsequently became secretary of state. Nelson Rockefeller also hired many former OSS operatives, such as Charles Fahs, who became head of the humanities division in 1950, and his assistant, Chadbourne Gilpatric (who also worked for the CIA).[83] To take one last example, David Rockefeller, Nelson's brother, served in a special army intelligence unit during the war tasked with spying on the anticolonial movement in Algeria, before becoming a spook in Paris, where he surveilled resistance communists and set up an espionage network within de Gaulle's provisional government. A close friend of Dulles and high-ranking CIA officer Thomas Braden, the latter often debriefed

---

80. James Petras, "The Ford Foundation and the CIA: A Documented Case of Philanthropic Collaboration with the Secret Police," *The James Petras Website* (blog), December 15, 2001, https://petras.lahaine.org/the-ford-foundation-and-the-cia-a-documented-case-of-philanthropic-collaboration-with-the-secret-police/. Also see Saunders, *The Cultural Cold War*, particularly 142 where she discusses the fact that "the [Ford] [F]oundation's archives reveal a raft of joint projects [with the CIA]."

81. Barry M. Katz, *Foreign Intelligence: Research and Analysis in the Office of Strategic Services 1942–1945* (Cambridge, MA: Harvard University Press, 1989), 2.

82. See Donald W. Rowland et al., *History of the Office of the Coordinator of Inter-American Affairs* (Washington, DC: U.S. Government Printing Office, 1947).

83. See Saunders, *The Cultural Cold War*, 145.

him informally, with Dulles's permission. In a confession that reveals the inner workings of this dark world of the plutocratic elite, Braden explained that David Rockefeller "was of the same mind as us, and very approving of everything we were doing. He had the same sense as I did that the way to win the Cold War was *our* way. Sometimes David would give me money to do things which weren't in our budget. He gave me a lot of money for causes in France."[84]

The Carnegie Foundation also had similar ties to the U.S. national security state. Inderjeet Parmar has provided a detailed overview of many of the links between the Big Three and their government, which brings this pattern clearly into view.[85] The connections have been so tight between the CIA and the major foundations of the capitalist ruling class, as well as with the leadership of premier educational corporations, that sociologist Pierre Grémion described in the following terms the decision-making elite that was responsible for U.S. cultural diplomacy:

> The State Department, the senior management of the major foundations, their trustees, as well as the trustees of the major universities involved in the nationalization and internationalization of the American intellectual system, were fully informed [regarding the CIA's funding of the CCF, and thus its involvement in collaborative cultural warfare with the foundations]. In the 1950s, when a senior executive of the Ford Foundation took up their post, not three weeks went by before they were aware of "Cord" (Meyer's) programs [i.e. CIA programs]. The quality of CIA personnel, surpassing... that of the State Department, made the agency a super-foundation, if not the Foundation of foundations.[86]

Rather than the capitalist foundations and the bourgeois state operating in separate spheres, according to the liberal ideology of the private and public sectors, they function as two elements within an organic totality, which generally work in concert with one another toward common objectives.

Although this investigation uncovers a number of direct links between intellectuals and their financial backers in the ruling class and bourgeois states, this should not obscure a broader phenomenon of which they form

---

84. Cited in ibid., 145.
85. See Parmar, *Foundations of the American Century*, 31–64.
86. Pierre Grémion, *Intelligence de l'anticommunisme: Le Congrès pour la liberté de la culture à Paris 1950–1975* (Paris: Librairie Arthème Fayard, 1995), 453.

a decisive part: there is a relationship of ideological confluence between the bourgeois regime of knowledge production and its leading producers. This means that direct intercession or additional resources are not always necessary if the system of bourgeois knowledge simply functions as it is supposed to by providing uplift to those who excel at giving to the system what it demands. In concrete terms, at least for academics, uplift means perks like prestigious appointments, lucrative book deals, academic awards, lavish junkets, funded translations, major grants, coverage by the bourgeois press, international fame, and much more. Many of these rewards are simply part of the normal functioning of the bourgeois system of knowledge production, and there is not an exceptional money trail revealing extraordinary interventions by ruling class foundations or the state. This is crucially important to emphasize because many of the imperial sophists under scrutiny in this study have not received special treatment from the men and women of the shadows. They have simply reaped the benefits of the system of bourgeois knowledge by giving to it what it requires for preferment. They are, in brief, the highest performing—and thus the highest paid—ideologues. This is an essential aspect of the political economy of bourgeois knowledge.

Conspiracy Theories and Conspiratorial Realities

Often the term "conspiracy" is applied dismissively whenever one suggests that people who occupy positions of political and economic power are consciously dedicated to advancing their elite interests. Even when they openly profess their designs, there are those who deny that intent is involved.

—MICHAEL PARENTI[87]

Labels like "conspiratorial thinking" and "conspiracy theory," as they are generally used in public discourse, are often mobilized as weapons of class warfare whose principal objective is to peremptorily exclude as beyond the pale certain forms of materialist analysis. By labeling them as conspiracy theories they can be banished from the realm of rational discourse as heretical without even having to look at the evidence. Such an act nips sober scientific scrutiny in the bud, in favor of an ideologically conditioned reflex that requires absolutely no knowledge. In a benighted

87. Michael Parenti, *Dirty Truths: Reflections on Politics, Media, Ideology, Conspiracy, Ethnic Life and Class Power* (San Francisco: City Lights Books, 1996), 173.

"gotcha" moment, an entire materialist analysis can be disregarded as preposterous in a split second by someone who is completely ignorant of the facts. They simply need to say, perhaps with a disdainful smirk to affectively communicate their dimwitted sense of intellectual superiority: "That sounds conspiratorial."

One of the ways that conspiracy theories have been used as ideological weapons of war against scientific investigation is by affiliating the materialist examination of actually existing conspiracies on the part of the capitalist class and its state managers with superstitious conspiracy theories that traffic in the most bizarre forms of free association and magical thinking. Imagined UFO landings and convoluted cabals based on wacky assumptions and crackpot theories are thereby put under the same umbrella as concrete investigations into ruling-class collusion, thereby discrediting the latter as unscientific and unworthy of being taken seriously. Moreover, since conspiracy theories are associated with mental illness and paranoia, using the label serves to pathologize those who proffer them as irrational crazies whose evidence should not even be considered.

It is important to recognize, in this regard, that the capitalist ruling class has widely supported and promoted certain forms of conspiratorial thinking, such as the idea of an international communist conspiracy, or what used to be referred to as the Judeo-Bolshevik conspiracy to destroy Western civilization. The problem is not, then, with conspiracy theories per se, but rather with the scientific examination of the ways in which the capitalist class and its political elite act behind the scenes in their own self-interest and lie about it to the general public in order to advance their agenda. What is verboten is the study of capitalist conspiracy.

Yet there are a number of conspiracies of precisely this nature, including some that have even been proven by bourgeois courts and governmental commissions. The 1934 "Business Plot," as I have detailed in a long article on the topic, was a conspiracy on the part of some of the leading U.S. robber barons—the Morgan, Dupont, Rockefeller, Pew, and Mellon families—to establish a fascist dictatorship in the United States.[88] This was proven by the McCormack-Dickstein committee, and it is therefore part of the public record, even though none of the conspirators were prosecuted for their actions. The General Motors (GM) streetcar conspiracy was proven to exist in a court case that took place

---

88. See Gabriel Rockhill, "Fascist Plots in the U.S.: Contemporary Lessons from the 1934 'Business Plot,'" *Liberation School*, June 6, 2021, https://www.liberationschool.org/fascist-plots-in-the-u-s-contemporary-lessons-from-the-1934-business-plot/.

in 1949. GM and related companies had monopolized the sale of buses and supplies to National City Lines and subsidiaries as part of a largely successful effort to destroy streetcar transit systems. Operation Gladio is a well-documented conspiracy of the most heinous sort in which the CIA collaborated with MI6 to commit brutal acts of terrorism against an innocent civilian population and blame those acts on communists in order throw them in prison and pressure the public into support-ing authoritarian anticommunist governments.[89] This was proven in Italian courts, and there was also a European Parliament resolution on Gladio.[90] Although too few people are aware of this fact, it was demon-strated in a court of law in 1999 that Martin Luther King Jr. was assas-sinated in a "conspiracy" involving "governmental agencies."[91] Similarly, in *Hunt vs. Liberty Lobby*, a U.S. court of law found that "President Kennedy had indeed been murdered by a conspiracy involving, in part, CIA operatives E. Howard Hunt and Frank Sturgis, and FBI informant Jack Ruby."[92] There are many other examples that could be pointed to, including conspiracies that are highly probable but not proven beyond a reasonable doubt or as part of the public record. The most important point, though, is that it is possible for the capitalist ruling class and its state managers to conspire in their own interest, and they have done this so regularly that it makes perfect sense to keep capitalist conspiracies within the realm of scientific investigation instead of banishing them as beyond the pale of reason.

Moreover, a scientific analysis of conspiracy theories allows us to

---

89. See Daniele Ganser, *NATO's Secret Armies: Operation Gladio and Terrorism in Western Europe* (London: Frank Cass, 2005) and Allan Francovich, *Gladio*, 1992, film, https://www.youtube.com/watch?v=GGHXjO8wHsA.i

90. The European Parliament resolution on Gladio is available at https://eur-lex.europa.eu/legal-content/EN/TXT/?uri=CELEX%3A51990IP2021&qid=1723588321217 and https://en.wikisource.org/wiki/European_Parliament_resolution_on_Gladio.

91. "Complete Transcript of the Martin Luther King, Jr. Assassination Conspiracy Trial," available on the King Center's website: https://thekingcenter.org/wp-content/uploads/2019/05/King_Family_Trial_Transcript.pdf. Also see William F. Pepper Esq, *The Plot to Kill King: The Truth Behind the Assassination of Martin Luther King Jr.* (New York: Skyhorse, 2018).

92. Parenti, *Dirty Truths*, 184. Also see Mark Lane, *Plausible Denial: Was the CIA Involved in the Assassination of JFK?* (New York: Thunder's Mouth Press, 1991) and H. P. Albarelli Jr, with Leslie Sharp and Alan Kent, *Coup in Dallas: The Decisive Investigation into Who Killed JFK* (New York: Skyhorse Publishing, 2021). For the first-person testimony of another CIA participant, see Robert Morrow, *First Hand Knowledge: How I Participated in the CIA-Mafia Murder of President Kennedy* (New York: S.P.I. Books, 1992).

better understand the inner workings of the bourgeois state. This is particularly important when examining the dark underside of the state apparatus. After all, as Michael Parenti pointed out, "In most of its operations, the CIA is by definition a conspiracy, using covert actions and secret plans."[93] According to former CIA officer John Stockwell, between 1947 and 1987 the Agency launched some 3,000 major operations and 10,000 minor operations.[94] These cannot, therefore, be interpreted as mere exceptions, but they are rather fundamental aspects of how the bourgeois state functions. Parenti drew the pertinent conclusion: "National security state conspiracies are components of our political structure, not deviations from it."[95]

Dual governance is one of the best descriptions of how the bourgeois state actually operates. In bourgeois democracies, there is, on the one hand, the public face of the visible government and, on the other, the invisible government of agencies that work in the shadows to guarantee the rule of capital. They function in tandem with one another to maintain the extant system and advance the interests of the capitalist class. There was a brief moment in the 1954 CIA-orchestrated coup d'état in Guatemala that perfectly illustrates this. After Jacobo Árbenz was deposed, Colonel Díaz took power and publicly vowed to continue the struggle against imperialism. It only took a few hours before he received a visit from John Doherty and Enno Hobbing, the two principal CIA operatives overseeing the operation. The latter explained to Díaz that he was "not convenient for the requirements of American foreign policy."[96] When Díaz protested and demanded to see the U.S. ambassador, Hobbing laid out the essence of dual governance in very simple terms to his ill-fated interlocutor: "Well, Colonel, there is diplomacy and then there is reality. Our ambassador represents diplomacy. I represent reality. And the reality is we don't want you."[97] Within a few days, reality prevailed, Díaz was removed from power, and Castillo Armas became president, unleashing a brutal reign of terror.

In order to discourage reductivist and simplistic readings of this book

---

93. Parenti, *Dirty Truths*, 185–86.

94. John Stockwell mentions these numbers in the lecture excerpted under the title "CIA's War on Humans," https://www.youtube.com/watch?v=m3ioJGMCr-Y.

95. Parenti, *Dirty Truths*, 188.

96. Stephen Kinzer, *Overthrow: America's Century of Regime Change from Hawaii to Iraq* (New York: Times Books, 2006), 146

97. Ibid.

and its companion tomes, let me be crystal clear: there is not some mysterious cabal of capitalists and state agents who control absolutely everything from behind the scenes, including the entire intellectual world. Scholars are not just puppets on strings, with master spies playing the role of puppeteers. Moreover, agencies like the CIA are not omnipotent, and they do not manipulate and regulate the entirety of social life from the shadows. They have regularly failed in their missions, and they continue to do so. To cite one telling example, the Cuban writer and university professor, Raúl Antonio Capote, revealed in his 2015 book *Enemigo* that he had worked for the CIA for years on its destabilization campaigns targeting intellectuals, writers, artists, and students in Cuba.[98] Although the cocksure master spies considered him one of their agents engaged in their sordid bag of dirty tricks to continue their non-stop imperialist war on the small island country, Capote was actually pulling one over on his supercilious handlers: he was working undercover for Cuban intelligence the entire time. This is a clear sign that the imperialist intelligence agencies, in spite of some partial victories on the battlefield, are ultimately fighting a war that has proven itself to be extremely difficult to win: they are desperately attempting to impose a global order that is detrimental to the overwhelming majority of the world's population.

Cuba's Directorio General de Inteligencia (DGI) has been so successful in routing U.S. intelligence that it was revealed, in 1987, that every agent the CIA had recruited in Cuba since 1961 was a DGI double agent. The United States only learned this, however, when Cuban intelligence officer Florentino Aspillaga Lombard defected there.[99] Knowing that this had become common knowledge, the Cubans then released an eleven-part television series on their successful operations against the U.S. empire, showing footage from hidden cameras that captured the supposedly clandestine activities of the CIA aimed at turning Cuba back into a colony.[100] Between 1985 and 2001, Anna Belen Montes, a senior analyst with

---

98. See Raúl Antonio Capote, *Enemigo* (Madrid: Ediciones Akal, S.A., 2015).

99. James Olson, the head of CIA counterintelligence at the time, said "Aspillaga told me some very disturbing things. . . . He said that the Cuban DGI had successfully run 38 double agents against us. So every agent that we thought we'd recruited on the island was, in fact, being controlled by the DGI." Cited in Will Grant, "The Cuban Spying Case That Has Shocked the US Government," *BBC*, January 8, 2024, https://www.bbc.com/news/world-latin-america-67913465.

100. Former CIA officer Philip Agee discusses this series in his lecture "The CIA in the Post Cold War World," California State University Fullerton, C-SPAN, November 7, 1995, https://www.youtube.com/watch?v=197Op8BMAwE.

the Defense Intelligence Agency (a key producer of intelligence for the Pentagon), "spied for the Cubans from inside the U.S. intelligence community itself."[101] In 2023, Manuel Rocha, who served as U.S. ambassador to Bolivia and had access to "a wealth of classified and sensitive intelligence information," was arrested and admitted to working as a Cuban agent for 40 years.[102] According to U.S. Attorney General Merrick Garland, Rocha's alleged crimes constituted "one of the highest-reaching and longest-lasting infiltrations of the U.S. government by a foreign agent."[103] These are but some of the examples that led James Olson, who headed counterintelligence at the CIA when Aspillaga Lombard defected, to admit in 2024: "They [the Cubans] owned us. They beat us. . . . They have been so successful in operating against us."[104] When Gerardo Hernández Nordelo—one of the five Cuban agents who infiltrated terrorist groups in Miami that organize attacks against Cuba—was asked to comment on Rocha's case, he said that "ideological spies" like him "are harder to detect and more skilled at their trade than those who are in it for the money": "Someone that does something not out of money or profit but for his ideals is always a better professional in this area."[105]

The Dialectics of Agency

Far from being a reductivist account, the analysis that follows is a meticulous study of a complex material system of knowledge production, circulation, and consumption in which special attention is paid to all of the different types of agency at work, including their various levels of determinacy, their particular ranges of efficacy, their specific sites of operation, and their struggles in relationship to a larger force field of agencies. The methodology deployed is thus explicitly multi-agential, which is an important aspect of dialectics, and it openly rejects reductive determinism. Bourgeois ideology postulates a reified opposition between objective determinants and the subjective freedom of the individual, assuming *either* that there is an external force controlling

---

101. See the FBI's online record of "Famous Cases and Criminals," titled "Ana Montes: Cuban Spy," https://www.fbi.gov/history/famous-cases/ana-montes-cuba-spy.
102. Grant, "The Cuban Spying Case That Has Shocked the US Government."
103. Cited in ibid.
104. Cited in ibid.
105. Cited in ibid. Regarding Hernández Nordelo, see his profile on *EcuRed*: https://www.ecured.cu/Gerardo_Hern%C3%A1ndez_Nordelo#La_misi.C3.B3n.

the subject *or* that there is an individual acting freely. Neither is the case, and this opposition is the consequence of pre-dialectical thought. The dialectical approach advocated here examines the intricacies of a complex force field of agencies, while also clearly identifying the hierarchical relationship between them and bringing to the fore the deepest, driving forces.

In the case of the CIA, it needs to be understood first and foremost as one among many other agents of ruling-class power. When addressing the liberal outrage over CIA funding of university activities, the French journalist Claude Julien appropriately raised the following rhetorical question:

> Is there such a difference between Michigan State University accepting money from the CIA to train police forces in Vietnam, and the University of California receiving $363 million in 1965 from the Pentagon with $246,470,000 going into atomic research for military purposes? ... 53 per cent of the budget of the University of California in 1965 came from the government of the empire.[106]

The CIA is part of a much broader institutional network of agencies within the bourgeois state that work with the representatives of the bourgeoisie to advance a common agenda (part of which includes presenting bourgeois society as free, open, and devoid of any ruling-class program). The detailed lists of governmental agencies involved in psychological warfare are incredibly long, as attested to by internal documents that are over seventy pages in length.[107] These agencies have many different strategies for advancing their work.

If we were forced to use the metaphor of puppets since it is so often invoked when discussing the CIA, it would be more appropriate to say that state agencies like this generally prefer to build and manage marionette theaters, allowing the puppets to come of their own accord. This has the distinct advantage of eliminating the strings and maximizing the impact of their agenda, while allowing the marionettes to exercise their

---

106. Claude Julien, *America's Empire*, trans. Renaud Bruce (New York: Pantheon Books, 1971), 317, translation slightly modified.

107. There are many documents that could be cited, but this one provides an interesting overview: "Inventory of Cold War Weapons," October 17, 1951, the CIA FOIA Electronic Reading Room, https://www.cia.gov/readingroom/document/cia-rdp80r 01731r0035 00170002-8.

own agency. Jason Epstein, the co-founder of the *New York Review of Books*, grasped this point well in an article written in the wake of the 1966 revelations concerning CIA interventions in the cultural field: "It was not a matter of buying off and subverting individual writers and scholars, but of setting up an arbitrary and factitious system of values by which academic personnel were advanced, magazine editors appointed, and scholars subsidized and published, not necessarily on their merits, though these were sometimes considerable, but because of their allegiances."[108] In the case of the Congress for Cultural Freedom (CCF) and the CIA's many other front organizations, Pierre Grémion described the standard operating procedure in the following terms: "Money is channeled through foundations to organizations, and the agency limits itself to controlling their administrative secretariats."[109]

It is important to note, finally, that the dominant system of knowledge production in the capitalist world nonetheless allows for—to some degree—vital space within which critical scholarship can operate. This is the result of class struggle and valiant efforts to keep the university open to forms of critique that overstep the boundaries of the dominant ideology. It is also due, in part, to the fundamental contradiction highlighted earlier: the academic system needs to appear to be democratic and meritocratic, while actually being tightly controlled by those who own the means of intellectual production. Critical scholarship can therefore be tolerated to some degree because it can be used as supposed proof of the system's openness, thereby contributing to the myth that it is not primarily a system of power. There is, in any case, a margin of maneuver for research that contests this system from within. The imperial academy is far from being omnipotent, and it is incapable of controlling all of those who operate within it.

It is imperative to take full advantage of this vital space and attempt to expand it. As Lenin argued, intellectuals play an essential role in the revolutionary transformation of society because they have the skills and training necessary to serve as the cartographers of class struggle, mapping the extant play of forces and providing a systemic apprehension of the social totality. However, they cannot perform this duty properly if they are deprived of the material conditions necessary to do so. The

---

108. Jason Epstein, "The CIA and the Intellectuals," *New York Review of Books*, April 20, 1967.
109. Grémion, *Intelligence de l'anticommunisme*, 448.

intellectual class traitor is thus a crucial figure in the history of Marxism. and there are many such renegades at work around the world, including within the imperial core.

CHAPTER 2

Imperial Intellectual Apparatus

Imperial Ideological Warfare

We should use ideas as weapons.
—JOHN FOSTER DULLES, U.S. SECRETARY OF STATE (AND
BROTHER OF CIA DIRECTOR ALLEN DULLES)[1]

When the United States emerged in the mid-twentieth century as the world's leading imperialist power, it had to contend with wide public support for communism since the USSR had just played the leading role in defeating fascism. Waging an open war on the anti-fascists in the name of expanding empire was a hard sell. Therefore, the mind managers had their work cut out for them because they needed to quickly change the narrative, depicting the United States as the greatest purveyor of democracy in the world, which had just defeated fascism, while smearing the Soviet Union as an evil empire intent on global domination, very much like the fascists. The full force of its powerful industries of indoctrination had to be unleashed in this process in order to present empire building as democracy promotion and counter-revolution as the fight for freedom. For such a colossal feat, the United States had to become the global information superpower that it is.

This war for hearts and minds took on a specific form in the imperial core as the United States sought to integrate the former imperialist powers of Western Europe, which had been ravaged by the war, as junior partners in an international war on communism. That way, the imperial looting of the Third World could continue unabated, with the United States taking

---

1. Cited in David Talbot, *The Devil's Chessboard: Allen Dulles, the CIA, and the Rise of America's Secret Government* (New York: Harper Perennial, 2016), 201.

the leading role. Since the communists were the principal anti-fascist force in Europe, there was a serious risk that they would become the leaders of Western European countries. Prohibiting this was of the utmost importance, and the United States thereby undertook to lead an overt and covert war on communism in every possible sector, including economics (the Marshall Plan), the military (NATO, fascist stay-behind armies as part of Operation Gladio, military interventions to prop up anticommunist forces in Greece, etc.), politics (support for anticommunist governments, including fascist ones, and clandestine control of parties and unions), society (extensive propaganda and control of organizations of civil society), culture (cultural imperialism and the spread of anticommunist culture), and academia (support for anticommunist institutions, organizations, and intellectuals). The broad aims of this expansive psychological warfare campaign were spelled out in a 1952 CIA paper:

1 Eliminate Communist influence.
2 Reduce neutralist sentiments.
3 Transmute nationalism from a single country basis to identification with membership of the large European community.
4 Unite WE [Western Europe] with Atlantic world.
5 Demonstrate to non-Europeans that Atlantic Community is not a white man's club but rather the democratic bastion of the free world.[2]

In what follows, we will focus on the cultural and intellectual aspects of the war on communism, with a particular concentration on the North-Atlantic relationship between the United States and Western Europe. This is where the imperial superstructures of the contemporary world were forged, notably by the gradual development of a dominant system of ideological production, distribution, and consumption, which arose out of the imperial economic base. While each society has its own specific superstructure, the United States, as the foremost imperialist state, has developed the most powerful superstructure, and it has engaged in cultural imperialism to extend its influence as much as possible around the world.

Given that this book, like the rest of the trilogy, focuses on the intellectual apparatus, meaning the sector of the superstructure that regulates the production and dissemination of knowledge, it is essential to understand

---

2. "The Problem," November 4, 1952, the CIA FOIA Electronic Reading Room, https://www.cia.gov/readingroom/document/cia-rdp80-01065a000200080038-7.

this apparatus as a systemic, objective totality in order to be able to situate subjects within it. This is not to deny that the subjects of knowledge production and consumption have agency. However, subjects and their agency do not exist in the abstract, or in some pristine ethereal domain. They only exist as concrete subjects acting within specific material realities. As we will see, the imperial intellectual apparatus systematically fosters particular types of subjects, while defining, in general terms and under normal conditions, the range and conditions of their agency.

One of the fundamental patterns that will emerge is the use of professional academics, writers, journalists, and other cultural producers to launder state propaganda and present it to the public as the autonomous result of free intellectual inquiry. Disinformation is thereby given academic, journalistic, or artistic credentials, and many others in the same networks often end up circulating it as authentic or corroborating its claims in their own work. Propaganda spreads in this way through multiple forms and is broadcast by various sources, creating the illusion of a reasoned consensus on the part of the broader intelligentsia. Those involved certainly exercise their agency, either by being directly implicated or by recirculating and promoting—perhaps unwittingly—the work of the propagandists. Their actions, however, are conditioned by the material system in which they operate. If they do not feel the constraints, and therefore have the impression that they are free, it is simply because they are not pushing up against them. You only feel a leash if you run far enough from your owner.

This system for the production, distribution, and consumption of ideas is artificially constructed and managed, from behind the scenes, but in such a way that it appears to be a natural development animated by free cultural producers and consumers. Given the ideological consensus required for participating in this system, it fosters the illusion that anticommunism—instead of being an ideology promoted by imperialist powers and their minions—is an organic occurrence and the inevitable result of open-minded inquiry. Moreover, due to the number of institutions, organizations, networks, and individuals participating in this system, the dominant ideology is regularly corroborated by numerous sources, and it thereby maintains a remarkable consistency and ubiquity. Calling it into question comes to look, from within the system, like a complete aberration, as if someone were simply unhinged or irrational, and it is also an affront to the democratic consensus of the established community of the broader intelligentsia. It therefore appears as if it must obviously be driven by ideology. In fine, the dominant ideology becomes reason itself, and actual reason is dismissed as ideology. The material system of ideo-logical production thereby succeeds in turning the world upside-down.

A Model of Imperial Disinformation

The Information Research Department (IRD) in the British Foreign Office was a powerful propaganda agency that served as one of the models for the U.S.-led empire of ideas. The IRD was established by the Labour government in 1948; it grew out of the disinformation agencies founded during the Second World War. SO1, the propaganda arm of the Special Operations Executive (SOE) that had been set up in 1940, became a sepa-rate entity known as the Political Warfare Executive (PWE). "By 1941," according to Paul Lashmar and James Oliver, the PWE "was housing some 458 propagandists," mainly from universities and the press corps.[3] It exercised "full political control" over the BBC's foreign broadcasts and, during the war, this nominally independent news agency "became an instrument of state information policy, 'guided' by the MOI [Ministry of Information] and the PWE in all of its activities."[4] The MOI and the PWE, which also worked extensively with other media outlets, were closed down after the war. The rebirth of the latter, which was focused on covert rather than overt propaganda like the MOI, emerged out of Christopher Mayhew's proposal to develop an anticommunist propaganda agency in the Foreign Office, that would target the general public but also distrib-ute its materials to ministers, Labour Party officials, union delegates, and other community leaders. Mindful of the risks of straightforward anti-communism in a context of strong pro-socialist sentiments due to the Soviet defeat of Nazism and the electoral success of the Labour Party, Mayhew cleverly proposed a "Third Force" propaganda campaign that "would attack capitalism as well as Communism and promote the Social Democratic values associated with the Labour government."[5] This sup-port for the compatible left and its social-democratic agenda were, for Mayhew, "purely tactical—a cover designed to undermine any left-wing opposition."[6]

The Information Research Department (IRD) emerged out of Mayhew's

---

3. Paul Lashmar and James Oliver, *Britain's Secret Propaganda War* (Phoenix Mill, UK: Sutton Publishing, 1998), 14.
4. Ibid., 17, 18.
5. Ibid., 27.
6. Ibid..

proposal, and it was financed through the budget of the Secret Intelligence Service (SIS, also known as MI6). The IRD "made use of the intelligence coming into MI6," "worked closely with the anti-Soviet Section IX of the Secret Service," and later collaborated with the CIA.[7] The role of this governmental organization was to run an international anticommunist propaganda campaign, which was as clandestine as it was far-reaching. Its sprawling networks engulfed newspapers, magazines, news agencies, radio stations, publishing houses, academic institutions, and more. It was in constant contact with the BBC and worked directly with such significant bourgeois outlets as London Press Service and Reuters. The IRD also placed its people in the media and the academic world, who would publish IRD content under their own name, dissimulating its true origin. It established working relationships with several British publishers and even set up its own publishing house (Ampersand Limited).

The IRD was one of the largest and best-funded departments in the Foreign Office, and its staff grew to an estimated 400 to 600 professional anticommunist propagandists. "By 1950," Hugh Wilford writes, "the IRD had succeeded in establishing permanent channels for the routine transmission of its by now considerable output of anti-Communist propaganda all over the world."[8] As Lashmar and Oliver explain: "While to the man in the street, it appeared that a diverse range of media were separately coming to similar conclusions about Communism and the nature of the Cold War, in fact much of the media was singing from a hymn sheet which was provided by IRD."[9] This is a particularly potent psychological warfare strategy because if sources from different perspectives, which might have significant disagreements, all concur on certain fundamentals, it sends the message that these agreements are based on fact, not ideological persuasion when, in reality, the exact opposite is the case.

---

7. Ibid., 28, also see 67. It is equally worth consulting Jonathan Bloch and Patrick Fitzgerald, *British Intelligence and Covert Action: Africa, Middle East and Europe since 1945* (Dingle, Ireland: Brandon Book Publishers, 1983). The director of the IRD from 1953 to 1958 was John Rennie, who would later head MI6. Bloch and Fitzgerald, *British Intelligence and Covert Action*, 91. From 1966 to 1969 the IRD was directed by MI6 agent Nigel Clive. Lashmar and Oliver, *Britain's Secret Propaganda War*, 141.

8. Hugh Wilford, "The Information Research Department: Britain's Secret Cold War Weapon Revealed," *Review of International Studies*, Vol. 24, No. 3 (July 1998): 353–69. Also see Hugh Wilford, *The CIA, the British Left and the Cold War: Calling the Tune?* (New York: Routledge, 2013).

9. Lashmar and Oliver, *Britain's Secret Propaganda War*, 175.

MI6 and the CIA both use journalism as a form of deep cover for their officers, and they also hire journalists as agents.[10] In the case of the IRD, from the mid-1950s it "developed a hard core of trusted and like-minded journalists and academics who were to remain remarkably consistent throughout its existence."[11] "A circulation list for 1976," report Lashmar and Oliver in their analysis of IRD networks, "lists ninety-two British journalists working for publications including the *Observer*, the *Guardian*, the *Financial Times*, *The Times*, the *Daily Mirror*, the *Daily Mail*, the *Telegraph*, and the *Sunday Express*, as well as freelance journalists and journalists working for ITN and Reuters."[12] Many of these reporters passed off Foreign Office research as if it was their own, thereby laundering state propaganda as independent journalism.[13] MI6 had penetrated the "English mass media on a wide scale," according to double agent Kim Philby, with scores of paid agents.[14] The BBC was completely controlled at multiple levels, and MI5—the UK's domestic Security Service—vetted "its staff for 'subversives' from the 1930s until the practice was revealed in 1985."[15]

The IRD also established, penetrated, subsidized, collaborated with, or took control of numerous news agencies in order to disseminate its propaganda around the world, including Reuters, Foreign News Service, Britanova, Arab News Agency, Near and Far East News, International News Rights and Royalties, and World Feature Services Ltd.[16] In the early 1960s, the IRD "became involved in supporting wider media projects in the 'private' sector, including TV programs," and it provided disguised support for non-governmental organizations (NGOs).[17] In 1970, the IRD's Brian Crozier founded the Institute for the Study of Conflict (ISC), which joined a team of private anti-left organizations producing anticommunist propaganda, like the Economic League and Aims in Industry.[18] The reactionary oligarch Richard Mellon Scaife funded the ISC, and Crozier also

---

10. See, for instance, Bloch and Fitzgerald, *British Intelligence and Covert Action*, 35.
11. Lashmar and Oliver, *Britain's Secret Propaganda War*, 118.
12. Ibid., 119.
13. See ibid., 120.
14. Cited in ibid., 75.
15. Ibid., 59.
16. See Bloch and Fitzgerald, *British Intelligence and Covert Action*, 94–96 and Lashmar and Oliver, *Britain's Secret Propaganda War*, 73, 77–82.
17. Lashmar and Oliver, *Britain's Secret Propaganda War*, 138–39.
18. See ibid., 163.

secured money from Shell and British Petroleum.[19] The IRD became both a customer and a source of information for the ISC, which increasingly came to fill the role that the IRD was playing.[20]

The IRD also collaborated with the U.S. State Department and the CIA, and it was part of a broad international anticommunist network. The Agency took a leading role in the cultural war against communism beginning around the early 1950s, and its Congress for Cultural Freedom (CCF), discussed below, borrowed much of its structure and *modus operandi* from the IRD. The UK chapter of the CCF, the British Society for Cultural Freedom, founded in 1951, had ample connections to the IRD.[21] The overlapping international networks fed off and supported one another in numerous ways, and they all contributed to the common objective of an intellectual world war on communism.

It was to the IRD that George Orwell submitted his infamous list of suspected communists in 1949.[22] The author of *1984* and *Animal Farm*, widely celebrated as a left critic of state power and propaganda, was up to his eyeballs in them himself. While writing books that purportedly denounced them, or rather, decried their supposed totalitarian perversions in the East, he was cozying up, quite literally, to Western state power and propaganda. He pursued an IRD officer, Celia Kirwan, courting her and then even asking for her hand in marriage.[23] It was to her and her fellow Thought Police that he denounced those whom he suspected of communism. He also, according to internal documents, "expressed his wholehearted and enthusiastic approval of the department's [the IRD's] aims."[24] He was repaid in full for his dutiful service as an anticommunist snitch. The Ministry of Truth, known in the real world as the IRD, gained the foreign rights to a significant portion of Orwell's literary output, and it spent years distributing his anticommunist literature all over the world, translating it into at least twenty languages, creating an animated film version of *Animal Farm*, and collaborating with the CIA on a feature-length

19. Scaife, it is worth noting, "was listed as the owner of record of Forum World Features, a news service, which a 1975 article in the *Washington Post* identified as being C.I.A.-funded." John S. Friedman, "Public TV's CIA Show," *The Nation*, July 19–26, 1980, 76. Also see Bernard D. Nossiter, "CIA News Service Reported," *Washington Post*, July 3, 1975, A26.

20. See Lashmar and Oliver, *Britain's Secret Propaganda War*, 164–65.

21. See Wilford, *The CIA, the British Left and the Cold War*, 196–98.

22. See Lashmar and Oliver, *Britain's Secret Propaganda War*, 95–98.

23. See ibid., 95.

24. Ibid., 97.

film based on the same book.[25] Big Brother had Orwell's back and was one of the principal forces that made him into a literary superstar whose books are still obligatory reading in many schools. Orwell was, however, by no means the only one. The Thought Police at the IRD also enrolled many other writers and academics to publish anticommunist propaganda under their own name. It also bought, translated, and distributed their work around the world in order to guarantee their fame. In addition to Orwell, these authors included figures like Bertrand Russell, Arthur Koestler, Czesław Miłosz, Victor Kravchenko, and hundreds of others.

Many of the leading bourgeois historians of communism were products of the IRD. Robert Conquest, an acclaimed scholar and longtime research fellow at Stanford University's Hoover Institution, served in the IRD and drew extensively on its files for his famous work *The Great Terror: Stalin's Purge of the Thirties* (1968). He also "edited seven volumes of material from IRD on Soviet politics, without acknowledgment that the books' source was a secret government agency or that the publisher, Frederick A. Praeger, was subsidized by the CIA."[26] Journalist David Barzilay similarly presented the IRD's propaganda material in his writings as if it were his own.[27] Oxford historian A. J. P. Taylor and Leanard Schapiro, a professor at the London School of Economics (LSE), both had strong IRD ties, and the latter was a member of its inner circle.[28] Brian Crozier, a well-known bourgeois historian of communism, was actually one of the central staff members of the IRD. In his autobiography, *Free Agent*, he admitted to working with MI6 and the CIA on numerous projects, as well as to using IRD files as the basis for some of his books.[29] MI6 officer Robert Carew Hunt was also in on the state-backed anticommunist propaganda war, and he penned a widely circulated IRD book titled *The Theory and Practice of Communism* (1950).[30] Maurice Cranston, a professor at the LSE, contributed books to the IRD's Background Books

25. In addition to Lashmar and Oliver's *Britain's Secret Propaganda War*, see Hugh Wilford, *The Mighty Wurlitzer: How the CIA Played America* (Cambridge, MA: Harvard University Press, 2008), 118–20.

26. Ronald Grigor Suny, *Red Flag Unfurled: History, Historians, and the Russian Revolution* (London: Verso, 2017), 94.

27. See Lashmar and Oliver, *Britain's Secret Propaganda War*, 161.

28. See ibid., 122–23.

29. See Brian Crozier, *Free Agent: The Unseen War 1941–1991* (London: HarperCollins, 1993) and Lashmar and Oliver, *Britain's Secret Propaganda War*, 101.

30. See Lashmar and Oliver, *Britain's Secret Propaganda War*, 98.

series.[31] In fact, the LSE "formed a center for anti-communist academics" (Conquest had a research fellowship there in the 1950s).[32] St. Antony's College, Oxford, was another anticommunist outpost with many connections to the intelligence community. Sir William Deakin, the Warden of St. Antony's College, was involved in IRD projects, and former SOE man David Footman headed the Soviet Studies Department.[33]

The British agency not only selected authors and often provided them with propaganda material to sanitize, but it "also subsidized production through bulk orders amounting to tens of thousands of pounds."[34] This guaranteed massive distribution and high visibility for an impressive number of scholarly books, which were actually little more than undercover Foreign Office propaganda (the IRD's Background Book series, for instance, published "nearly 100 titles … over two decades").[35] "By promoting and supporting specific intellectuals, politicians and trade unionists it [IRD] helped shape and define the political consensus of a generation."[36]

It is important to apprehend this overall system of knowledge production, circulation, and consumption, as well as its specific *modus operandi*, because it was widely used by the CIA and other disinformation agencies. One of its key features was the academic or cultural laundering of state propaganda. The IRD fabricated anticommunist misinformation, which it would whitewash through the academy or the broader cultural world by finding a professor or writer who would put their name on it, removing all references to its original source. Academic or journalistic imprimatur was thereby accorded to imperial lies, which would be consumed by readers as if they were the autonomous and informed opinion of an independent researcher. To ensure that its laundering would have maximum impact, the IRD, sometimes along with other agencies, would buy and distribute tons of copies of the publications, often making the author famous in the process. This stratagem, which was widely employed by other capitalist propaganda agencies, was remarkably simple and effective. All that it required was sufficient lucre and authors interested in fame and glory.

---

31. See ibid., 123.
32. Ibid.
33. See ibid., 102 and 123.
34. Ibid., 101.
35. Ibid.
36. Ibid., 175.

Marshall Plan for the Mind

The cold war was and is a war, fought with ideas instead of bombs.
—CIA OFFICER TOM BRADEN[37]

"No one before [the Congress for Cultural Freedom (CCF)] had tried to mobilize intellectuals and artists on a worldwide scale in order to fight an ideological war against oppressors of the mind."[38] This was Nicholas Nabokov's opinion on the expansive operation in which he played a central role. Born to landed Russian gentry who had fled the Bolshevik Revolution, he was the cousin of the writer Vladimir Nabokov. In 1951, he became the General Secretary of the CCF, which was at the center of the international ideological war on communism, as we shall see. However, it is important to note at the outset that the CCF was only one part of a larger operation.

For instance, the Psychological Strategy Board (PSB), formed in 1951 to "provide for the more effective planning, coordination and conduct ... of psychological operations," ran an anticommunist "Doctrinal Program" that aimed to develop "a more extensive and intensive use of serious books and of highly intellectual periodical materials, as well as the fostering of associations and meetings among intellectuals."[39] Wary that "any intellectual effort which might be identified as 'selling the U.S.' or as a strictly American propaganda effort would be doomed to stagnation and defeat," the program sought to manipulate nationalist feelings "to the advantage of American objectives and the weakening of Communist influences," which included unofficial assistance to "indigenous authors and publishers to produce and circulate critical analyses of Communist doctrine and the viewpoints of the West."[40]

---

37. Thomas W. Braden, "I'm Glad the CIA Is 'Immoral,'" *Saturday Evening Post*, May 20, 1967.
38. Saunders, *The Cultural Cold War*, 100. Nabokov added: "This kind of ideological war had so far been the appanage of Stalinists and Nazis."
39. Cited in Psychological Strategy Board, "The Psychological Program," White House Office, Office of the Special Assistant for National Security Affairs: Records, 1952–1961, NSC Series, Status of Projects Subseries, Box 3, Folder NSC 142 (5), Dwight D. Eisenhower Library; "Communist Influence Among Students and Intellectuals," June 26, 1953, White House Office, National Security Council Staff: Papers, 1948–61, NSC Registry Series, 1947–62, Box 16, Folder PSB Documents, Master Book of—Vol. IV (10), Dwight D. Eisenhower Library, 4. Also see Dwight D. Eisenhower: Records as President, White House Central Files (Confidential File), 1953–1961, Subject Series, Box 61, Folder Psychological Strategy Board, Dwight D. Eisenhower Library.
40. Ibid., 3–4.

The Marshall Plan played a particularly important role in integrating Western Europe into the U.S. zone of influence and control, including ideologically. The $13.3 billion in economic recovery (the equivalent of $173.7 billion in 2024), far from being a benevolent expenditure, sought to develop capitalism in Western Europe as a bulwark against communism. It also had the benefit of producing extensive markets for U.S. goods in order to alleviate crises of overproduction. Powerful figures in the U.S. administration, including General George C. Marshall himself (Secretary of State at the time) and Secretary of Defense James Forrestal, argued that there was a need for covert actions that could complement the imperial endeavors of the Marshall Plan.

On June 18, 1948, the National Security Council (NSC) approved NSC 10/2 and established the Office of Policy Coordination (OPC), which would be used to clandestinely funnel Marshall Plan funds into sub-rosa political activities in Europe, including psychological and political warfare operations. "From its creation in 1948 until 1952 when the Marshall Plan was terminated," explains Sallie Pisani, "the OPC operated as the plan's complement. Its actions were meant to be and remain covert so that they could be plausibly denied by the government."[41] Richard Bissell was the deputy administrator of the Economic Cooperation Administration (ECA) at the time, which oversaw the management of the Marshall Plan, and he later became, following a stint at the Ford Foundation, the CIA's Deputy Director for Plans, who is responsible for clandestine activities. Interviewed by Pisani in 1983, he explained how the OPC siphoned funds from the Marshall Plan for covert actions:

> OPC was formed right after the Marshall Plan. . . . It was a complementary operation to secure Western Europe. . . . [Frank] Wisner [the OPC's Director] got counterpart funds for the OPC from the Marshall Plan. Recipient governments had to deposit 100 percent of the value of their received aid in their own banks. . . . Five percent in each country was tapped privately. . . . When I was deputy administrator of the Marshall Plan, counterpart funds were funneled to the OPC. Wisner came for the funds but said I didn't have to know what for. My feeling was that we needed this procedure because we needed a political action arm.[42]

---

41. Sallie Pisani, *The CIA and the Marshall Plan* (Lawrence: University Press of Kansas, 1991), 70–71.
42. Cited in ibid., 72–73.

The ECA thus collaborated with the OPC to secretly use Marshall Plan funds "to influence Europe without their actions being attributed to the United States."[43] There was a particular focus on political, economic, and psychological warfare. We know from the files of the Psychological Strategy Board that the ECA had 69 employees working in psychological warfare in the United States (the State Department had 2,724) and "there were 180 Americans working on propaganda in the Paris Office."[44]

The OPC, the ECA's close collaborator on this Marshall Plan for the mind, originally functioned semi-autonomously to maintain plausible deniability, though it was given quarters and rations by the CIA and received guidance from the Departments of State and Defense.[45] However, it was gradually integrated into the CIA beginning in 1950.[46] The International Organizations Division (IOD) was a department set up within the OPC to manage the CIA's relationships with unions, the media, student and professional associations, and other organizations. It was headed by Tom Braden, who had served in the OSS during the war, taught English at Dartmouth College, worked as Executive Secretary at the Museum of Modern Art, pursued his career in the CIA, and later worked as a journalist. Braden was what some scholars call a professional psy-warrior, meaning an official dedicated to the psychological war for hearts and minds, which was generally judged to be more important than military warfare.[47] In his covert operations, he strived to bring together intellectuals, writers, artists, and other cultural producers in a common front against communism:

> We wanted to unite all the people who were artists, who were writers, who were musicians, and all the people who follow those people, to demonstrate that the West and the United States was devoted to freedom of expression and to intellectual achievement, without any rigid barriers as to *what you must write* and *what you must say* and *what you must do* and *what you must paint*, which was what was going on in the Soviet Union.[48]

---

43. Ibid., 92.
44. Ibid., 129.
45. See ibid., 72.
46. See ibid., 78.
47. On the deep connections between MoMA and, more generally, the New York art world, on the one hand, and the CIA, on the other, see Gabriel Rockhill, *Radical History & the Politics of Art* (New York: Columbia University Press, 2014), 191–217.
48. Quoted in Saunders, *The Cultural Cold War*, 98.

In a classic case of projection, the CIA man was apparently convinced that the direct control that he exercised, with his organization, over cultural production was preserving freedom (even though communist culture was banned and excluded), whereas the cultural system that operated outside of the Agency's control was fundamentally lacking in liberty. This is not to suggest that there were not cultural barriers erected in the Soviet Union; it is only to point out the hypocrisy of defining *control* as *freedom* in the U.S. case, while claiming that *control* was *unfreedom* in the USSR.

THE CENTERPIECE FOR THE IOD's and CIA's cultural cold war was the Congress for Cultural Freedom (CCF). Run by undercover CIA operative Michael Josselson from its Paris headquarters, the CCF "evolved into one of the most important artistic patrons in world history, sponsoring an unprecedented range of cultural activities."[49] According to CCF documentation, the organization's budget rose from $860,619 in 1955 to over $2 million in 1966 (which is about $19 million in 2024).[50] Frances Stonor Saunders estimated the CIA's investment in the CCF at tens of millions of dollars. Braden claimed that there were never any budgetary limits for this or other projects, a point corroborated by CIA officer Gilbert Greenway, who also noted that they were not required to obtain authorization from the U.S. Congress or account for their spending.[51] There was so much pelf floating around for psychological warfare that Frank Wisner started calling it *candy*.[52] Braden did note that he was cautious to cover his tracks as much as possible, which appears to be the only limit he had on spending. One of his rules was: "Use legitimate existing organizations; disguise the extent of American interest; protect the integrity of the organization by not requiring it to support every aspect of official American policy."[53]

Support for left-wing forces that were non-communist was a key tactic, which is an important fact for understanding the intellectual world war. Given the strong leftist sentiments across Europe in the wake of the communist defeat of fascism, which had also discredited much of the liberal left for its role in aiding and abetting fascism, the cold warriors sought

49. Wilford, *The Mighty Wurlitzer*, 101–2.
50. See Peter Coleman, *The Liberal Conspiracy: The Congress for Cultural Freedom and the Struggle for the Mind of Postwar Europe* (New York: Free Press, 1989).
51. See Saunders, *The Cultural Cold War*, 105.
52. See ibid., 68, 106.
53. Braden, "I'm Glad the CIA Is 'Immoral,'" 13.

to create or enhance divisions in the left between the pro-Soviet and the anti-Soviet camps. The former, composed of Communist Party members and fellow travelers, were the true enemies. The latter, made up of socialists of various stripes who did not support actually existing socialism in the East, were considered to be part of the "compatible" or "respectable" left. This meant that their orientation was ultimately compatible with capitalism and the interests of U.S. imperialism. They were precisely the ones who could be relied upon, at least in many instances, to shield Europe from communism. According to Braden: "In much of Europe in the 1950s, socialists, people who called themselves 'left'—the very people whom many Americans thought no better than Communists—were the only people who gave a damn about fighting Communism."[54] This explains why covert cold warriors like Braden went behind the back of the U.S. Congress, which was too anticommunist to appreciate the nuances and difficulties of the ideological struggle in Europe, to fund, support, and promote the non-communist left. Braden used the unlimited funds at his disposal to clandestinely finance a vast array of activities, including political parties, unions, women's organizations, media outlets, cultural endeavors, intellectual work, and much more. The compatible left's hostility to actually existing socialism made it a natural ally of U.S. imperialism.

Braden's frank insider account, "I'm Glad the CIA Is 'Immoral'" (1967), is what is called in Company parlance a "limited hangout," which is a propaganda tactic that consists in providing restricted insider information to stem the tide of further investigations and take control of the narrative.[55]

---

54. Ibid., 10. Cord Meyer, the head of the CIA's IOD, explained things in the following terms: "Our help went mainly to the democratic parties of the left and of the center. The right wing and the conservative forces had their own financial resources: the real competition with the communists for votes and influence lay on the left of the political spectrum, where the allegiance of the working class and the intelligentsia was to be decided." Cited in Peter Finn and Petra Couvée, *The Zhivago Affair: The Kremlin, the CIA, and the Battle Over a Forbidden Book* (New York: Vintage, 2015), 118.

55. As former executive assistant to the Deputy Director of the CIA Victor Marchetti explained, a limited hangout is a public relations tactic used by clandestine professionals: "When their veil of secrecy is shredded and they can no longer rely on a phony cover story to misinform the public, they resort to admitting—sometimes even volunteering—some of the truth while still managing to withhold the key and damaging facts in the case. The public, however, is usually so intrigued by the new information that it never thinks to pursue the matter further." Marchetti, "CIA to Admit Hunt Involvement in Kennedy Slaying," *The Spotlight*, August 14, 1978, https://archive.org/details/marchetti-victor-cia-to-admit-hunt-involvement-in-

The story of CIA involvement in all of these activities had been broken by investigative journalists in the mid-1960s, and the Agency sought to nip them in the bud and run a faith-in-government campaign by confessing to some abuses. Braden's story, published in the Agency-connected *Saturday Evening Post*, was thus vetted by the CIA and even shared with the president prior to publication.[56] Although he had officially left the Company in 1954, it is likely that this was simply to go undercover as a journalist and, in any case, he continued to collaborate with the Agency.[57] His article should thus be understood for what it is: a series of limited admissions regarding activities whose depth and breadth likely surpassed what he claimed.

"Our Big Family"

The Cold War may well be termed a battle for the minds of men.

—CIA MEMORANDUM[58]

In the wake of the Second World War, France, like Italy, had one of the strongest Communist parties in Europe. If it had been integrated into the socialist camp, this would have been catastrophic for the imperialists. This helps explain why "it was no accident that the European headquarters for Marshall Plan activity was in Paris."[59] It is likely for the same reason that the CIA's CCF was headquartered there as well, not to mention the fact that Paris was considered by many to be the cultural capital of the world at the time, and thus an ideal imperial outpost.

---

kennedy-slaying-the-spotlight-aug.-14-1978/mode/2up.

56. On April 19, 1967, National Security Advisor W. W. Rostow sent a secret memo to the president informing him of "the forthcoming Braden Article" and sharing with him "the story from [CIA Director] Dick Helms."

57. In a 1973 memo, CIA man John M. Maury, serving as Legislative Counsel, recounted how he had a phone conversation with Braden, whom he described as a journalist and "one-time Agency staffer and personal friend." After saying that the CIA officially had "no comment" regarding a story concerning Howard Hunt, they had an off-the-record discussion in which they shared information about their common interests. See "Conversation with Tom Braden re Howard Hunt," December 20, 1973, the CIA FOIA Electronic Reading Room, https://www.cia.gov/readingroom/document/01482352.

58. "Inventory of Cold War Weapons," October 17, 1951, the CIA FOIA Electronic Reading Room, https://www.cia.gov/readingroom/document/cia-rdp80r01731r003 500170002-8.

59. Pisani, *The CIA and the Marshall Plan*, 82.

Established in 1950, the CCF promoted on the international scene the research of collaborationist academics such as Raymond Aron and Hannah Arendt, over and against their Marxian enemies like Jean-Paul Sartre and Simone de Beauvoir. The material support poured into the CCF far outstripped, and stood in stark contrast to, the meager resources available for cultural projects in war-torn Europe. As Frances Stonor Saunders explains:

> At its peak, the Congress for Cultural Freedom had offices in thirty-five countries, employed dozens of personnel, published over twenty prestige magazines, held art exhibitions, owned a news and features service, organized high-profile international conferences, and rewarded musicians and artists with prizes and public performances. Its mission was to nudge the intelligentsia of western Europe away from its lingering fascination with Marxism and Communism towards a view more accommodating of "the American way."[60]

The CCF's honorary presidents included renowned thinkers and politicians like Benedetto Croce, John Dewey, Theodor Heuss, Karl Jaspers, Jacques Maritain, Bertrand Russell, and Léopold Senghor. The reach of the organization was so broad that Saunders claims that, wittingly or not, almost every intellectual, writer, and cultural producer in postwar Western Europe was somehow caught up in its web.[61]

Some continue to debate how many people knew that the CCF was a CIA front organization, and at what time they realized it. Editor Jason Epstein asserted that by the middle of the 1960s everyone basically knew who was paying the bills. After all, it did not take a genius to figure out, in a war-ravaged and destitute Western Europe that had been overtly funded by the Marshall Plan, who had an interest in and was capable of lavishly funding non-communist international conferences and seminars, prestige magazines, scholarly journals, book publications, art exhibits and concerts, media campaigns, and much more. Those intellectuals who claimed that they were ignorant of what was going on, such as Aron and Arendt, were either being disingenuous—which seems highly probable—or

---

60. Saunders, *The Cultural Cold War*, 1. Also see Summary of Seventeen Years of the CCF, November 1967, International Association for Cultural Freedom Records, Box 659, Folder 33, IACF 1967–1968, Hanna Holborn Gray Special Collections Research Center at the University of Chicago.
61. See Saunders, *The Cultural Cold War*, 2.

simply admitting that their philosophic views were so out of touch with material reality that one should question the validity of their philosophies in general. Retired CIA official E. J. Applewhite understood their opportunist attitude in the following terms: "We knew they wanted to have it both ways: to be walking with the devil in the shadows secretly, and to be walking in the sun."[62] A "former official of a CIA conduit" apparently told Richard Elman: "They [the writers] knew where it [the money] was coming from, and in a general way what was happening all along. If anybody says they didn't they were just being naïve ... or false naïve [*sic*]."[63] When shown the 1967 public statement, signed by Arendt and sixteen others who claimed to openly oppose the CIA's subsidization of culture (in the wake of the revelations concerning the CCF), CIA officer Tom Braden "laughed out loud."[64] Looking at the list of signatories, the man who was one of the Agency's leading cultural warriors in Western Europe bluntly stated, "Of course they knew."[65]

They also knew, because it was publicly disclosed, that the CCF was being financed by the capitalist ruling class in the United States via its foundations. Internal documents reveal that CIA officer Michael Josselson even shared with Aron, who was his close friend and with whom he went on at least one family vacation, the budget allocated to the CCF by two of the biggest robber barons in U.S. history: Ford and Rockefeller (in 1957, the former provided $500,000 and the latter $40,000).[66] This funding, as everyone knew, was to promote non-communist scholarship in Western Europe that served the interests of its American benefactors. Although the CCF's connections to the CIA demonstrate that it was a psychological warfare operation overseen by the U.S. government, it is essential to recognize that, even if it had not received Agency sponsorship, the CCF was publicly recognizable as an anticommunist organization engaged in intellectual subcontracting for the capitalist class of the world's leading imperialist power. Moreover, it had open ties to the U.S. government and

62. Richard Elman, "The Aesthetics of the CIA," 1979, http://richardelman.org/cia, 2 (this unpublished article was written for a magazine that went under after it had commissioned the essay).

63. Ibid., 2.

64. Saunders, *The Cultural Cold War*, 410.

65. Quoted in ibid., 411.

66. See Michael Josselson, letter to Raymond Aron, October 23, 1957, International Association for Cultural Freedom Records, Box 80, Folder Raymond Aron 1955–1957, Hanna Holborn Gray Special Collections Research Center at the University of Chicago.

its political operators in Europe, including major figures like the State Department operative renowned for advocating a policy of containment of the USSR, George Kennan, who participated in its conferences and internal deliberations.[67]

The international conferences organized by the CCF were not humble affairs, as they drew on its seemingly unlimited budget. They often brought together scores of intellectuals from numerous continents, provided simultaneous translations in multiple languages, partnered with prestigious institutions, and benefited from ample media coverage in the international press. According to Peter Coleman's selective list, thirty-seven conferences were sponsored by the CCF, and they often led to major publications, sometimes in more than one language.[68] The same organization hosted "some fifty international seminars in addition to a large number of local meetings" around the world, from Tokyo, Cairo, and Pune to Kampala, Madrid, and Oxford.[69] The Ford Foundation stepped in to support this program, and some of the most prestigious universities collaborated. Coleman's partial list of institutions that co-sponsored CCF seminars includes thirty-eight, among them the Free University of Berlin, St. Antony's College of Oxford, University of California Berkeley, University of Montevideo, Bengali Academy, and the University of Khartoum.[70] The CCF also began sponsoring university chairs, granting scholarships, and financing study trips. The list of participants is much too long to summarize here, but some of the most well-known intellectuals involved in CCF networks included, in addition to Aron and Arendt, Max Horkheimer, Sidney Hook, Friedrich von Hayek, Daniel Bell, Arthur Koestler, Czesław Miłosz, Roger Caillois, and Edgar Morin.

The flagship enterprise of the CCF was its network of prestige magazines. It "created or helped sustain more than twenty monthlies, bimonthlies, and quarterlies," and its financial largesse allowed it to influence a

---

67. Kennan admitted to knowing about CIA funding in a November 9, 1967, letter to the Ford Foundation's Shepard Stone: "I never felt the slightest pangs of conscience about it, from the standpoint of the organization. This country has no ministry of culture, and CIA was obliged to do what it could to try and fill the gap. It should be praised for having done so, and not criticized." International Association for Cultural Freedom Records, Box 318, Folder Central Intelligence Agency 1967, Hanna Holborn Gray Special Collections Research Center at the University of Chicago.

68. See Coleman, *The Liberal Conspiracy*, 253–57.

69. Summary of Seventeen Years of the CCF, November 1967, International Association for Cultural Freedom Records.

70. See Coleman, *The Liberal Conspiracy*, 259–60.

broad circle of secondary journals and magazines aligned on its agenda.[71] The CCF's funding supported exquisite publications and large print runs, which contributed to making its magazines some of the most influential in the postwar era. CIA agent Melvin Lasky ran *Der Monat* in Germany, which had been launched before the CCF and also received funding from the Office of Military Government, United States (OMGUS) and the Ford Foundation. Replete with illustrations on glossy paper, it was able to reach a circulation of 25,000 copies in the mid-1950s, making it the largest journal of its sort and the model for the CCF's other publications. Its mission was cultural and transatlantic, and it aimed at orienting the intelligentsia against communism, while boasting on its presentation page that it was a "forum for open debate and discussion based on the free expression of opinion."

The network of magazines and journals included *Encounter* (UK and U.S.), *Minerva* (UK), *Soviet Survey* (UK), *The China Quarterly* (UK), *Preuves* (France), *Tempo presente* (Italy), *Forum* (Austria), *Partisan Review* (U.S.), *Commentary* (U.S.), *Mundo Nuevo* (Latin America), *Cuadernos* (Latin America), *Quest* (India), and *Quadrant* (Australia).[72] Although there were variations, they generally took the CCF's soft-sell approach by avoiding unhinged anticommunism and allowing minor criticisms of the United States in order to maintain their credibility and reinforce their cover. In general, however, they tended to follow the CCF's editorial line by being opposed to communism and neutralism, while supporting Atlanticism, a unified Europe, NATO, and the United States. They also regularly boasted, of course, that they were tribunes of free cultural expression.

The CCF had an annual budget of around $15,000 (approximately

---

71. Summary of Seventeen Years of the CCF, November 1967, International Association for Cultural Freedom Records.

72. On the CCF's journals, as well as its broader cultural war, see Giles Scott-Smith's work, particularly Giles Scott-Smith and Charlotte Lerg, eds., *Campaigning Culture and the Global Cold War: The Journals of the Congress for Cultural Freedom* (London: Palgrave Macmillan, 2017) and Giles Scott-Smith, *The Politics of Apolitical Culture: The Congress for Cultural Freedom, the CIA and Post-War American Hegemony* (New York: Routledge, 2002). Also see the document titled "Journals Funded by or Associated with the Congress," International Association for Cultural Freedom Records, Box 318, Folder 3, Central Intelligence Agency, Hanna Holborn Gray Special Collections Research Center at the University of Chicago, as well as Summary of Seventeen Years of the CCF, November 1967, International Association for Cultural Freedom Records.

$160,000 in 2024) for book publishing, and it produced 170 titles according to Coleman's calculations (Coleman was the editor of the CCF journal *Quadrant*).[73] The books were published in nineteen countries and at least seven languages. The CIA front collaborated on these projects with some of the leading publishers in the world, including, in the Anglophone sphere: Oxford University Press, MIT Press, Beacon Press, Free Press, Routledge, and Frederick A. Praeger. It was also directly involved in covert psychological warfare operations like running book and magazine programs in communist or communist-leaning countries, where it sent thousands upon thousands of its publications to institutions and intellectuals who represented "a potential force for liberalization" (while also creating publishing opportunities for them in the West).[74]

The authors implicated in the book and magazine programs are too numerous to summarize, but they included figures like Arendt, Aron, Bell, Dewey, Jaspers, Koestler, Orwell, Theodor Adorno, Albert Camus, André Malraux, and Richard Wright. The CCF, given its means and connections, was able to offer incredibly lucrative deals and opportunities for intellectual fame. To take but one revealing example, in 1961 it invited anthropologist Clifford Geertz to present a series of lectures at the University of Khartoum, where it also planned to invite half a dozen equally eminent scholars from around the world, and the same number of "the most outstanding scholars of the region."[75] The lectures would then be collected into a book that "the Congress would help to have published or which would be published under its auspices by a reputable commercial press."[76]

73. See Coleman, *The Liberal Conspiracy*, 261–74.

74. Summary of Seventeen Years of the CCF, November 1967, International Association for Cultural Freedom Records.

75. Edward Shils, letter to Clifford Geertz, December 21, 1961, International Association for Cultural Freedom Records, Box 659, Folder 27 Clifford Geertz 1961, Hanna Holborn Gray Special Collections Research Center at the University of Chicago. Shils mentions that Bertrand de Jouvenel was invited to give a series of such lectures in Geneva. It is not clear what came of the offer to Geertz, but he continued to be referenced in CCF plans in 1965, and he felt compelled to later sign a public letter stating that he knew nothing of the CIA connections. See Pierre Grémion, *Intelligence de l'anticommunisme: Le Congrès pour la liberté de la culture à Paris, 1950–1975* (Paris: Librairie Arthème Fayard, 1995), 530, and Nicolas Nabokov, letter to anonymous, May 27, 1966, International Association for Cultural Freedom Records, Box 318, Folder 1, Central Intelligence Agency 1966, Hanna Holborn Gray Special Collections Research Center at the University of Chicago.

76. Shils to Clifford Geertz, December 21, 1961.

All of the expenses connected to the trip would be covered by the CCF. Geertz would receive $1,500 for the lectures (the equivalent of $15,700 in 2024) and "all royalties arising from the publication of a book" would be his.[77]

Among those involved in such projects, the cases of Aron and Bell are particularly revealing, since they are both major figures in the postwar social sciences. Aron was arguably France's most prominent conservative public intellectual, and Bell was an esteemed Harvard professor renowned for his theses on the end of ideology and post-industrialism. Thanks in part to funding from the world's most notorious spy agency, ten books that Aron contributed to were published, including his manuscript *Three Essays on the Industrial Age* and the Japanese translation of his anticommunist classic *Opium of Intellectuals*.[78] The CCF also covered all-expenses-paid trips, which it treated as major public relations campaigns to promote Aron's work around the world. For instance, on his first voyage to Tokyo in 1953, the CCF planned news releases to be sent to all the leading outlets, a large press conference, interviews in the "Big Three newspapers" and one of the main magazines, lectures to students, and negotiations with the "Big Three" to see if one of them would regularly translate Aron's column in *Le Figaro*, as well as meetings with various organizations, intellectuals, political figures, union leaders, journalists, and artists.[79] His international renown was thus due in no small part to Company business.

Bell's most famous book, *The End of Ideology*, asserted that the grand humanistic ideologies of yesteryear—Marxism was a particular target— were exhausted and revolutionary movements would no longer be able to attract the working class. As he indicated in the acknowledgments, deftly leaving aside any reference to the CIA, many of the chapters in the book were either published in Agency journals or presented at its conferences. He also expressed his gratitude to major CIA cultural warriors like Aron, Irving Kristol, and Sol Levitas. Without ever mentioning the Company, he referred to CIA agent Melvin Lasky as "an old comrade," stated that he "owe(d) much" to Agency operator Michael Josselson for his "practical political wisdom," and praised CIA consultant Sidney Hook as "one of

---

77. Ibid.

78. See Coleman, *The Liberal Conspiracy*, 261–74.

79. Untitled document on Aron's trip to Japan, International Association for Cultural Freedom Records, Box 80, Folder Raymond Aron 1951–1954, Hanna Holborn Gray Special Collections Research Center at the University of Chicago.

the great teachers of the generation."[80] This was in the 1988 edition of the book, when many of these Company connections had been public knowledge for over twenty years.

With such a record shilling for the most infamous spy agency in history, known for its record of overthrowing foreign governments and assassinating political leaders, one might assume that the scholarly reputations of Aron and Bell would have suffered from their affiliations. Nothing could be further from the truth. They both remain major intellectual reference points in the postwar social sciences. Bell's anticommunist screed, which he explicitly framed as part of the "war of ideas" between Marxists and CIA-affiliated intellectuals in the 1988 Afterword to *The End of Ideology*, was included in the *Times Literary Supplement*'s list of the most influential 100 books since the Second World War.[81] Aron, for his part, was showered with some of the highest forms of public praise in France, including being named Officier de la Légion d'honneur, Commandeur de l'ordre des Palmes académiques, and Professor at the Collège de France (the highest academic honor).

ALL OF THE PEOPLE INVOLVED in these programs were part of what undercover CIA officer and CCF director Michael Josselson referred to, in an expression reminiscent of the mafia, as "our big family."[82] They collaborated within a vast network of knowledge production and dissemination capable of promoting the work of intellectuals whose worldviews were compatible with the CIA's agenda. This global web included the Latin American Institute of International Relations (LAIIR), which established seven national centers in capital cities across South America that pursued activities similar to those of the CCF: study groups, publications, seminars, art exhibits, and lecture tours.[83] It also comprised major feature services:

---

80. Daniel Bell, *The End of Ideology: On the Exhaustion of Political Ideas in the Fifties* (Cambridge, MA: Harvard University Press, 1988), 448–49.

81. Ibid., 410. Also see *Times Literary Supplement*, October 6, 1995.

82. See, for instance, Coleman, *The Liberal Conspiracy*, 101.

83. See the summary of the LAIIR's activities available in "The Latin American Institute of International Relations," November 1967, International Association for Cultural Freedom Records, Box 659, Folders 33, IACF 1967–1968, Hanna Holborn Gray Special Collections Research Center at the University of Chicago. According to this document, the LAIIR was running four journals, was associated with another five journals, and was involved in publishing at least eighteen books that came out of its study groups.

"Forum Information Service based in London and Preuves-Informations and El Mundo en Español based at CCF headquarters in Paris."[84] Its largest endeavor appears to have been an international press service called Forum Service or Forum World Features (depending on the source) that distributed around the world, free of charge, reports and analyses by its venal intellectuals in twelve languages, which served 600 newspapers and reached five million readers.[85] These included at least thirty domestic newspapers.[86] The anticommunist journalist and historian Brian Crozier oversaw the Forum's daily operations.[87] CIA agent Melvin Lasky served as its editorial director, and "career C.I.A. man" Robert G. Gately worked as "Forum's executive director in the early 1960s."[88]

All of this infrastructure provided a powerful social elevator that allowed scholars to travel the world indulging in junkets, obtain funding for their research, present their work in prestigious international settings, publish their ideas in esteemed outlets with wide readerships, gain privileged access to the global media, have their work translated into multiple languages, receive favorable book reviews and press coverage, and quickly ascend to influential positions in the world's most prominent institutions. This covertly manufactured intellectual apparatus could—and did—make major academic reference points and even celebrities out of theoretical toadies. However, they often were not perceived as imperialist sycophants, due in large part to the expansive and compartmentalized nature of this system, its clandestine manipulation, and the prevalence of the bourgeois ideology of meritocracy. This Cyclopean network thereby fostered the illusion that anticommunist worldviews were freely embraced by those who promulgated them, as well as by those who consumed them. The net effect was that an artificially constructed intellectual consensus often passed itself off as a natural development based on the freedom of cultural production and consumption purportedly characteristic of the West.

Soon after it was publicly revealed, in 1966, that the CCF was a

---

84. Lashmar and Oliver, *Britain's Secret Propaganda War*, 133.
85. See Coleman, *The Liberal Conspiracy*, 102, as well as Lashmar and Oliver, *Britain's Secret Propaganda War*, 133; Saunders, *The Cultural Cold War*, 311–12; Nossiter, "CIA News Service Reported."
86. See John Crewdson, "Worldwide Propaganda Network Built by the C.I.A.," *New York Times*, December 26, 1977.
87. See Nossiter, "CIA News Service Reported."
88. Crewdson, "Worldwide Propaganda Network Built by the C.I.A.," 37. Also see Lashmar and Oliver, *Britain's Secret Propaganda War*, 133.

CIA-front organization, the Ford Foundation, which had been co-funding the operation, took over its financing. To try to save the psywar enterprise from sinking, the President of the Ford Foundation and former national security advisor, McGeorge Bundy, asked Aron to become the president of the revamped organization, whose name would henceforth be the International Association for Cultural Freedom (IACF). It is worth noting that, in their correspondence on the topic, Bundy admitted that he was "a little stunned to learn, after the recent *New York Times* investigation, that the Executive Committee was unaware of what had been the subject of café gossip in New York for years."[89] He knew, in other words, that most thinking people had long understood that the CCF was a propaganda platform discreetly funded by the U.S. government. To navigate the choppy waters that came with the official revelations, the CCF thus proposed to make a minor change to its name, assign a new director (replacing a CIA officer by one of his agents and his close friend), slightly reconfigure the executive committee, and replace Agency funding by the support of one of its most faithful accomplices, the Ford Foundation.

Aron eventually turned down the presidency after a second wave of revelations, but the organization's mild makeover allowed it to persist until 1979. Its legacy continued much longer. To take but a few concrete examples, a number of its magazines went on publishing with alternative sources of funding, such as *Encounter* (until 1991), as well as *Quadrant* and *China Quarterly*, which still exist.[90] In 1998, Encounter Books was launched. Explicitly drawing on the name and orientation of the CIA's *Encounter* magazine, it seeks to "advance its love of liberty and the cultural achievements of the West against a rising tide of collectivist sentiment and the soft totalitarianism of intellectual conformity."[91] The European Intellectual Mutual Aid Fund (*Fondation pour une entraide intellectuelle européenne*), originally established as an affiliate of the CCF

---

89. Cited in Grémion, *Intelligence de l'anticommunisme*, 467.
90. See Roderick MacFarquhar, "The Founding of *The China Quarterly*," *China Quarterly*, No. 143 (September 1995): 692–96.
91. See the About page on its website: https://www.encounterbooks.com/about/. One of Encounter Books' notable publications is *NextGen Marxism: What It Is and How to Combat It* (https://www.encounterbooks.com/books/next-gen-marxism/). Its authors have both served in the Heritage Foundation, a powerful conservative think tank, and worked for the State Department and the Department of Homeland Security respectively. Regarding Encounter Books' relationship to the MAGA movement, see John Bellamy Foster, "The MAGA Ideology and the Trump Regime," *Monthly Review*, Vol. 77, No. 1 (May 2025).

to imbue Eastern European scholars with anti-totalitarian and pro-capitalist ideas, later merged with George Soros' Open Society Foundation.[92] Moreover, the Katzenbach Commission, convened by President Johnson in 1967 to examine the relationships between the CIA and civil society organizations, recommended the creation of a public-private mechanism that would allow for the overt distribution of governmental funds. State agencies like the National Endowment for Democracy (NED) and NGOs like Freedom House have since taken up the CCF's work of promoting so-called cultural freedom around the world. Allen Weinstein, a former professor and co-founder of the NED, clearly explained the shift when discussing his organization: "A lot of what we do today was done covertly 25 years ago by the CIA."[93]

Although the lid was blown on the CCF in 1966, the structures and strategies that it established have thereby continued, sometimes under slightly different and more overt forms. Furthermore, institutional inertia carried forth a number of its projects by promoting its venal intellectuals into major positions of power and shoring up an anticommunist network of institutions, associations, and networks. One of the greatest legacies of the CCF has thus been the consolidation of an anticommunist system of intellectual production, circulation, and consumption, which continues to serve as one of the best guarantees for preserving capitalist hegemony. Intellectuals and cultural producers in need of employment will thereby be forced to find their place within it, conforming to its constraints for very material reasons. Such a system has no strings attached, so to speak, because there are no puppet masters or marionettes, only a tightly controlled theater with actors acting as if—and often believing—that they are free to say whatever they want (since their lines never stray far from the anticommunist script).

---

92. See Nicolas Guilhot, "A Network of Influential Friendships: The Fondation pour une entraide intellectuelle européenne and East-West Cultural Dialogue, 1957–1991," *Minerva*, Vol. 44, No. 4 (December 2006): 379–409.

93. Cited in David Ignatius, "Innocence Abroad: The New World of Spyless Coups," *Washington Post*, September 22, 1991, C4. Also see William Blum, *Rogue State: A Guide to the World's Only Superpower* (London: Zed Books, 2014), 238–43, as well as former CIA case officer Philip Agee's discussion of the NED on "Alternative Views," a program that also has an expansive archive of excellent interviews on the U.S. national security state: https://www.youtube.com/watch?v=nvZQa0hkfgw&t=1655s.

The Mighty Wurlitzer

Deception is a state of mind and the mind of the state.

—JAMES JESUS ANGLETON,
HEAD OF CIA COUNTERINTELLIGENCE 1954–1974[94]

CIA officer Michael Josselson's "big family" was just a small part of what his colleague, Frank Wisner, called his "mighty Wurlitzer": the international jukebox of media and cultural programming controlled by the Company.[95] Wisner wanted to be able to press a single button at CIA headquarters in Langley, Virginia, and have the same propaganda tune play in all of the Agency's media assets around the world. To take but a few examples of this gigantic program of psychological warfare, Carl Bernstein marshaled ample evidence in a well-known article to demonstrate that at least 400 U.S. journalists worked surreptitiously for the CIA between 1952 and 1977.[96] Following these revelations, the *New York Times* undertook a three-month investigation and concluded that the CIA "embraced more than eight hundred news and public information organizations and individuals."[97] These two exposés were published

---

94. Cited in Allan Francovich, *Gladio*, 1992, film, https://www.youtube.com/watch?v=GGHXjO8wHsA.

95. Earlier versions of a few of these paragraphs were published in Gabriel Rockhill, "Imperialist Propaganda and the Ideology of the Western Left Intelligentsia: From Anticommunism and Identity Politics to Democratic Illusions and Fascism," Interview by Zhao Dingqi, *Monthly Review*, Vol. 75, No. 7 (December 2023), https://monthlyreview.org/2023/12/01/imperialist-propaganda-and-the-ideology-of-the-western-left-intelligentsia/. The information in these paragraphs was compiled from multiple sources, including archival research, numerous FOIA requests, and works such as Coleman, *The Liberal Conspiracy*; Grémion, *Intelligence de l'anticommunisme*; Saunders, *The Cultural Cold War*; Scott-Smith, *The Politics of Apolitical Culture*; Wilford, *The Mighty Wurlitzer*; Philip Agee and Louis Wolf, eds., *Dirty Work: The CIA in Western Europe* (New York: Dorset Press, 1978); Frédéric Charpier, *La C.I.A. en France: 60 ans d'ingérence dans les affaires françaises* (Paris: Editions du Seuil, 2008); Ray S. Cline, *Secrets, Spies, and Scholars* (Washington, DC: Acropolis, 1976); Allan Francovich, *On Company Business*, 1980, film; Victor Marchetti and John D. Marks, *The CIA and the Cult of Intelligence* (New York: Dell Publishing, 1974); and John Stockwell, *The Praetorian Guard: The U.S. Role in the New World Order* (Boston: South End Press, 1991).

96. See Carl Bernstein, "The CIA and the Media," *Rolling Stone*, October 20, 1977, https://www.carlbernstein.com/the-cia-and-the-media-rolling-stone-10-20-1977.

97. Crewdson, "Worldwide Propaganda Network Built by the C.I.A."

in establishment venues by journalists who themselves operated in the same networks they were analyzing, so these estimates were likely low.

Arthur Hays Sulzberger, the director of the *New York Times* from 1935 to 1961, worked so closely with the CIA that he even signed a confidentiality agreement (the highest level of collaboration). William S. Paley's Columbia Broadcasting System (CBS) was unquestionably the Agency's greatest asset in the field of audiovisual broadcasting. It worked so regularly with the Company that it installed a direct phone line to CIA headquarters, which was not routed through its central operator. Paley himself had worked as the Deputy Chief of the Psychological Warfare Division of the Supreme Headquarters Allied Expeditionary Force during the war, so he was deeply familiar with the U.S. national security state's psy-war operations.[98] Henry Luce's Time Inc. was the CIA's most powerful collaborator in the weekly and monthly arena (including *Time*—where Bernstein later published—*Life, Fortune, Sports Illustrated*). Luce agreed to hire Agency operatives as journalists, which became very common cover.[99] As we know from the Task Force on Greater CIA Openness, convened by Agency Director Robert Gates in 1991, these types of practices continued in later years (and up to the present): "PAO (Public Affairs Office) [of the CIA] now has relationships with reporters from every major wire service, newspaper, news weekly, and television network in the nation.... In many instances, we have persuaded reporters to postpone, change, hold, or even scrap stories."[100] In the contemporary world, we should note that CNN's Anderson Cooper interned with the CIA, and Tucker Carlson apparently applied to join the Agency (and, in any case, he has operated to some extent like a modern-day incarnation of the CIA's beloved William F. Buckley Jr.). It was revealed, more generally, that in 2023 the U.S. Agency for International Development (USAID), which has a long history of covert collaboration with the CIA, "funded training

98. See the memo regarding "Radio Propaganda to Allied Occupied Germany," April 16, 1945, Jackson, C.D.: Papers, 1931–67, Box 11, Folder Paley, William—Paris, Dwight D. Eisenhower Library.

99. The mainstream media has also had extensive ties to other governmental agencies involved in psychological warfare, and it is important to situate the CIA as part of a much larger public-private propaganda partnership. See, for instance, Nicholas J. Cull, *The Cold War and the United States Information Agency: American Propaganda and Public Diplomacy, 1945–1989* (Cambridge: Cambridge University Press, 2010).

100. Task Force on Greater CIA Openness, "Memorandum for Director of Public Affairs," November 18, 1991, http://www.takeoverworld.info/cia-openness.html.

and support for 6,200 journalists, assisted 707 non-state news outlets, and supported 279 media-sector civil society organizations."[101] It had a budget of $43 billion, and its foreign aid budget in 2025 "included $268,376,000 allocated by Congress to support 'independent media and the free flow of information.'"[102] The same year, Wikileaks revealed that USAID financed the shadowy group Internews Network, which had a "$472 million budget to quietly work with 4,291 media outlets and more than 9,000 individual journalists around the world," promoting pro-Western views.[103]

The CIA also took control of the American Newspaper Guild, and it became the owner of press services, magazines, and newspapers that it used as cover for its agents. It has owned, at least in part, *Rome Daily American, Okinawa Morning Star, Manila Times, Bangkok World, Tokyo Evening News*, and other outlets in Athens and Rangoon.[104] It has also had officers in other press services, such as LATIN, Reuters, Associated Press, United Press International, and Ritzhaus in Scandinavia. William Schaap, an expert on governmental disinformation, testified that the CIA "owned or controlled some 2,500 media entities all over the world. In addition, it had its people, ranging from stringers to highly visible journalists and editors, in virtually every major media organization."[105] "We 'had' at least one newspaper in every foreign capital at any given time," one CIA man told journalist John Crewdson.[106] Furthermore, the source related, "Those that the agency did not own outright or subsidize heavily it infiltrated with paid agents or staff officers who could have stories printed that were useful to the agency and not print those it found detrimental."[107] "Most CIA stations," former CIA officer Philip Agee explained, "pay journalists to publish the CIA's propaganda as if it were the journalist's own work."[108] John Stockwell, another former case officer, spoke out candidly about the

101. Clayton Weimers, "USA: Trump's Foreign Aid Freeze Throws Journalism around the World into Chaos," *Reporters without Borders*, February 3, 2025, https://rsf.org/en/usa-trump-s-foreign-aid-freeze-throws-journalism-around-world-chaos.
102. Ibid.
103. See journalist Nury Vittachi's tweet and accompanying video on February 24, 2025, https://x.com/NuryVittachi/status/1894217287768707254.
104. See Crewdson, "Worldwide Propaganda Network Built by the C.I.A."
105. Quoted in William F. Pepper, *The Plot to Kill King* (New York: Skyhorse, 2018), 186.
106. Crewdson, "Worldwide Propaganda Network Built by the C.I.A."
107. Ibid.
108. Philip Agee, "West Germany: An Interview with Philip Agee," interview by Informations Dienst in *Dirty Work*, ed. Agee and Wolf, 186.

work of the Agency in recruiting journalists, sometimes setting them up, and he also explained how the CIA directly manufactures propaganda stories and places them in press outlets around the world.[109] In the digital age, this process has continued. Yasha Levine, Alan MacLeod, and other scholars and journalists have detailed the extensive involvement of the U.S. national security state in the realms of big tech and social media. They have demonstrated, among other things, that major intelligence operators occupy key positions at Facebook, X (Twitter), TikTok, Reddit, and Google.[110]

Books have been particularly important to the intellectual world war on communism. According to the Chief of the CIA's Covert Action Staff in 1961:

> Books differ from all other propaganda media, primarily because one single book can significantly change the reader's attitude and action to an extent unmatched by the impact of any other single medium. . . . Books [are] the most important weapon of strategic (long-range) propaganda.[111]

The Agency has therefore engaged extensively in commissioning, subsidizing, producing, translating, publishing, distributing, buying, reviewing, and promoting books, without acknowledging its role in any of this.[112] Before the end of 1967, "well over a thousand books were produced, subsidized or sponsored by the CIA." [113] In some cases, its officers oversaw the project from start to finish: the "advantage of direct contact

---

109. See "Former CIA Agent John Stockwell Talks about How the CIA Worked in Vietnam and Elsewhere," https://www.youtube.com/watch?v=NK1tfkESPVY, as well as Stockwell's books.

110. See Yasha Levine, *Surveillance Valley* (New York: PublicAffairs, 2018) and Alan Macleod's articles in *MintPress News*: "National Security Search Engine: Google's Ranks Are Filled with CIA Agents," July 25, 2022; "Meet the Ex-CIA Agents Deciding Facebook's Content Policy," July 12, 2022; "The Federal Bureau of Tweets: Twitter Is Hiring an Alarming Number of FBI Agents," June 21, 2022; "The NATO to TikTok Pipeline: Why Is TikTok Employing so Many National Security Agents?," April 29, 2022.

111. Cited in Senate Select Committee to Study Governmental Operations with Respect to Intelligence Activities, *Final Report*, Book I, *Foreign and Military Intelligence* (Washington, DC: U.S. Government Printing Office, 1976), https://www.intelligence.senate.gov/sites/default/files/94755_I.pdf, 193.

112. See ibid., 192–95.

113. Ibid., 193.

with the author is that we can acquaint him in great detail with our intentions; that we can provide him with whatever material we want to include and that we can check the manuscript at every stage."[114] In other words, the Agency can more or less ghostwrite a book and have its propaganda academically laundered by passing it off as the work of a purportedly autonomous intellectual. This is the case, according to Mark Lane, for Christopher Andrew—the author of numerous high-profile books on the history of intelligence agencies, including the KGB—who "makes a living writing books for the CIA that are favorable to the CIA . . . [and] is paid to write reviews denouncing books that are critical of the CIA."[115]

This is only one example, however, of a systemic series of arrangements involving multiple state agencies, not just the CIA. The deputy director of the United States Information Agency (USIA), Reed Harris, explained, for instance, that his agency has anticommunist books written according to its specifications, and that it controls every aspect of the books, from their conception to the final edited manuscript.[116] One of Reed's associates added: "We try to obtain the assistance of renowned writers in the literary world. We ask them to write books for us. Their stature gives the book greater credibility."[117]

These factitious forms of scholarly production have gone hand in hand with the artificial manipulation of the circulation and consumption of cultural products. The CIA has collaborated with USIA, the United States Information Service (USIS), and U.S. embassies across the globe to buy up books for millions of dollars, thereby guaranteeing widespread distribution or even best-seller status for chosen publications (while also marshaling its power to shower them with awards). In 1965, for example, the "USIS spent several million dollars to distribute 14,453,000 books throughout the world."[118] Analysts have also noted "the practice whereby one CIA operative or asset would write a book and others review it for selected newspapers and magazines," thereby creating hype by producing the illusion that different sources appreciate the same book.[119] If there is

---

114. Quoted in Finn and Couvée, *The Zhivago Affair*, 127.
115. Mark Lane, *Last Word: My Indictment of the CIA in the Murder of JFK* (New York: Skyhorse Publishing, 2011), 89.
116. See Claude Julien, *America's Empire*, trans. Renaud Bruce (New York: Pantheon Books, 1971), 313.
117. Ibid., translation slightly modified.
118. Ibid., 310.
119. William F. Pepper, Esq., *The Plot to Kill King: The Truth Behind the Assassination of Martin Luther King Jr.* (New York: Skyhorse, 2018), 60.

an invisible hand governing the supposedly free market of cultural goods, it should be clear whose it is.

Franklin Publications, "a group representing the most important trade, university and educational publishers in the United States," was launched as a "private non-profit corporation created for the purpose of avoiding either the stigma of an official agency of propaganda or the tyranny of the balance sheet."[120] With a private nonprofit façade to maintain credibility, it was discreetly funded from behind the scenes by the U.S. government, including the CIA (via the Asia Foundation).[121] It also "worked closely with the . . . USIA to promote American values."[122] Opening offices all over the globe, including "in Egypt, Iran, Nigeria, Indonesia, Pakistan, Bangladesh and Afghanistan," it built an extensive network of international publishing infrastructure for the cultural Cold War by using the private sector as cover for government-funded propaganda efforts.[123] One of its objectives was to establish an overseas network to ensure wider distribution of its books, "particularly in foreign languages."[124] As the vice president of one of the textbook publishers involved (Silver Burdett Company) explained in a letter to the Psychological Strategy Board, the secret funding allowed it to "compete with prices of books in the local market . . . [to guarantee] wider distribution of American ideals which is the primary purpose of our operations."[125]

---

120. Amanda Laugesen, "This Cold War–Era Publishing House Wanted to Share American Values with the World," *Smithsonian Magazine*, July 13, 2018, https://www. smithsonianmag.com/history/cold-war-government-funded-publishing-house-took-american-literature-world-180969624/; Harold Lasswell, Memo to Executive Committee, Franklin Publications, September 26, 1952, Edward P. Lilly: Papers, 1928–1992, Box 54, Folder Book Programs, Dwight D. Eisenhower Library, 2.

121. Internal documents reveal discussions concerning the advantages of nonprofit front organizations for book projects, including one involving the State Department and three book trade associations. See "Suggestion for Improving Facilities for Ideological Warfare," March 6, 1952, the CIA FOIA Electronic Reading Room, https://www.cia.gov/readingroom/document/cia-rdp80-01065a000200080057-6.

122. Laugesen, "This Cold War-Era Publishing House."

123. Ibid. On Franklin Publications and some parallel projects, also see the Book Programs Folder in Edward P. Lilly: Papers, 1928–1992, Box 54, Dwight D. Eisenhower Library.

124. Memo for the Record re 3rd Meeting of Doctrinal Warfare Panel, December 12, 1952, Edward P. Lilly: Papers, 1928–1992, Box 54, Folder Doctrinal Programs 1952, Dwight D. Eisenhower Library, 1.

125. Charles E. Griffith, letter to Edward P. Lilly, Psychological Strategy Board, March 16, 1953, Edward P. Lilly: Papers, 1928–1992, Box 54, Dwight D. Eisenhower Library, 2.

Furthermore, the CIA distributed "roughly ten million books and other publications," generally free of charge, to six Warsaw Pact countries between 1956 and 1991.[126] George Minden, who oversaw the project, explained that some 500 publishers, institutions, and individuals were involved by the end of 1962.[127] The Agency also set up multiple fronts, such as the International Advisory Council, to conceal its hidden hand, and it funded the creation of publishing houses like Bedford Publishing Company.[128] In 1991, the "annual expenditures for books and handling reached $1,850,900" (the equivalent of $4.3 million in 2024).[129]

According to the plan published by the Free Europe Press, one of the principal organizations involved, the goal was to "to reduce the efficiency of the communist administration by weakening loyalty of the Party and state cadres."[130] This was done subtly, however, by systematically presenting materials under sponsorship of a cover organization and avoiding "total attacks on communism."[131] The project sought instead to promote "'revisionist' trends among the new elites" and prioritize "practical alternatives to doctrinaire Marxist principles," while demonstrating "the superior achievements of the West."[132] Among the very long list of books sent, prominent members of the Western left intelligentsia were well represented: Arendt, Orwell, Isaiah Berlin, Herbert Marcuse, and Karl Wittfogel, among others.[133] The book program was "demonstrably effective" according to the CIA, and it remained largely unexposed until 1991.[134] "Millions of people," Alfred Reisch concluded, "were affected one way or another by the book project without ever hearing about its existence."[135]

---

126. Alfred A. Reisch, *Hot Books in the Cold War: The CIA-Funded Secret Western Book Distribution Program Behind the Iron Curtain* (Budapest: Central European University Press, 2013), xi.

127. See John P.C. Matthews, "The West's Secret Marshall Plan for the Mind," *International Journal of Intelligence and Counterintelligence*, Vol. 16, No. 3 (2003): 422. The domestic "sponsors" included the American Council of Learned Societies, the AFL-CIO, Barnes and Noble, Brookings Institution, Doubleday, *Encyclopedia Britannica*, Funk and Wagnalls, Grove Press, Harper and Row, Harvard University Press (see ibid.).

128. See Finn and Couvée, *The Zhivago Affair*, 125–27.

129. Matthews, "The West's Secret Marshall Plan for the Mind," 425.

130. Cited in ibid., 412.

131. Cited in ibid.

132. Cited in ibid.

133. See Reisch, *Hot Books in the Cold War*, 34.

134. Cited in Finn and Couvée, *The Zhivago Affair*, 263.

135. Reisch, *Hot Books in the Cold War*, 525.

While the CIA was promoting the work of the Western anticommunist left in the East, it was simultaneously engaged in publishing, distributing, and promoting the writings of Eastern dissidents. To cite one of the most important examples, the CIA was responsible for the publication of Boris Pasternak's *Dr. Zhivago* in Russian as a propaganda ploy after it had been rejected for publication by the Soviet literary journal *Novyi Mir*, which judged that it was anti-socialist and condemned the October Revolution, as well as everything that followed from it.[136] The Company promoted Pasternak's work through its expansive channels, in various formats and translations into other languages. "Agency officials congratulated themselves that 'in one form or another, including full-length and condensed books and serials in indigenous languages, this book has been spread throughout the world, with assistance from this agency in a number of areas where interest might not normally be great.'"[137]

Such stalwart support for Eastern dissidents contrasted sharply with the CIA's open assault on Western dissidents. The cases of Victor Marchetti and Philip Agee are particularly remarkable. They had both been recruited into the CIA as university students and spent years as case officers, but their pangs of conscience led them to break ranks with the Company. Marchetti was "served with an official censorship order" in order to prevent him from exercising his right to free speech by publishing his book *The CIA and the Cult of Intelligence*.[138] He was only able to bring it to the light of day by agreeing to let the CIA vet its contents, and his former employer deleted 140-plus passages.[139] In Agee's case, the Agency undertook a global harassment, defamation, and surveillance campaign, and it even had plans to assassinate him.[140] All of this was in order to prohibit him from writing *Inside the Company: CIA Diary*. After he managed to publish it, "he was hunted, arrested, threatened, expelled from country after country (often illegally) and sometimes prosecuted."[141] The former

---

136. See "Letter to Boris Pasternak from the Editors of *Novyi Mir*," *Daedalus*, Vol. 89, No. 3, The Russian Intelligentsia (Summer 1960): 649, and Finn and Couvée, *The Zhivago Affair*.

137. Finn and Couvée, *The Zhivago Affair*, 216.

138. Victor Marchetti and John D. Marks, *The CIA and the Cult of Intelligence* (New York: Dell Publishing, 1974), 19.

139. See ibid., 9.

140. Agee mentions the plot in a 1992 lecture at Carnegie Mellon University, available at https://www.youtube.com/watch?v=yWnsqjaoinU&t=808s.

141. Philip Agee, *On the Run* (Secaucus, NJ: Lyle Stuart Inc., 1987), front flap.

CIA officer had definitively gone too far in his freedom of thought and speech, because he dared to situate the U.S. police state within the social totality and draw the most coherent conclusion:

> American capitalism, based as it is on exploitation of the poor, with its fundamental motivation in personal greed, simply cannot survive without force—without a secret police force. The argument [in this book] is with capitalism and it is capitalism that must be opposed, with its CIA, FBI and other security agencies understood as logical, necessary manifestations of a ruling class's determination to retain power and privilege.[142]

In addition to publishing, the CIA has also been deeply involved in the art world.[143] For instance, it promoted U.S. American art, particularly Abstract Expressionism and the New York art scene, over and against socialist realism.[144] It funded art exhibits, musical and theatrical performances, international art festivals, and more in a bid to disseminate what was touted as the free art of the West. The Company worked closely with major art institutions in these endeavors. To take but a single telling example, one of the major CIA officers involved in the cultural cold war, Thomas Braden, was the executive secretary of the Museum of Modern Art (MoMA) before joining the Agency. MoMA's presidents have included Nelson Rockefeller, who became the super-coordinator for clandestine intelligence operations and allowed the Rockefeller Fund to be used as a conduit for CIA money. Among MoMA's directors, we find René d'Harnoncourt, who had worked for Rockefeller's wartime intelligence agency for Latin America. John Hay Whitney of the eponymous museum and Julius Fleischmann sat on MoMA's board of trustees. The former had worked for the CIA's predecessor organization, the OSS, and allowed his charity to be used as a conduit for Company money. The latter served as the president of the Agency's Farfield Foundation. William S. Paley, the president of CBS and one of the major figures in U.S. psychological warfare programs, including those of the CIA, was on the members' board of MoMA's International Program. As this web of relations indicates, the

---

142. Philip Agee, *Inside the Company: CIA Diary* (New York: Stonehill Publishing, 1975), 597.

143. Regarding some of the CCF's contributions to these efforts, see Summary of Seventeen Years of the CCF, November 1967, International Association for Cultural Freedom Records.

144. See Rockhill, *Radical History and the Politics of Art*, 191–217.

capitalist ruling class works closely with the U.S. national security state in order to tightly control the cultural apparatus.

A copious body of literature has demonstrated the depth and breadth of the U.S. government's penetration of the entertainment industry.[145] Matthew Alford and Tom Secker have documented that the Department of Defense (DOD) has supported—with complete and absolute censorship rights—a minimum of 814 movies, with the CIA involved in at least 37 and the FBI 22.[146] Regarding TV shows, some of which have been very long running, the DOD totals 1,133, the CIA 22, and the FBI 10. Above and beyond these quantifiable cases, there is also the qualitative relationship between the national security state and Tinseltown. John Rizzo explained as much in 2014: "The CIA has long had a special relationship with the entertainment industry, devoting considerable attention to fostering relationships with Hollywood movers and shakers—studio executives, producers, directors, big-name actors."[147] Having served as the Deputy Counsel or Acting General Counsel of the CIA for the first nine years of the war on terror, during which time he was involved in overseeing global rendition, torture, and drone-assassination programs, Rizzo was well placed to understand how the culture industry could provide cover for imperial butchery.

Promotion and Repression

The IRD and the CCF were two major, well-funded organizations for psychological warfare that both enrolled and targeted intellectuals in a global war on the very idea of communism. They were so expansive and powerful that leading specialists on the CCF have described it as one of the greatest cultural patrons in world history (Hugh Wilford) that likely left almost no Western European intellectual of the time unaffected (Frances Stonor Saunders).[148] Due to institutional inertia and normalization, integration

---

145. See, for instance, Matthew Alford, *Reel Power: Hollywood Cinema and American Supremacy* (London: Pluto Press, 2010); Matthew Alford and Tom Secker, *National Security Cinema: The Shocking New Evidence of Government Control in Hollywood* (n.p.: CreateSpace, 2017); Tricia Jenkins, *The CIA in Hollywood: How the Agency Shapes Film and Television* (Austin: University of Texas Press, 2013); David L. Robb, *Operation Hollywood: How the Pentagon Shapes and Censors the Movies* (Amherst, NY: Prometheus, 2004).
146. See Alford and Secker, *National Security Cinema*.
147. Quoted in ibid., 49.
148. See Wilford, *The Mighty Wurlitzer*, 101–2, and Saunders, *The Cultural Cold War*, 2.

into later organizations, and a generalized proliferation of overt operations over the last fifty years or so, the practices of the IRD and CCF are alive and well in the contemporary world, although they have taken on different forms.

These two state propaganda organizations were, as we have seen, part of a much broader attempt to establish monopoly control over the world of ideas. They were nested within, and intertwined with, the CIA's mighty Wurlitzer, another global network that persists to this day. Although there are many other components, the IRD, the CCF, and the mighty Wurlitzer are all part of an overall superstructural framework for the production, circulation, and consumption of ideas. They have helped foster a compatible left intelligentsia, while dividing it from the incompatible left, by providing uplift to the former and demotion for the latter.

The promotional networks of the ruling class go hand in hand with the direct repression of alternative material systems of knowledge production. This takes many forms and would require volumes to document. In the interest of space, suffice it to say that for every intellectual promoted by these networks, there have been many that have been demoted, sidelined, discredited, and, in certain cases, killed. Such repression does not simply occur on an individual level, however; it has been systematically organized as a global war on the very idea of communism and knowledge networks that promote it, or even simply want to examine it scientifically.

In the United States, the so-called Red Scare is a euphemism for a war on the Reds that took many forms, began well before Senator McCarthy, and continues today. To cite but three telling examples, the documentary history of the FBI's Counter-Intelligence Program (COINTELPRO) exposes

> the secret, systematic, and sometimes savage use of force and fraud, by all levels of government, to sabotage progressive political activity supposedly protected by the U.S. constitution. They [the documents] reveal ongoing, country-wide CIA-style covert action—infiltration, psychological warfare, legal harassment, and violence—against a very broad range of domestic dissidents.[149]

Operation Chaos was a domestic spying operation run by the CIA, which segued with COINTELPRO. Ostensibly focused on "foreign influence

---

149. Ward Churchill and Jim Vander Wall, *The COINTELPRO Papers: Documents from the FBI's Secret Wars Against Dissent in the United States* (Boston: South End Press, 1990), 10.

upon American dissent," it targeted leftists, amassed "thousands of files on Americans," and sought to eliminate incompatible news and information networks.[150] "Chaos," Joel Whitney explained, "was a scheme to spy on and destroy a large, independent strain of the American free press, bluntly quashing all homespun editorial opposition and preemptively striking against embarrassing stories."[151] Project Resistance fed into Chaos by focusing more specifically on radicals in the university, and it set up collaborative networks between campus officials and governmental authorities in order to do so.[152]

Promotion and repression are thus two sides of the same war of ideas. Although this study primarily focuses on the former by detailing the global material networks that promoted the compatible left intelligentsia, it must never be forgotten that these have gone hand in hand with repressive networks aimed at destroying the so-called incompatible left and alternative systems of knowledge. Whereas promotion seeks to shore up hegemony, repression strives to exclude—and ideally eliminate—counter-hegemonic voices. The overall objective is to produce, more or less from behind the scenes, the illusion of a scholarly, journalistic, and cultural consensus that has been freely arrived at across society at large.

150. Senate Select Committee to Study Governmental Operations with Respect to Intelligence Activities, *Final Report*, Book III, *Supplementary Detailed Staff Reports on Intelligence Activities and the Rights of Americans* (Washington, DC: U.S. Government Printing Office, 1976), https://www.intelligence.senate.gov/sites/default/files/94755_III.pdf, 681, 682.

151. Joel Whitney, *Finks: How the C.I.A. Tricked the World's Best Writers* (New York: OR Books, 2016), 241.

152. See Senate Select Committee, *Final Report*, Book III, *Supplementary Detailed Staff Reports*, 721–23.

CHAPTER 3

The Imperial Theory Industry

Toward a Systemic Analysis

Theodor Adorno and Max Horkheimer provided some insightful criticisms of the culture industry, excoriating the system operative behind mainstream capitalist culture, without subjecting the industry within which they worked—the theory industry—to the same blistering critique.[1] Michel Foucault wrote at length about the historical relationship between knowledge and power, even introducing his own concept of knowledge/power to underscore the intertwined nature of "the deployment of force and the establishment of truth," but he never rigorously examined the principal powers at work within the knowledge networks that promoted *him*.[2] This lack of self-reflective critique, in which tools of critical analyses applied to external objects of study are turned back on the subject, reveals the existence of a significant blind spot, and it is a clear sign that their approaches are non-systematic and undialectical. They are subjects who have criticized systems while shunning the critique of the very systems that produced the subjects performing such critiques.

---

1. Although much of their work could be cited, see in particular their canonical critique of the culture industry in Theodor W. Adorno and Max Horkheimer, *Dialectic of Enlightenment*, trans. John Cumming (New York: Continuum Publishing Company, 1993), 120–67, as well as Theodor Adorno, *The Culture Industry: Selected Essays on Mass Culture*, ed. J. M. Bernstein (New York: Routledge, 1991).

2. Michel Foucault, *Discipline and Punish: The Birth of the Prison*, trans. Alan Sheridan (New York: Vintage Books, 1979), 184. Foucault wrote so much on this topic that innumerable passages could be cited. Suffice it here to reference his discussion of the "nexus of knowledge-power" in Michel Foucault, *The Politics of Truth*, ed. Sylvère Lotringer, trans. Lysa Hochroth and Catherine Porter (Los Angeles: Semiotext(e), 2007), 60–61.

In the case of Adorno and Horkheimer, it is surely their bourgeois background and petty-bourgeois class position that drove them to denigrate the entertainment industry to which the masses are subjected while generally exonerating the realm of high art and theory, which are forms of bourgeois culture in which they willingly indulged and participated, as well as celebrated (at least in certain forms).[3] Paul Baran's biting critique of their work in his personal correspondence with Herbert Marcuse brings this clearly into view:

> The dialectic of these gentlemen, from which all history and all philosophy has fallen away, has been transformed into pure obscurantism despite all of Adorno's sharp-sighted observations and deep insights. With Horkheimer, even all of these have disappeared and what remains is an old well-to-do gentleman who yearns for the good old days when there were servants and when one could pursue his "fine self-cultivation [*feine Bildung*]."[4]

Foucault's orientation is not dissimilar, and it further reveals the difficulty that the imperial intelligentsia has in perceiving the imperial power that supports it. If it is, as Upton Sinclair famously stated, "difficult to get a man to understand something when his salary depends upon his not understanding it," it is next to impossible to get an imperially promoted intellectual to apprehend the powers undergirding their social status and the global prominence of their discourse.[5]

The class position of these intellectuals and their specific standing within the international relations of intellectual production go a long way to explaining their blind spots, as well as their ideological alignment. As the leading luminaries of the radical theory industry, they are not only members of the intellectual labor aristocracy, but they are its crème de la crème. Their purported knowledge is, in other words, completely saturated with power, and more specifically the power of the theory industry

---

3. It is worth recalling that Adorno's father was a "wealthy wine merchant" and Horkheimer's was a "millionaire." Thomas Wheatland, *The Frankfurt School in Exile* (Minneapolis: University of Minnesota Press, 2009), 24, and Ingar Solty, "Max Horkheimer, a Teacher Without a Class," *Jacobin*, February 15, 2020.
4. Paul Baran and Herbert Marcuse, "The Baran Marcuse Correspondence," ed. John Bellamy Foster, trans. Joseph Fracchia, *Monthly Review Online*, March 1, 2014, https://mronline.org/2014/03/01/baran-marcuse-correspondence/. I would like to thank John Bellamy Foster for drawing my attention to this important exchange.
5. Upton Sinclair, "I, Candidate for Governor and How I Got Licked," *Oakland Tribune*, December 11, 1934.

that promotes them. Perched atop a global pyramid of symbolic value creation, they had lucrative positions at elite institutions with significant platforms and perks. Destined to go down in bourgeois history as the greatest thinkers of their generation, they had no material or intellectual incentive to seriously combat the system that continues to promote them.

For those on the left fringe of the imperial intelligentsia, who desire to be seen on the side of the people without, however, losing their superior social standing, petty-bourgeois symbolic gestures of radicality can easily serve as an ersatz for any real investment in substantive social change. In this way, they can recuperate their reputation as radicals, while simultaneously using their discourse to try and co-opt revolutionaries within the consumerist and symbolic realm of bourgeois culture. This is one of the social functions of the radical fringe of the intellectual labor aristocracy, namely to serve as the radical recuperators who reintegrate potentially insurgent forces within the anticommunist—and ultimately pro-capitalist—camp. As knowledge brokers who are power brokers, they police the left border of critique, excluding communism as beyond the pale.

It is for these reasons, ultimately, that they have not diagnosed and critically assessed the theory industry, which is the capitalist-driven system of knowledge and power that promotes them. Their blind spot is not accidental: it is a constitutive feature of their ideology as imperial intellectuals. As the leading lights of the theory industry, they have been trained, and they train others, not to see the imperial power structures that have promoted their—anticommunist—knowledge as the most sophisticated form of critical theory in the world.

The Theory Industry

Everything becomes saleable and purchaseable. Circulation becomes the great social retort into which everything is thrown, to come out again as the money crystal. Nothing is immune from this alchemy, the bones of the saints cannot withstand it, let alone more delicate *res sacrosanctae, extra commercium hominum* [consecrated objects, beyond human commerce].

—KARL MARX[6]

6. Karl Marx, *Capital: A Critique of Political Economy*, Vol. 1, trans. Ben Fowkes (New York: Vintage Books, 1977), 229.

Just as there is a movie industry and a music industry, there is a theory industry. Intellectual production is not the result of individuals thinking on their own or entering a free marketplace of ideas. It is a consequence of the overall social relations of theoretical production and thus, under modern capitalism, an entire industry that not only creates and distributes intellectual products, but also manufactures the people who produce and consume them. This industry has evolved significantly over time. Whereas the commodification of ideas has accompanied capitalism like its shadow, there has been a veritable industrialization of knowledge production in the modern age. Although this has been a process devoid of sharp breaks, at least within the capitalist world, the imperialist phase of capitalism has brought with it a global intellectual industry whose level of development far surpasses that of the nineteenth century. In our day and age there is a tremendously powerful industry with global networks for the production, circulation, and consumption of ideas. Its apex is situated in the imperial core, led by the United States.

The leading producers for the imperial industry of ideas are part of the intellectual labor aristocracy, meaning a group of privileged thinkers in the imperial core who are elevated socially and economically above those in society at large, as well as those situated in the periphery and semi-periphery (where a comprador intellectual labor aristocracy exists that garners value from its subservience to the core's theoretical nobility). To become a member of this labor aristocracy, not unlike in other industries, you need to spend years, even decades, proving your fealty to the establishment and being tested on your ability to perform and conform. The highest echelons of this academic aristocracy are generally occupied by those who—like Samuel Huntington and Francis Fukuyama—have made the greatest contributions to the ideological agenda of those who own and control the means of intellectual production. They are the leading thinkers of the day because they are the top manufacturers of ideological products. This is how we need to understand what is often, rather naively, referred to as the star system.

The distinguished careers of Huntington and Fukuyama illustrate one of the important themes of this book and its subsequent volumes: the military-industrial-academic complex, which is an outgrowth of a more general phenomenon, the state-financial-intellectual nexus (or, in a more logical order, the financial-state-intellectual network). This expression refers to the deeply intertwined, dialectical relationship between the bourgeoisie, the bourgeois state, and the bourgeois intelligentsia. In the case under examination, it seeks to capture the extent to which the theory industry (intellectual), far from functioning as an autonomous sphere of theoretical production, is bound up with and largely conditioned and driven by, various governmental forces (state) and ultimately the capitalist ruling class (financial). Like so many other business sectors in the United States, the theory industry is connected to a model of capitalist development that is profoundly militaristic and imperialist, meaning that it is embedded within the permanent war economy. This is clear in the case of the dominant figures of the theory industry, as we will see below. However, the theory industry's radical fringe is no less linked to these imperatives, although the primary form that this takes is an intellectual war on communism, meaning a theoretical battle waged against the greatest impediment to imperialism.

This complex is perfectly illustrated by Huntington and Fukuyama's renowned careers as professors at Harvard and Stanford respectively. Huntington, to begin with, spent half a century at Harvard's Center for International Affairs, which was founded by Henry Kissinger and Robert Bowie. The former had numerous CIA ties, and the latter was a Rockefeller Foundation advisor, head of the principal strategic arm of the State Department known as the Policy Planning Staff, and deputy director of the CIA.[7] Huntington himself had ties to the CIA's Congress for Cultural Freedom (CCF) via its chief administrative officer, Warren D. Manshel, with whom he would later found *Foreign Policy*.[8] Archival documents reveal that in 1954 Huntington provided comments on at least one of Raymond Aron's CCF-incubated papers.[9] Much later, the world-famous Harvard professor was actually "'uncloaked as a CIA 'asset,' working secretly with a CIA consultant and publishing documents that were both paid for and censored by the Agency.'"[10] In the late 1970s,

---

7. See Tim B. Müller, *Krieger und Gelehrte: Herbert Marcuse und die Denksysteme im Kalten Krieg* (Hamburg: Hamburger Edition, 2011), 345.

8. See Warren D. Manshel, letter to Raymond Aron, July 22, 1954, International Association for Cultural Freedom Records, Box 80, Folder 1, Raymond Aron 1951–1954, Hanna Holborn Gray Special Collections Research Center at the University of Chicago, and "W. D. Manshel, 66; Magazine Publisher Was an Ambassador," *New York Times*, February 27, 1990.

9. See Samuel P. Huntington, "Comments on 'Nations and Ideologies' by Raymond Aron," International Association for Cultural Freedom Records, Box 80, Folder 1, Raymond Aron 1951–1954, Hanna Holborn Gray Special Collections Research Center at the University of Chicago.

10. Ami Chen Mills, *CIA Off Campus: Building the Movement against Agency Recruitment and Research* (Boston: South End Press, 1991), 32. Also see Robert Witanek, "The CIA on

his friend and colleague Zbigniew Brzezinski, who had been appointed National Security Adviser in the Carter administration, invited him to become White House Coordinator of Security Planning for the National Security Council (NSC). In addition to playing this role for the NSC, Huntington also did research for some of the most reactionary elements of the capitalist ruling class. He openly admitted, for instance, that his most famous book, *The Clash of Civilizations* (1996), "was made possible by the financial support of the John M. Olin Foundation and the Smith Richardson Foundation."[11] Both of these organizations are major funders of the American Enterprise Institute, as well as hawkish neoconservativism and the anticommunist right more generally.[12] Moreover, the Smith Richardson Foundation has a history of collaborating with the Company, including having Agency officials among its consultants and providing training to CIA and Department of Defense (DOD) officials.[13] As an intellectual subcontractor for such interests, Huntington delivered the theoretical consumer product they had paid for by advancing an antidialectical culturalist framework of analysis (the longtime enemy of Marxism). This was supposed to explain geopolitics, but its primary objective was clearly to obscure international class struggle, promote hackneyed myths regarding the West and the rest, foster cultural divisions within the global working class, and thereby aid the advance of imperialism.[14]

Fukuyama was Huntington's student, and his career reveals the same basic pattern of the financial-state-intellectual complex. He operated, like his mentor, in a network where national security agencies (state) collaborated with the capitalist ruling class (financial) on psychological warfare operations (intellectual) to advance their interests. In his case, he admitted

Campus," *CovertAction Information Bulletin*, No. 31 (Winter 1988).

11. Samuel P. Huntington, *The Clash of Civilizations and the Remaking of World Order* (New York: Simon & Schuster, 2003), 15.

12. See the profiles by the Militarist Monitor: "Smith Richardson Foundation," May 5, 2015, https://militarist-monitor.org/profile/smith_richardson_foundation/ and "John M. Olin Foundation," May 7, 2015, https://militarist-monitor.org/profile/john_m_olin_foundation/.

13. See John S. Friedman, "Public TV's C.I.A. Show," *The Nation*, Vol. 231, No. 3 (July 19–26, 1980): 73–77.

14. "In the post–Cold War world," Huntington asserted, "the most important distinctions among peoples are not ideological, political, or economic. They are cultural." Huntington, *The Clash of Civilizations*, 21. On this issue, and Huntington more specifically, see Samir Amin, "Imperialism and Culturalism Complement Each Other," *Monthly Review*, Vol. 48, No. 2 (June 1996): 1–11.

that he owed much of his academic career to Paul Wolfowitz, George W. Bush's hawkish Deputy Secretary of Defense. Fukuyama worked for him on two occasions, "first at the U.S. Arms Control and Disarmament Agency and later at the State Department."[15] Wolfowitz then recruited him to the Johns Hopkins School of Advanced International Studies when he was a dean there, and both of them worked for several years as analysts at the Rand Corporation.[16] Rand is a conservative think tank that came out of the Air Force and has ties to the CIA; it was created with bank guarantees provided by the Ford Foundation. Fukuyama's most well-known work, *The End of History and the Last Man* (1992), "would never have existed" if its author had not been invited to deliver a lecture at the John M. Olin Center for Inquiry into the Theory and Practice of Democracy at the University of Chicago.[17] James Thomson, president of RAND and former employee of the DOD and the White House, provided Fukuyama with office space during the writing of the book.[18] Unsurprisingly, this theoretical product of the financial-state-intellectual complex attempts to repurpose a reductivist version of teleology, incorrectly affiliated with Marx, to consecrate a triumphalist anticommunist narrative that makes capitalism and pseudo-democracy into the end of history.[19] The book is thoroughly idealist and, like Huntington's, its historical narrative reads like a propagandistic fairy tale forged in the halls of power. Both authors, however, are leading imperial intellectuals that occupy pole positions within the theory industry and have had a broad and profound public impact thanks to the knowledge networks of the ruling class and its managers. It is not in the least bit surprising, given that these networks include an expansive system for circulation and consumption, that their two major works were *New York Times* bestsellers (Fukuyama's also won the *Los Angeles Times* book prize).

---

15. Francis Fukuyama, *America at the Crossroads: Democracy, Power, and the Neoconservative Legacy* (New Haven: Yale University Press, 2006), ix.

16. See ibid.

17. Francis Fukuyama, *The End of History and the Last Man* (New York: Avon Books, 1992), ix.

18. Ibid.

19. "Liberal democracy," according to Fukuyama, "remains the only coherent political aspiration that spans different regions and cultures around the globe. In addition, liberal principles in economics—the 'free market'—have spread, and have succeeded in producing unprecedented levels of material prosperity, both in industrially developed countries and in countries that had been, at the close of World War II, part of the impoverished Third World." Ibid., xiii.

Although this book, like its companion volumes, provides a framework for understanding these ideologues of empire, it does not take them as its principal focal point. Instead, it concentrates on the left wing of the imperial intellectual industry by examining the work of those who have been marketed as radical theorists in various ways. Some of them are self-declared Marxists or even communists, while others present themselves as anti-capitalists inspired more directly by anarchist or libertarian socialist traditions, and still others are progressive liberals or they proffer forms of radical critique that openly refuse to be contained within any of these categories. What they all share in common is that they have been promoted internationally as the most important leftist intellectuals of the day. They are the leading luminaries of a sector of intellectual production that might best be described as the industry of compatible left critical theory.

Compatible Left Critical Theory

> There are Marxists who have become legal or armchair Marxists, who would like to see Marxism as merely another variant of philosophy and who treat it in a very eclectic fashion, as though one is free to draw from Marxism as one draws from Greek thought and its equivalent, without looking at the class base and without looking at whether an ideology is supportive of the status quo or not.
>
> —WALTER RODNEY[20]

One of the fundamental ideological objectives of the bourgeoisie in the imperialist phase of capitalism has been to isolate, discredit, and attempt to crush the communist left. This has been particularly difficult given the proven ability, on the part of the communists, to address the most serious problems facing the working and oppressed masses of the world. One of the key tactics that has been developed by the imperialist powers has been to support socialists of the non-communist sort, which has been facilitated by their social chauvinist tendencies, particularly in the imperial core.

These propensities had come clearly into view when the left split during the First World War between what Vladimir Lenin incisively diagnosed as the social chauvinists of the European labor aristocracy and

---

20. Walter Rodney, *Decolonial Marxism: Essays from the Pan-African Revolution* (London: Verso, 2022), 44–45.

those who would become known as the communists (though they were still sometimes called social democrats at the time). The former lined up and supported their national bourgeoisies in the war, whereas the latter, dedicated to anticolonial and anti-imperialist liberation, followed Lenin in embracing the slogan "No war but class war!" It is essential to recognize, then, that there are material forces that drive specific class strata toward particular ideologies, and this continues to be true, of course, in the contemporary world. There is often a powerful confluence of interests between the imperial intelligentsia and anticommunist ideology.

The intelligence agencies of the imperialist powers have done everything they can to foster splits on the left by driving a wedge between what they consider to be the compatible left of the socialists, who traffic in capitalist and imperialist accommodation, and the incompatible left of communism. This book, like the two to be published in its wake, focuses on the intellectual—and particularly the academic—front of this war on communism and, more specifically, on the endeavor to shore up a form of compatible left critical theory. Since it has not been possible to simply eliminate Marxism due to its broad public appeal, clear explanatory power, and proven ability to transform the socioeconomic order, the managers of bourgeois society have been faced with the dilemma of how best to deal with its existence. As we shall see, their preferred tactic has been to use their monopoly control over the superstructure to internationally promote a commodified version of Marxism, often referred to as Western or cultural Marxism, as well as forms of edgy theory that purport to surpass Marxism in their radicality and sophistication. If we simplify things, we might say that the implicit mantra driving the imperial theory industry has been: if you cannot beat your competitors (the actual Marxists), then flood the market with seductive but cheap knockoffs, promote them to no end, and try to bury your competitors as passé.

Intellectual Imperialism

Imperialism cannot be understood merely as an economic-military system of control and exploitation. Cultural domination is an integral dimension to any sustained system of global exploitation.

—JAMES PETRAS[21]

---

21. James Petras, "Cultural Imperialism in Late 20th Century," *Economic and Political Weekly*, Vol. 29, No. 32 (August 6, 1994): 2070.

The intellectual labor aristocracy that occupies the radical niche of the imperial theory industry is aristocratic in more ways than one. Its highest ranks are composed of a small coterie of intellectuals who are elevated above all others as worthy investments, and they receive a long series of economic and symbolic rewards for their work. To share some concrete numbers that are part of the public record, the radical liberal theorist Judith Butler received a gross salary of $341,927 in 2020 from the University of California Berkeley.[22] Invited professors like Étienne Balibar, Catherine Malabou, and Gayatri Spivak regularly received around $50,000 as visiting professors for offering mini-courses in California.[23] The Tanner Lectures at Cambridge University come with an honorarium of tens of thousands of dollars for two presentations, as well as a book deal (Butler, Wendy Brown, Bruno Latour, and James Scott have all presented Tanner Lectures).[24]

These are by no means the most lucrative deals, and it is important to remember that celebrities of the imperial intellectual apparatus usually accumulate from multiple sources at the same time.[25] Nevertheless, these numbers are very large compared to the average salaries of full-time professors in the United States ($101,810 in 2020–21), and they tower over the income of the majority of the university teaching staff.[26] Most adjunct faculty, according to a 2020 report, make under $3,500 per class and less than $50,000 a year, usually with limited to no benefits and zero job security.[27] Graduate students who work as teaching assistants earned

---

22. This information is available on websites like the following: https://ucannualwage. ucop.edu/wage/. Cost of living and rank need to be factored in, of course, when comparing this salary to the national average.

23. See websites like "Transparent California," https://transparentcalifornia.com/.

24. Scott mentions that he received $20,000 for the Tanner Lectures he presented in 2011. See the documentary film by Todd Holmes, *In a Field of His Own: The Life and Career of James C. Scott*, https://www.youtube.com/watch?v=r-IgJJW5Fkc. Years ago, I was personally involved in arranging Jacques Rancière's keynote lecture at the annual conference of the Society for Phenomenology and Existential Philosophy, for which he received $15,000.

25. It is worth recalling that the income of top university administrators far outstrips that of its highest paid faculty.

26. These numbers are from the survey table released as part of the AAUP's "2020–21 Faculty Compensation Survey Results," and they are calculated for all ranks of full-time faculty and every category of university (with the exception of unranked ones): https://www.aaup.org/2020-21-faculty-compensation-survey-results.

27. These calculations are from the American Federation of Teachers, "An Army of Temps: AFT 2020 Adjunct Faculty Quality of Work/Life Report," https://www.aft.org/

on average $38,040 in 2021.[28] These numbers only indicate income and do not account for the major differences in workload, as well as research and teaching support, not to mention many other factors like supplemental pay, research budgets, grants, benefits, retirement, etc. Moreover, they are only national comparisons, and the discrepancy between the upper echelons of the intellectual labor aristocracy and the global professoriate would also need to be taken into account. It is worth mentioning in this regard that the average monthly salary for a professor at a public institution in the United States in 2012 was $6,054, whereas in Armenia it was $538 and in Russia $617 (in U.S. purchasing power parity dollars).[29]

Furthermore, the prized theorists in the imperial core are situated at the apex of pyramidal structures of intellectual labor, with broad masses of scholars positioned beneath them, who often contribute directly to their work but rarely receive credit: university staff and office assistants, less prominent and junior colleagues, students at various levels (including former students who have become professors), editors, translators, etc. The intellectual value streams flow up, with the menial labor being performed at the bottom and the value being extracted at the top. Intellectual property law, grounded in bourgeois ideology, guarantees that the individual at the summit receives the symbolic and monetary rewards for what is often collective labor. Furthermore, these material social hierarchies allow the lords of the theory industry to develop veritable fiefdoms within the imperial academy, establishing powerful networks of sycophantic collaborators and formidable allies that can have a far-reaching impact on the job market, the conference circuit, the publishing industry, and much more.

These pyramidal frameworks are international in scope, and they are part of a global hierarchy of knowledge production. The comprador intellectual labor aristocracy in the periphery garners value from its proximity to the guaranteed values of the imperial core. As James Petras insightfully explained:

Cultural imperialism functions best through colonized intermediaries,

sites/default/files/media/2020/adjuncts_qualityworklife2020.pdf.

28. See Ryan Lane, "How Much Do Graduate Students Get Paid?," *NerdWallet*, February 23, 2023, which summarizes data from the Bureau of Labor Statistics, https://www.nerdwallet.com/article/loans/student-loans/how-much-do-graduate-students-get-paid.

29. Philip G. Altbach, et al., eds., *Paying the Professoriate: A Global Comparison of Compensation and Contracts* (New York: Routledge, 2012), 11.

cultural collaborators. The prototype imperial collaborators are the upwardly mobile third world professionals who imitate the style of their patrons. These collaborators are servile to the west and arrogant to their people.[30]

The intellectual labor aristocracy, and particularly its upper echelons, is generally empowered to vet the compradors, thereby engaging in what is ultimately a form of intellectual neocolonialism. Jennifer Ponce de León has perceptively diagnosed how this operates in the case of decolonial theory, where scholars at elite institutions in the North filter theoretical production from the Global South, celebrating work that is ultimately counter-revolutionary like their own, and casting a long shadow over those who do not conform to their ideological orientation.[31] This is equally the case for the other radical theoretical discourses promoted by the imperial academy: the intellectual patriciate is endowed with the authority to judge all of those beneath it, at least within its immediate market niche.

These veritable stars of the imperial system of knowledge production, in the case of the radical theorists who will interest us here, are also aristocratic and imperial in another sense: they have historically come from—or at least been strongly influenced by—Western Europe. As the home of the former leading imperialist powers, Western Europe still boasts a level of cultural cachet within the symbolic economy that is a consequence of having the most developed cultural apparatus historically. There is, thus, a persistence of the *ancien regime* in the cultural world: Western European bourgeois culture is still widely respected for its added value of suave sophistication in the realms of art, literature, culture, and theory.[32] These relationships have been changing, however, as the United States has continued to assert itself as the leading imperialist power and has sought to become the global center of cutting-edge bourgeois cultural

---

30. Petras, "Cultural Imperialism in Late 20th Century," 2072.

31. See Jennifer Ponce de León's presentations on this topic, which are available via the Critical Theory Workshop's video archive (https://www.youtube.com/@criticaltheoryworkshop5299), as well as her forthcoming book. Although there are limits to her overall orientation, Silvia Rivera Cusicanqui has provided an insightful critique of decolonial discourse in "*Ch'ixinakax utxiwa*: A Reflection on the Practices and Discourses of Decolonization," *The South Atlantic Quarterly*, Vol. 111, No. 1 (Winter 2012): 95–109.

32. On this topic, see Arno J. Mayer, *The Persistence of the Old Regime: Europe to the Great War* (London: Verso, 2010).

production.[33] Today, it is increasingly the principal site of radical anti-communist theoretical fabrication.

These imperial structures of knowledge production are seconded by an imperial logic of circulation and consumption. The products of the empire's theory industry are available everywhere in the world, and they are usually marketed as innovative, iconoclastic, cutting-edge, and even sexy and edgy. While it is often difficult, if not impossible, to find certain classic works in the history of Marxism, the distribution of radical theory is very much like that of other imperial products, and it is readily on offer even to those looking for something more substantial. Moreover, there is enormous pressure, at least within certain sectors of the intelligentsia and the broader world of cultural production, to consume them. The equation is simple: if one wants to be a sophisticated cultural creator conversant in cutting-edge theoretical developments, it is imperative to consume the leading work from the empire. In fact, many intellectual communities will not even take you seriously if you have not expressed your bona fides by communicating a basic familiarity with the consumer products of the imperial theory industry.

Marxism, by contrast, can be systematically ignored and dismissed as "old school." In fact, it is common to criticize it without ever seriously engaging with it, particularly as a vast international tradition including innumerable figures beyond Marx. The guiding assumption is that you do not have to because it has already been proven to be so fundamentally flawed. Walter Rodney, discussing the English tradition that has had a significant impact on regions around the world, explains this phenomenon with biting wit and insight:

> It is fashionable to glory in one's ignorance, to say that we are against Marxism. When pressed about it one responds—but why bother to read it? It is obviously absurd. So, one knows it is absurd without reading it and one doesn't read it because one knows it is absurd, and therefore one glories in one's ignorance of the position.[34]

The products of the theory industry, by contrast, are frequently objects of the most extreme forms of cultish cultural commodity fetishism. They require sycophantic worship and will not tolerate the slightest criticism

---

33. See Gabriel Rockhill, *Radical History & the Politics of Art* (New York: Columbia University Press, 2014), 191–217.
34. Rodney, *Decolonial Marxism*, 35.

(unless, perhaps, it is only a minor amendment by an acolyte, or a critique formulated in favor of another imperial intellectual product). Moreover, the theory industry abides by a temporal logic similar to other culture industries, where tried and true values anchor consumerist traditions while an endless stream of new products vie for that status in the future. This means that scholars who want to or need to play the game are forced to stay up on the latest fads of imperial intellectual fabrication, otherwise they come off as backward and unsophisticated. In many cases, they have little to no time for any serious materialist scholarship because they are so busy studying the latest chameleonic permutations of the dominant ideology.

These international material networks of knowledge production, circulation, and consumption have a particularly pernicious effect on the intelligentsia of the Global South. Since the imperial core, due to the history of the capitalist underdevelopment of the rest of the planet, has the most developed intellectual apparatus, with the greatest symbolic and monetary value attached to it, many intellectuals from around the world are drawn to study, work, and publish in the capitalist core. Those who are more progressively oriented and in search of radical ideas that might help address the effects of imperialism in their home countries are led to drink from the poisoned well of the imperial theory industry.[35] If they return to their countries of origin, or share their intellectual work with them from abroad, instead of being able to deliver the weapon of revolutionary theory as the antidote to imperialism, they have nothing but this poison to spread, though they often believe it to be a novel form of social medicine that surpasses the supposed toxin of Marxism. Unfortunately, since the countries most brutalized by imperialism have generally seen their working-class movements crushed and leftist culture decimated, these imperially trained intellectuals, with their prestigious credentials, sometimes have an easy job selling their nostrums as if it were a proven cure (thereby bolstering the sense of success of the snake oil salespeople).

Finally, if the intellectuals who are the stars of the radical theory industry are revolutionary thinkers, as they are often presented, we need to ask a simple question: would an empire really promote its enemies to such an extent, showering them with lucrative awards and fame? Is that what it did, for instance, with major Marxist intellectuals like Michael Parenti,

---

35. I would like to express my gratitude to Ali Kadri for encouraging me to integrate this aspect into my analysis, and more generally for having read an earlier draft of this manuscript and provided insightful feedback.

George Jackson, or Walter Rodney? Parenti, arguably one of the greatest political analysts in the contemporary United States, was never able to secure a tenured faculty position, and the other two were killed in assassinations linked to state forces. In situating the radical theorists promoted by empire within the social totality, we also have to ask another basic question: do they have any material interest in overthrowing a system that promotes them as the greatest intellectuals of the day and provides them with ample financial and symbolic rewards, ensuring that they will go down in bourgeois history as philosophical grandees? Even for those who know nothing about their work, examining the social relations of intellectual production should make at least one thing obvious: these theorists are not at all considered to be a real threat by the capitalist ruling class. The opposite is the case.

Dialectical Analysis of Theoretical Production

A dialectical analysis of the social totality always situates the subjective theoretical practices of intellectuals within the objective world of international class struggle. It does not accept the arbitrary dividing line that many desperately try to erect between intellectual production and the extant socioeconomic reality, as if someone's thought could—and should—be separated from their life, as well as from the material system of theoretical production, circulation, and reception. Such a non-dialectical assumption is little more than a symptom of an idealist approach to theoretical work, which presumes that there is a spiritual and conceptual realm that functions independently of material reality and the political economy of knowledge.

This presupposition perpetuates intellectual commodity fetishism, in the sense of the idolization of the sacred products of the theory industry, and it fosters the development of cults of personality around their producers, both of which inhibit the ability to situate theoretical production within the overall social relations of production and class struggle. This assumption also serves the interests of those who have bought into, or aspire to be part of, a particular franchise within the imperial theory industry—whether it be Frankfurt School critical theory, French Theory, contemporary U.S. critical theory, or any other—because it protects the brand image of the franchise itself (which remains unsullied by the actual social relations of production). Whereas intellectual commodity fetishism is a principal feature of consumption within the theory industry, brand image management is the hallmark of production.

The satraps of the franchise defend it with the ferocity of intellectual guard dogs.

For a dialectical analysis, it is important to acknowledge that the intellectuals under scrutiny here have indeed mobilized their subjective agency in various ways. Far from simply being pawns on empire's chessboard, they have even, in certain instances, formulated critiques of capitalism, neoliberalism, consumer society, postmodernism, and the culture industry. Some of them have also taken public political positions that are worthy of support, such as opposition to the U.S. imperialist war in Vietnam, certain NATO interventions, or Israel's settler colonial war. They do not all share the exact same political orientations, and there is even a relatively broad spectrum within the radical theory industry, stretching from self-declared Maoists like Alain Badiou or other versions of Western Marxism to the more or less liberal neo-Habermasians. Moreover, they have all evolved over time, and it is rare for them to maintain a single position throughout their lives. Sometimes, their stances waver even within a single text. Slavoj Žižek, for instance, has jumped, within the same paragraph, from ultra-leftist posturing to an open embrace of fascism.

Dialectical hermeneutics does not, however, reduce interpretation to simply bearing witness to the infinite complexity of the object of interpretation. As a method of materialist analysis, it seeks to account for all of these intricacies while also synthetically conceptualizing them at a higher level, moving from sense-perception and brute empirical description to understanding, which itself is part of an ongoing process of reasoned reflection and nuanced refinement. In the case of the compatible critical theorists, all of their petty disagreements and minor differences, which can be traced out empirically, could easily distract us from where they stand on the most fundamental questions of international class struggle. A dialectical approach to hermeneutics thereby allows us to shed light on all of the complex differences operative at an empirical level, while also synthetically grasping the fundamental ideological orientation of particular theoretical practices and situating them in relationship to the overall social relations of production.

Before turning to an examination of this orientation, it is important to note that the approach taken here is not purely negative or critical but does recognize some positive contributions. Given their conditions of intellectual production—which are, quite simply, the best in the world— it would be surprising if this crème de la crème of the intellectual labor aristocracy was not capable of making contributions that could, in some way, be of use. It is worth noting that many of the most important insights advanced by the compatible left theorists result from materialist analysis or have been borrowed from the Marxist tradition. To take a few examples, Adorno has provided insightful accounts of the impact of recording technologies and industrial commercialization on musical production. Bourdieu's conceptualization of practical sense and the habitus could be drawn on to advance a more developed account of the practically oriented, dispositional, and embodied aspects of ideology. Badiou has intervened in the French political scene with incisive and important critiques of the establishment. Other examples could surely be pointed to from the thinkers in question, and there has been ample scholarship praising their contributions. Dialectical hermeneutics accounts for this and the other differences mentioned above, and much of my earlier research has analyzed some of their work in minute detail. However, this is not the principal goal of this book and its accompanying tomes, which are instead focused on engaging in a dialectical ideology critique that examines how their subjective output has largely been conditioned and shaped by the objective forces of the imperial intellectual apparatus that has promoted them, and to which they have made significant contributions.

There is always, of course, a play of forces between objective elements and subjective agency. The simple fact that someone works for a corporation or receives a grant from a foundation does not mean that they are a complete sellout who needs to be publicly tarred and feathered. Everyone has to survive and find means to do so, if they can, which often leads to inevitable compromises, at least within the capitalist world. This is particularly the case with intellectual labor, which requires substantial material support. The argument advanced here, then, is not a reductive form of guilt by association, where anyone who received a Ford grant, collaborated with a compromised intellectual, or published in a journal secretly backed by the CIA is a spirited contributor to a global anticommunist conspiracy. There have been many different levels and degrees of collaboration, and it is important to distinguish between them. A direct CIA collaborator and Agency apologist like Gloria Steinem did not play the same historical role as an anticommunist intellectual like Hannah Arendt. The latter did not work directly for an intelligence agency, but she operated in, and profited handsomely from, the CCF networks, colluded with the IRD and the British Foreign Office for at least one of her publications, received perks from the capitalist ruling class, and was a stalwart anticommunist in her later work (which went hand in hand with her abominable positions on racial segregation and slavery).[36]

While registering these differences, one of the primary objectives of this study is to bring into relief a remarkably consistent pattern: the leading, purportedly leftist luminaries, who are perched at the top of the intellectual labor aristocracy, tend to agree with the most fundamental aspects of the dominant ideology. In many cases, they have a history of collaborating, to various degrees, with the powerbrokers that promote this ideology, if it be the capitalist class or bourgeois state managers. However, there is, more generally, a confluence of interests between the intellectual system's overseers and those who successfully work within it, which means that direct ties are often not even necessary between these elements. Intellectuals who want to advance within the imperial academic world are trained to give to it what it wants because a powerful system of rewards and punishments induces them to do so.

ABS Theory: Imperial Uplift and Opportunism

The failure of *all* socialist and communist experiences in the last century had as its consequence that we have not [*sic*] today a great and clear idea of another world.

—ALAIN BADIOU[37]

Like many other bourgeois cultural products, radical theory has, at times, formulated significant criticisms of capitalism. If we situate these within the objective social world, it makes perfect sense to ask a simple and practical question that is rarely raised in academic circles: if capitalism is recognized as having negative effects, what is to be done about it? The deeper one drills down into the lives and work of the radical theorists, sifting through the deliberate obscurantism that characterizes some of their discourses, the more obvious their response becomes, and the easier it is to

---

36. See the discussion of Arendt in Frances Stonor Saunders, *The Cultural Cold War* (New York: New Pres, 2000). Regarding her views on racial segregation and slavery, consult Hannah Arendt, "Reflections on Little Rock," *Dissent* (Winter 1959): 45–56 and Hannah Arendt, *On Revolution* (London: Penguin Books, 1990), as well as the German edition of this book, whose discrepancies are revealing: *Über die Revolution* (Munich: Piper Verlag GmbH, 1965).
37. Alain Badiou, interview on HARDtalk, BBC, March 24, 2009, available in two parts online: https://www.youtube.com/watch?v=NPCCNmE7b9g and https://www.youtube.com/watch?v=OpH5GTTIZ3k (my emphasis).

understand their primary social function. Although they often gesture toward a world beyond capitalism, they all regularly affirm that *there is no real alternative* in the sense of a concrete project of collectively constructing a socialist world through anti-imperialist state-building projects. In this regard, they tend to condemn actually existing socialism, usually in the most categorical terms and without the least sense of having to seriously research it in order to cultivate an informed opinion. They regularly genuflect, in this way, to anticommunist dogma in totalizing, universal judgments based on what they present as absolute, objective truths. In extreme cases, those on the left fringe occasionally identify lost opportunities or golden moments, but even these are explainable exceptions that confirm the rule (the French Maoism of the intelligentsia is a good example insofar as it has tended to fetishize the Chinese Cultural Revolution as a battle within and, crucially, *against* the revolution). In any case, these theorists' criticisms of the capitalist world generally pale in comparison to their uncompromising condemnation of all—or nearly all—socialist projects in the real world. Their brand of radical theory ultimately leads, implicitly or explicitly, to a politics of capitalist accommodation since socialism is judged to be far worse than the extant capitalist order. They therefore proffer what we might refer to as ABS Theory: Anything But Socialism.

The theorists examined in this book and its companion volumes have exercised their agency in dedicating themselves to specific political and ideological struggles. Many of them have worked explicitly within the anticommunist tradition of Friedrich Nietzsche and Martin Heidegger in order to combat Marxism, and a few have directly participated in anticommunist subversion operations, including Derrida, Foucault, and Žižek. Some, including many members of the Frankfurt School, worked directly for the U.S. national security state or for soft power psychological warfare projects funded by the ruling class (such as Marcuse). Others have primarily participated in the ideological and cultural efforts to discredit communism, with the support of the capitalist class and within the Agency's knowledge networks, as is clearly visible in the work of Adorno and Horkheimer. Still others, like those drawn together around Badiou's supposedly new idea of communism (which is, in fact, a very old idea that Engels aptly described, nearly 150 years ago, as utopian socialism), have presented themselves as communists, or even the only real communists, by advocating for a mysterious third way beyond both capitalism and real-world socialism.[38] Although they are critical of the former, they condemn the latter in the most resolute terms. They have positioned themselves on an idealist stairway to heaven in an attempt to convince their readership that a magical path transcends the terrestrial class struggle between imperialism and actually existing socialism. Even if they are devoid of direct ties to the overt or covert machinations of the ruling class and its state managers, they nonetheless do the type of ideological work that their institutions support.

A significant portion of this projected trilogy elucidates the objective social forces that have encouraged and fostered these kinds of activities. However, it is absolutely essential to recognize and account for the agency of those involved, and much of what follows will be dedicated to tracking this in great detail. After all, the intellectuals who succeed and advance within the imperial theory industry have sometimes worked very hard in order to do so. Far from acting as simple automatons, they have met the system halfway, a third of the way, or some other ratio. In doing so, they have received uplift in return, meaning opportunities to advance within the academic establishment and ultimately occupy a position in the pantheon of bourgeois history. Given the extensive development of the theory industry and its imperial dominion, the uplift it provides far surpasses simple career preferments. It literally makes individual theorists into global superstars perched at the very top of the intellectual labor aristocracy, which is an extremely lucrative position accompanied by an awesome power of cultural influence, at least within the academic world, but often more broadly. One of the principal forms of agency that these thinkers have mobilized is therefore opportunism.

It is not the least bit surprising, in this regard, that these intellectuals have been so widely supported and promoted within the capitalist world. To shore up the compatible, non-communist left over and against the threat of actually existing socialism, what better tactic than to champion scholars like these as some of the most important, and even most radical, thinkers of the contemporary world? Critical theory, as well as Marxism, can thereby be redefined as a kind of anticommunist radical theory that is not directly connected to class struggle from below. Instead, it freely

---

38. I am thinking in particular of some of the most famous theorists who participated in this series of books: Costas Douzinas and Slavoj Žižek, eds., *The Idea of Communism* (London: Verso, 2010); Slavoj Žižek, ed., *The Idea of Communism 2: The New York Conference* (London: Verso, 2013); Alex Taek-Gwang Lee and Slavoj Žižek, eds., *The Idea of Communism 3: The Seoul Conference* (London: Verso, 2016).

criticizes all forms of domination, including so-called authoritarian socialism, and it thereby ultimately sides with capitalist control societies over and against what figures like Adorno and Horkheimer described as the fascist horrors of powerful socialist states.

In this regard, the compatible left theorists promoted by the imperial theory industry have played the role of radical recuperators in both senses of this expression: they occupy the left, radical fringe of capitalist recuperation, and they help recuperate potentially real radicals who are seeking system change. What they have on offer—and this is one of the reasons why they have been so widely marketed—are discourses whose revolutionary symbology belies their counter-revolutionary substance. Under the guise of radicality, they ultimately work to recuperate potentially insurgent forces within the extant system by denying the existence of a real, concrete alternative. Their purported radicality can take different forms. Some openly identify with the radically reactionary philosophies of Nietzsche and Heidegger, while others are insurgent anarchists or openly engage in communist cosplay. Still others are simply progressive liberals or social democrats who think they are radicals due, in large part, to how far right the political spectrum is within the imperial core. Many of them combine elements from these orientations or shift back and forth between them based on the needs of the moment.

What these extremes demonstrate is the instability of petty-bourgeois ideology, which can quickly jump from one position to another. The petty bourgeoisie finds itself sandwiched between the bourgeois politics of capitalism and the proletarian politics of socialism, often dreaming of an enchanting but nonexistent third way beyond this pitched class struggle. Fearful of proletarianization, but attracted to a bourgeois lifestyle, the petty bourgeoisie is sometimes resentful of its corporate overlords and capable of celebrating jacqueries, while nonetheless lacking a concrete, long-term collective political project of its own.[39] Its members generally content themselves with promoting greater access to power for their social group while explicitly or implicitly rejecting system change because they do not want to undermine their privileged social standing (this is particularly the case for the imperial petty bourgeoisie). It is for this reason that they generally guide their followers toward symbolic, culturalist, or discursive solutions that ultimately maintain the status quo of extant material reality. It is here that we see that their ABS Theory and

---

39. On this issue, see Nicos Poulantzas, *Classes in Contemporary Capitalism*, trans. David Fernbach (London: Verso, 1979), 287–99.

their practical support for Anything But Socialism in the real world is ultimately ABS Theory: it is a BS theory aimed at preserving their class standing in the imperialist world.

Theoretical Practices: For Use-Value or Exchange-Value?

> The frivolous way in which some intellectuals who call themselves leftists (and who, nonetheless, don't seem to give a damn about the masses) rush forth shamelessly to repeat word for word the same critiques of the socialist world proposed and promulgated by capitalism only demonstrates that they have not broken with capitalism as radically as they might perhaps think.
>
> —ROBERTO FERNÁNDEZ RETAMAR[40]

The industry of compatible left theory maintains a specific logic of production, circulation, and consumption. If one concretely abstracts to the highest possible level, then it becomes clear that production is assumed to be driven by individual producers and is ultimately grounded in the liberal ideology of the free subject as the source of meaningful theoretical creation. In the most extreme cases, the producer is elevated to the status of a genius who transcends his or her historical context. The products of these individuals are, as cult objects subjected to collective worship, isolated from the overall social relations of production through a process of intellectual commodity fetishism. The connection between these products and their producer is diligently maintained through the legal and social framework of bourgeois intellectual property, which binds them together under the same trademark. Each brand, with all its various products, is circulated in the marketplace of ideas, where it competes with the other marques. Intellectual consumerism is thereby mediated, among other things, by brand identification and established canons of guaranteed values.

Within this overall framework, the dominant form of theoretical practice is based on exchange-value. The objective is to develop marketable theoretical products and, ideally, a unique brand that allows one to outshine one's rivals. This, at least, is what occurs at the pinnacle of the intellectual labor pyramid mentioned above. Most intellectuals, however, work at much lower levels, and they contribute to brand values, and profit

---

40. Roberto Fernández Retamar, *Caliban and Other Essays*, trans. Edward Baker (Minneapolis: University of Minnesota Press, 1994), 42.

from them, as members of a particular franchise or in other ways. If we only focus on those in the highest echelons of the radical theory industry, they are compelled to develop their own brand of thinking, replete with an idiosyncratic conceptual vocabulary, a unique theoretical framework, and their own referential basis among established trademarks. Their system of thinking has to be singular in order to differentiate itself from other marques, even if they can join forces on certain fronts for mutual brand enhancement. Another essential aspect of this exchange-value-driven theoretical practice is discursive proliferation and an undying devotion to the cult of the new. It is imperative to "get one's name out there" by constantly sharing new and innovative work, or simply hot takes and blurbs.

There is a specific symbolic economy operative in the forms of intellectual production analyzed in this book and the rest of the trilogy. A premium is placed on sophistication and what is presented as a higher order of thought that supposedly surpasses the ability of most people to even understand it. This is readily visible in the obscurantist language and convoluted phraseology of the authors who, very much like the clergy, implicitly communicate that only the initiated can fully understand their mysterious message. Clarity and science based on collective communication and the use-value of ideas are generally scoffed at as beneath the high priests of theory. They adorn their discourses with endless references to the bourgeois canon, constructing complicated intertexts that can only be parsed by advanced scholars (and even that is uncertain). They also openly indulge in a cult of complexification where nothing is quite as it appears, and many of them have an unbridled passion for paradoxes. Although there are some at least partial exceptions to these tendencies, they generally avoid mobilizing dialectics to overcome contradictions, preferring instead to freeze dialectics at a standstill and regress to a pre-dialectical world of reified oppositions and metaphysical abstractions.[41] They sometimes do indulge, however, in the doggerel dialectics of endless rhetorical inversions—"And what if it was precisely the opposite?!"— which attempts to reduce dialectics to a sophistic device and a pseudo-intellectual show of sophomoric sophistication. Overall, this idealism for the initiated implicitly communicates the class standing of those who proffer it: they are members of the intellectual labor aristocracy and, more specifically, the high priests of the imperial theory industry.

---

41. On this issue, see Néstor Kohan's excellent article, "Fetichismo y hegemonía desde la teoría marxista," in *Sujeto y conflicto en la teoría política*, ed. Atilio A. Boron (Buenos Aires: Ediciones Luxemburg, 2011), 13–42.

This idealism often goes hand in hand with subjectivism. The dominant theoretical practice within the theory industry is not oriented toward scientifically elucidating the objective world. It focuses instead on the subjective construction of personal conceptual systems and individual philosophies (hence the proliferation of references to such things as "a Deleuzian perspective," "Badiou's vocabulary," "Adorno's way of thinking," etc.). Although there are many different variations and degrees of subjectivism, these discourses do not principally take their bearings from material reality, but rather from the bourgeois cultural canon and the marketplace of ideas. The value of one's philosophy, in this regard, does not depend, first and foremost, on its ability to adequately describe and potentially transform the world, but rather on its capacity to construct a singular system of ideas that resonates with the bourgeois canon, meaningfully contributes to its ongoing historical elaboration, and carves out a market niche as a unique theoretical contribution. The latter is sometimes celebrated for providing a new perspective or a novel way of thinking and speaking. However, the subjectivism of this theoretical practice—meaning the fact that it is developed, at a practical level, by subjects invested in their own individual projects rather than the collective elucidation of objective reality—reveals how profoundly undialectical it is. The world of subjective theoretical practice is primary, and it is severed from, and operates separately from, the objective world. The latter is either treated as secondary or ignored as non-existent (such as in cases where the factual world is replaced by endless fictions). These subjectivist discourses are thus grounded in exchange-value within the universe of bourgeois culture rather than use-value for class struggle within the broader, material world. They are, of necessity, doomed to scientific failure. Intellectual practices developed in the subjectivist bubble of bourgeois culture will inevitably be less capable of grasping the objective world than those practices undertaken by subjects dialectically engaged with the objective world, who are dedicated to collectively understanding and changing it. This is yet another reason why subjectivist discourses have recourse to obscurantism, namely, to create the illusion that their word webs magically reveal something special about the world when, in fact, they are largely disconnected from it.

The obscurantism of these theorists, which comes in many forms, is not accidental. They are quite literally in the business of turning the world upside down by saying X equals non-X, so it makes perfect sense that they would be professionals in confusion. Socialism in practice, for them, is—with almost no exception—equivalent to slavery, not liberation. There is not a real-world alternative to capitalism, despite the fact that as much as one-third of the global population has lived under socialist governments. What drives the world is not the material forces of class struggle but the realm of ideas and culture. These are but a few examples of the ideological inversions that characterize the work of many of these thinkers. In methodological terms, they also suffer—to varying degrees, and in a manner that would need to be spelled out in each case—from what György Lukács described as irrationalism:

> Irrationalism is merely a form of reaction (reaction in the double sense of the secondary and the retrograde) to the dialectical development of human thought. Its history therefore hinges on that development of science and philosophy, and it reacts to the new questions they pose by designating the mere problem as an answer and declaring the allegedly fundamental insolubility of the problem to be a higher form of comprehension. This styling of the declared insolubility as an answer, along with the claim that this evasion and side-stepping of the answer, this flight from it, contains a positive solution and "true" achievement of reality is irrationalism's decisive hallmark.[42]

John Bellamy Foster has incisively drawn on Lukács's foundational critique in order to diagnose the persistent forms of irrationalism operative in the era of late imperialism. This includes the work of those directly inspired by the reactionary German traditions of thought studied by Lukács, namely "post-Marxists, postmodernists, and posthumanists from Derrida to Deleuze to Latour."[43]

Instead of reifying the opposition between thinking and being like the irrationalists, a dialectical approach recognizes that "objective reality

---

42. György Lukács, *The Destruction of Reason*, trans. Peter Palmer (London: Verso, 2021), 104. Although Lukács did not engage with the Frankfurt School in any detail in this book from 1954, his 1962 preface to *The Theory of the Novel* famously claimed that "a considerable part of the leading German intelligentsia, including Adorno, have taken up residence in the 'Grand Hotel Abyss' which I described [in *The Destruction of Reason*] in connection with my critique of Schopenhauer as 'a beautiful hotel, equipped with every comfort, on the edge of an abyss, of nothingness, of absurdity. And the daily contemplation of the abyss between excellent meals or artistic entertainments, can only heighten the enjoyment of the subtle comforts offered." György Lukács, *The Theory of the Novel: A Historico-Philosophical Essay on the Forms of Great Epic Literature*, trans. Anna Bostock (Cambridge, MA: MIT Press, 1971), 22.
43. John Bellamy Foster, "The New Irrationalism," *Monthly Review*, Vol. 74, No. 9 (February 2023), https://monthlyreview.org/2023/02/01/the-new-irrationalism/.

is fundamentally richer, more diverse and more intricate than the best developed concepts of our thinking can ever be," while at the same time it strives to improve our apprehension of the real through an ongoing process of scientific elucidation.[44] Moreover, unlike the forms of market-driven brand thinking based on exchange-value, dialectical and historical materialism (DHM) as a theoretical practice is grounded in use-value. It puts intellectual labor in the service of developing the best possible understanding of the world and optimal strategies for practically transforming it. This undertaking, even when constrained by the confines of a bourgeois world, is necessarily collective, and it is recognized as such. Instead of cultivating or supporting an idiosyncratic brand in order to market oneself, intellectuals in this scientific tradition strive to contribute to a common project that requires clear communication, collaboration, and the collective testing of hypotheses. In other words, they are invested in science. This should not be understood in terms of the bogeyman constructed by radical theorists where science is ignorantly equated with positivism or some naïve and unmediated belief in being able to apprehend pure objective reality once and for all. Science qua *Wissenschaft* is an ongoing process of collective elucidation of the world. One of the strengths of the materialist approach is precisely that it dialectically situates subjects within a broader objective world and understands full well that the former cannot completely and absolutely grasp the latter. "A system of natural and historical knowledge, embracing everything, and final for all time," Engels insisted, "is a contradiction to the fundamental laws of dialectic reasoning."[45]

These theoretical practices, one based primarily on exchange-value and the other principally on use-value, are largely incompatible. One is a product of the intellectual sector of the bourgeois superstructure. The other endeavors to develop a scientific apprehension of reality in order to transform it. In any other domain, most people would recognize that it does not make sense to combine ideology with science, or to confuse brand thinking with useful inquiry. However, intellectual eclecticism within the bourgeois canon is one of the hallmarks of the theoretical practices of the radical theory industry. Thinkers in this orbit have gone to great lengths to combine, at will, various traditions in order to enhance the cachet of their conceptual products with a veritable potpourri of cultural

---

44. Lukács, *The Destruction of Reason*, 99.

45. Karl Marx and Friedrich Engels, *Collected Works*, Vol. 25, *Anti-Dühring and Dialectics of Nature* (New York: International Publishers, 1987), 25.

references, symbols taking clear precedence over substance. Marx and some elements of the Marxist tradition have even been subjected to such treatment, in an endeavor to turn them into fodder like any other within the bourgeois canon. DHM should not, however, be reduced to a decoration for bourgeois discourses, thereby serving to enhance pseudo-science. Class struggle also exists in theory and, although the two positions outlined know many shades of gray, we should be able to clearly identify who is dedicated first and foremost to collectively elucidating and transforming the world, and who is not.

Actually Existing Ignorance (Regarding Socialism)

The important tradition of socialism is to be fundamentally called into question, since everything that this socialist tradition has produced in history is to be condemned.

—MICHEL FOUCAULT[46]

Since benighted anticommunism has been so widely promoted within capitalist culture, and the imperial theory industry more specifically, major swaths of the population have been inculcated with the knee-jerk response of uninformed calumny, rather than rigorous analysis, when it comes to actually existing socialism. This ignorance has been industrially produced through the imperial superstructure, and it is an excellent example of its awesome power of ideological indoctrination. The intelligence services of the imperialist powers have played a central role in developing and disseminating anticommunist scholarship in the academy, as well as throughout the media. Indeed, an incredible number of leading experts on communism within the imperial core have been revealed to have been working for the disinformation services of imperialist states. As a matter of fact, the premier institutions for studying the Soviet Union in the United States, as we will see, were established by the CIA, with funding from the capitalist ruling class. It would thus be unwise to take the work of these imperial institutions and ideologues—which dominates the market—as objective scholarship devoid of an ideological agenda.

Unfortunately, this is precisely what the compatible critical theorists have done. They have generally accepted imperialist propaganda regarding socialism as if it was scientifically accurate, while deriding communist

---

46. Michel Foucault, *Dits et écrits*, Vol. 3, *1976–1979* (Paris: Éditions Gallimard, 1994), 398.

scholarship as thoroughly ideological. Some of them have even gone so far as to maintain that this disinformation is undeniably and absolutely true, while regularly calling into question the very idea of being able to establish historical truths in other areas. Foucault, for instance, was famous for celebrating the Nietzschean view that everything is fiction, but he stalwartly dug in his heels regarding the historical truth inherent in the claims of anticommunist dissidents resolutely supported by the imperial powers. The so-called "specificity of the question of the gulag" needed to be recognized as an absolute historical fact characteristic of "every socialist society," which therefore needed to be condemned à la André Glucksmann.[47] This supposed verity, which Foucault did not even attempt to prove, could not be contextualized, mediated, or explained away in any manner, but instead needed to be recognized as a universal reality that stood as a total factual refutation of Marxism (a position he shared with Glucksmann, his fellow anticommunist regime-change activist).[48]

Many Marxists saw through the promotion of dissident propaganda at the time, which demonstrates the superior practical applications of their theoretical framework. Now, however, it has been clearly demonstrated that the anticommunist disinformation accepted—and produced—by the compatible radical theorists has largely been manufactured and financially backed by imperialist states and the capitalist ruling class. In other words, it is part of the historical record that they were simply wrong and, perhaps even more important, that they were the ideological dupes of the capitalist spin doctors. What kind of critical theory are they doing if they are not even capable of being critical of the most fundamental aspects of imperialist propaganda? How could they possibly be trusted to elucidate the relationship between knowledge and power if they have been incapable of knowing how the power dynamics that have conditioned their own purported knowledge claims function?

Moreover, since the imperial theorists who were alive at the time almost all celebrated the destruction of the Warsaw Pact countries, which many of them heralded as a liberation from slavery, we also now have a very clear understanding of what post-socialism looks like. Far from being a utopia of democratic freedom that the leftist intelligentsia should celebrate, it has been a fiesta for the ruling class, which unleashed a horrific

---

47. Ibid., 420.

48. See ibid., 420–21. Also see Gabriel Rockhill, "Foucault: The Faux Radical," *Los Angeles Review of Books*, "The Philosophical Salon," October 12, 2020, https://thephilosophicalsalon.com/foucault-the-faux-radical/.

juggernaut of destruction on the overwhelming majority of the popula-tion.[49] If we judge theories by their use-value for apprehending reality and thereby allowing us to gain traction over it, the theories of the compat-ible left intelligentsia did not grasp the true nature of socialism or post-socialism. Therefore, they are of a distinctly inferior value. Rather than providing us with a correct understanding of actually existing socialism, with all of its complexities and contradictions, they have proffered actu-ally existing ignorance regarding socialism, care of the imperialist ruling class that funded the propaganda they peddle.

For the purposes of the argument that follows, readers do not have to have strong convictions regarding the value of real socialism. They only need to be willing to question the dominant dogma and remain open to the idea that socialism in reality has not been an unmitigated disaster, but that it has, instead, at a minimum, had some positive effects in particular cases. The value of socialism, for those who would doubt it, should not be considered in absolute and non-dialectical terms, but rather relationally: compared to the horrors of actually existing capitalism, with its bound-less waste of human life and nature. Isn't socialism preferable for the over-whelming majority of people and the planet? According to David Michael Smith's calculations, the expansion of capitalism in North America and the imperial endeavors of the United States have led to the death of some 300 million people in an unending U.S.-American Holocaust.[50] This, of course, is only one of the leading capitalist countries. Taking the others into account and analyzing how they function as a metabolic system, it would be very difficult not to concur with one of Ali Kadri's major contri-butions: capitalism is an international regime of waste that systematically destroys human life and nature for the profit of a very small coterie of people.

In approaching socialism dialectically, situating it in relationship to capitalism, it is important to look at the historical facts. In a major study

---

49. See, for instance, David Kotz and Fred Weir, *Revolution From Above: The Demise of the Soviet System* (New York: Routledge, 1998), 161–99; Michael Parenti, *Blackshirts and Reds: Rational Fascism and the Overthrow of Communism* (San Francisco: City Lights Publishers, 1997), 87–120; Ludo Martens, *L'URSS et la contre-révolution de velours* (Brussels: Éditions EPO, 1991). Although the overall framing is skewed, Adam Curtis's seven-part 2022 BBC documentary television series, *Russia 1985–1999: TraumaZone*, provides an intimate portrait of some of the destruction unleashed by the capitalist counter-revolution.

50. David Michael Smith, *Endless Holocausts: Mass Death in the History of the United States Empire* (New York: Monthly Review Press, 2023), 15.

based on what is likely the most comprehensive body of data (which is from the World Bank and could not be suspected of communist sympathies), Shirley Cereseto and Howard Waitzkin found that socialism has far outperformed capitalism. They used the Physical Quality of Life Index (PQLI), a composite indicator calculated from life expectancy, infant mortality, and literacy rates. The PQLI is used extensively in cross-national research because it provides a useful X-ray of a country's infrastructure and social services, as well as a general sense of what it is like to live there. Cereseto and Waitzkin also distinguished between different levels of economic development so that the comparisons were coherent. What they found is that "at the same level of economic development, the socialist countries showed more favorable outcomes than the capitalist countries in nearly all the PQL variables. The more favorable performance of the socialist countries was evident in 22 of 24 comparisons."[51] In some cases, socialist countries outperformed capitalist ones by two or three times. Importantly, given how socialism has been a struggle against imperialist underdevelopment: "Differences between capitalist and socialist countries in PQL were greatest at lower levels of economic development."[52]

It is imperative to note, moreover, that socialism has played a leading role in lifting up the most exploited and oppressed of the global working class: women and national minorities or racialized groups.[53] The socialist struggle has always been pitted, as Domenico Losurdo has powerfully argued, against exploitation as well as oppression, and communists have

---

51. Shirley Cereseto and Howard Waitzkin, "Capitalism, Socialism, and the Physical Quality of Life," *International Journal of Health Services*, Vol. 16, No. 4 (1986): 648.

52. Ibid. Also see Vicente Navarro, "Has Socialism Failed? An Analysis of Health Indicators under Capitalism and Socialism," *Science & Society*, Vol. 57, No. 1 (Spring 1993): 6–30.

53. A large body of literature could be cited to support this claim, from Marx and Engels' writings on colonialism and the family to the work of Lenin, Zetkin, Mao, and so many others on the national and woman questions, as well as many historical accounts of the practical struggles to lift up the most oppressed and exploited members of the global working class. In the interests of space, I will simply cite a few representative works: Walter Rodney, *The Russian Revolution: A View from the Third World*, ed. Robin D. G. Kelley and Jesse Benjamin (London: Verso, 2018); Robin D. G. Kelley, *Hammer and Hoe: Alabama Communists during the Great Depression* (Chapel Hill: University of North Carolina Press, 2015); Clara Zetkin, *Clara Zetkin: Selected Writings*, ed. Philip S. Foner (Haymarket Books, 2015); Angela Y, Davis, *Women, Race & Class* (New York: Vintage Books, 1983); Vijay Prashad, *Red Star Over the Third World* (London: Pluto Press, 2019); Fidel Castro and Vilma Espín, *Women and the Cuban Revolution: Speeches and Documents by Fidel Castro, Vilma Espín, and Others* (New York: Pathfinder Press, 1981).

been at the vanguard of the fight to truly universalize the hypocritical liberal claim that *all* human beings are free and equal.[54] The best elements of the dialectical and historical materialist tradition, from Marx and Engels to Lenin and beyond, have conceived of and acted on socialism as an anticolonial and feminist struggle for universal human liberation. They have also been dedicated to overcoming the metabolic rift introduced by capitalism between human beings and nature.[55] Imperialist identity politics, and the theory industry more generally, have disingenuously misrepresented these histories, but they have been well documented for anyone interested in informing themselves. Such work is anathema to the dominant ideology, however, and for good reason: it scientifically examines the evidence, rather than relying on hoary tropes and uninformed ideological reflexes. It is grounded in the type of historical and materialist research, moreover, that has largely been overshadowed by the speculative forms of critical theory promoted by the imperial theory industry.

This study is based on the recognition that socialism in the real world, not just in the thoughtscape of intellectuals, is of some value. This does not imply that it is perfect or has solved all problems. It also does not mean that there is one monolithic bloc of actually existing socialism that needs to be accepted or rejected *in toto*, as if there were not ongoing struggles between and within various socialist state-building projects. This overall history has not been easy, and there have been many setbacks, contradictions, and complications. It should always be remembered, moreover, that these histories have not unfolded smoothly due to the persistence of racist, misogynist, and homophobic ideologies driven by capitalism

---

54. See, in particular, Domenico Losurdo, *Class Struggle: A Political and Philosophical History*, trans. Gregory Elliott (New York: Palgrave Macmillan, 2016).

55. See John Bellamy Foster's groundbreaking work on this topic, including books such as John Bellamy Foster, *The Dialectics of Ecology* (New York: Monthly Review Press, 2022); John Bellamy Foster, *Capitalism in the Anthropocene: Ecological Ruin or Ecological Revolution* (New York: Monthly Review Press, 2022); John Bellamy Foster, Richard York, and Brett Clark, *The Ecological Rift: Capitalism's War on the Earth* (New York: Monthly Review Press, 2010); John Bellamy Foster, *Marx's Ecology Materialism and Nature* (New York: Monthly Review Press, 2000); John Bellamy Foster, *Marx's Ecology: Materialism and Nature* (New York: Monthly Review Press, 2000). Also see the following works: Salvatore Engel-Di Mauro, *Socialist States and the Environment: Lessons for Eco-Socialist Futures* (London: Pluto Press, 2021); Carlos Martinez, *The East Is Still Red: Chinese Socialism in the 21st Century* (Glasgow: Praxis Press, 2023); Helen Yaffe, *Cuba's Life Task: Combatting Climate Change*, 2023, film; Helen Yaffe, "Cuba Shows How to Take Action on Climate Change," *Jacobin*, January 10, 2022.

and sharp contradictions generated by the need to develop the productive forces to fend off imperialist onslaught. Major tactical sacrifices have had to be made along the way, and internal struggles persist. To understand these histories, they need to be approached from the point of view of the dialectics of socialism and the recognition that it is a complex historical process of transforming a capitalist world to make it more egalitarian and ecologically sustainable.[56] It is not an ideal society based on a theoretical blueprint, but rather, as Losurdo cogently argued, a practical, collective, ongoing process of learning.

This book does not, however, mount an explicit and systematic defense of actually existing socialism for three reasons. The first is that it would have required additional volumes, above and beyond the two subsequent tomes that are forthcoming. The second is that significant elements for such a defense were incorporated into this study as fundamental correctives to the theoretical and practical positions taken by the compatible left intelligentsia. The reader will find, then, in every chapter, copious references to DHM analyses whose strengths are made evident in contrast to the unresearched and superficial accounts of Western critical theorists. If one checks the notes, there are numerous sources that provide rigorous material histories of socialist state-building projects, with all of their ups and downs, rather than mythological horror stories propagandistically constructed around a communist bogeyman (see, for instance, the work of Samir Amin, Atilio Borón, Radhika Desai, Cheng Enfu, John Bellamy Foster, Georges Gastaud, Bruno Guigue, Ali Kadri, Annie Lacroix-Riz, Torkil Lauesen, Domenico Losurdo, Ludo Martens, Carlos Martinez, Aymeric Monville, Immanuel Ness, Michael Parenti, Jacques Pauwels, Walter Rodney, Albert Szymanski, and many others who will be cited in the following pages). Finally, my methodology seeks to concretely demonstrate the superiority of DHM by developing a counter-history of the Western intelligentsia—particularly its left-most wing—whose explanatory power surpasses that of the standard accounts found in the bourgeois humanities and social sciences, as well as those of the Western Marxists themselves. It thereby lays the necessary groundwork for drawing on the rich tradition of DHM to account for the history of socialism, rather than blithely relying on the antiscientific grand narratives and atrocity propaganda proffered by the imperial critical theorists.

---

56. On this topic, see Gabriel Rockhill, "Lenin and the Dialectics of Socialism," *World Marxist Review*, Vol. 4, No. 4 (2025): 5–10.

Ideologues of Empire

I am a "primordial [*primaire*]" anticommunist, since when one is a "secondary" anticommunist it's too late.

—MICHEL FOUCAULT[57]

In 1966, it was publicly revealed that the CIA had been running an expansive global psychological warfare operation through the Congress for Cultural Freedom (CCF) in order to clandestinely promote the non-communist left. As noted above, there was likely not a single Western European intellectual who was not, directly or indirectly, caught up in the CCF's web. Adorno and Horkheimer—to return to the figures discussed at the beginning of this chapter—had been actively weaving it, as we shall see. Foucault, the other figure invoked above, was known as a "violent anticommunist" at the time and was very much in line with the CCF's deeper agenda.[58] Although there is no proof that he directly collaborated with it, he had just published *The Order of Things* (1966), where he consigned Marxism to the nineteenth century and claimed that it was dead in the twentieth. Internal documents reveal, moreover, that the CIA identified Foucault by name, and French structuralism more generally, as major allies in the intellectual world war on communism.[59]

How, we might wonder, did these critical theorists of the culture industry and knowledge/power react to the revelation that the theory industry of global knowledge production within which they operated was clandestinely driven by imperial power dynamics? Since this sparked such wide public debate at the time, across the bourgeois press, they were most certainly aware of the CIA's direct role in promoting the non-communist left intelligentsia, within which they occupied a very prominent place. The news clippings in the CCF archive include eight folders across two boxes that are filled with articles from the most well-known outlets around the world, which published cascading revelations at the time, including *Le Monde, Le Nouvel Observateur, Die Welt, New York Times, Newsweek, New York Herald Tribune, Time,* and many more.[60] As world-famous criti-

---

57. Didier Eribon, *Michel Foucault* (Paris: Flammarion, 1989), 415–16. As the author, who was Foucault's biographer and confidant, explains, this was one of Foucault's oft-repeated jokes.
58. Ibid., 237. Also see Rockhill, "Foucault: The Faux Radical."
59. See "France: Defection of the Leftist Intellectuals," the CIA FOIA Electronic Reading Room, https://www.cia.gov/readingroom/document/cia-rdp86s00588r000300380001-5.
60. See International Association for Cultural Freedom Records, Boxes 318–319, Hanna

cal theorists with a reputation for radical, anti-establishment thinking, this was a prime opportunity for them to bring their theories to bear on a concrete, contemporary problem and demonstrate their use-value.

The opposite, however, was the case. As far as I know, they did not so much as utter a peep about what was arguably the greatest knowledge/power scandal of their generation. Their fellow critical theorists of the imperial theory industry were equally silent. It was only those who were explicitly named as CIA collaborators, like Arendt and Aron, who felt compelled to make a public statement (they denied any knowledge of the Agency's role, which is laughable according to the leading Agency man involved).[61] For the others, there was nothing to be discussed, analyzed, or criticized, let alone changed. It was simply business as usual.

This moment brings starkly into relief the social function and ideological orientation of the imperial critical theorists, as well as their position within global class struggle in theory. By acting as if nothing had happened, they ran cover for one of the CIA's greatest covert operations within the intelligentsia. Even years later, none of them mentioned that their knowledge networks had been so deeply infiltrated and manipulated by the Agency. Pierre Bourdieu, who was Aron's assistant and owed much of his academic career to his support, even left out any reference to the CIA in a rare mention of the CCF.[62] Given their global prominence, it would have been sufficient for someone like Foucault—or anyone else—to mention it, even in passing, for it to have become common knowledge around the world, at least within the intelligentsia. Instead, their silence has been so systematic that to the ears of many intellectuals it sounds conspiratorial to discuss what is actually just part of the public record. Refusing to speak out at the time and then running cover for the Agency—intentionally or not—through their silence, the dons of the theory industry practically demonstrated the complicity between their forms of knowledge and the power of empire.

Holborn Gray Special Collections Research Center at the University of Chicago.

61. See Saunders, *The Cultural Cold War*, 410–11.

62. See Pierre Bourdieu, "Préface" in Brigitte Mazon, *Aux origines de l'École des Hautes Études en Sciences Sociales: Le rôle du mécénat américain (1920–1960)* (Paris: Les Éditions du Cerf, 1988), iii.

Western Marxism: A Product of the Imperial Superstructure

The expression "Western Marxism" is widely used to refer to the specific form of Marxism that has developed in the imperial core. According to Perry Anderson's well-known Trotskyist account, it was a "product of *defeat*": the failure of the socialist revolution to move westward after 1917 led to a situation in which Marxists in the West tended to turn away from Communist Party organizing and the analysis of political economy toward an investment in the academic world and a predilection for cultural and philosophic issues.[1] While these are indeed characteristics of Western Marxism, Anderson failed to situate its emergence in relationship to the totality of social relations of intellectual production, as well as production more generally. By tracing the division between Western and Eastern Marxism back to what Lenin referred to as the split in the socialist movement around the First World War, Domenico Losurdo shed light on the socioeconomic underpinnings of this ideological divide: Western Marxism emerged historically as a social chauvinist version of Marxism within the imperial core, which superciliously derided the anticolonial and anti-imperialist Marxism of the East.[2]

Anderson's account, very much like the Western Marxists with whom he largely identifies, is primarily superstructural because it does not provide a coherent analysis of the economic base of imperialism out of which

---

1. Perry Anderson, *Considerations on Western Marxism* (London: Verso, 1989), 42.
2. See Domenico Losurdo, *Western Marxism: How It Was Born, How It Died, How It Can Be Reborn*, ed. Gabriel Rockhill (New York: Monthly Review Press, 2024).

Western Marxism emerged. Losurdo's approach, drawing on Lenin, centers the imperial system and thereby elucidates why it is that Western Marxists tend to accommodate imperialism and even capitalism, while rejecting the real-world socialist alternative. In developing a detailed, materialist account of the inner workings of the superstructure of the world's leading imperialist power, this investigation seeks, among other things, to extend and further develop Losurdo's work by providing a political economy of knowledge production, circulation, and consumption. It is precisely by foregrounding the dialectical play between the objective forces of the imperial superstructure, on the one hand, and the subjective agency of intellectuals, on the other, that we can bring more fully into relief the phenomenon known as Western Marxism, which would be better described as imperial Marxism.[3]

The second part of this book shifts its focus from the imperial superstructure in general to a particular development within it, which made a major contribution to so-called Western Marxism: the Frankfurt School of critical theory. Chapter 4 examines the lives and careers of Theodor Adorno and Max Horkheimer, who are widely recognized as its leading intellectual figures, in large part because they collaborated on a common intellectual project and directed the Institute for Social Research (the institution colloquially known as the Frankfurt School). Far from being Marxist revolutionaries, as we shall see, they opportunistically integrated themselves into the bourgeois order and curried favor with powerful elements of the capitalist class and leading imperialist states. Indeed, they rose to global prominence within the elite networks of the anticommunist compatible left, which was promoted by intelligence agencies like the CIA (with which they collaborated). By equating communism with fascism and defending at least certain acts of imperialism, the founding fathers of the Frankfurt School were precisely the kinds of "Marxists" that the imperialist ruling class and its state managers wanted to—and did—support, as an ideological weapon of war against the anti-imperialist Marxists and actually existing socialism.

Chapter 5 examines the integration of the Frankfurt School into the U.S. military-industrial-academic complex in the 1940s, when no less than seven Frankfurt School affiliates went directly to work for the U.S. national security state and its propaganda agencies. Examining the

---

3. On these and related issues, see John Bellamy Foster and Gabriel Rockhill, "Western Marxism and Imperialism: A Dialogue," *Monthly Review*, Vol. 76, No. 10 (March 2025), https://monthlyreview.org/2025/03/01/western-marxism-and-imperialism-a-dialogue/.

intimate ties between the bourgeoisie, the bourgeois state, and the bourgeois academy, it situates these scholars within the broader world of wea-
ponized research and soft power politics, to which they made a decisive
contribution. One thing that becomes clear, through the course of the
analysis, is that the Institute for Social Research's collaboration with the
U.S. government, meaning its role as a veritable Washington School, functioned as a springboard for its national and international prominence after
the war. Its version of Marxism served the interests of the U.S. empire,
and the Frankfurt scholars' contributions to the latter catapulted them
into prestigious academic positions, helped them secure major grants
from the ruling class, and generally contributed to their fame within the
theory industry. This chapter examines, as well, the complex cases of the
Frankfurt School affiliates who had ties to Soviet intelligence and appear
to have been playing a double game. Finally, it addresses the most widespread myth regarding the Institute's governmental work, namely that it
was simply fighting fascism and was therefore contributing to a noble
cause and beyond reproach.

The last chapter studies the life and work of the figure who is reputed
to be the most radical member of the Frankfurt School: Herbert Marcuse.
It is a deep dive that begins with an examination of the most controversial aspect of his career, namely the eleven years that he spent working
for the Office of Strategic Services (the predecessor to the CIA) and the
State Department. By comparing the archival record to Marcuse's later
misrepresentations of his career, an image emerges that calls into question his status as an anti-establishment intellectual who embodied what
he called the "Great Refusal." This leads to a broader reassessment of his
work as a whole, including his extensive and persistent ties as a professor
to the U.S. national security state, his long and close collaborations with
the capitalist ruling class in internationally promoting an anticommunist
version of Marxism, his anarchist-inflected radicalization in the 1960s,
his surveillance by the FBI and harassment by conservative forces, and
his promotion as the so-called godfather of the New Left by the bourgeois
media. To understand the complexities of his case, a thoroughly dialectical approach is taken in order to sedulously track the nuances of his trajectory, while always situating his reorientations within the broader social
totality. What will become clear is that, although Marcuse's radicalization
made him into an enemy of certain sectors of the U.S. government, he was
simultaneously identified as a useful enemy by other elements because he
remained a dedicated anticommunist until the end.

Overall, the second part of this book should thus be understood as an

examination of a specific field of intellectual production within the imperial superstructure, that contributed to the development of Western or
imperial Marxism. Although this section, and even individual chapters,
can be read independently, the first half of this book provides the overall
framework within which they need to be understood. In other words, the
Frankfurt School can only be fully elucidated if it is situated within the
social totality, and more specifically the evolution of the imperial superstructure in the twentieth century.

PART II

COMPATIBLE CRITICAL
THEORY

CHAPTER 4

Anticommunist Critical Theory: Adorno and Horkheimer

Foundations of the Imperial Theory Industry

Frankfurt School critical theory has been, along with French theory, one of the hottest commodities of the imperial theory industry.[1] Together, they serve as the common source for so many of the trend-setting forms of theoretical critique that currently dominate the academic market in the capitalist world, from postcolonial and decolonial theory to queer theory, Afro-pessimism, new materialism, and beyond. The Frankfurt School's political orientation has therefore had a foundational effect on the globalized Western intelligentsia.

The luminaries of the first generation of the Institute for Social Research—particularly Theodor Adorno and Max Horkheimer, who will be the focus of this chapter—are towering figures of Western or cultural Marxism. For those familiar with Jürgen Habermas's reorientation away from historical materialism in the second and then third generations of the Frankfurt School, this early work often represents a veritable golden age of critical theory, when it was still—though perhaps passive or pessimistic—dedicated in some capacity to radical politics. If there is a grain of truth in this assumption, it is only insofar as the early Frankfurt School is compared to later generations that refashioned critical theory as radical liberal—or even just blatantly liberal—ideology.[2] However, this point of comparison is

---

1. An earlier, much abbreviated version of this essay was published as Gabriel Rockhill, "The CIA & the Frankfurt School's Anti-Communism," *Los Angeles Review of Books*, "The Philosophical Salon," June 27, 2022, https://thephilosophicalsalon.com/the-cia-the-frankfurt-schools-anti-communism/.
2. See my analysis of Jürgen Habermas, Axel Honneth, and Nancy Fraser, as well as the

setting the bar much too low, as is the case whenever one reduces politics to academic politics. After all, the first generation of the Frankfurt School lived through some of the most cataclysmic clashes in global class struggle of the twentieth century, when a veritable intellectual world war was being fought over the meaning and significance of communism.

To avoid being the dupes of history, or of the parochialism of the imperial academy, it is therefore important to recontextualize the Institute for Social Research's work in relationship to international class struggle. One of the most significant features of this context was the desperate attempt, on the part of the capitalist ruling class, via its state managers and ideologues, to redefine the left—in the words of cold warrior CIA officer Thomas Braden—as the "compatible," meaning non-communist, left.[3] As Braden and others involved have explained in detail, one important facet of this struggle consisted in the use of foundation money and Agency front groups like the Congress for Cultural Freedom (CCF) to promote anticommunism and lure leftists into taking positions against actually existing socialism.

Adorno and Horkheimer were caught up in various ways in the CCF's global networks. Horkheimer participated in at least one of its junkets (in Hamburg).[4] Adorno published in the CIA-funded journal *Der Monat*, which was openly sponsored by the U.S. occupying force in his home country, the Office of Military Government, United States (OMGUS), and the High Commission for Occupied Germany (HICOG). *Der Monat* was the largest review of its kind in Europe and the model for many of the Agency's other publications. Adorno's articles appeared, as well, in at least two other CIA magazines: *Encounter* and *Tempo presente*. He also hosted in his home, corresponded, and collaborated with the "'witting' CIA agent" who was arguably the leading figure in the German

---

first generation of the Frankfurt School, in Gabriel Rockhill, "Critical and Revolutionary Theory: For the Reinvention of Critique in the Age of Ideological Realignment," in *Domination and Emancipation: Remaking Critique*, ed. Daniel Benson (Lanham, MD: Rowman & Littlefield Publishers, 2021), 117–61.

3. See, for instance, Thomas W. Braden, "I'm Glad the CIA Is 'Immoral,'" *Saturday Evening Post*, May 20, 1967. As mentioned earlier, there are clear signs that Braden's article is what the Agency calls a "limited hangout."

4. See Gabriel Rockhill, *Radical History & the Politics of Art* (New York: Columbia University Press, 2014), 207–8 and Giles Scott-Smith, "The Congress for Cultural Freedom, the End of Ideology, and the Milan Conference of 1955: 'Defining the Parameters of Discourse,'" *Journal of Contemporary History*, Vol. 37, No. 3 (2002): 437–55.

anticommunist *Kulturkampf*: Melvin Lasky.[5] An employee of the U.S. military government in West Germany, Lasky was the founder and chief editor of *Der Monat* and a member of the original steering committee for the CIA's CCF. This powerful Cold War operative told Adorno that he was open to every form of collaboration with the Frankfurt School, including publishing articles and any other declaration as quickly as possible in his pages.[6] Adorno took him up on the offer and sent him four unpublished manuscripts, including Horkheimer's *Eclipse of Reason*, in 1949.[7] Adorno also advocated for publishing his work and Horkheimer's simultaneously in *Der Monat* since this would constitute an official statement by the Institute and position it in contemporary debates.[8] Although he said in his private correspondence that he was not enthusiastic about the collaboration (Horkheimer concurred), he immediately added that "in the current circumstances, it's a very important relationship."[9] Among other things, the intellectual duo wanted to publicly clarify their position on "homeopathy [their term for Marxism dedicated to the East]," meaning their hostility toward it.[10] The CIA-backed prestige journal was not only there to serve them, but the Agency point person (Lasky) running it personally translated Horkheimer's texts and procured Adorno an official invitation "by the Americans" to present a lecture in Berlin.[11] In the cultural cold war, Adorno and Horkheimer were squarely situated in Lasky's camp.

It is important to recall, in this context, that the Paris branch of the Institute for Social Research collaborated closely with Raymond Aron,

---

5. Hugh Wilford, *The CIA, the British Left and the Cold War* (New York: Routledge, 2014), 275. Lasky admitted to working as a witting agent of the CIA (see the press clippings in the International Association for Cultural Freedom Records, Box 319, Folder 2, Hanna Holborn Gray Special Collections Research Center at the University of Chicago). Some of Lasky's correspondence with Adorno is available in Theodor Adorno and Max Horkheimer, *Correspondance: 1927–1969*, Vols. 1-4, ed. Christoph Gödde and Henri Lonitz, trans. Didier Renault (Paris: Klincksieck: 2016). I cite the French edition here and elsewhere because Adorno and Horkheimer's complete correspondence is not available in English, as far as I know, and it does not appear that these letters were published in German.

6. See Adorno and Horkheimer, *Correspondance*, Vol. 3, 291.

7. See ibid., 348.

8. See Adorno and Horkheimer, *Correspondance*, Vol. 4, 647.

9. Adorno and Horkheimer, *Correspondance*, Vol. 3, 291.

10. Ibid., 278.

11. Ibid., 292.

who was in charge of overseeing which work was appropriate for a French audience, and who was himself invited to lecture at the Institute.[12] In the postwar era, Aron became the philosophic figurehead of the CCF and an indefatigable anticommunist ideologue whose public visibility was immensely enhanced by CIA support. He was so intimately connected with the Agency that he even went on family vacations with the spook who directed the entire CCF operation from its Paris headquarters (Michael Josselson). One of the Institute's other research associates, Franz Borkenau, was also very active in the CCF.[13]

Adorno's name appears on a document, likely from 1958/59, that outlined plans for an all-German committee of the CCF.[14] Indeed, he was not only connected with the German CCF, but Michael Hochgeschwender identifies Adorno as one of the "most important contacts" for the man put in charge of setting up the CCF in Frankfurt: Hans Schwab-Felisch.[15] The latter "was closely associated with the Berlin CCF office and *Der Monat* in the early 1950s," and he candidly described Lasky's U.S.-backed journal as "an organ in the cultural struggle of the Cold War."[16] It is interesting to note that Schwab-Felisch also worked as a journalist for *Die Neue Zeitung*, the newspaper published in the U.S. occupation zone in Germany, and then the Suhrkamp publishing house in Frankfurt.[17] Adorno, for his part, had an old friendship with Ruby d'Arschot, the secretary of the CCF's

---

12. See Adorno and Horkheimer, *Correspondance*, Vol. 1,   146, and Leo Löwenthal, *An Unmastered Past: The Autobiographical Reflections of Leo Löwenthal*, ed. Martin Jay (Berkeley: University of California Press, 1987), 55.

13. Among other sources, see Frances Stonor Saunders, *The Cultural Cold War: The CIA and the World of Arts and Letters* (New York: New Press, 2000), 71, 78–79.

14. See Michael Hochgeschwender, *Freiheit in der Offensive? Der Kongreß für kulturelle Freiheit und die Deutschen* (Munich: R. Oldenbourg Verlag, 1998), 488. Although the classification system has changed, making it nearly impossible to use Hochgeschwender's references to locate the file in question, I was able to find another untitled document with Adorno's name on it along with other major CCF collaborators in Germany like Heinrich Böll and Karl Löwith (see International Association for Cultural Freedom Records, Box 145, Folder 1, Germany 1959, Hanna Holborn Gray Special Collections Research Center at the University of Chicago). Adorno is also listed as a potential participant in a CCF planning document for a 1959 conference titled "Memorandum on a Conference on the Topic of 'Tolerance,'" International Association for Cultural Freedom Records, Box 145, Folder 1, Germany 1959, Hanna Holborn Gray Special Collections Research Center at the University of Chicago (the conference did not end up receiving CCF funding).

15. Hochgeschwender, *Freiheit in der Offensive?*, 481.

16. Ibid., 176, 175.

17. See ibid., 366, 481.

Arts Committee, and it was through her that he "had signaled his will-ingness to collaborate" with the U.S.-backed propaganda organization.[18] What is more, even after it was revealed in 1966 that the CCF was a CIA front, Adorno continued to be "included in the expansion plans of the Paris headquarters [of the CCF]," as it was "business as usual" in the part of Germany overseen by the United States.[19]

In perfect line with this orientation, Adorno published an interview highly critical of the student movement in the CCF's *Encounter* maga-zine in 1969, when CIA agent Melvin Lasky was still the editor. Since Lasky and Adorno had known one another personally for years, and Lasky had agreed to translate Horkheimer, it is highly likely that Adorno granted translation and publication rights directly to this Agency opera-tive (if not, it was to one of his underlings).[20] In the interview, Adorno openly eschewed practice in favor of theory, and he condemned Stalinism along with Nazism. He forcefully rejected the violence of "the totalitarian states," which he claimed were responsible for "the murder of countless millions."[21]

He never, to my knowledge, publicly expressed regret or self-criticism regarding his role in directly contributing to the CIA's anticommunist propaganda, nor did Horkheimer. Perhaps this is unsurprising, since they both rose to global prominence within the elite networks of the anticom-munist left, buoyed by the U.S. national security state and the capitalist ruling class.

Intellectuals in the Age of Revolution and Global Class War

> The Frankfurt School perpetrated a bourgeois sleight of hand by posturing as a Marxist institute while at the same time insisting that revolution could no longer depend on insurrection by the working class, and declining to take part in the overthrow of capitalism.
>
> —BERTOLT BRECHT[22]

---

18. Ibid., 481. Regarding d'Arschot's work for the CCF, see International Association for Cultural Freedom Records, Box 123, Folders 3–6, Ruby d'Arschot 1960–1963, Hanna Holborn Gray Special Collections Research Center at the University of Chicago.

19. Hochgeschwender, *Freiheit in der Offensive?*, 563.

20. The interview was conducted by an editor of *Der Spiegel*.

21. Theodor W. Adorno, "On Barricades and Ivory Towers," *Encounter*, September 1969, 67. "Philosophy in so far as it remains philosophy," Adorno asserted, "cannot recommend direct steps or changes. It brings about changes in so far as it remains theory" (ibid., 68).

22. Cited in Stuart Jeffries, *Grand Hotel Abyss: The Lives of the Frankfurt School* (London:

Although their early lives were marked by the world-historical events of the Russian Revolution and the attempted revolution in Germany, Adorno and Horkheimer were esthetes wary of the supposed morass of mass politics. While their interest in Marxism was piqued by these incidents, it was primarily of an intellectual nature. Horkheimer did become marginally involved in activities around the Munich council republic after the First World War, particularly by providing support for some of those involved after the council had been brutally suppressed. However, he—the same is true *a fortiori* of Adorno—"continued to maintain his distance from the explosive political events of the time and to devote himself primarily to his own personal concerns."[23]

Their class standing was far from insignificant in this regard, for it positions them and their political outlook within the larger, objective world of the social relations of production. Both Frankfurt School theorists were from affluent families. Adorno's father was a "wealthy wine merchant" and Horkheimer's was a "millionaire" who "owned several textile factories."[24] Adorno "had no personal ties at all to socialist political life" and systematically maintained "a deep aversion to formal membership of any party organization."[25] Similarly, Horkheimer was never "an overt member of any working-class party" or trade union.[26] The same is generally true of the other Frankfurt School figures close to Horkheimer: "None of those belonging to the Horkheimer circle was politically active; none of them had his origins either in the labor movement or in Marxism."[27]

In the words of John Abromeit, Horkheimer sought to preserve the

---

Verso, 2017), 77.

23. John Abromeit, *Max Horkheimer and the Foundations of the Frankfurt School* (Cambridge: Cambridge University Press, 2011), 42.

24. Thomas Wheatland, *The Frankfurt School in Exile* (Minneapolis: University of Minnesota Press, 2009), 24; Ingar Solty, "Max Horkheimer, a Teacher without a Class," *Jacobin*, February 15, 2020, https://www.jacobinmag.com/2020/02/max-horkheimer-frankfurt-school-adorno-working-class-marxism; Wheatland, *The Frankfurt School in Exile*, 13.

25. Perry Anderson, *Considerations on Western Marxism* (London: Verso, 1989), 33; Steven Müller-Doohm, *Adorno: A Biography*, trans. Rodney Livingstone (Cambridge: Polity Press, 2005), 94.

26. Anderson, *Considerations on Western Marxism*, 33. Also see Bertus Mulder and Lolle Nauta, "Working-Class and Proletariat: On the Relation of Andries Sternheim to the Frankfurt School," *Praxis International*, Vol. 9, no. 4 (January 1990): 433–45.

27. Rolf Wiggershaus, *The Frankfurt School: Its History, Theories, and Political Significance*, trans. Michael Robertson (Cambridge, MA: MIT Press, 1995), 104.

supposed independence of theory and "rejected the position of Lenin, Lukács, and the Bolsheviks that critical theory must be 'rooted'" in the working class, or more specifically working-class parties.[28] He encouraged critical theorists to operate as intellectual free agents rather than grounding their research in the proletariat, which was a type of work that he disparaged as "totalitarian propaganda."[29] Adorno's overall position, like Herbert Marcuse's, was summarized by Marie-Josée Levallée in the following terms: "The Bolshevik party, which Lenin made the vanguard of the October Revolution, was a centralizing and repressive institution which would shape the Soviet State in its image and turn the dictatorship of the proletariat into its own dictatorship."[30] In an interesting—though debatable—formulation, Leo Löwenthal described the Institute's form of critical theory as one that rejected both "the Social Democratic and the Bolshevik versions of Marxism" in favor of continuing "the radical Enlightenment tradition."[31]

Horkheimer became the director of the Institute for Social Research in 1930, even though he was a thirty-five-year-old junior scholar who was "an almost unknown philosopher at the time, with no credentials in the social sciences, to say nothing about Marxism and related topics."[32] According to Bertus Mulder and Lolle Nauta, this was because he had the advantage of not being a communist, which would have provoked protest

---

28. Abromeit, *Max Horkheimer*, 150. Any scant and circumspect hope that Horkheimer had placed in the Soviet Union dissipated in the early 1930s, and "after 1950, Horkheimer began defending the liberal-democratic political traditions of the West in a manner that was … one-sided" (ibid., 15, also see 181).

29. "Critical theory," Horkheimer claimed, "is neither 'deeply rooted' like totalitarian propaganda nor 'detached' like the liberalist intelligentsia." Max Horkheimer, *Critical Theory: Selected Essays*, trans. Matthew J. O'Connell and others (New York: Continuum, 2002), 223–24.

30. Marie-Josée Levallée, "October and the Prospects for Revolution: The Views of Arendt, Adorno, and Marcuse," *The Russian Revolution as Ideal and Practice: Failures, Legacies, and the Future of Revolution*, ed. Thomas Telios, et al. (Cham, Switzerland: Palgrave Macmillan, 2020), 173.

31. Löwenthal, *An Unmastered Past*, 65. In the 1930s, Löwenthal explained, the few defenders of the USSR in their circles—Karl Wittfogel, Henryk Grossman, and Ernst Bloch—referred to Horkheimer's group as the "swine on 117th Street" (the location of their Columbia University house) (ibid., 66). Horkheimer had even claimed that "it would not surprise him if an alliance developed between Hitler and Stalin, if Hitler made only the least overture" (ibid.).

32. Christian Fleck, "The Political Economy of the Frankfurt School," *Society*, Vol. 60 (2023): 108.

on the part of the university.[33] The administration actually did initially refuse to accept Horkheimer, but not for his politics. It was because of his lack of training in the requisite areas of economics and political science. The Frankfurt School's wealthy patron, Felix Weil, convinced them, however, to greenlight his appointment by making them an offer they could not refuse: he would fund two chairs instead of one, and Horkheimer would occupy the one in social philosophy.[34]

His stewardship of the Institute was characterized by speculative concerns with culture and authority rather than rigorous historical materialist analyses of capitalism, class struggle, and imperialism. In the words of Gillian Rose, "instead of politicizing academia," the Institute under Horkheimer "academized politics."[35] This was perhaps seen nowhere more clearly than in "the constant policy of the Institute under Horkheimer's direction," which "continued to be abstinence, not only from every activity which was even remotely political, but also from any collective or organized effort to publicize the situation in Germany or to support émigrés."[36] With the rise of Nazism, Adorno attempted to go into hibernation, assuming that the regime would only target "the orthodox pro-Soviet Bolshevists and communists who had drawn attention to themselves politically" (they would indeed be the first to be put in the concentration camps).[37] He "refrained from public criticism of any kind of the Nazis and their 'great power' policies."[38]

Critical Theory U.S.-American Style

There is a kind of dominant stratum in the East compared to which [U.S. Secretary of State] John Foster Dulles is an amiable innocent.

—MAX HORKHEIMER[39]

---

33. See Mulder and Nauta, "Working-Class and Proletariat," 435.

34. See Fleck, "The Political Economy of the Frankfurt School," 108.

35. Gillian Rose, The Melancholy Science: An Introduction to the Thought of Theodor W. Adorno (New York: Columbia University Press, 1978), 2.

36. Wiggershaus, The Frankfurt School, 133. Also see Solty, "Max Horkheimer, a Teacher without a Class" and Rose, The Melancholy Science, 2.

37. Müller-Doohm, Adorno, 181.

38. Ibid. "Even in his private letters," Müller-Doohm writes, "until well into the mid-1930s, we find no more than rather generalized, pessimistic mood-pictures, and no unambiguous statements on the political situation" (ibid.).

39. Theodor Adorno and Max Horkheimer, "Towards a New Manifesto?" New Left Review 65 (September-October 2019): 39. This statement was made in 1956, when Dulles

The refusal to overtly participate in progressive politics was intensified when the leaders of the Institute moved it to the United States in the early 1930s. The Frankfurt School adapted itself "to the local bourgeois order, censoring its own past and present work to suit local academic or corporate susceptibilities."[40] Horkheimer had words like *Marxism*, *revolution,* and *communism* expunged from its publications in order to avoid offending its U.S. sponsors.[41] Löwenthal, the managing editor of the Institute's *Zeitschrift für Sozialforschung*, publicly admitted that "we stylistically reformulated certain expressions that might have been misunderstood politically."[42] In a telling example, when the Institute published Walter Benjamin's well-known article on "The Work of Art in the Age of Mechanical Reproduction," it changed the final sentence: "Benjamin had written: 'This is the situation which Fascism is rendering aesthetic. Communism responds by politicizing art.' In the *Zeitschrift* version, though, 'the totalitarian doctrine' was substituted for 'Fascism' and 'the constructive forces of mankind' for 'communism.'"[43]

Furthermore, any type of political activity was strictly forbidden, as Marcuse later explained.[44] Horkheimer put his energy into securing corporate and state funding for the Institute, and he even hired a public relations firm to promote its work in the United States. Another émigré from Germany, Bertolt Brecht, was thus not fully unjustified when he critically described the Frankfurt scholars as—in the words of Stuart Jeffries—"prostitutes in their quest for foundation support during their American exile, selling their skills and opinions as commodities in order to support the dominant ideology of oppressive U.S. society."[45] They were indeed intellectual free agents unrestrained by any working-class organi-

---

and the U.S. administration had already been involved in several coups d'état, including against Iran and Guatemala, as well as a global war on communism.

40. Anderson, *Considerations on Western Marxism*, 33. Thomas Wheatland explains that the Horkheimer Circle in New York chose to "remain silent about the major political questions of the day and . . . [concealed] its Marxism almost completely. . . . Horkheimer remained unwilling to risk the possible repercussions of political activism or even political engagement with the major topics of the era." *The Frankfurt School in Exile* (Minneapolis: University of Minnesota Press, 2009), 99.

41. See Jeffries, *Grand Hotel Abyss*, 72 and 197.

42. Löwenthal, *An Unmastered Past*, 69.

43. Jeffries, *Grand Hotel Abyss*, 197 (also see 72).

44. See Wheatland, *The Frankfurt School in Exile*, 72 (also see 141).

45. Jeffries, *Grand Hotel Abyss*, 136.

zations in their pursuit of corporate and state sponsorship for their brand of market-savvy critical theory.

Todd Cronan has argued that there was a palpable shift in the Frankfurt School's overall political orientation around 1940—the year Pollock wrote "State Capitalism"—as it increasingly turned its back on class analysis in favor of privileging race, culture, and identity. "It often seems to me," Adorno wrote to Horkheimer that year, "that everything that we used to see from the point of view of the proletariat has been concentrated today with frightful force upon the Jews."[46] According to Cronan, Adorno and Horkheimer "opened up the possibility from within Marxism of seeing class as a matter of power, of domination, rather than economics (the Jews were not a category defined by economic exploitation). And once that possibility was raised, it became the dominant mode of analysis on the left at large."[47] In other words, the Frankfurt theorists helped set the stage for a more general shift away from historical materialist analysis grounded in political economy toward culturalism and identity politics. While there is certainly some truth to this, it is important to add that elements of culturalism were nonetheless operative earlier within the social chauvinism of the European left, so Adorno and Horkheimer were picking up on traditions that were already at work.

It is highly revealing in this regard that the Institute undertook a massive study of "Anti-Semitism in American Labor" in 1944–45, under Pollock's stewardship. Fascism had risen to power with extensive financial backing by the capitalist ruling class, and it was still on the warpath around the world. Yet, the Frankfurt scholars were hired to focus on the purported anti-Semitism of U.S. workers rather than on the capitalist funders of fascism or the actual Nazis who were fighting a war against the Soviets. They reached the remarkable conclusion that the "communist-run" unions were the worst of all, and that they thus had "fascist" tendencies: "The members of these unions are less communist than fascist-minded."[48] The study in question was commissioned by the Jewish Labor Committee (JLC). One of the JLC's leaders, David Dubinsky, had numerous ties to the CIA and was involved, along with the likes of Agency operatives Jay Lovestone and Irving Brown, in the Company's expansive campaign to

---

46. Quoted in Jack Jacobs, *The Frankfurt School, Jewish Lives, and Antisemitism* (Cambridge: Cambridge University Press, 2014), 59–60.
47. Todd Cronan, *Red Aesthetics: Rodchenko, Brecht, Eisenstein* (Lanham, MD: Rowman & Littlefield Publishers, 2021), 132.
48. Cited in ibid., 151.

take over organized labor and purge it of communists.[49] In fact, the JLC served as one of the conduits by which CIA funds were channeled to the anticommunist Free Trade Union Committee (FTUC).[50] By identifying the communist unions as the most anti-Semitic, and even "fascist," the Frankfurt School appears to have provided some of the ideological justification for destroying the communist labor movement.

Some might consider the Institute for Social Research's collaboration with U.S. authorities and self-censorship justified due to the anticommunist, and sometimes philofascist, attitudes of the U.S. ruling class and its managers, not to mention the enemy alien acts and decrees.[51] Indeed, based on a detailed overview of the Institute's history and activities on January 21, 1944, the Federal Bureau of Investigation (FBI) mobilized numerous stool pigeons to spy on the scholars for about ten years due to the concern that the Institute might be serving as a communist front.[52] The informants included close associates of the Institute like Karl Wittfogel, other professional colleagues, and even neighbors. The Bureau found little to no evidence of suspicious behavior, however, and its officers appear to have been reassured when some of their snitches, who were personally close to the Frankfurt scholars, explained to them that the critical theorists "believe there is no difference between Hitler and Stalin as to purpose and tactics."[53] Indeed, as we will see below, they would claim as much in some of their writings, including when they had settled in West Germany and were no longer under the direct threat of FBI surveillance and potential detainment or deportation. In anticipation, here is one of Horkheimer's claims in 1970: "The '*Führer* [Nazi leader],' whether he is named Stalin

---

49. On the JLC's leadership, see Catherine Collomp, "'Anti-Semitism Among American Labor': A Study by the Refugee Scholars of the Frankfurt School of Sociology at the End of World War II," *Labor History*, Vol. 52, No. 4 (November 2011): 417–39. On Dubinsky's work with the CIA, see the documents available via the CIA's FOIA Electronic Reading Room (https://www.cia.gov/readingroom/home), as well as Allan Francovich's documentary film *On Company Business* (1976); Hugh Wilford, *The CIA, the British Left and the Cold War: Calling the Tune?* (London and New York: Routledge, 2014); Hugh Wilford, *The Mighty Wurlitzer: How the CIA Played America* (Cambridge, MA: Harvard University Press, 2008); and Saunders, *The Cultural Cold War*.

50. See Wilford, *The CIA, the British Left and the Cold War*, 93–94.

51. See David Jenemann, *Adorno in America* (Minneapolis: University of Minnesota Press, 2007), 181–82.

52. See Theodor Adorno's FBI file, obtained through a FOIA request and available here: https://vault.fbi.gov/theodor-adorno/theodor-adorno-part-01-of-01/view.

53. See ibid.

[*sic*] or Hitler, describes his nation as the highest, he claims to know what is absolutely good, and the others are absolutely bad" (which begs the question of the status of the leader of the Frankfurt School, since he here claims to know that Stalin is as "absolutely bad" as Hitler).[54]

Propaganda Research for the Robber Barons

Adorno originally emigrated to the United States at the behest of Paul Lazarsfeld, a research associate of the Institute, in order to work for the Princeton Radio Research Project (PRRP).[55] Funded by the Rockefeller Foundation, the PRRP studied the effects of radio on society, with obvious implications for psychological warfare. It brought together major propaganda operatives who made prominent careers at the intersection of the U.S. national security state and the corporate media. Frank Stanton served as the co-director of the PRRP. He worked as a research director at the CIA-connected CBS, becoming its president in 1946, and he served as the chairman of the Rand Corporation (the Air Force's think tank).[56] The other co-director was Hadley Cantril, who became a consultant for Nelson Rockefeller's Office of the Coordinator of Inter-American Affairs (CIAA), the propaganda and intelligence agency overseeing Latin America.

Lazarsfeld, who became and remained friends with Stanton, regularly collaborated with the U.S. government and the foundations of the ruling class, including on international projects (he was close to Fernand Braudel and helped set up, with support from the Ford Foundation, the Maison des Sciences de l'Homme in Paris).[57] During the war, he served with other Frankfurt School associates in the Office of War Information (OWI).[58] The PRRP, to return to this key project, later evolved into the

---

54. Max Horkheimer, *Gesellschaft im Übergang* (Frankfurt: Anthenäum Fischer Taschenbuch Verlag, 1972), 168.

55. See Wiggershaus, *The Frankfurt School*, 168, and Christian Fleck, *A Transatlantic History of the Social Sciences: Robber Barons, the Third Reich and the Invention of Empirical Social Research*, trans. Hella Beister (London: Bloomsbury Academic, 2011), 166.

56. CBS had such deep ties to the U.S. National Security State that its directors established a private phone line to the CIA that "bypassed the CBS switchboard," provided cover for CIA agents as reporters or staff, used the William S. Paley Foundation to launder Agency funds, and "CBS correspondents joined the CIA hierarchy once a year for private dinners and briefings." Wilford, *The Mighty Wurlitzer*, 227; Saunders, *The Cultural Cold War*, 221.

57. See Fleck, *A Transatlantic History of the Social Sciences*, 175 and 202.

58. See Gerald Sussman, *Branding Democracy: U.S. Regime Change in Post-Soviet Eastern*

Office of Radio Research (ORR) and the Bureau of Applied Research (BASR), both of which were housed at Columbia University, where Lazarsfeld became a professor in 1940. There, he cooperated closely with Horkheimer, and "they agreed on a common strategy for dealing with their financial sponsors."[59] Indeed, "during the Institute's period of exile in the United States, Lazarsfeld served as a mediator between it and the academic environment there."[60]

Lazarsfeld received substantial grants from the Rockefeller Foundation, and BASR worked so closely with the U.S. national security state and propaganda agencies that it was considered one of the "de facto adjuncts of government psychological warfare programs."[61] By 1950–51, some 75 percent of its annual budget "consisted of contracts with U.S. military and propaganda agencies," including the Air Force, the Office of Naval Research, the United States Information Agency (USIA), and Voice of America (VOA).[62] Columbia's War Documentation Project, for instance, was funded by the CIA in 1954, and it was administered by BASR.[63] A VOA project run by BASR involved surveys conducted in the Middle East, including in two countries that "experienced CIA-supported coups d'état while the study was underway" (Iran and Egypt).[64] The Frankfurt School's Leo Löwenthal was the research director at the VOA, and he also worked for BASR and the OWI.[65] It is not clear if he was involved in

---

Europe (New York: Peter Lang, International Academic Publishers, 2010), 38.

59. Wiggershaus, *The Frankfurt School*, 168.

60. Ibid., 168. Also see Fleck, *A Transatlantic History of the Social Sciences*, 353n37: "In a letter to Löwenthal, 24 July 1944, Horkheimer expressed the hope that the institute would later profit from what Löwenthal would learn in the BASR."

61. Christopher Simpson, *Science of Coercion: Communication Research and Psychological Warfare 1945–1960* (Oxford: Oxford University Press, 1996), 4.

62. Ibid., 56, also see 72–73. One revealing example was the German Radio Project. Funded to the tune of $25,000 by the Rockefeller Foundation, Lazarsfeld oversaw the training of six German broadcasters at Columbia University. He collaborated with the Director of the Information Control Division of OMGUS (Gordon E. Textor), a psychological warfare expert (General Robert A. McClure), and the U.S. State Department allowed the broadcasters to visit VOA and fully observe its operations. This financial-state-academic collaboration aimed to train West German journalists to operate like U.S. Americans. See RG 1.1, Series 717, Box 19, Folders 173–74, Rockefeller Archive Center.

63. Jim Schachter, "Documents Disclose CIA Research: Agency Financed Covert Studies in '50s and '60s," *Columbia Daily Spectator*, April 17, 1980, 1.

64. Simpson, *Science of Coercion*, 56.

65. See Fleck, *A Transatlantic History of the Social Sciences*, 244.

this specific project, but his job consisted in evaluating "the effects of the Voice of America radio programs . . . for a broad, international area."[66] He worked with his immediate superiors in the State Department on this, and his office "employed many experts in the social sciences and maintained contracts with university institutes and commercial research firms."[67] Löwenthal was very close to Lazarsfeld, whom he referred to affectionately as his "ever-faithful friend," and the latter was responsible for getting him invited to work at Stanford's Center for Advanced Studies.[68]

The Institute for Social Research, it is worth noting in passing, contributed directly to this type of propaganda research by working with BASR at Columbia on a pilot study on reactions in Germany to VOA, BBC, and the major Russian broadcasting station.[69] It was also involved in a number of other surveys and research projects with obvious propaganda, pro-business, or counter-insurgency implications: a radio study on the effectiveness of broadcasts; a Ford-funded Oslo project on "reactions to threat"; a public survey aimed at constructing a "tension barometer" that tells the government "where there are likely to be trouble spots"; a study "for a big corporation of the attitude of its personnel towards its social welfare program"; a survey "of the impact of democratic propaganda on the refugees from the eastern sector of Berlin."[70] As Horkheimer explained in a 1952 letter to Professor Frederic Lane of the Rockefeller Foundation, which had provided the Institute with a grant of $5,000: "Our real aim is to study conditions in Germany and their effect upon German ideology, with emphasis on the ultimate reintegration of Germany into the community of nations."[71] The Frankfurt School was thus dedicated to the same fundamental objective as the capitalist ruling class and the bourgeois states that funded it, namely the dismantling of socialism in the East and the reincorporation of all of Germany into the capitalist West.

Lazarsfeld's propaganda research at Columbia was so important that it came up, years later, in the correspondence between CIA Director

---

66. Löwenthal, *An Unmastered Past*, 83.

67. Ibid.

68. Ibid., 138.

69. See LCD, Diary, May 11, 1951, RG 1.2, Series 717, Box 15, Folder 155, Rockefeller Archive Center.

70. Frederic C. Lane, Diary, February 19, 1953, RG 1.2, Series 717, Box 15, Folder 155, Rockefeller Archive Center.

71. Max Horkheimer, letter to Frederic C. Lane, January 21, 1952, RG 1.2, Series 717, Box 15, Folder 155, Rockefeller Archive Center.

William Casey and an unnamed contact. The former wanted to know "the foremost practitioners of psychological warfare of the late 1940s and early 1950s," surely to learn from their techniques.[72] His correspondent concurred that psywar was "a prerequisite if democracy is to prevail over totalitarianism," and Lazarsfeld's group was the first he referenced: "Your recollections are quite right. Back in the 1930s [sic], there was a group of sociologists at Columbia University, led by Harold Lasswell and Paul Lazarsfeld, who were concerned with propaganda analysis."[73] Here we have, then, according to the archival record, the Director of the CIA recalling the propaganda contributions of the research associate of the Frankfurt School who served as a liaison between the Institute and U.S. universities, as well as the person responsible for arranging Adorno's first job in the United States.[74]

Adorno directed the "Music Study" for the PRRP for two and a half years, with support from the Rockefeller Foundation.[75] In his later description of his activities, he explained that "this was about collecting data that were supposed to be of benefit for the planning agencies in the field of mass media, either directly in the industry or by way of cultural advisory boards and similar bodies."[76] There were some methodological conflicts, and by the end of the project Adorno became convinced that "the stereotypical production mechanisms of popular culture molded the expectations of consumers to maximize profits for its shareholders," which was in line with his general critique of the culture industry.[77] There were also complaints about Adorno's obscure writing

---

72. (Sanitized), June 19, 1984, the CIA FOIA Electronic Reading Room, https://www.cia.gov/readingroom/document/cia-rdp86m00886r002800010009-5.

73. Ibid. There are gaps in the correspondence, and it is unclear why there is a discrepancy in the decades they reference (1930s versus 1940s and 1950s). In any case, Casey's interlocutor appears to be unaware of the fact that Lazarsfeld was only hired at Columbia in 1940.

74. "Horkheimer and the Institute," notes Wiggershaus, "were closely in touch with him [Lazarsfeld] during the whole period of their stay in the United States." *The Frankfurt School*, 165.

75. See Fleck, *A Transatlantic History of the Social Sciences*, 182.

76. Cited in ibid., 182.

77. Jeffries, *Grand Hotel Abyss*, 206. This quote is, in many ways, a summary of Müller-Doohm's biography of Adorno, which can be consulted for more details. On the culture industry, see in particular Theodor W. Adorno and Max Horkheimer, *Dialectic of Enlightenment*, trans. John Cumming (New York: Continuum Publishing Company, 1993), 120–67, as well as Theodor Adorno, *The Culture Industry: Selected Essays on Mass Culture*, ed. J. M. Bernstein (New York: Routledge, 1991).

style, but Lazarsfeld nonetheless recognized that he had made important contributions, and he "tried to keep Adorno in the project."[78] However, Rockefeller refused to further employ him or fund him separately "due to the reservations expressed about him by various people inside and outside the RF [Rockefeller Foundation] as well as Adorno's own failure to come up with a final report after the two-and-a-half years working on the project."[79] Nevertheless, the Rockefeller Foundation played an important role in supporting the Frankfurt School in the United States, as well as after it returned to Germany. Indeed, it funded Horkheimer's first trip back to Europe in April 1948, when he took up a guest professorship at Frankfurt University.

The Rockefellers use their foundation as a tax shelter that allows them to mobilize a portion of their stolen wealth "in the corruption of intellectual activity and culture."[80] They were, moreover, directly involved in the national security state during the time of the Frankfurt School's sponsorship. After serving as the director of the CIAA (a federal propaganda agency whose work resembled that of the OSS and the CIA), Nelson Rockefeller became, in 1954, the "'super-coordinator' for clandestine intelligence operations, with the title of Special Assistant to the President for Cold War Strategy."[81] He also allowed the Rockefeller Fund to be used as a conduit for CIA money, very much like a large number of other capitalist foundations that have an extensive history of working hand-in-glove with the Company (as revealed by the Church Committee report and other sources). As one of the world's major investors in soft power politics and propaganda, the Rockefeller Foundation clearly identified the Frankfurt School as an ally in the ideological war on communism.

Bye-Bye Blue Skies: Leaving Your Marxist Friends to Die

Bertolt Brecht's close friend, Walter Benjamin, was one of the Frankfurt scholars' most important Marxist interlocutors at the time. He was not able to join them in the United States because he tragically committed suicide in 1940 at the border between France and Spain, the night before

---

78. Fleck, *A Transatlantic History of the Social Sciences*, 185. Also see Jeffries, *Grand Hotel Abyss*, 203–7, which discusses some of the conflicts.

79. Fleck, *A Transatlantic History of the Social Sciences*, 185.

80. Wiggershaus, *The Frankfurt School*, 397.

81. John Loftus, *America's Nazi Secret* (Walterville, OR: Trine Day, 2011), 228.

he faced near certain apprehension by the Nazis. According to Adorno, he "killed himself after he had already been saved" because he had "been made a permanent member of the Institute and knew it."[82] He was "flush with funds" for his trip, in the words of the famous philosopher, and knew "that he could rely completely on us materially."[83]

This version of history, which presents Benjamin's suicide as an incomprehensible personal decision, was an exercise in mendacity for the sake of personal and institutional exoneration, according to a detailed analysis published by Ulrich Fries. Not only were the leading figures of the Frankfurt School unwilling to assist Benjamin financially for his flight from the Nazis, Fries argues, but they also ran an extensive cover-up campaign to disingenuously present themselves as his benevolent benefactors.

Prior to his suicide, Benjamin was financially dependent on the Institute for a monthly stipend. However, the Frankfurt scholars despised the influence of Brecht and revolutionary Marxism on his work. Adorno had no compunction about describing Brecht with the anticommunist epithet "savage" when explaining to Horkheimer that Benjamin needed to be "definitively" liberated from his influence.[84] "During the late 1930s," Helmut Dubiel notes in his dialogue with Löwenthal, "the Institute in a sense blackmailed Benjamin ideologically, threatening to cut off funds in order to make him give up his allegedly strict Marxist course."[85] It is not surprising, then, that Benjamin feared losing his stipend, which was due, in part, to Adorno's critiques of his work and refusal to publish a section of his Baudelaire study in 1938.[86] Horkheimer explicitly told Benjamin

---

82. Cited in Ulrich Fries, "Ende der Legende: Hintergründe zu Walter Benjamins Tod," *The Germanic Review: Literature, Culture, Theory*, Vol. 96, No. 4 (2021): 421, 422. I would like to express my sincere gratitude to Helmut-Harry Löwen, who drew my attention to this important article and shared his partial translation of it with me.

83. Cited in ibid., 422, 422.

84. See Adorno's letter to Horkheimer on January 26, 1936, published in Adorno and Horkheimer, *Correspondance*, Vol. 1, 110.

85. Löwenthal, *An Unmastered Past*, 67. Also see Silvia Holz-Markun, "Kulturelle Volksfront: Der Philosoph Ernst Bloch im antifaschistischen Widerstand," *Unsere Zeit*, January 5, 2024, https://www.unsere-zeit.de/kulturelle-volksfront-4787206/. According to Holz-Markun, "The vehement anticommunism that began to increasingly dominate the Institute's team meant that Horkheimer and Adorno were unwilling to give [Ernst] Bloch a remunerated commission within the Institute" (ibid). Special thanks to Helmut-Harry Löwen for drawing my attention to this article.

86. See the epistolary exchange between them in Ronald Taylor, ed., *Aesthetics and Politics* (London: Verso, 1977), 100–41.

around the same time, as fascist forces were closing in around him, that he should prepare for the discontinuation of his sole source of income since 1934. He claimed, moreover, that his hands were "unfortunately tied" when he refused to fund Benjamin's journey to safety by paying for a steamship ticket to the United States that would have cost under $200.[87]

This was literally "a month after transferring an extra $50,000 to an account at his exclusive disposal," which was the "second time in eight months" that he had secured an additional $50,000 (the equivalent of just over $1.1 million in 2024).[88] In July 1939, Pollock also obtained an additional $130,000 for the Institute from Felix Weil, the affluent son of a capitalist millionaire whose profits from a grain enterprise in Argentina, property speculation, and meat trading funded the Frankfurt School. At the moment of its founding, Weil had promised university officials in Frankfurt to pay for the cost of a new building and library himself, while guaranteeing that his father would cover personnel and other costs. The foundation they established for this purpose, *Gesellschaft für Sozialforschung*, received the equivalent today of half a million dollars annually (and additional payments like the one mentioned above were sometimes made, including for the funding of various professorships).[89] Hanns Eisler summed up the political economy of the Frankfurt School with remarkable concision in a suggestion he made to Brecht for his "Tui Novel" (see below): "A rich old man (Weil, the speculator in wheat) dies; disturbed at the poverty in the world, in his will he leaves a large sum to set up an institute which will do research on the source of this poverty, which is, of course, himself."[90]

It was political will, not money, that was lacking. Indeed, Ulrich Fries concurs with Rolf Wiggershaus that Horkheimer's cruel decision to abandon Benjamin was part of a broader pattern according to which the directors "systematically placed the realization of their private life goals above the interests of everyone else," while propagating the false appearance of "outstanding commitment to those persecuted by the Nazi regime."[91] As if to put the last nail in Benjamin's coffin, his literary estate was later purged

---

87. Cited in Fries, "Ende der Legende," 409.

88. Ibid., 409, 424.

89. See Christian Fleck, "The Political Economy of the Frankfurt School," *Society*, Vol. 60 (2023): 108.

90. Bertolt Brecht, *Journals 1934–55*, ed. John Willett, trans. Hugh Rorrison (London: Bloomsbury, 1993), 230.

91. Fries, "Ende der Legende," 414.

of its more explicit Marxist elements. According to Helmut Heißenbüttel, "In everything Adorno did for Benjamin's work, the Marxist-materialist side remains erased. . . . The work appears in a reinterpretation in which the surviving controversial correspondent imposes his view."[92]

One of the other members of the Frankfurt School who was not able to emigrate and, like Benjamin, ended up dying in Europe was Andries Sternheim. Unlike Adorno and Horkheimer, he was of working-class origin. He was also deeply involved in the labor movement and was a member of the Dutch Social Democratic Labor Party. Bertus Mulder and Lolle Nauta have described him as "more practically oriented than his philosophically trained German colleagues":

> His reviews [in the Institute's journal] deal with subjects like unemployment and its social and psychological consequences; rationalization in industry; the role of trade unions in the different countries; the position of women in society and the way the attainments of the labor unions are monopolized by fascist dictatorship.[93]

Sternheim directed the Geneva branch of the Institute from 1931 to 1938. Anticipating the war, he expressed interest in emigrating to the United States. However, he was not invited by the Institute, and its director refused to help him survive in Switzerland.[94] In June 1938, Horkheimer proceeded to dismiss him as director of the Geneva branch on the pretext of the Institute's bad financial situation, which was disingenuous as we have seen.[95] Sternheim therefore had to return to Amsterdam, where Horkheimer apparently thought he would be safe because he "did not expect a war in Europe."[96] After returning to the Netherlands, Sternheim and his wife were captured by the Nazis and sent to Auschwitz, where they were both put to death.

Two intellectuals on the left end of the Frankfurt School's political spectrum, both of whom engaged in Marxist analysis, were thus left to die in Europe, despite the fact that the Institute had the necessary financial resources to save them. Instead of using the hundreds of thousands

---

92. Cited in ibid., 410.
93. Mulder and Nauta, "Working-Class and Proletariat," 436.
94. See ibid., 136, and Fleck, "The Political Economy of the Frankfurt School," 110.
95. Mulder and Nauta, "Working-Class and Proletariat," 436.
96. Bertus Mulder, "A Dutch Diamond Worker in the Frankfurt School of Sociology," *The Netherlands' Journal of Social Sciences*, Vol. 28, No. 2 (1992): 136.

of dollars that had been gifted to them by a millionaire to help their colleagues avoid certain death, the leaders of the Frankfurt School used these
unearned funds for personal enrichment:

> They [Horkheimer and Pollock] managed to use Weil's money to fund a
> life of luxury over a very long period of time, starting with a house in the
> suburbs of Frankfurt in the 1920s, to condominiums in Manhattan, a newly
> built bungalow in Pacific Palisades, and lastly, since 1957, residences in
> Montagnola in the Tessin region of Switzerland (finally, Pollock married a
> cousin of Felix [Weil] who did not donate money to any opaque enterprise
> but rather enjoyed it herself).[97]

Based on the principle of the primacy of practice, these activities shed
more light on their practical political orientation and their moral com-
pass as human beings than their theoretical ruminations on politics and
morality.

Malign the East, Defend—While in the Pay of—the West

> The Institute of Social Research at Frankfurt University was founded
> with the support of HICOG [High Commission for Occupied
> Germany] and largely supported by American means. It is the aim of
> this Institution to develop an integration of American and German
> research methods and to help in the education of German students
> in the spirit of American democracy.
>
> —THEODOR ADORNO[98]

In 1949–50, the intellectual front men of the Frankfurt School moved the
Institute back to West Germany, one of the epicenters for the intellectual
world war on communism. "In this milieu," writes Perry Anderson, "in
which the KPD [Communist Party] was to be banned and the SPD [Social
Democratic Party] formally abandoned any connection with Marxism,
the depoliticization of the Institute was completed."[99] No less than Jürgen
Habermas—who occasionally outflanked Adorno and Horkheimer to
the left in the early years—accused the latter of "opportunist conformity

---

97. Fleck, "The Political Economy of the Frankfurt School," 111.
98. Cited in Jenemann, *Adorno in America*, 184.
99. Anderson, *Considerations on Western Marxism*, 34.

which was at odds with the critical tradition."[100] Indeed, Horkheimer continued his censorship of the Institute's work, refusing to publish two articles by Habermas that were critical of liberal democracy and spoke of "revolution," daring to suggest the possibility of an emancipation from "the shackles of bourgeois society."[101] In his private correspondence, Horkheimer candidly submitted to Adorno that "it is simply not possible to have admissions of this sort in the research report of an Institute that exists on the public funds of this shackling society."[102] This appears to be a forthright admission that the economic base of the Frankfurt School was the driving force behind its ideology, or at least its public discourse.

It is important to recall, as we shall see, that seven research associates of the Institute worked as analysts and propagandists—often alongside future foundation managers like the Rockefeller Foundation's Charles Fahs and its CIA-connected Chadbourne Gilpatric—for the U.S. government, which "had a vested interest in the continuing loyalty of the Frankfurt School because a number of its members were working on sensitive government research projects."[103] In 1954, Adorno met with the Estimates Group in order to discuss the possibility of doing contract research for the U.S. State Department.[104] The Estimates Group, at the time, was a committee of division chiefs who contributed directly to strategic discussions at the highest level of the government (Marcuse began regularly attending the Estimates Group's meetings when he worked for the State Department). It is not clear what came of these conversations. What is known, as we saw above, is that Adorno did propaganda research for the ruling class and the Frankfurt School's principal academic liaison in the United States, Lazarsfeld, and was deeply involved in research for the military-industrial-academic complex.

With all of these ties to the capitalist class and the national security state, it is not surprising that the U.S. government supported the Institute's move back to Germany with a very significant grant of 236,000 DM for

---

100. Jeffries, *Grand Hotel Abyss*, 297. Habermas himself, we should recall, was a member of the Hitler Youth and would later support the Persian Gulf War and NATO's intervention in Yugoslavia.

101. See Horkheimer's jeremiad against Habermas and Marxism in his letter to Adorno on September 27, 1958, in Adorno and Horkheimer, *Correspondance*, Vol. 4, 386–99.

102. Quoted in Wiggershaus, *The Frankfurt School*, 554.

103. Jenemann, *Adorno in America*, 182. On Fahs and Gilpatric, including the fact that the latter worked for the CIA, see Saunders, *The Cultural Cold War*, 145.

104. See Tim B. Müller, *Krieger und Gelehrte: Herbert Marcuse und die Denksysteme im Kalten Krieg* (Hamburg: Hamburger Edition, 2011), 170.

the building of the Institute and 204,300 DM in 1950 for its research work (the total of 440,300 DM, or $104,958, is equivalent to just over $1.3 million in 2024).[105] These funds were administered by John McCloy, the U.S. High Commissioner of Germany. McCloy had worked as a jurist and banker for big oil and IG Farben, before serving as the Assistant Secretary of War. After the end of hostilities, he granted extensive pardons and commutations to Nazi war criminals. Sometimes referred to as "the chairman of the American Establishment," he went on to become the chairman of Chase Manhattan Bank, of the Council on Foreign Relations, and of the Ford Foundation.[106] In addition to the funds provided by McCloy, the Institute also received support from the German Federal Government, UNESCO, the Society of Social Research, private donors, the government of Hesse, and the city of Frankfurt.[107]

The Rockefeller Foundation, surely enticed by Adorno and Horkheimer's claim to be on a mission as "apostles of American empirical methods," also made a modest contribution to the Institute in the early 1950s.[108] Professor Louis Wirth told a representative of the Rockefeller Foundation that Adorno and Horkheimer were "carrying on a tremendous campaign to get support from [the] UN, UNESCO, the German government, American occupying forces, foundations, and everybody else, and that they [were] representing themselves as the last word in the latest thing in American social science."[109] The representative shared with Wirth the view of associates like Philip Mosely (a high-level CIA advisor and Rockefeller consultant), namely that Adorno and Horkheimer "nevertheless do know

---

105. See Philip E. Mosely, Diary, November 3–6, 1950, RG 1.2, Series 717, Box 15, Folder 155, Rockefeller Archive Center. Also see Wiggershaus, *The Frankfurt School*, 434, whose number is just slightly lower (435,000 DM). Since Mosely acquired this information directly from Frederick Burkhard at HICOG, it is likely more exact.

106. Inderjeet Parmar, *Foundations of the American Century: The Ford, Carnegie, and Rockefeller Foundations in the Rise of American Power* (New York: Columbia University Press, 2012), 54.

107. In addition to Wiggershaus, see Müller, *Krieger und Gelehrte*, 365; Philip F. Mosely, Diary, November 3–6, 1950; and Fabien Link, "Cooperation and Competition: Re-establishing the Institute of Social Research and the Emergence of the 'Frankfurt School,'" *NTM Zeitschrift für die Geschichte der Wissenschaften, Technik und Medizin*, Vol. 24 (2016): 225–49.

108. Müller, *Krieger und Gelehrte*, 365. Philip Mosely used the same vocabulary in his diary on November 3–6, 1950, claiming that Horkheimer is "obviously quite an apostle of American empirical methods among Germans."

109. LCD, interview with Louis Wirth, April 13, 1951, RG 1.2, Series 717, Box 15, Folder 155, Rockefeller Center Archive.

something about empirical research methods and are perhaps one of the very few potential avenues for developing interest and effort along these lines in the German social science scene."[110] Another Rockefeller executive interviewed professor Arnold Bergstraesser about the Institute, asking him if it was still Marxist, as it had claimed to be in the pre-Nazi days, "although without any implications of its being communistic."[111] Bergstraesser replied that "he did not think it was Marxist, and gave some examples."[112] Vetted by multiple sources, the leaders of the Frankfurt School were thus identified as anticommunist intellectuals worthy of support because they were making a unique contribution to intellectual imperialism, and more specifically the dissemination of U.S.-style bourgeois social science (which was being promoted as a weapon of ideological warfare against dialectical and historical materialism).

The Institute for Social Research received support from the occupying force of its home country, the High Commission for Occupied Germany (HICOG), for a study of political attitudes in Germany.[113] It also cooperated with the Bureau of Applied Social Research at Columbia for "a pilot study of reactions in Germany to the Voice of America, BBC, and the major Russian broadcasting station."[114] As an intellectual subcontractor for government and business interests, it provided research with obvious propaganda and counter-insurgency implications. In 1954, the Institute even signed a research contract with the Mannesmann corporation, which "had been a founding member of the Anti-Bolshevik League and had financed the Nazi Party."[115] During the Second World War, Mannesmann used slave labor, and its chairman of the board was the Nazi Wilhelm Zangen, the War Economy Leader of the Third Reich.[116] Although Zangen was briefly imprisoned after the war for his reliance on slave labor and his role arming the Nazi regime, he only served four months of his sentence, and he continued working for Mannesman. At the beginning of 1949, he even became "chairman of the board of directors in one of his own

---

110. Ibid.

111. Excerpt from EFD's Diary, Arnold Bergstraesser, August 4, 1953, RG 1.2, Series 717, Box 15, Folder 155, Rockefeller Center Archive.

112. Ibid.

113. See LCD Diary, Institute for Social Research, May 11, 1951, RG 1.2, Series 717, Box 15, Folder 155, Rockefeller Center Archive.

114. Ibid.

115. Wiggershaus, The Frankfurt School, 479.

116. See Robert S. Wistrich, Who's Who in Nazi Germany (New York: Routledge, 2002), 283.

former Mannesmann factories," where he "immediately began to put the old corporation back together."[117] He continued to climb the ranks and became the overall chairman of the board of Mannesman from 1957 to 1966.[118] The Frankfurt School's postwar contract with this company was for a sociological study of worker opinions, with the implicit implication that such an analysis would help management stall or prevent socialist organizing.

This was not the only time that the Institute financially benefited from Nazis and their collaborators. As Christian Fleck has demonstrated, the Weil empire protected its investments under the Third Reich by establishing an anonymous container for its activities innocuously entitled ROBEMA, which was entrusted to two administrators. This entity not only sheltered their finances from Nazi theft, but it performed better than Pollock's catastrophic investments on Wall Street, which lost "about one million dollars in 1937 alone."[119] In the final ROBEMA transaction, one of the administrators transferred several thousand German marks to Pollock in 1963. The money came from "dividends for the years 1941 to 1944 from IG Farben, the famous business conglomerate that had been broken apart after 1945 because of its close collaboration with the Nazi system."[120] IG Farben had relied on slave labor from concentration camps during the war and was involved in medical experiments on inmates. One of its subsidiaries produced the poison gas Zyklon B that was used in the gas chambers.

The precise nature of these social relations of intellectual—and more specifically ideological—production and how they relate to the Holocaust industry should not be lost on us.[121] This industry has distorted the history of the Nazi Holocaust, and fascism more generally, by promoting a culturalist and exceptionalist misrepresentation of it that works to shore up imperialist interests (especially Zioimperialism), while obscuring the actual history of fascism as an anticommunist project bankrolled by the capitalist class and deeply rooted in Western colonial traditions.[122]

---

117. Wiggershaus, *The Frankfurt School*, 480.

118. See Wistrich, *Who's Who in Nazi Germany*, 283.

119. Fleck, "The Political Economy of the Frankfurt School," 110.

120. Ibid., 111.

121. On the Holocaust industry, see Norman Finkelstein, *The Holocaust Industry: Reflections on the Exploitation of Jewish Suffering* (London: Verso, 2024) and Tony Greenstein, *Zionism during the Holocaust: The Weaponization of Memory in the Service of State and Nation* (n.p.: New Generation Publishing, 2022).

122. See all of Domenico Losurdo's writings on these and related issues, as well as

The Frankfurt School, for its part, caught the rising postwar wave of the Holocaust industry, under the forlorn banner of the impossibility of poetry after Auschwitz, while writing theory that was funded in part by investments in the corporation that produced the poison gas used at Auschwitz. The Holocaust industry—in both the Nazi and the Western imperialist meaning of this expression—played no small role in bolstering this school of thought within the imperial theory industry.

Perhaps the clearest explanation of why capitalist governments and the corporatocracy supported the Institute for Social Research is to be found in the words of Shepard Stone. He had a background in journalism and military intelligence before going on to serve as Director of International Affairs at the Ford Foundation, where he worked closely with the CIA in funding cultural projects around the world. Described by Hugh Wilford as "a psychological warfare expert with close ties to the CIA," Stone even became the president of the International Association for Cultural Freedom, which was the new name given to the CCF in a rebranding effort after its CIA origins had been revealed (Stone was initially recommended for the job by the Agency operative who directed the CCF, Michael Josselson).[123] In fact, "many believed he [Stone] was an Agency man."[124] When Stone was the director of public affairs for HICOG in the 1940s, he sent a personal note to the U.S. State Department to encourage it to extend Adorno's passport: "The Institute of Frankfurt is helping to train German leaders who will know something of democratic techniques. I believe it is important for our over-all democratic objectives in Germany that such men as Professor Adorno have an opportunity to work in that country."[125] The Institute was doing the kind of ideological work that the U.S. state and capitalist ruling class wanted to—and did—support. Its members were contributing, albeit to varying degrees and with some minor exceptions, to pro-Western "democracy promotion" and propaganda efforts, the fulsome rejection of actually existing socialism, and the displacement of dialectical and historical materialism in favor of U.S.-style bourgeois social science.

Meeting, and even surpassing, the dictates of ideological conformity to the "shackling society" that funded the Institute, Horkheimer openly

Greenstein, *Zionism during the Holocaust*.

123. Wilford, *The CIA, the British Left and the Cold War*, 230. On Josselson's recommendation, see Saunders, *The Cultural Cold War*, 411.

124. Saunders, *The Cultural Cold War*, 143.

125. Cited in Jenemann, *Adorno in America*, 184.

expressed his support for the United States' anticommunist puppet government in West Germany, whose intelligence services had been stocked with former Nazis.[126] As has been well documented, there was deep continuity between the Nazi era and the period of Western patronage after the war insofar as there was "renewed control of German public, social, economic and cultural life by forces which only partially and temporarily had been deprived of the influence they had exerted under the Nazi regime" (we should add, at a minimum, military, intellectual, and educational life).[127] "While in the East a genuine de-Nazification process did take place," explain Bruni de la Motte and John Green, "in the West it was desultory to begin with and later non-existent: many leading Nazis merely donned the new 'democratic' clothing and continued to occupy or reoccupy influential positions."[128]

Antifascists in Theory, Collaborators with Erstwhile Nazis in Practice

Without the collaboration with German social researchers, some of whom had worked for Nazi organizations, the establishment of the Institute [for Social Research] as a renowned institution for social-empirical research in West Germany would hardly have been possible.

—FABIAN LINK[129]

When the Frankfurt School moved to occupied West Germany, Adorno and Horkheimer did, on certain occasions, resist specific cases of academic continuity with the Nazi regime. For instance, they lobbied to keep ex-Nazis from gaining leadership positions in the German Society of Sociology, and they "prevented the appointment of [former Nazi Arnold]

126. See, for instance, Philip Agee, "West Germany: An Interview with Philip Agee," interview by Informations Dienst, *Dirty Work: The CIA in Western Europe*, ed. Philip Agee and Louis Wolf (New York: Dorset Press, 1978), 184–87.

127. John H. Herz, "The Fiasco of Denazification in Germany," *Political Science Quarterly*, Vol. 63, No. 4 (December 1948): 569. Among many other possible sources, see Victor Grossman, *A Socialist Defector: From Harvard to Karl-Marx-Allee* (New York: Monthly Review Press, 2019).

128. Bruni de la Motte and John Green, *Stasi State or Socialist Paradise? The German Democratic Republic and What Became of It* (London: Artery Publications, 2022), 21.

129. Fabian Link, *Demokratisierung nach Auschwitz: Eine Geschichte der westdeutschen Sozialwissenschaften in der Nachkriegszeit* (Göttingen: Wallstein Verlag, 2022), 275.

Gehlen as professor at the University of Heidelberg in 1958."[130] At the same time, however, the Institute for Social Research collaborated with scholars who had worked under the Nazi regime, some of whom were ardent supporters. Heinz Sauermann, Ludwig Neundörfer, and Gerhard Wurzbacher were all members of Nazi organizations and contributed sociological knowledge to national socialist projects, including Heinrich Himmler's settlement policy (in the case of Neundörfer). After the war, they worked with the Institute for Social Research, including on a common project with Neundörfer's Sociographic Institute.[131] The Frankfurt School also collaborated with other institutes that "regrouped several sociologists who had been die-hard Nazis or had worked for Nazi organizations."[132] One of these was the Institut für Demoskopie Allensbach. The think tank in Frankfurt cooperated with it "in a planned project for the Office of the Federal Chancellor in 1953/54, with the aim to recruit officials for a new West German army."[133] This was in line with the general position taken by Adorno and Horkheimer, who advocated "the establishment of the *Bundeswehr* [West German armed forces]," emphasizing "that the liberal West had to be defended against totalitarian attacks by force of arms if necessary" (Horkheimer also "later repeatedly defended Israel's military actions").[134]

Between 1950 and 1952, Adorno directed the Darmstadt Study with Max Rolfes. He "was a former scientific adviser to Heinrich Himmler, who had been conducting research in Alsace and Lorraine for Himmler's settlement politics during the early 1940s."[135] This was a project of ethnic cleansing whose first wave of expulsions in Alsace in late 1940 led to the forced displacement of 105,000 people, who were, according to a Nazi memo on the topic, "in the main Jews, gypsies, and other foreign racial elements, criminals, asocial, and incurably insane persons, and in addition, Frenchmen and Francophiles."[136] Since the *Führer* had given permis-

---

130. Link, "Cooperation and Competition," 237.

131. See Link, "Cooperation and Competition." On the relationship between the Frankfurt School and Nazi collaborators, also see Link, *Demokratisierung nach Auschwitz*.

132. Link, "Cooperation and Competition," 231.

133. Ibid.

134. Link, *Demokratisierung nach Auschwitz*, 562.

135. Link, "Cooperation and Competition," 231.

136. Memorandum by Dr. Stier, 7 August 1942, Concerning a Conference on "General Directions for the Treatment of Deported Alsatians" Attended by Representatives of the Land Office and Settlement Staff, Strasbourg, the Office for the Repatriation of Ethnic Germans, the Reich Security Main Office, and the DUT, in *Trials of War Criminals Before*

sion to "cleanse Alsace of all foreign, sick, or unreliable elements," additional deportations followed, and the same is true of Lorraine.[137]

The Frankfurt School's collaborations with erstwhile Nazi researchers were, in the words of Fabian Link, "based on shared political sentiments, such as 'anti-totalitarianism.'"[138] Both parties were invested in *Westbindung*: the alliance with the US-led West against the communist East. Whereas leading Frankfurt scholars like Adorno and Horkheimer embraced the Western anti-totalitarian ideology that identified fascism and communism, the scholars who had pursued their careers under the Nazis "exchanged their anti-Bolshevist views for anti-totalitarian attitudes, opposing the Soviet communist state and welcoming Western democracy."[139] There was plenty of anticommunist common ground. Sociologist Helmut Schelsky, for instance, had been "a fervent anti-Bolshevist" and a member of several Nazi organizations, including the *Stürmabteilung*, or stormtroopers and the Nazi Party.[140] He also "fought enthusiastically as a soldier in the Second World War."[141] In the postwar era, he and his assistant Wurzbacher had several meetings with the leaders of the Frankfurt School, who "invited them to conferences and workshops to exchange ideas, research results, and methods."[142] In his well-researched 638-page book on the topic, Link provides a detailed account of all of the common ground, both theoretically and practically, between Schelsky's group, which included Arnold Gehlen, and Adorno and Horkheimer's. His overall conclusion is that "the similarities [between these two groups] clearly predominated in the early 1950s," though around 1960 "the cooperative relationships and content-related agreements between the two intellectual collectives became fragile."[143]

Adorno and Horkheimer not only presented themselves as leading critical theorists of fascism, but their writings on the topic have been widely celebrated. Their conceptualization of fascism is notoriously rather

---

the Nuremberg Military Tribunals Under Control Council Law, No. 10, Vol. 13: *United States of America v. Ernst von Weizsaecker, et al.* (Case 11: 'Ministries Case') (Washington, D.C.: U.S. Government Printing Office, 1952), 611–14, https://forum.axishistory.com/viewtopic.php?t=66094.

137. Ibid.
138. Link, "Cooperation and Competition," 231.
139. Ibid.
140. Ibid., 232.
141. Link, *Demokratisierung nach Auschwitz*, 54.
142. Link, "Cooperation and Competition," 232.
143. Link, *Demokratisierung nach Auschwitz*, 559, 568.

obscure, but they had a tendency to privilege psychological and cultural factors over and against the collectively resourced analysis of capitalist crisis and global class struggle that was being developed at the time by the dialectical and historical materialist tradition. Lars Fischer, in a capacious review article on "The Frankfurt School and Fascism," highlights the looseness of its theoretical work but nonetheless identifies a coherent unity of purpose: "What all the contributions to the debates among the members and associates of the Frankfurt School had in common . . . was the fact that they were meant to serve one purpose before all others: to facilitate the most effective possible opposition to Nazi Germany and its fascist allies."[144] If this was the unifying goal of their theoretical work, there can be little doubt that they practically failed, particularly if one examines their postwar collaborations.

In a revealing exchange, fellow émigré intellectual Günther Anders had the opportunity to ask Adorno how he, as a self-declared antifascist, could have concluded a truce with former Nazis like the philosophical anthropologist Arnold Gehlen. The Frankfurt School luminary replied that Gehlen's case was ambiguous and that he did not intend to defame him for his participation in the Nazi regime (Gehlen signed the university vow of allegiance to Hitler and the Nazis, joined the Nazi Party, and served in the *Wehrmacht*).[145] "It is quite indifferent to me with whom I shake hands," Adorno opined, "as long as nothing of this remains sticking to the paper upon which I write."[146] This is an obscure statement, but it appears to mean that practical collaboration with those who had sworn allegiance to the Third Reich was acceptable, so long as it did not sully his prose, thereby besmirching the reputation of his intellectual commodities.

It is not only that major figures like Adorno, Horkheimer, and Pollock worked closely with German professors who were Nazi collaborators. The latter also came to occupy leadership positions within the Institute for Social Research. Boris Rajewsky, a member of the board of the Institute's foundation and its legal representative, was "a former *Oberscharführer* (technical sergeant) in the SA [*Sturmabteilung* or stormtroopers] and member of the NSDAP [Nazi Party]."[147] As university rector, his "support

---

144. Lars Fischer, "The Frankfurt School and Fascism," in *The Sage Handbook of Frankfurt School Critical Theory*, ed. Beverley Best, et al. (London: Sage Publications, 2018), 800.

145. See Ernst Klee, *Das Personenlexikon zum Dritten Reich: Wer war was vor und nach 1945* (Frankfurt: Fischer Taschenbuch Verlag, 2005), 176.

146. Cited in Link, "Cooperation and Competition," 233.

147. Ibid.

was essential for the re-establishment of the Institute for Social Research" in Germany.[148] Lawyer Hellmut Becker, a one time member of the Nazi Party, "proved to be absolutely loyal to the Institute for Social Research as a lawyer and adviser, attending almost every meeting with potential clients and linking Horkheimer and Adorno to industrialists and politicians."[149] Since a genuine de-Nazification did not take place in occupied West Germany, connections to quondam Nazis facilitated the financial, political, and social success of the Institute.

According to a 1951 Rockefeller Foundation overview of the work being done by Adorno and Horkheimer, they wanted to recruit Ludwig von Friedeburg to "the staff of the Institute."[150] The Rockefeller report mentions that "von Friedeburg's father was the supreme commander of the German navy."[151] Hans-Georg von Friedeburg was, indeed, the deputy commander of Nazi U-boat forces and the last Commander-in-Chief of the navy of the Third Reich. He was "the only co-signatory of both *Wehrmacht* surrender documents," and he committed suicide soon thereafter.[152] His son, Ludwig, had the distinction of serving as the youngest submarine commander in the Second World War, and he became a first lieutenant in the navy.[153] This is the man whom Adorno recommended "in glowing terms," only six years after his service to the Nazi cause, claiming that he was "the most talented of the young people who have studied at the Institute."[154]

In 1949, Ludwig von Friedeburg attended the Salzburg Seminar, which was, in part, a scheme on the part of U.S. intelligence veterans "to foil the communist bid for ideological hegemony."[155] He began coursework at the Institute for Social Research in 1951, and Adorno successfully

---

148. Ibid.

149. Ibid., 235.

150. LCD, Diary, May 11, 1951, RG 1.2, Series 717, Box 15, Folder 155, Rockefeller Archive Center.

151. Ibid.

152. Manuel Ruoff, "Vom U-Boot zum Katheder und zur Rednertribüne," *Preußische Allgemeine*, May 21, 2024, https://paz.de/artikel/vom-u-boot-zum-katheder-und-zur-rednertribuene-a11363.html.

153. See the information compiled on the website uboat.net: https://uboat.net/men/commanders/321.html and Ruoff, "Vom U-Boot zum Katheder und zur Rednertribüne." On Friedeburg's life and work, also see Alex Demirovic and Heinz Steinert, "In Memoriam Ludwig von Friedeburg," *Soziologie*, Vol. 39, No. 4 (2010): 485-92.

154. LCD, Diary, May 11, 1951, RG 1.2, Series 717, Box 15, Folder 155, Rockefeller Archive Center.

155. Wilford, *The Mighty Wurlitzer*, 129.

recruited him in 1954 (he received Rockefeller support at the Institute).[156] Friedeburg became an assistant to Adorno and then director of empirical research at the Frankfurt School. Having lost "HICOG as its main donor" in 1953 and facing stiffer competition for contracts from politicians and industry, as well as for research grants from the major foundations, the Institute "responded by shifting its research focus": "its empirical social researchers henceforth tailored their projects more closely to regional politics and industry-related topics."[157] It is for this reason that "two proven social empiricists were appointed as co-directors of the Institute: von Friedeburg in 1954 and [Rudolf] Gunzert in 1956, who became the second director of the Institute three years later" (Gunzert had joined the Nazi party and was given a teaching position at the University of Heidelberg by the Reich Ministry of Science, Education and Culture).[158] This allowed the Frankfurt School to more successfully develop the kinds of anticommunist, empirically-driven social scientific research that served the political and business interests of occupied West Germany, as well as those of its imperial overseers in the United States.

Friedeburg's "first task was to bring the Mannesmann study to a successful conclusion."[159] This means that a former Nazi was put in charge of doing Institute research for a Nazi-connected corporation, which contributed—at least potentially—to the company's forestalling of socialist organizing. The erstwhile fascist first lieutenant became so integral to the Institute's leadership that one of the major historians of the Frankfurt School states that "he more or less independently kept the day-to-day business of research going."[160] Although Friedeburg temporarily left to Berlin in 1962, he returned to Frankfurt in 1966 to become one of the directors of the Institute for Social Research, as well as of the associated university seminar, together with Adorno and Habermas (the latter had, like Friedeburg, served in the Hitler Youth).[161]

---

156. See Ruoff, "Vom U-Boot zum Katheder und zur Rednertribüne" and Wiggershaus, *The Frankfurt School*, 438, 480, and 537.

157. Link, *Demokratisierung nach Auschwitz*, 298.

158. Ibid. Regarding Gunzert, see Link, *Demokratisierung nach Auschwitz*, 275 and this online biography: https://wiki.studiumdigitale.uni-frankfurt.de/SOZFRA/index.php/Rudolf_Gunzert.

159. Wiggershaus, *The Frankfurt School*, 481. See also Alex Demirovic and Heinz Steinert, "In Memorium Ludwig von Friedeburg," *Soziologie*, Vol. 39, No. 4 (January 2010): 485–92.

160. Wiggershaus, *The Frankfurt School*, 563.

161. See Demirovic and Steinert, "In Memorium Ludwig von Friedeburg," as well as

As Friedeburg later averred: "it was my close friendship and solidarity with Adorno that determined my basic relationship with the Institute for Social Research."[162] In an ironic twist of fate, this one time Nazi published and wrote the preface to the 1973 German edition of Adorno's contribution to the Frankfurt School's classic study of fascism, *The Authoritarian Personality*, and he also served as Adorno's literary executor after his death.[163] Given Friedeburg's high caliber Nazi pedigree, which contrasted sharply with Adorno's Jewish heritage and Marxian intellectual interests, these two were a peculiar postwar pair. Friedeburg had joined the Hitler Youth at the age of twelve and voluntarily embarked on a military career four years later, whereas Adorno went into exile during National Socialism. "In 1942—the year in which Adorno and Max Horkheimer began their work on *Dialectic of Enlightenment*—Friedeburg cheered Hitler at the Sportpalast."[164] When Adorno later lambasted, in a text ironically titled "The Meaning of Working through the Past," the "idiocy" of those who shift the "responsibility for the atrocities of Hitler … onto those who tolerated his seizure of power and not to *the ones who cheered him on*," had he forgotten about the past of his close friend and collaborator, who had enthusiastically supported the *Führer*?[165] By the time Friedeburg was hired and then began moving into leadership positions at the Institute, he had spent more years of his life (eleven) being a Nazi than a former Nazi (nine).

Adorno was actually fully aware of his friend's past, but he relied on a doggerel version of dialectics in a deplorable effort to convert a vice

the biography available on this well-documented website on the student movement at Frankfurt University: https://studentenbewegung-frankfurt.de/ludwig-von-friedeburg/.

162. Cited in the following online biography: https://studentenbewegung-frankfurt.de/ludwig-von-friedeburg/.

163. See Theodor W. Adorno, *Studien zum autoritären Charakter*, trans. Milli Weinbrenner, preface by Ludwig von Friedeburg (Frankfurt: Suhrkampf, 1973); Link, *Demokratisierung nach Auschwitz*, 321; and Wiggershaus, *The Frankfurt School*, 633. It is true that Friedeburg joined the German Social Democratic Party (SPD) in 1969. However, as Fabian Link rightly points out, the conversion of anti-Bolshevism into anti-totalitarianism was facilitated by the SPD, which "announced the party's anti-communist and anti-Soviet program on 6 May 1945" (Link, "Cooperation and Competition," 232).

164. See the biography available here: https://studentenbewegung-frankfurt.de/ludwig-von-friedeburg/.

165. Theodor Adorno, *Critical Models: Interventions and Catchwords*, trans. Henry W. Pickford (New York: Columbia University Press, 2005), 91 (my emphasis).

into a virtue. In a report penned by the critical theorist, he explained that Friedeburg "is certainly not one of the many people who, having grown up in the specific atmosphere of the Hitler dictatorship, have freed themselves from it out of genuine inner strength."[166] Instead, the world-renowned philosopher went on to write, it was the "qualities that developed in the officer milieu, such as loyalty, a sense of duty and a collective sense of responsibility" that had evolved in Friedeburg to such an extent that they "allowed him full emancipation."[167] Nazi discipline, it seems, is what permitted him to free himself from Nazism.

It would be interesting to compare this statement, and more generally the Institute's collaboration with (former) fascists, to the famous fascism (F) scale developed by Adorno in *The Authoritarian Personality*. This scale was part of a questionable endeavor to identify psychological variables that were likely to foster a "potentially antidemocratic personality."[168] "Conventionalism" and "authoritarian submission" are the first two variables on the F scale, which appear to be what Adorno was emphasizing in his description of Friedeburg as a loyal officer. He was a Nazi, after all, so he presumably would have ranked rather high on the F scale, like the Institute's other collaborators. This begs the question, however, of how a high ranking on the F scale would have helped him—or others—overcome fascism, when the opposite is supposed to be the case. Was the F scale used to vet collaborators with the Frankfurt School and, if so, to what avail?

It is a remarkable fact, then, that the Institute renowned for antifascist critical theory not only collaborated with erstwhile Nazi researchers after the war. It also integrated several of them into powerful leadership positions within the Institute, including its legal representative, members of its board, and its directors. Rather than an established antifascist directing the Institute after Adorno and Horkheimer, it is highly revealing that the man put in charge was an intellectual who had received eleven years of well-disciplined training by the Third Reich. Friedeburg became, in fact, the longest serving managing director of the Frankfurt School, a

166. Cited in the biography available here: https://studentenbewegung-frankfurt.de/ludwig-von-friedeburg/.
167. Ibid.
168. Theodor Adorno, Else Frenkel-Brunswik, et al., *The Authoritarian Personality* (New York: Norton, 1969), 228.

position he held from 1975 to 2001.[169] These close collaborations with former Nazis and their recruitment into leadership positions in the Institute
were integral to the economic, political, social, and intellectual success of
the Frankfurt School during its postwar integration into occupied West
Germany.[170]

Imperial Critical Theory

Horkheimer expressed his support for the imperial project in Vietnam,
which he judged necessary to stop the Chinese.[171] Speaking at one of
the *Amerika Häuser* in Germany, which were propaganda outposts in
the anticommunist *Kulturkampf*, he solemnly declared in May 1967: "In
America, when it is necessary to conduct a war, – and now listen to me
… it is not so much a question of the defense of the homeland, but it is
essentially a matter of the defense of the Constitution, the defense of the
rights of man."[172] The high priest of critical theory is here describing a
country that was founded as a settler colony, whose genocidal elimination
of the Indigenous population seamlessly merged with a project of imperialist expansion that has arguably left the bloodiest footprint—as Martin

---

169. See Demirovic and Steinert, "In Memorium Ludwig von Friedeburg" and the online
biography available here: https://www.lagis-hessen.de/pnd/116791950.

170. See Link, *Demokratisierung nach Auschwitz* and "Cooperation and Competition."

171. According to Wiggershaus: "Horkheimer did not, like Paul Tillich, defend socialism
or, like Hugo Sinzheimer or Hermann Heller, belong to the committed democrats and
declared opponents of Nazism" (*The Frankfurt School*, 112). On Adenauer, see Rockhill,
"Critical and Revolutionary Theory," as well as Agee and Wolf, ed., *Dirty Work*, 184–87,
and De la Motte and Green, *Stasi State or Socialist Paradise?*, 19. Douglas Kellner aptly
described the late Horkheimer as someone "who increasingly sought refuge in religion
and assumed incredibly reactionary political positions, defending the U.S. role in Viet
Nam [sic], warning of the Red Chinese 'yellow peril' and taking an anticommunist stance
in the Cold War." Douglas Kellner, "The Frankfurt School Revisited: A Critique of Martin
Jay's the *Dialectical Imagination*," *New German Critique*, No. 4 (Winter 1975): 151. On
Horkheimer's anticommunism, also see Helmut Dubiel, *Theory and Politics: Studies in
the Development of Critical Theory*, trans. Benjamin Gregg (Cambridge, MA: MIT Press,
1985).

172. Quoted in Wolfgang Kraushaar, ed., *Frankfurter Schule und Studentenbewegung: Von
der Flaschenpost zum Molotowcocktail 1946–1995*, Vol. 1: *Chronik* (Hamburg: Rogner &
Bernhard Verlags KG, 1998), 252–53. On the *Amerika Häuser* as the "crown jewels" of
the U.S. occupation of Germany and its cultural war on communism, see Nicholas J.
Cull, *The Cold War and the United States Information Agency: American Propaganda and
Public Diplomacy, 1945–1989* (Cambridge: Cambridge University Press, 2010), 27.

Luther King Jr. had just publicly argued in April 1967—on the history of the modern world (including some 37 military and CIA interventions between the end of the Second World War and 1967, when Horkheimer broadcast this ignominious claim via a U.S. propaganda platform).[173] As Domenico Losurdo pointed out in his insightful critique of Horkheimer, he framed the Cold War as a battle between civilized and totalitarian states, and he argued for the defense of the former against the barbarism of the latter.[174] Losurdo also drew attention to Horkheimer's assessment of the Black liberation struggle in the United States since the critical theorist maintained—based on an anecdote about his "Negro friend" and his experience on a panel with U.S. American scholars—that "Negroes" are angrier at other "Negroes" than at whites, claiming that "the terror of Negro activists against other Negroes is much fiercer [*stärker*] than one suspects."[175]

Although Adorno often indulged in the petty-bourgeois politics of complicit passivity, avoiding public pronouncements on major political events, the few statements he did make were strikingly reactionary. For instance, in 1956, he co-authored an article with Horkheimer in defense of the imperialist invasion of Egypt by Israel, Britain, and France, which aimed at seizing the Suez Canal and overthrowing Gamal Abdel Nasser (an action condemned by the United Nations).[176] Referring to Nasser, one of the prominent anticolonial leaders of the non-aligned movement, as "a fascist chieftain . . . who conspires with Moscow," they exclaimed: "No one even ventures to point out that these Arab robber states have been on the lookout for years for an opportunity to fall upon Israel and to slaughter the Jews who have found refuge there."[177] According to this

---

173. See William Blum, *Killing Hope: US Military and CIA Interventions since World War II* (London: Zed Books, 2014).

174. See Domenico Losurdo, *Western Marxism: How It Was Born, How It Died, How It Can Be Reborn*, ed. Gabriel Rockhill (New York: Monthly Review Press, 2024), 114.

175. Horkheimer, *Gesellschaft im Übergang*, 174.

176. On the Suez War, see Richard Becker, *Palestine, Israel and the U.S. Empire* (San Francisco: PSL Publications, 2009), 71–78.

177. Quoted in Jeffries, *Grand Hotel Abyss*, 297. Adorno and Horkheimer's statements on Nasser are perfectly in line with the propaganda produced by the Western media and intelligence agencies. As Paul Lashmar and James Oliver have convincingly argued, the Information Research Department—a secret anticommunist propaganda office closely tied to MI6 and the CIA—pressured the BBC and its other news assets to present Nasser as "a Soviet dupe," which was "the favored all-purpose propaganda line for anti-colonial leaders." *Britain's Secret Propaganda War: 1948-1977* (Phoenix Mill, UK: Sutton

pseudo-dialectical inversion, it is the Arab states that are "robbers," not the settler colony working with core imperialist countries to infringe upon the self-determination of Arabs. We would be well served to recall Lenin's trenchant rejection of such sophistry, which is characteristic of much of what counts for "dialectics" in the imperial theory industry: "Not infrequently have dialectics served . . . as a bridge to sophistry. But we remain dialecticians and we combat sophistry not by denying the possibility of all transformations in general, but by analyzing the *given* phenomenon in its concrete setting and development."[178] Such concrete, materialist analysis is precisely what is lacking in idealist inversions à la Adorno and Horkheimer.

Marcuse, renowned for his later radicalization, also expressed his support for Israel's settler colonial imperialist project. It is true that he made very critical comments regarding its founding, and he even condemned what he called the "Jewish fascists in Israel."[179] However, in a debate a few weeks after the Six-Day War of 1967, he asserted: "I feel in solidarity and identify myself with Israel for personal reasons."[180] He described Israel's assault on Egypt, Jordan, and Syria as a "preventive war" that "could and must be understood and justified."[181] Such a conclusion, as Losurdo pointed out, was "entirely based on the assumption of a 'war of annihilation' that the Arab states are scolded for."[182] It was sorely lacking in rigorous materialist analysis. Indeed, one of the Israeli commanders in the 1967 war, General Matityahu Peled, made the following candid admission to the Israeli newspaper *Haaretz* on March 19, 1972: "The thesis that

---

Publishing, 1998), 64. Colin Legum of the *Observer*, which regularly collaborated with British intelligence, recalled that: "the favorite official line was to discredit any militant anticolonial leader as a Communist. We were fed confidential reports from MI6 proving the Moscow links with all these colonial agitators." Cited in Jonathan Bloch and Patrick Fitzgerald, *British Intelligence and Covert Action: Africa, Middle East and Europe since 1945* (Dingle, Co. Kerry, Ireland: Brandon Book Publishers, 1984), 92. Ernst Bloch similarly supported Israel and the war on Egypt, and he accused Nasser of following a "Nazi model." See Losurdo, *Western Marxism*, 127.

178. Vladimir Lenin, *Collected Works*, Vol. 22 (Moscow: Progress Publishers, 1966), 309.

179. Cited in Müller, *Krieger und Gelehrte*, 654.

180. Quoted in Barry Kätz, *Herbert Marcuse and the Art of Liberation: An Intellectual Biography* (London: Verso, 1982), 207.

181. Cited in Losurdo, *Western Marxism*, 129.

182. Ibid.

the danger of genocide was hanging over us in June 1967 and that Israel was fighting for its physical existence is only a bluff, which was born and developed after the war."[183]

Adorno and Horkheimer published one of their most overtly political texts in 1956. Rather than supporting the global movement for anticolonial liberation and the building of a socialist world, they celebrate—with only a few minor exceptions—the superiority of the West, while repeatedly disparaging the Soviet Union and China. Invoking stock racist descriptions of the purported barbarians in the East, whom they describe using the overtly subhumanizing vocabulary of "beasts," they flatly proclaim that they are "fascists" who have chosen "slavery."[184] Adorno even chastises Germans who mistakenly think that "the Russians stand for socialism," reminding them that the Russians are actually "fascists," adding that the "industrialists and bankers"—with whom he identifies—already know this.[185]

"Everything the Russians write slips into ideology, into crude, stupid twaddle," Adorno brazenly asserts in this text, as if he had read *everything* they wrote, even though, per usual, he does not cite a single source (nor did he even read Russian, as far as I know).[186] Claiming that there is "an element of re-barbarization" in their thinking, which is also to be found in Marx and Engels according to him, he unabashedly proclaims

183. Quoted in Richard Becker, "June 1967 War: A Turning Point in Palestine's Liberation Struggle," *Liberation News*, June 5, 2007, https://www.liberationnews.org/07-06-05-june-1967-war-turning-point-in-html/.

184. Adorno and Horkheimer, "Towards a New Manifesto?," 40, 49, 35. The racialization of communists has been an important part of anticommunist ideology, as Domenico Losurdo explained in *War and Revolution*, trans. Gregory Elliott (London: Verso, 2015). Leonardo Acosta has provided a similar analysis in which he directly identified the broader social tendency of imperialist ideology that influenced Adorno and Horkheimer, and to which they contributed in turn: "Since the worst enemy of capitalism resides in the force of the exploited masses, the repertory of working-class stereotypes in the imperialist press is very broad. The first rule that the press seems to follow is that the exploited masses are never composed of human beings, hence the analogies with animal or subhuman attitudes and characteristics. A typical example is the 'Communist hordes' or 'Chinese hordes,' which imperialism tried to use to explain its defeat in Korea." Leonardo Acosta, "Mass Media and Imperialist Ideology," in *Communication and Class Struggle*, Vol. 1, *Capitalism, Imperialism*, ed. Armand Mattelart and Seth Siegelaub (New York: International General, 1979), 147.

185. Adorno and Horkheimer, "Towards a New Manifesto?," 49.

186. Ibid., 59.

that it is "more reified than in the most advanced bourgeois thought."[187] As if this was not enough disingenuous grandstanding, Adorno has the chutzpah to describe this writing project with Horkheimer as a "strictly Leninist manifesto."[188] This is in a discussion in which they affirm that they "are not calling on anyone to take action," and Adorno explicitly elevates bourgeois thought and what he refers to as "culture at its most advanced" above the supposed barbarism of socialist thinking.[189] Moreover, it is in this context that Horkheimer doubled down on their social chauvinism by averring, in a world-historical conclusion that provoked no rebuttal on the part of his "Leninist" collaborator: "I believe that Europe and America are probably the best civilizations that history has produced up to now as far as prosperity and justice are concerned. The key point now is to ensure the preservation of these gains."[190] In 1956, it is worth recalling, the United States was still largely racially segregated, was involved in anticommunist witch hunts and destabilization campaigns around the world, and had recently extended its imperial reach by overthrowing democratically elected governments in Iran (1953) and Guatemala (1954), while the European powers were waging violent struggles to hold onto their colonies or convert them into neocolonies.

---

187. Ibid.

188. Ibid., 57.

189. Ibid., 57, 59.

190. Ibid., 41. Horkheimer expressed similar pro-capitalist, anticommunist views on numerous occasions. For instance, in a long letter to Adorno dated September 27, 1958, he claimed that "revolution really means the passage to terror" and asserted that what must be defended is "the remainder of bourgeois civilization where the idea of individual freedom and authentic society still has its place." Adorno and Horkheimer, *Correspondance*, Vol. 4, 395. In 1968, to cite another example, he explicitly described his position as counter-revolutionary: "An open declaration that even a dubious democracy, for all its defects, is always better than the dictatorship which would inevitably result from a revolution today, seems to me necessary for the sake of truth." Horkheimer, *Critical Theory*, viii. After recalling Horkheimer's condemnation of the "savage barbarism of the East," Stefan Müller-Doohm writes in his 700-page biography of Adorno that "Adorno and Horkheimer were in agreement in their assessment of the so-called Eastern bloc, i.e. the Soviet Union, but also communist China" (415). Regarding colonialism, Horkheimer wrote to Adorno that although "the European dream of permanent superiority in the colonial era" was "abominable," it nevertheless had "its good sides." Adorno and Horkheimer, *Correspondance*, Vol. 4, 466.

"Fascism and Communism Are the Same"

In the East . . . they have chosen slavery. . . . We have to reject . . . Marxism.

—MAX HORKHEIMER[191]

One of the most consistent political claims advanced by Adorno and Horkheimer is that there is a "totalitarian" equivalence between fascism and communism, if it manifests itself in socialist state-building projects, anticolonial movements of the Third World, or even New Left mobilizations in the West. In all three cases, those who think they are breaking out of the "shackling society" are only making things worse. The patent fact that Western capitalist countries offered no significant bulwark against fascism, which arose *within* the capitalist world, and that it was precisely the Soviet Union and communists—including in China—that did the lion's share of the work to defeat it, does not seem to have caused them to reflect on the viability of this benighted and simplistic thesis (which is to say nothing of the importance of socialism to anticolonial movements and the uprisings of the 1960s). In fact, for all of his moral opining on the horrors of Auschwitz, Adorno appears to have forgotten who actually liberated the infamous concentration camp: the Red Army.

Horkheimer had formulated his version of horseshoe theory with particular clarity in a limited circulation pamphlet published in 1942, which broke with the Aesopian language of many of the Institute's other publications. Directly accusing Friedrich Engels of utopianism, he averred that the socialization of the means of production had led to an increase in repression, and ultimately to an authoritarian state. "The bourgeoisie earlier held the government in check through its property," according to this millionaire's son, whereas in new societies socialism simply "did not function," except to produce the mistaken belief that one was—through the Party, honored leader, or the supposed march of history—"acting in the name of something greater than oneself."[192] Horkheimer's position in this piece is perfectly in line with anarcho-anticommunism, which is a widespread ideology within the Western left: a "classless democracy" is supposed to emerge spontaneously from the people through "free agreement," without the supposedly pernicious influence of parties or states. As Losurdo insightfully pointed out, the Nazi war machine was ravaging the

---

191. Adorno and Horkheimer, "Towards a New Manifesto?," 35–36.
192. Max Horkheimer, "The Authoritarian State," *Telos* 15 (Spring 1973): 16.

USSR in the early 1940s, and Horkheimer's call for socialists to abandon the state and party centralization therefore amounted to nothing less than a demand that they capitulate before the Nazis' genocidal rampage.[193]

Whereas there are vague suggestions at the end of Horkheimer's 1942 pamphlet that there might be something desirable in socialism, later texts would bring into full relief Adorno and Horkheimer's unequivocal rejection of it. For instance, when they were considering making a public statement on their relationship to the Soviet Union, Adorno sent the following draft of a planned co-authored piece to Horkheimer: "Our philosophy, as a dialectical critique of the overall social tendency of the age, stands in the sharpest opposition to the politics and doctrine that emanates from the Soviet Union. We are unable to see anything in the practice of the military dictatorships disguised as people's democracies other than a new form of repression."[194] It is worth noting in this regard, given the overwhelming lack of materialist analysis of actually existing socialism on the part of Adorno and Horkheimer, that even the CIA recognized that the Soviet Union was not a dictatorship. In a 1955 report, the Agency clearly stated that the Western idea of a Soviet dictatorship was exaggerated because there was collective leadership in the USSR, even in Stalin's time.[195]

In 1959, Adorno published a text titled "The Meaning of Working through the Past" in which he recycled the "shameful truth" of "philistine wisdom" referenced in this earlier draft, namely that—in complete conformity with the dominant Cold War ideology—fascism and communism are the same because they are two forms of "totalitarianism."[196] Openly rejecting the vantage point of "political-economic ideology," which distinguishes these two warring camps, Adorno claimed to have privileged access to a deeper social-psychological dynamic that unites them.[197] As

---

193. See Losurdo, *Western Marxism*.

194. Max Horkheimer, *Gesammelte Schriften*, ed. Alfred Schmidt and Gunzelin Schmid Noerr, Vol. 18 (Frankfurt: S. Fischer, 1985), 73. Also see Müller-Doohm, *Adorno*, 334. Adorno went so far as to explicitly endorse the position of the militant anticommunist and CIA collaborator Arthur Koestler, writing that "communism has become a 'rightwing party' (which Koestler highlighted) and . . . it has completely identified itself with Russian imperialism." Adorno and Horkheimer, *Correspondance*, Vol. 4, 655.

195. See "Comments on the Change in Soviet Leadership," March 2, 1955, the CIA FOIA Electronic Reading Room, https://www.cia.gov/readingroom/document/cia-rdp80-00810a006000360009-0. I would like to express my gratitude to Colin Bodayle for drawing my attention to this document.

196. Adorno, *Critical Models*, 94.

197. Ibid.

"authoritarian personalities," he asserted ex cathedra, fascists and communists "possess weak egos" and compensate by identifying themselves with "real-existing power" and "great collectives."[198] The very idea of an "authoritarian personality" is thus a deceitful notion aimed at synthesizing opposites via psychologizing pseudo-dialectics. It begs the question, moreover, of why psychology and particular ways of thinking appear, at least here, to be more central to historical explanation than material forces and class struggle.

Given Adorno's collaboration with erstwhile Nazis, particularly in the case of his close friendship with future Institute director Ludwig von Friedeburg, one might wonder whether they were diagnosed with weak egos. Was it for this reason that, after dutifully serving the Nazi cause (for eleven years in Friedeburg's case), they pursued *Westbindung*, or alliance with the West, via the Frankfurt School after the war? Did they simply, like so many other Nazis, identify with the "real-existing power" of the world's leading imperialist force, which was militarily occupying their country, as well as with the "great collective" of the imperial West, which was pursuing an anticommunist agenda like its Nazi forebears? Does the Frankfurt School, and Adorno more specifically, have a better way of explaining this shift in allegiance, if one is to rely on his psychologizing forms of explanation? Why, finally, did so many Nazis ally with the West after the war, like Friedeburg, rather than with the communists, whom they continued to fight?

In spite of this attempt to psychologically identify fascists and communists through an idealist amalgamation, Adorno nonetheless suggested, in the same text, that the Nazi assault on the Soviet Union could be retrospectively justified due to the fact that the Bolsheviks were—like Hitler himself had said—a menace to Western civilization. "The threat that the East will engulf the foothills of Western Europe is obvious," the famed philosopher proclaimed, "and whoever fails to resist it is literally guilty of repeating Chamberlain's *appeasement*."[199] The analogy is revealing because, in this case, it would mean appeasing the "fascist" communists if one did not directly fight against them. In other words, as obscure and convoluted as his phraseology is, this appears to be a clarion call for military opposition to the spread of communism (which is perfectly in line with Horkheimer's support for the U.S. empire's war in Vietnam).

Adorno's fierce rejection of actually existing socialism was also on full

198. Ibid.
199. Ibid.

display in his exchange with Alfred Sohn-Rethel. The latter asked him if *Negative Dialectics* had anything to say about changing the world, and if the Chinese Cultural Revolution was part of the "affirmative tradition" he condemned. Adorno replied that he rejected the "moral pressure" from "official Marxism" to put philosophy into practice.[200] "Nothing but despair can save us," he asserted with his signature panache of petty-bourgeois melancholia.[201] Adding, for good measure, that the events in communist China were no cause for hope, he explained with memorable insistence that his entire thinking life had been resolutely pitted against this form—and presumably others—of socialism: "I would have to deny everything I have thought my whole life long if I were to admit to feeling anything but horror at the sight of it."[202]

Adorno's open indulgence in despair and simultaneous abhorrence of actually existing socialism are not simply idiosyncratic, personal reactions but are common affective ideologies within his class position. "The representatives of the modern labor movement," Lenin wrote in 1910, "find that they have plenty to protest against but nothing to despair about."[203] In a description that anticipated Adorno's petty-bourgeois gloom, the leader of the world's first successful socialist revolution then proceeded to explain that "despair is typical of those who do not understand the causes of evil, see no way out, and are incapable of struggle."[204]

Adorno also pursued this line of thinking, or rather feeling, in his criticisms of anti-imperialist and anti-capitalist student activism in the 1960s. He agreed with Habermas—who had himself been a member of the Hitler Youth and studied for four years under the "Nazi philosopher" (his description of Heidegger)—that this activism amounted to "left fascism." He defended West Germany as a functioning democracy rather than a "fascist" state, as some of the students argued.[205] At the same time, he quarreled with Marcuse over what he judged to be the latter's misguided support for the students and the antiwar movement, explicitly claiming that the answer to the question "What is to be done?" for good dialecticians is *nothing at all*: "The goal of real praxis would be its own

---

200. Müller-Doohm, *Adorno*, 438.

201. Ibid.

202. Ibid.

203. V. I. Lenin, *Collected Works*, Vol. 16 (Moscow: Progress Publishers, 1977), 332.

204. Ibid.

205. As I have argued in "Critical and Revolutionary Theory," this assessment on the part of the students was justified, at least to a large extent.

abolition."[206] He thereby inverted, through dialectical sophistry, one of the central tenets of Marxism, notably the primacy of practice. It is in this context of turning Marx on his head that he repeated, once again, the ideological mantra of the capitalist world: "Fascism and communism are the same."[207] Even though he referred to this slogan as a "petit bourgeois truism," apparently acknowledging its ideological status, he unabashedly embraced it.[208]

Idealism is the hallmark of Adorno and Horkheimer's reflections on actually existing socialism and, more generally, progressive social movements. Rather than studying the projects that they denigrate with any of the rigor and earnestness with which they sometimes approach other topics, they rely on stock misrepresentations and anticommunist canards devoid of concrete analysis (although they occasionally reference a few of the anticommunist publications, like those by the rabid cold warrior Arthur Koestler, which were amply funded and supported by imperialist states and their intelligence services).[209] This is particularly true in the case of their vilification of socialist state building projects. Their writings on the topic are not only remarkably devoid of references to any rigorous scholarship on the matter, but they proceed as if such serious engagement was not even necessary. These texts genuflect to the dominant ideology, stalwartly insisting on the anti-Stalinist bona fides of their

---

206. Adorno, *Critical Models*, 267. Adorno's pseudo-dialectical praise of inaction as the best form of action is reiterated in his correspondence with Marcuse regarding the student protests: "We withstood in our time, you no less than me, a much more dreadful situation—that of the murder of the Jews, without proceeding to praxis; simply because it was blocked to us.... To put it bluntly: I think that you are deluding yourself in being unable to go on without participating in the student stunts, because of what is occurring in Vietnam or Biafra. If that really is your reaction, then you should not only protest against the horror of napalm bombs but also against the unspeakable Chinese-style tortures that the Vietcong carry out permanently." Adorno and Marcuse, "Correspondence on the German Student Movement," *New Left Review* 233 (January–February 1999): 127. He made similar statements elsewhere, such as in his 1969 text on "Resignation" where he celebrated the "utopian moment in thinking" over and against any form of action: "The uncompromisingly critical thinker, who neither signs over his consciousness nor lets himself be terrorized into action, is in truth the one who does not give in.... Thinking is actually the force of resistance." Adorno, *Critical Models*, 293.

207. Adorno, *Critical Models*, 268.

208. Ibid.

209. Koestler was a major figure in the networks of the CIA's Congress for Cultural Freedom (CCF) and MI6's Information Research Department (IRD).

authors, without being concerned with any of the details, nuances, or complexities.[210] They thereby attempt to provide intellectual credibility to the dogmatic propaganda that was aggressively being promoted by Western intelligence agencies like the Information Research Department (IRD). One of its key themes was precisely "equating Communism with Nazism," while intentionally ignoring any positive contributions made by the communists.[211] The IRD had several hundred propagandists pushing out this line in their expansive network of media assets, and it came to work closely with the CIA and train its operatives in the dark arts of psychological warfare.

Given how directly Adorno and Horkheimer parroted the Western propaganda being put out by agencies like this, one cannot help but wonder, then, if the students were not correct when, in the late 1960s, they circulated leaflets asserting that these Frankfurt scholars were "left idiots of the authoritarian state" who were "critical in theory, conformist in practice."[212] Hans-Jürgen Krahl, one of Adorno's doctoral students, went so far as to publicly besmirch his mentor and the other Frankfurt professors as "Scheißkritische Theoretiker [shit-critical theorists]."[213] He voiced this lapidary critique of these stalwart defenders of ABS (Anything But Socialism) Theory when he was being arrested, at the behest of Adorno, for a university occupation related to his involvement in the Socialist German Students' League. The fact that the author of Negative Dialectics called the police to have his own students arrested is a standard reference point among his political critics. As we have seen, however, it is only the very tip of the iceberg. Far from being a bizarre anomaly, it is consistent with his politics, his social function within the intellectual apparatus, his class standing, and his overall orientation within global class struggle.

Although it is rarely mentioned, Adorno was not alone in summoning the police to arrest his students. He was joined by none other than his close friend and colleague, the former Nazi first lieutenant Ludwig von

---

210. For an excellent overview of the German Democratic Republic, see De la Motte and Green, Stasi State or Socialist Paradise?

211. Lashmar and Oliver, Britain's Secret Propaganda War, 29.

212. Quoted in Esther Leslie, "Introduction to Adorno/Marcuse Correspondence on the German Student Movement," New Left Review 233 (January-February 1999): 119 and Kraushaar, Frankfurter Schule und Studentenbewegung, Vol. 1, 374.

213. Kraushaar, Frankfurter Schule und Studentbewegung, Vol. 1, 398. Krahl was the only activist not released from jail the same night, and Adorno decided to press charges against him, as he had in 1964 against the student group Subversive Aktion, in spite of pressure to drop the charges.

Friedeburg.[214] The latter was at the time one of the three members of the Institute's board, along with another quondam Nazi, Rudolf Gunzert.[215] The irony of this situation should not be lost on us: the students accused of "left fascism" by the leaders of the Frankfurt School for their opposition to fascism in West Germany were arrested at the behest of a former Nazi and his longtime collaborator and supporter, both of whom were co-directing the Institute for Social Research, alongside yet another one time Nazi.[216]

The Tuis of Western Marxism

> If those who have plenty were to hand some over to the needy, they would ultimately find themselves overwhelmed by them.
>
> —MAX HORKHEIMER[217]

Brecht proposed the neologism "Tuis" to refer to intellectuals (*Intellektuellen*) who, as subjects of a commodified culture, get everything backwards (hence *Tellekt-Uellen-In*). He had shared his ideas for a *Tui-Novel* with Benjamin in the 1930s, and he later wrote a play that emerged out of his earlier notes: *Turandot or The Whitewashers' Congress*. Brecht returned to the German Democratic Republic after the war to contribute to the socialist state building project, unlike the Frankfurt scholars who settled in West Germany with funding from the capitalist ruling class and imperialist states. He wrote *Turandot*, in part, as a satirical critique of these Western "Marxists."

In the play, the Tuis are presented as professional whitewashers who receive handsome salaries for making things appear the opposite of what they are. "The whole country is governed by injustice," Sen states in *Turandot*, before providing a concise summary of ABS Theory: "And in the Tui Academy all you get to learn is why it has to be that way."[218] Tui training, like the work of the Institute for Social Research, teaches us that *there is no alternative* to the dominant order, and it thereby forecloses the possibility of system change. In one of the most striking scenes, the Tuis

---

214. See Wiggershaus, *The Frankfurt School*, 633.
215. See ibid.; Link, *Demokratisierung nach Auschwitz*, 275; and this online biography: https://wiki.studiumdigitale.uni-frankfurt.de/SOZFRA/index.php/Rudolf_Gunzert.
216. See https://studentenbewegung-frankfurt.de/rudolf-gunzert/.
217. Adorno and Horkheimer, "Towards a New Manifesto?," 61.
218. Bertolt Brecht, *Collected Plays: Six*, ed. John Willett and Ralph Manheim (London: Random House, 1998), 189.

are shown preparing for the whitewashers' congress. Nu Shan, one of the teachers in the Academy, operates a pulley system that can raise or lower a basket of bread in front of the speaker's face. In training a young man named Shi Me to become a Tui, he tells him to speak on the topic "Why Kai Ho's position is false" (Kai Ho is a revolutionary resembling Mao Zedong). Nu Shan explains that he will raise the breadbasket above his head when Shi Me says something wrong and lower it in front of his face when it is correct. After much raising and lowering in relation to Shi Me's ability to conform to the dominant ideology, his arguments crescendo to the point of shrill anticommunist slander devoid of rational argumentation: "Kai Ho isn't a philosopher at all, but just a loudmouth—*the basket sinks*—a troublemaker, a power-hungry good-for-nothing, an irresponsible gambler, a muckraker, a rapist, an unbeliever, a bandit and a criminal. *The basket is hovering just in front of the speaker's mouth.* A tyrant!"[219] This scene presents, in microcosm, the relationship between professional intellectuals and their financial backers within class societies: the former earn their bread as academic free agents by providing the best possible ideology for the latter. It is a matter of literal food for thought.

What the Frankfurt School had to offer the bread givers of "the shackling society" was by no means insignificant. Mobilizing pseudo-dialectical sophistry, they defended in highfalutin academic language the propagandistic idea that communism is indistinguishable from fascism, even though some thirty-five million Soviets had given their lives to defeat the Nazi war machine (to mention but one of the most blatant forms of opposition between communism and fascism, although there are of course many others since they are mortal enemies).[220] Moreover, by displacing class struggle in favor of an idealist critical theory severed from practical political engagements, they shifted the very foundations of analysis away from dialectical and historical materialism toward a generalized theoretical critique of domination, power, and identity thinking. They also made significant contributions to the West's imperial project of "democracy promotion," the development of imperialist propaganda,

---

219. Ibid., 145.

220. Approximately twenty million Chinese also gave their lives to defeat fascism, and then the communists went on to consolidate a socialist state in 1949 to—among other things—protect themselves against further fascist and imperialist incursions. Regarding the Soviet death toll of thirty-five million, see Annie Lacroix-Riz's lecture, "Le rôle de l'URSS dans la Seconde Guerre mondiale—80 ans de la Victoire!," Café marxiste, https://www.youtube.com/watch?v=uh8I-proRAY&t=1801s.

the whitewashing and integration of Nazis in occupied West Germany, and the displacement of Marxism in favor of U.S.-style bourgeois social science (along with idealist speculation unmoored from material reality).

Adorno and Horkheimer thus ultimately played the role of radical recuperators. Cultivating an appearance of radicality, they recuperated the very activity of critique within a pro-Western, anticommunist ideology. Like other members of the petty-bourgeois intelligentsia in Europe and the United States, which formed the basis of Western or imperial Marxism, they publicly expressed their social-chauvinistic disgust with what they described as the savage barbarians in the East, who dared to take up the weapon of Marxist theory à la Lenin and use it to act on the principle that they could rule themselves. From the relative comforts of their capitalist-funded professorial citadel in the imperial core, they defended the superiority of the Euro-American world that promoted them against what they referred to as the levelling project of the bolshevized barbarians in the uncivilized periphery.

György Lukács, who had participated in the preliminary seminar out of which the Institute for Social Research emerged, notoriously implied that the Frankfurt scholars' pessimistic resignation and complicity with imperialism was the price they paid for their luxurious lifestyles as leading Western luminaries. He described them as having taken up residence in the "Grand Hotel Abyss": "a beautiful hotel, equipped with every comfort, on the edge of an abyss, of nothingness, of absurdity. And the daily contemplation of the abyss between excellent meals or artistic entertainments, can only heighten the enjoyment of the subtle comforts offered."[221] When Helmut Dubiel asked Löwenthal about this criticism in a long dialogue in which the latter discussed his experience in V.I.P. hotels and is described as living in "a very pretty house in one of the most attractive areas of the United States," the professional propagandist—who spent six years as research director of Voice of America (VOA)—explained where things stood for the Frankfurt scholars: "We were always of a different opinion: luxury is not an evil. The proletarian resentment of the upper strata is not productive for theory."[222] As his interlocutor struggled to articulate his next question, Löwenthal clarified what he meant: "I don't sympathize with the proletariat."[223]

221. György Lukács, *The Theory of the Novel*, trans. Anna Bostock (Cambridge, MA: MIT Press, 1999), 22.

222. Löwenthal, *An Unmastered Past*, 156.

223. Ibid., 157. To be fair, Löwenthal immediately added the following qualification: "Marx

Furthermore, the Frankfurt School's generalized critique of domination is part of a larger embrace of an anti-party and anti-state ideology, which ultimately leaves the left bereft of the tools of disciplined organization necessary to wage successful struggles against the well-funded political, military, and cultural apparatus of the capitalist ruling class. This is perfectly in line with its overall politics of defeat, which Adorno explicitly embraced through his anti-Marxist defense of inaction as the highest form of praxis. The leaders of the Tui Academy in Frankfurt, amply funded and supported by the bourgeoisie and imperialist states, including the U.S. national security state, were thus ultimately global spokesmen for an anticommunist politics of capitalist accommodation. Wringing their hands at the infelicities of consumer society, which they sometimes described in remarkable detail, they nonetheless refused to do anything practical about them because of the bedrock assumption that the socialist cure for such misfortunes is much worse than the disease itself.

---

didn't sympathize with the proletariat either: the proletariat was to be abolished!" This is, however, a cheap play on words. Löwenthal quickly clarified his position, in any case, by explaining that his life of luxury was somehow prefiguring utopia: "Proletarian lifestyles are hardly a model worth imitating, nor are petit-bourgeois lifestyles that attempt to emulate the lifestyles of the upper classes. Today, however, many members of these upper classes engage in the glorification of a rural communal life in primitive circumstances. I reject that as well. I would say quite directly that luxury is the anticipation of utopia."

CHAPTER 5

The Washington School of Critical Theory

The Frankfurt School's Integration into
the U.S. Military-Industrial-Academic Complex

During their wartime and immediate postwar exile in the United States, the majority of the core members of the Frankfurt School were not working as professors or full-time researchers with the Institute for Social Research. Instead, they were in the employ of the U.S. government, serving various state agencies for years on end, including the Office of Strategic Services (OSS), which was the wartime predecessor to the Central Intelligence Agency (CIA), the State Department, and propaganda agencies like the Office of War Information (OWI) and Voice of America (VOA). They were thus intellectuals and purported Marxists who labored in the service of the capitalist state that would emerge from the war as the leading imperialist power.

Although some have raised questions regarding this performative contradiction, the Frankfurt scholars themselves have tended to defend their record of government service and, in certain cases, they have even proudly pointed to it as one of the major attempts to put Frankfurt School critical theory to work in a practical political struggle.[1] What they have in mind is the fight against fascism. Within the imperial academy, this has led to a relative consensus that their efforts were for a noble cause and

---

1. See, for instance, Raffaele Laudani, "Introduction" in Franz Neumann, et al., *Secret Reports on Nazi Germany: The Frankfurt School Contribution to the War Effort*, ed. Raffaele Laudani, trans. Jason Francis Mc Gimsey (Princeton: Princeton University Press, 2013), 1.

therefore beyond reproach. Such justifications are often expedient, how-ever, and they generally do not dwell on any of the details or situate these intellectuals within the social totality through materialist analysis. They are usually motivated by brand management within the theory industry.

Isn't it a remarkable fact, though, and one worthy of critical scrutiny, that what is arguably the most famous school of Western Marxism was very largely integrated into the intelligence and propaganda agencies of the U.S. government? As we will see, seven affiliates of the Frankfurt School worked for the world's leading imperialist government for a combined total of over fifty years. They formed a veritable "Washington School" at the time, so their governmental work is by no means a marginal or minor aspect of the history of the Frankfurt School. What is more, their ser-vice to the United States cannot be arbitrarily severed from their schol-arly careers and international notoriety. As a matter of fact, Washington was, in many ways, their career springboard because it financially sup-ported the development of their research agendas, launched them into prestigious positions in the academy, gave them access to major soft power operators who doled out ruling class funds for the correct kind of research, and connected them to some of the most powerful figures in the military-industrial-academic complex and, more generally, the financial-state-intellectual nexus. In other words, serving as the Washington School helped make the Frankfurt School into what is arguably the most inter-nationally renowned school of Western—or rather, imperial—Marxism.

It is important, therefore, to resist the standard account of their work within the capitalist academy, which tends to be reductive, simplistic, and undialectical, while skating gingerly over the complexities of the archival record. In delving into the intricacies of their government work, a more nuanced picture emerges. It becomes clear, to begin with, that the relation-ship between the U.S. government and institutions of higher education is so intimate that a lot of the orientation of postwar social science was actu-ally forged in the crucible of wartime intelligence agencies. Rather than understanding the university as an ivory tower insulated from the realm of state power and, moreover, the economy, the image that emerges is one of a veritable military-industrial-academic complex. The bourgeois state (military) and big capital (industrial) work together with universi-ties (academic) in an organic system of knowledge production and dis-semination. The Frankfurt scholars in question worked for state agencies (military), benefited individually or collectively—via the Institute—from foundation grants offered by the capitalist ruling class (industrial), and pursued research at major universities (academic). Rather than separating

their governmental work from their later academic scholarship, or severing both of these from the capitalist interests driving them, they all need
to be seen as part of the organic totality within which these scholars operated. At its highest level of generality, it makes sense to describe it as a
financial-state-intellectual complex.

Prior to their intelligence and propaganda work, the Frankfurt intellectuals were rather marginal figures in the U.S. academy, with a single enclave
at Columbia University, where they originally worked in German and
were generally cut off from broader anglophone academic debates. Max
Horkheimer, as we know from his correspondence with Herbert Marcuse,
saw collaboration with the U.S. government—at least in his case—as an
opportunity to advance the Institute and its agenda (Friedrich Pollock
also urged Marcuse to begin working for the OWI).[2] "I am convinced
that this time [working for the OWI and OSS]," Horkheimer wrote to
Marcuse in 1942, "will not be lost with regard to our common philosophical work both under *practical* and theoretical aspects" (my emphasis).[3]
Indeed, when the Frankfurt scholars supposedly returned to civilian life
after the war, they not only secured premier positions at elite U.S. institutions on both coasts, but they continued to collaborate with many of the
same people, organizations, and financial backers. This intricate network
of the financial-state-intellectual complex needs to be brought to the fore
to fully understand the material history of the Frankfurt School, as well
as the reasons why its particular version of Marxism—which served the
interests of the world's leading imperialist state while traducing communism—became so prominent in the United States and the world.

This more nuanced, dialectical approach will also allow us to be attentive to struggles within the Frankfurt School and around its relationship
to the U.S. government. As we will see, not everyone was playing the same
game. Many of the Frankfurt intellectuals involved were anticommunists
aligned on the U.S. side of the Cold War, but they were generally more
progressive than some of their colleagues, and they tended to oppose
crass forms of right-wing anticommunism. Moreover, there were significant differences within the Frankfurt School itself, and the individuals

2. See Herbert Marcuse, letter to Max Horkheimer, December 2, 1942, and Max
Horkheimer, letter to Herbert Marcuse, December 19, 1942, in Max Horkheimer,
Gesammelte Schriften, Vol. 17, *Briefwechsel 1941–1948*, ed. Gunzelin Schmid Noerr
(Frankfurt: Fischer Verlag GmbH, 1996), 388.
3. Horkheimer, letter to Marcuse, December 19, 1942, in Horkheimer, *Gesammelte
Schriften*, Vol. 17, 390.

involved were not all on the exact some ideological page. Their intellectual and political trajectories differed in various ways, and it is not the goal in this chapter to advance a reductivist interpretation of their work. In many ways, each one of them is deserving of a fine-grained analysis to bring out these differences, which is one of the reasons that the next chapter will do precisely this for the most prominent among them (Marcuse). In describing their work here, then, the focus is on general tendencies, with the full understanding that there are sometimes exceptions or additional nuances that would need to be added in individual cases. Among these complexities, we will see that a few of the Frankfurt intellectuals were playing a double game, at least to some extent: they had connections to Soviet espionage networks.

The Washington School

An intellectual partnership between scholars and spies is the best formula for successful intelligence collection and evaluation.
—RAY CLINE, FORMER DEPUTY DIRECTOR OF THE CIA[4]

The OSS, where many Frankfurt scholars found employment, served as the model for the CIA. It was founded in 1942, along with the Office of War Information (OWI), the psychological warfare agency that also hired many of the Institute's researchers. These two organizations resulted from a split in the Office of the Coordinator of Information (COI), the intelligence and propaganda agency established in 1941 by President Roosevelt. The man named at its head, William "Wild Bill" Donovan, was a millionaire Wall Street lawyer and a Republican admirer of J. Edgar Hoover. Roosevelt apparently enjoyed his blend of capitalist orthodoxy and nationalism. However, his enthusiasm for sub-rosa operations and military intelligence, as well as his anti-New Deal political orientation, created conflicts with Robert Sherwood, the liberal playwright who headed the COI's propaganda service. Hence the split, in 1942, of the COI into two agencies: the OSS and the OWI, which was responsible for propaganda, a task relayed by the United States Information Agency (USIA) from 1953.[5] The COI's Research and Analysis Branch (R&A) was inte-

---

4. Ray S. Cline, *Secrets, Spies, and Scholars: Blueprint of the Essential CIA* (Washington, D.C.: Acropolis Books, 1976), 161.
5. See ibid., esp. 46–47. Also see the internal documents describing the relationship between the OWI and the OSS, such as Edward P. Lilly: Papers, 1928–1992, Box 23,

grated into the OSS, and it "was conceived as the heart of the intelligence organization."[6] The OSS's other principal branches, Secret Operations and Special Operations, were to function "as veins and arteries, feeding into and supplied by it [R&A], respectively."[7]

In 1941, "the Germanist Walter Dorn, first chief of the Europe-Africa Division's Central European Section [of the OSS], had taken the initiative of requesting from the exiled scholars of the International Institute for Social Research at Columbia a list of experts on Germany to be found within the refugee community."[8] Franz Neumann, who offered to share the Institute's research materials with Donovan, recommended Horkheimer, Adorno, Pollock, Marcuse, Otto Kirchheimer, Leo Löwenthal, and Arkadij Gurland.[9] Horkheimer supported himself with funds from the Institute, which was sustained by Wall Street investments and donations from its wealthy patron Felix Weil. Adorno had been employed in a joint appointment at the Institute and the Rockefeller-funded Princeton Radio Research Project (PRRP). Neither of them required additional employment. However, due to Horkheimer's budgetary cuts, the others were in need of work.

In the months following Neumann's recommendations to Dorn, the Frankfurt scholars "bombarded the OSS with applications, manuscripts, and research proposals."[10] Marcuse, for instance, "sent to the Chief of the Psychology Division manuscripts he had written on 'The New German Mentality' and 'Private Morale in Germany.'"[11] They actively wanted to collaborate with the U.S. government, and their entreaties eventually bore fruit. As early as 1942, five affiliates of the Frankfurt School "had begun to supplement their incomes with part-time consulting jobs for various of the new war agencies: Marcuse and Löwenthal with the German Section

---

Folder Office of Strategic Services (OSS), Dwight D. Eisenhower Library; White House Office, Office of the Special Security Affairs: Records, 1952–1961, NSC Series, Policy Papers Subseries, Box 3, Folder NSC 127/1 Psychological Warfare Planning, Dwight D. Eisenhower Library; Dwight D. Eisenhower: Records of the President, White House Central Files (Confidential File), 1953–1961, Subject Series, Box 14, Folder Office of Strategic Services, Dwight D. Eisenhower Library.

6. Barry M. Katz, *Foreign Intelligence: Research and Analysis in the Office of Strategic Services 1942–1945* (Cambridge, MA: Harvard University Press, 1989), 3.

7. Ibid.

8. Ibid., 10.

9. See ibid., 10–11.

10. Ibid., 11.

11. Ibid.

of the Office of War Information, Neumann, Gurland, and Pollock with the Board of Economic Warfare."[12]

Marcuse, Neumann, and Kirchheimer then began working regularly for the OWI. Before accepting the job, Marcuse told Horkheimer that his function would be to "make suggestions on 'how to present the enemy to the American people,' in the press, movies, propaganda, etc."[13] The Institute's director encouraged Marcuse to take the position, saying that they would continue to collaborate and that Marcuse could "use his government position to advance Institute projects."[14] Marcuse not only concurred, but he explained to Horkheimer that he would serve as the Frankfurt School's semi-official liaison in the U.S. government, making invaluable connections and developing this state-intellectual nexus so as to assist the Institute:

> Even in my position in Washington, I would have plenty of opportunities actually to function as a member of the Institute: not only because of the connections I will make, but more specifically because I could regularly turn to you for advice, suggestions, etc. The nature of my work there would be such that this collaboration could be very close, very logical, and even to some extent "official." I feel strongly that . . . I would be of much compensating service to the Institute in many respects. I would be a kind of liaison man between various offices, particularly between the Office of War Information and the Office of Strategic Services. In both, we are well known, and I would like to develop and utilize this asset.[15]

One small indication of how this direct collaboration between the Frankfurt School and the U.S. government bore fruit is that one of the Institute's manuscripts that Marcuse shared with the OSS, "The Elimination of German Chauvinism," received feedback from the state agency in 1942.[16] Horkheimer found it "most interesting" and referred to the OSS input as "the first really valuable and substantial advice we

---

12. Ibid., 33.
13. Herbert Marcuse, *Collected Papers of Herbert Marcuse*, Vol. 1: *Technology, War and Fascism*, ed. Douglas Kellner (London; New York: Routledge, 1998), 234. The same book includes some of Marcuse's work for the U.S. propaganda agency.
14. Ibid., 17.
15. Marcuse, letter to Horkheimer, December 2, 1942, in Horkheimer, *Gesammelte Schriften*, Vol. 17, 388–89.
16. See Marcuse, *Technology, War and Fascism*, 17.

received in this matter."[17] He indicated his support for further work on the project, along the lines suggested by the predecessor organization to the CIA.[18] The point person in the OSS for their exchange, Edward Yarnall Hartshorne, Jr., later became the primary education officer in charge of the reopening of German universities in the U.S. occupation zone after the war.[19]

"Wild Bill" Donovan soon recruited Marcuse, Neumann, and Kirchheimer into the Research and Analysis Branch (R&A) of the COI-OSS. Pollock was hired by the Anti-Trust Division of the Department of Justice (DOJ) and was "an advisor for the War Production Board."[20] Löwenthal found a job at the OWI, alongside the famous anthropologist Ruth Benedict, and then at Voice of America (VOA).[21] Those working in R&A all moved to the State Department when it was relocated there. That makes five Frankfurt School intellectuals in government service, out of the eight whom Thomas Wheatland identifies as part of Horkheimer's primary circle.[22] As for the other three, Erich Fromm was in New York with Horkheimer and Adorno, before the latter two settled in well-to-do areas of Los Angeles. Siegfried Kracauer, whose life and work intersected with the Frankfurt School in various ways, worked at the Museum of Modern Art in New York and was supported by Guggenheim and Rockefeller for his research on German film. Arkady Gurland, an associate of the Institute, also worked at the OSS. Rolf Wiggershaus summarized the situation as follows:

> In 1943 six more or less full associates of the Institute were in full- or part-time government service, and were in this way visibly contributing to the war effort: Neumann as deputy chief of the Central European Section of the Office of Strategic Services (OSS), and consultant at the Board of Economic Warfare; Marcuse as senior analyst at the OSS; Kirchheimer and Gurland, also as members of staff at the OSS; Löwenthal as a consultant at the Office of War Information; and Pollock as consultant at the Department of Justice's

---

17. Horkheimer, letter to Marcuse, December 19, 1942, in Horkheimer, *Gesammelte Schriften*, Vol. 17, 391.
18. See Marcuse, *Technology, War and Fascism*, 17.
19. See Horkheimer, *Gesammelte Schriften*, Vol. 17, 394.
20. Leo Löwenthal, *An Unmastered Past: The Autobiographical Reflections of Leo Löwenthal*, ed. Martin Jay (Berkeley: University of California Press, 1987), 81.
21. See ibid., 82.
22. See Thomas Wheatland, *The Frankfurt School in Exile* (Minneapolis: University of Minnesota Press, 2009), xvii.

Anti-Trust Division. The only ones who were spared were Horkheimer and Adorno, the two principal theoreticians.[23]

Paul Lazarsfeld was also one of the Institute's research associates, and he served in the OWI. Depending on how strictly one defines the Frankfurt School and its networks, that makes seven affiliates working for the U.S. government (even Franz Neumann's wife, Inge, who would marry Marcuse after her husband's death, worked for the OSS).[24] Strictly speaking, therefore, it is not true that the Institute spent its wartime and immediate postwar exile in New York (and Los Angeles). The real refuge for the Frankfurt School at the time was Washington D.C., and more specifically the U.S. national security state and its propaganda agencies. The Frankfurt School, at least at the time, would have been more appropriately named the Washington School.

The Wartime Crucible of Postwar Social Science

The OSS's Research & Analysis branch (R&A) was, in Raffaele Laudani's opinion, "the biggest American research institution in the first half of the twentieth century."[25] It was in many ways, he claims, the birthplace of postwar U.S.-American social science. This is hardly an exaggeration since an incredible number of scholars who served in the OSS went on to become, after the war, major figures in their disciplines and preeminent

---

23. Rolf Wiggershaus, *The Frankfurt School: Its History, Theories, and Political Significance*, trans. Michael Robertson (Cambridge, MA: MIT Press, 1994), 301.

24. See Katz, *Foreign Intelligence*, 26. Although so peripheral that he generally is not even mentioned in the main histories of the Frankfurt School, and therefore is not considered part of it, Paul A. Baran had a research assistantship at the Institute, and he worked for the OSS (as well as for the Office of Price Administration and the Economic Effects Division of the U.S. Strategic Bombing Survey in Germany). His close friend and collaborator, Paul Sweezy, was not affiliated with the Institute, but he also served in the OSS, in its R&A in London. See John Bellamy Foster, "Introduction," in John Bellamy Foster, ed., *The Age of Monopoly Capital: Selected Correspondence of Paul M. Sweezy and Paul A. Baran* (New York: Monthly Review Press, 2017); John Bellamy Foster, ed., "The Baran-Marcuse Correspondence," trans. Joseph Fracchia, *Monthly Review Online*, March 1, 2014; John Bellamy Foster, "The Commitment of an Intellectual: Paul M. Sweezy (1910–2004)," *Monthly Review*, Vol. 56, No. 5 (October 2004); and Paul M. Sweezy, "Paul Alexander Baran: A Personal Memoir," *Monthly Review*, Vol. 16, No. 11 (March 1965).

25. Franz Neumann, et al., *Secret Reports on Nazi Germany: The Frankfurt School Contribution to the War Effort*, ed. Raffaele Laudani, trans. Jason Francis McGimsey (Princeton: Princeton University Press, 2013), 2.

power brokers at elite institutions, occupying leadership positions in academic associations and across the university system and publishing industry. Even for those who were renowned before the war, their careers were generally bolstered by their governmental service, which provided them with political backing as well as extensive contacts, including within the academic crème de la crème employed in Washington. This was very much the case for the Frankfurt scholars, whose long sojourn in the U.S. capital was integral to their postwar academic success.

With an "unlimited" budget, which rose to several hundred million dollars during the war according to former CIA officer R. Harris Smith, "Wild Bill" Donovan invested in the construction of a gigantic research center to put the intellectual world at the service of the war state.[26] "In a global and totalitarian war," Wild Bill opined, "intelligence must be global and totalitarian."[27] "The principal recruiting ground for the Research and Analysis Branch [of the OSS] was the American university establishment," as Bernard Katz explained.[28] Indeed, R&A was, according to Smith, "the first concerted effort on the part of any world power to apply the talents of its academic community to official analysis of foreign affairs," and "the branch resembled a star-studded college faculty."[29] With the help of the American Council of Learned Societies, the Social Science Research Council, and dense networks of academic association, R&A hired between 1,000 and 2,000 professional researchers (the precise numbers vary widely depending on the source).[30] This means that it was "one of the largest agencies in the intelligence apparatus with its 12,000 employees."[31] Moreover, "even the spies and technical

---

26. Richard Harris Smith, *OSS: The Secret History of America's First Central Intelligence Agency* (Berkeley: University of California Press, 1972), 5.
27. Cited in Tim Weiner, *Legacy of Ashes: The History of the CIA* (New York: Doubleday, 2007), 3.
28. Katz, *Foreign Intelligence*, 140.
29. Smith, *OSS*, 13.
30. See Katz, *Foreign Intelligence*, 5. Katz claims that there were "at peak strength, over nine hundred professionals" in the OSS's R&A (ibid., xiii). Laudani puts the number, at its zenith, between 1943 and 1945, at "twelve hundred employees, four hundred of whom were stationed abroad." "Introduction," in Franz Neumann, et al., *Secret Reports on Nazi Germany*, 2. Winks says that in 1945 "there were 1,500 in R&A in Washington and 450 overseas." Robin W. Winks, *Cloak and Gown: Scholars in the Secret War, 1939–1961* (New Haven: Yale University Press, 1987), 113. Cline offers the highest estimate of "nearly 2,000 research analysts." *Secrets, Spies, and Scholars*, 41.
31. Müller, *Krieger und Gelehrte*, 38. Cline claims that the total size of the OSS, including

experts in the OSS described R&A as 'the heart and soul' of the intelligence service."[32]

The research atmosphere was highly interdisciplinary, bringing together some of the most eminent or promising historians, economists, sociologists, political scientists, literary scholars, philosophers, and other academics. In the interest of space, let us briefly consider a few examples. The list of historians at the OSS, to begin with, reads like a roster of the cream of the crop of the discipline. Seven of them would later serve as presidents of the American Historical Association (AHA).[33] One of them, Professor Crane Brinton, wrote with two other OSS historians, John Christopher and Robert Lee Wolff, the influential textbook, *A History of Civilization*, which became "one of the two that dominated the market for the immediate postwar generation of undergraduate students."[34] Reflecting the synoptic worldview developed by these authors during their time at the OSS, it would not be totally revised until 1983. This state-backed approach to history was by no means exceptional, and we can point as well to OSS director William Langer's history of U.S. policy during the Second World War, which was closely coordinated by the State Department and funded by a substantial four-year grant that the Council on Foreign Relations had secured from the Rockefeller Foundation.[35] The model for this project was a collective war history in Britain overseen by the acclaimed academic Arnold Toynbee, who was employed by the intelligence department of the Foreign Office (FO) and was later financed by Rockefeller to work on this history in coordination with the FO.[36] It is remarkable, moreover, the extent to which historians trained in intelligence agencies were involved in writing some of the major historical encyclopedias and multivolume works on history and civilization that were published by prestigious presses and widely circulated during the Cold War (including

overseas staff, reached "about 13,000" (*Secrets, Spies and Scholars*, 53).

32. Müller, *Krieger und Gelehrte*, 38.

33. See Katz, *Foreign Intelligence*, xii, and Winks, *Cloak and Gown*, 495.

34. Winks, *Cloak and Gown*, 495.

35. See William L. Langer, *In and Out of the Ivory Tower* (New York: Neale Watson Academic Publications,1977), 200 and Müller, *Krieger und Gelehrte*, 191.

36. See Müller, *Krieger und Gelehrte*, 192. Toynbee received a lot of Rockefeller support throughout his career. See William H. McNeill, *Arnold J. Toynbee: A Life* (Oxford: Oxford University Press, 1989).

Brinton, Langer, and Toynbee). At the same time, and unsurprisingly, "R&A has been overlooked by professional historians."[37]

This pattern of governmental service followed by an ascension of the academic ladder to powerful leadership positions is also visible in other disciplines, as is the revolving door between Washington and elite universities. While some of this is surely due to the fact that many academics in the OSS already had prestigious positions before the war, the contacts they developed in the government, including with other influential intellectuals and foundation operatives, certainly contributed to enhancing their career trajectories in many cases. The economists in the OSS, for instance, included "five future AEA [American Economic Association] presidents and a Nobel Laureate."[38]

In the field of English literature and American Studies, Norman Holmes Pearson worked for the OSS and became head of the X-2 branch (the counterintelligence service) in London during the war. After the armistice, he returned to Yale, where he co-founded and headed the new American Studies program, which promoted U.S.-American interests during the Cold War, and he served as one of the university's most important CIA recruiters.[39] He twice won the prestigious Guggenheim Fellowship, became the president of the American Studies Association and Chancellor of the Academy of American Poets, and served on committees for the National Book Awards.[40]

To cite a final example, Evron M. Kirkpatrick became the first full-time director of the American Political Science Association (APSA) in 1954, serving until 1981 (he was praised by the *New York Times* for shielding APSA from campus controversies surrounding the war in Vietnam).[41] He had just come off a decade of leadership positions in the U.S. national security state, including serving as the assistant director of R&A in the OSS

---

37. Katz, *Foreign Intelligence*, xii.
38. Ibid., 9.
39. On Pearson, see Joel Whitney, *Finks: How the C.I.A. Tricked the World's Best Writers* (New York: OR Books, 2016) and Jefferson Morley, *The Ghost: The Secret Life of CIA Spymaster James Jesus Angleton* (New York: St. Martin's Press, 2017). According to Peter Matthiessen, the renowned American novelist who worked for the CIA: "Pearson recruited a great great many Yale seniors for the CIA." Cited in Whitney, *Finks*, 12.
40. See Winks, *Cloak and Gown*, 248 and 321.
41. See David Binder, "Evron Kirkpatrick, 83, Director of Political Science Association," *New York Times*, May 9, 1995, Section D, 23 and Evron M. Kirkpatrick's faculty profile on Indiana University's "Honors and Awards" page: https://honorsandawards.iu.edu/awards/honoree/561.html.

and, within the State Department, chief of External Research Staff, chief of Psychological Intelligence and Research, and deputy director of the Office of Intelligence Research.[42] These governmental connections were not abandoned as he moved into academia. Thirteen years into his twenty-seven year tenure as the executive director of APSA, it was revealed that he had been simultaneously serving for a decade as the "executive direc-tor of Operations and Policy Research, Inc., an organization established to help the United States Information Service, the government's propaganda arm, distribute more persuasive broadsides and magazines and books both in this country and abroad."[43] He employed more than a hundred profes-sors in this propaganda effort, many of them APSA members, and the funding came from the United States Information Service / United States Information Agency, "the Pentagon, the State Department and other gov-ernment agencies," as well as from foundations revealed to be CIA conduits and the Agency itself.[44] It is not surprising, given his work as an academic subcontractor for the U.S. national security state, that Kirkpatrick corre-sponded with the director of the CIA regarding APSA activities. In 1977, for instance, he wrote to the head of the Agency "on behalf of the Officers and Staff of the American Political Science Association" to invite him to attend APSA's annual meeting, sharing the program and encouraging him to bring it "to the attention of others who might be interested."[45] In any case, the CIA's Academic Relations Staff has a history of producing a "quarterly calendar of scheduled meetings of professional organizations that may be of interest" to its analysts.[46] Between January and October 1977, Agency oper-atives "attended 150 conferences, conventions, and symposia," and "more than 30 analysts presented scholarly papers as panelists at these meetings."[47]

---

42. See Kirkpatrick's faculty profile: https://honorsandawards.iu.edu/awards/honoree/561.html.

43. "The Professor and the CIA," *The Nation*, February 27, 1967, included in the press clippings available in International Association for Cultural Freedom Records, Box 318, Folder 4, Central Intelligence Agency 1968–1970, Hanna Holborn Gray Special Collections Research Center at the University of Chicago.

44. Ibid.

45. "Letter to Mr. Richard Martin Lyon Seyfarth, Shaw, Fairweather and Geraldson from Stansfield Turner," August 31, 1977, the CIA FOIA Electronic Reading Room, https://www.cia.gov/readingroom/document/cia-rdp80m00165a002400150002-1.

46. "Academic Relations," October 14, 1981, the CIA FOIA Electronic Reading Room, https://www.cia.gov/readingroom/document/cia-rdp85m00364r002003810016-4, 2–3.

47. "Activities in Academic Relations," November 3, 1977, the CIA FOIA Electronic Reading Room, https://www.cia.gov/readingroom/document/cia-rdp86b00985r000

OSS: "Oh So Socialist" in the Service of Capital

It was as if the left-Hegelian *Weltgeist* [world spirit] had taken up
temporary residence in the Central European Section of the OSS.

—JOHN HERZ, A COLLEAGUE OF
THE FRANKFURT SCHOLARS IN THE OSS[48]

"Oh So Socialist" was one of the nicknames given to the OSS because of the
number of leftist intellectuals like Marcuse, Neumann, and Kirchheimer
in its ranks. Although there were many liberals, Donovan thought it was
important to put socialists to work as well, as long as their research bore
fruit. He even "personally hired a young economist suspected of being
a communist by the FBI—Paul Sweezy."[49] As Tim Müller explained, the
objective was to have multiple perspectives, including from the socialist
or even communist left, in order to confront them and maximize input.
R&A activities were very collective, in any case, so the individual contributions of leftist scholars were part of a larger mix of vantage points.
Moreover, the United States was ostensibly allied with the Soviet Union
during the war, and Marxists are renowned for their rigorous materialist
analyses, so having them involved made sense for multiple reasons (not
least of which was the ongoing war on communism).

A veritable think tank, with an emphasis on the military meaning of
the second term, the OSS's R&A was chaired by two Republicans: James
Baxter, the president of Williams College, and William Langer, a Harvard
historian. Forging an alliance between the state, the capitalist class, and
the university in a military-industrial-academic complex, Donovan—a
wealthy Wall Street lawyer himself—peppered the OSS administration
with business magnates and corporate lawyers.[50] The *esprit de corps* of the
executive offices was nearly identical to that of company board rooms,
and major corporations lent their executives and often their funds, be it
Goldman Sachs, Standard Oil Company, Paramount Pictures, or J. Walter
Thompson Advertising Agency. Members of the wealthiest families in the
United States also worked in the administrative offices of the OSS, including the sons of Andrew Mellon and J. P. Morgan, and members of the
Vanderbilt, DuPont, Archbold (Standard Oil), and Ryan (Equitable Life

---

300010001-8, 3.

48. Katz, *Foreign Intelligence*, 33.

49. Müller, *Krieger und Gelehrte*, 44.

50. See Smith, *OSS*, 15.

Insurance) families.[51] The Rockefellers were notably absent, but they had their own propaganda and intelligence agency in Latin America: Nelson Rockefeller headed the Office of the Coordinator of Inter-American Affairs (CIAA).[52]

Intelligence agencies cannot be understood, nor can the inner functioning of the bourgeois state, without grasping the central and powerful role played by the capitalist ruling class. Leadership of the intelligence agencies, as can be seen, was not simply indirectly in the hands of the leading capitalists since, in many cases, they took direct control. The military-industrial-academic complex is not a level playing field since the state is controlled by the ownership class, and the intelligentsia—in this case—is in the employ of the bourgeois state. If the order of determinations was more clearly spelled out, and it was described at its highest level of concrete abstraction, it would be referred to as the financial-state-intellectual complex. All of this means that the "oh so socialist" researchers mentioned above were employed by the bourgeois state and overseen— directly or indirectly—by the bourgeoisie.

It is important to note that the CIA, founded in 1947, "is in many ways the mirror image of OSS."[53] It was established based on the same fundamental model and structure, triangulating and hierarchically organizing elements from the financial, state, and intellectual sectors. "The CIA took over the intelligence and covert psychological warfare activities of the OSS," meaning that it merged, like the OSS, secret intelligence and clandestine operations in the same organization.[54] Intellectuals and researchers thus remained just as important, and extensive recruitment from elite universities continued as before, as well as the revolving door between the academy and Washington. In fact, many of those who served in the OSS later continued their work for the CIA. For instance, the Frankfurt scholars' boss, William Langer, who was the Chief of R&A at the OSS, helped set up the Office of National Estimates (ONE) for the CIA in 1950 and

---

51. See ibid., 15.
52. See Harold B. Gotaas, et al., *History of the Office of the Coordinator of Inter-American Affairs: Historical Reports on War Administration* (Washington, DC: U.S. Government Printing Office, 1947).
53. Smith, *OSS*, 361.
54. "Summary of Psychological Warfare Arrangements within the U.S. Government since World War II," White House, Office of the Special Assistant for National Security Affairs: Records, 1952–1961, NSC Series, Policy Papers Subseries, Box 3, Folder NSC 127/1– Psychological Warfare Planning, Dwight D. Eisenhower Library. Also see Smith, *OSS*, 361.

served as its Assistant Director for its first year (ONE is a kind of R&A in the CIA). He was seconded in this endeavor by Yale history professor Sherman Kent, who was also a veteran of the OSS's R&A, and who then became ONE's director.[55] Langer continued to work as a CIA consultant in later years, including serving on the Board Panel on Covert Operations and participating in meetings, four times a year, to collaborate on National Intelligence Estimates with Kent, the powerful OSS/CIA operative Allen Dulles, and a group of professors.[56] There was thus deep continuity, and much of what has been outlined regarding the OSS equally applies to the CIA since "the Office of Strategic Services was the direct lineal ancestor of today's Central Intelligence Agency."[57]

De-Nazification as Re-Nazification

What were the Frankfurt School intellectuals doing in the OSS? They wielded the main intelligence weapon, according to the CIA's David Phillips: files. They prepared reports on Germany from the rise of Nazism to its collapse and the reconstruction of the country in the postwar period.[58] They analyzed various aspects of German society, the consequences of the defeat of the Third Reich, internal political opposition, and the new so-called threat of communism. Involved in de-Nazification and the preparation of the Nuremberg trials, they drew attention to the responsibility of industrialists and business leaders. Rather than a de-Nazification focused primarily on the upper echelons of the Nazi Party and the military, they advocated a broad program to de-Nazify the political, economic, administrative, and military spheres (duly rejected by their supervisors).[59] Donovan's team "did the lion's share of the American trial preparation," and Franz Neumann was "Donovan's right-hand man."[60] As head of the War Crimes Unit of the OSS, with people like Kirchheimer

---

55. On Langer and Kent, see Müller, *Krieger und Gelehrte* and Katz, *Foreign Intelligence*, esp. 197.

56. See John Cavanagh, "Dulles Papers Reveal CIA Consulting Network," *Forerunner*, Vol. 5, No. 9 (April 29, 1980) and White House, PFIAB, "Board Panel on Covert Action Operations," Top Secret Memo, September 10, 1963, National Archives, JFK Assassination Records, 2025 release, https://nsarchive.gwu.edu/document/32956-document-6-white-house-pfiab-board-panel-covert-action-operations-top-secret.

57. Smith, *OSS*, 361.

58. See Neumann, et al., *Secret Reports on Nazi Germany*.

59. See Laudani, "Introduction," 1–38.

60. Müller, *Krieger und Gelehrte*, 53.

and Marcuse working under him, Neumann played a central role in the collection of evidence and the constitution of the legal case for the main Nuremberg war crimes trials.

Marcuse later expressed regret that the U.S. government did not follow their advice. In an interview in which Jürgen Habermas asked him if his recommendations for de-Nazification had any consequence, he retorted: "On the contrary. Those whom we had listed first as 'economic war criminals' were very quickly back in the decisive positions of responsibility in the German economy."[61] John H. Herz, a German-born academic who served alongside the Frankfurt scholars in the OSS and the State Department, where he also took part in the Nuremberg trials, drew the following conclusion in an academic article published in 1948: de-Nazification "began with a bang" but "died with a whimper" because "it opened the way toward renewed control of German public, social, economic and cultural life by forces which only partially or temporarily had been deprived of the influence they had exerted under the Nazi regime."[62] In 1951, laws were passed to officially end any legal prosecution of former Nazis, while "the persecution of communists continued, with arrests and imprisonment" of around 10,000 suspected communists by the mid-1960s.[63] In 1956, the Communist Party of Germany was outlawed, as it had been in 1933, along with a number of communist and antifascist organizations.[64] This trajectory differed starkly from that of the German Democratic Republic (GDR), where a genuine de-Nazification process did take place and communists were empowered in society.

To return to the immediate postwar and the Frankfurt scholars' recommendations to the U.S. administration regarding the future of Germany, Herz explained that Marcuse and his associates:

> advocated a social democratic reformist position and not so much a Marxist one. They inclined toward a democratic (in the broad sense) constitution in Germany, which was first of all to eliminate the effects of authoritarian,

---

61. Quoted in Marcuse, *Technology, War, and Fascism*, 23. See also Herbert Marcuse, *Marxism, Revolution and Utopia*, Vol. 6 of *Collected Papers of Herbert Marcuse*, ed. Douglas Kellner and Clayton Pierce (New York: Routledge, 2014), 430.

62. John H. Herz, "The Fiasco of Denazification in Germany," *Political Science Quarterly*, Vol. 63, No. 4 (December 1948): 569.

63. Bruni de la Motte and John Green, *Stasi State or Socialist Paradise? The German Democratic Republic and What Became of It* (London: Artery Publications, 2022), 22.

64. See ibid.

illiberal tradition at all levels in German life. It was a position with which I, as a non-Marxist, could agree: a kind of Anglo-Saxon democracy, but one from which socialist measures could arise when conditions were right.[65]

The Federal Republic of Germany (FRG) was indeed bequeathed, on the surface, with a Western-style democracy and the possibility, but not the guarantee, of social welfare measures.[66] Konrad Adenauer, who had before the war called for a coalition government with the Nazis, became the FRG's first Chancellor. He was financially supported and controlled by the CIA, as former agent Philip Agee and others have explained in detail, and he packed his government "with other right-wing and conservative Catholic figures as well as high-ranking former Nazis."[67] The OSS/CIA also set up and controlled the FRG's postwar intelligence service. They put Nazi Brigadier General Reinhard Gehlen in charge, and he hired "some four thousand agents," of which a hundred, at least, "had clear ties to Nazi atrocities."[68] Moreover, the U.S. national security state funded, trained, and equipped fascist subversives to run brutal terror and destabilization campaigns against the GDR.[69] Additionally, the OSS/CIA recruited Nazis into secret fascist stay-behind armies as part of a broader strategy of tension in the West, which included committing acts of terrorism against civilians that were blamed on communists.[70]

---

65. Quoted in Marcuse, *Technology, War, Fascism*, 22.

66. In East Germany, by contrast, a strong socialist welfare state was established, which included: "–The abolition of class privilege and the introduction of greater equality of income distribution. –Elimination of land and property speculation. –Restricting the influence of banks and other large financial institutions. –Equal rights for women. –Access to education for all. –Promotion of the co-operative idea." De la Motte and Green, *Stasi State or Socialist Paradise?*, 160.

67. De la Motte and Green, *Stasi State or Socialist Paradise?*, 19. Also see Philip Agee and Louis Wolf, ed., *Dirty Work: The CIA in Western Europe* (New York: Dorset Press, 1978), 186, as well as Gabriel Rockhill, "Critical and Revolutionary Theory: For the Reinvention of Critique in the Age of Ideological Realignment," in *Domination and Emancipation: Remaking Critique*, ed. Daniel Benson (Lanham, MD: Rowman & Littlefield Publishers, 2021), 117–61.

68. Eric Lichtblau, *The Nazis Next Door: How America Became a Safe Haven for Hitler's Men* (New York: Mariner Books, 2015), 33.

69. See William Blum, *Killing Hope: U.S. Military and CIA Interventions since World War II* (London: Zed Books, 2014), 61–64.

70. See Daniele Ganser, *NATO's Secret Armies: Operation Gladio and Terrorism in Western Europe* (New York: Routledge, 2005) and Allan Francovich, *Gladio*, 1992, film, https://www.youtube.com/watch?v=GGHXjO8wHsA.

Horkheimer, the director of the Institute for Social Research, defended the Adenauer government and aligned himself with it.[71] Along with Adorno and Habermas, and likely some of the other Frankfurt scholars, Horkheimer maintained, against the left critics, that the FRG was a democracy, rebuffing in particular the students who accused it of complicity with fascism. In fact, Habermas would even later assert that "the *Bundesrepublik* was one of the six or seven most liberal countries in the world."[72] The real fascists, for these leading Frankfurt scholars, were not in the West German state, but rather in the left movements critical of the FRG, as well as in socialist states. Habermas infamously derided the students for engaging in "left fascism," an oxymoronic expression that Adorno proudly embraced. Marcuse was insightful enough to reject this fallacious assertion. However, even in one of his most radical books, *An Essay on Liberation*, he clearly distinguished West Germany from "the fascist and semifascist countries."[73]

These were some of the practical consequences of the world-renowned theorization of fascism in the writings of figures like Adorno and Horkheimer (though often with echoes in the work of some of the other Frankfurt intellectuals). Fascism was readily visible to them in leftwing movements and communism, which had been responsible for the wartime defeat of fascism, but not in bourgeois pseudo-democracies stocked with actual Nazis. Their ideological lens perfectly inverted the order of things. This positioned them very well for receiving U.S. government and ruling-class funding, as well as support from the West German government and private donors, in order to reestablish the Frankfurt School in the FRG. It became an anticommunist outpost in the battle of ideas and was part of a broader network of European institutions supported by the U.S. ruling class in its ideological war on communism.[74]

The Washington-to-Academic-Fame Pipeline

Many of the Frankfurt scholars continued to work for the state after the war. "Neumann, Marcuse, Kirchheimer, and some 900 other veterans of the defunct Research and Analysis Branch [were integrated] into the State

---

71. See Rockhill, "Critical and Revolutionary Theory."

72. Peter Dews, ed., *Autonomy and Solidarity: Interviews with Jürgen Habermas* (London: Verso, 1992), 231.

73. Herbert Marcuse, *An Essay on Liberation* (Boston: Beacon Press, 1969), 60.

74. See, for instance, Müller, *Krieger und Gelehrte*, 236.

Department's Interim Research and Intelligence Service."[75] However, the critical theorists did eventually find university positions, particularly as McCarthyism gradually came to grip the government. In 1948, Neumann became a professor of political science at Columbia University, and Marcuse began working there in 1952. Pollock returned to Frankfurt in 1950 to reestablish the Institute for Social Research. Kirchheimer landed a professorship in political science at the New School for Social Research in 1955. Löwenthal began teaching at the University of California, Berkeley in 1956, after a year at Stanford.

Government service and contacts in Washington not only eased their way into the U.S. academy. In many ways, their intelligence and propaganda work was a springboard for their intellectual careers at some of the most prestigious universities, which have ample ties to the political elite. They had spent years working with many of the most renowned academics on a common ideological project by doing research, analysis, and psychological warfare. Their connections to major academic power brokers could not have been better, and it is thus not at all surprising that they landed such prominent positions. Horkheimer was right, therefore, when he opportunistically encouraged Marcuse to accept his first job at the OWI because it could be used to help advance the Frankfurt School's projects.[76] Here's how Marcuse described his colleagues and the overall setting in the OSS: "Our division in the OSS was the best assembling of intellectuals ever gathered under one roof. Every single one of them has become a full professor of reputation, a writer, or whatever."[77]

The connections made in Washington were not only to powerful academics, but also to members of the political and media establishment, and they included direct or indirect ties to the managers of the major capitalist foundations. The latter tended to have prestigious academic training, and many of them worked for intelligence services during, and sometimes after the war. Shepard Stone, the longtime Director of International Affairs at the Ford Foundation who was deeply involved in its collaborations with the CIA and supported the Frankfurt School, was active in wartime intelligence work.[78] OSS veterans, as Frances Stonor Saunders explains,

---

75. Katz, *Foreign Intelligence*, 188.
76. See Marcuse, *Technology, War and Fascism*, 17.
77. Marcuse, *Marxism, Revolution and Utopia*, 430.
78. See Stone's biography in the guide to his papers: https://archives-manuscripts. dartmouth.edu/agents/people/739.

were recruited to the Rockefeller Foundation in droves. In 1950, OSS-er Charles B. Fahs became head of the foundation's division of humanities. His assistant was another OSS veteran named Chadbourne Gilpatric, who arrived there directly from the CIA. These two were the principal liaisons for the Congress for Cultural Freedom, and responsible for dispensing large Rockefeller subsidies to Josselson's outfit [the CCF].[79]

Fahs had become the chief of the Research and Analysis Division (Far East) of the OSS and then followed Marcuse, Neumann, and Kirchheimer to the State Department after the war, before moving on to the Rockefeller Foundation in 1950.[80] He also served on a secret CIA consultants board at Princeton alongside Marcuse's two greatest academic supporters (Philip Mosely and William Langer).[81] Edward D'Arms, who worked as the assistant and associate director of humanities for the Rockefeller Foundation from 1947 to 1957, and then the Ford Foundation, had earlier worked in the U.S. Army and then its Civil Affairs Division.[82]

It is not clear if the Frankfurt scholars met these foundation operatives during their sojourn in Washington. However, they ran in similar circles and were connected through the networks of the financial-state-intellectual complex. Even if these connections were distant in certain cases, the fact that the Frankfurt scholars had so dutifully served Washington was a reliable sign of their political bona fides. We do know, to take one example, that Marcuse interceded on the Institute's behalf by meeting and corresponding with D'Arms from the Rockefeller Foundation and connecting him with Horkheimer (who already knew him).[83] This was in 1953, when Marcuse was still officially a member of the State Department. Although

79. Frances Stonor Saunders, *The Cultural Cold War: The CIA and the World of Arts and Letters* (New York: New Press, 2000), 145.

80. See Fahs's biography via the Rockefeller Archive Center: https://dimes.rockarch.org/agents/8fgdhQozzVZpzKucKCQP9W.

81. See "Meeting of Princeton Consultants," April 25, 1953, the CIA FOIA Electronic Reading Room, https://www.cia.gov/readingroom/document/02233811 and "Princeton Consultants Meeting on 19 and 20 November," December 7, 1953, the CIA FOIA Electronic Reading Room, https://www.cia.gov/readingroom/document/02903581.

82. "Edward F. D'Arms, 87, Executive and Teacher," *New York Times*, May 3, 1991, https://www.nytimes.com/1991/05/03/obituaries/edward-f-d-arms-87-executive-and-teacher.html.

83. See Theodor Adorno and Max Horkheimer, *Correspondance: 1927–1969*, Vol. 4, ed. Christoph Gödde and Henri Lonitz, trans. Didier Renault (Paris: Klincksieck: 2016), 153–54.

he did not succeed in securing this particular grant, these overall connections certainly served the interests of the Frankfurt School, which continued to be supported by the U.S. government and its ruling class.

Whereas the members of the Institute for Social Research had been on the fringes of academic life and in search of work during their early exile, after their loyal service to the state, the Institute boasted an impressive national network of professors at the country's leading institutions: Columbia, Berkeley, the New School, Stanford, and Harvard. In Löwenthal's case, we know that it was Lazarsfeld who was "instrumental" in securing his invitation to Stanford's Center for Advanced Studies (Marcuse unsuccessfully beseeched Baran, an Institute affiliate who served in the OSS, to help him obtain a teaching position at the same university).[84] Lazarsfeld was an Institute associate, propaganda maven, Columbia professor, and a major academic subcontractor to the state and capitalist class. Marcuse, as we will see, was relocated to Columbia and Harvard, while initially still under contract with the State Department, to work at institutes created and controlled by the national security state, thereby launching an Ivy League academic career directly through his intelligence work. With its research associates securing such high-status positions, as well as with the corporate and state grants secured by Horkheimer, not to mention the public relations firm he hired to promote the Institute's work in the United States, the Frankfurt School was well positioned to become a dominant academic force in the world's leading empire. It is not an exaggeration to say that the Frankfurt School, insofar as it became the premier representative of Western Marxism, was to a certain extent the scion of empire.

Many of the Institute's researchers later defended their governmental service and claimed that they had no qualms about collaborating. Discussing Marcuse, Kirchheimer, and Neumann, Raffaele Laudani makes the following important point: "These thinkers never demonstrated any particular embarrassment in connection with their past government service. Rather, on more than one occasion, they proudly defended their participation as one of the few attempts to make the Frankfurt School's Critical Theory a practical tool in the fight against fascism."[85] Indeed, for a school of thought renowned for its defeatism and quietism, here was a moment of clear, practical political commitment on the part of the Frankfurt School.

---

84. Löwenthal, *An Unmastered Past*, 138. Also see John Bellamy Foster, ed., "The Baran-Marcuse Correspondence," *Monthly Review Online,* March 1, 2014.
85. Laudani, "Introduction," 1.

Löwenthal took a similar position, and he testified to the lack of scruples on the part of the other Frankfurt intellectuals. He spent six years, from 1949 to 1955, as research director of VOA, the governmental propaganda outlet under the control of the OWI (1943–45) and then the State Department (1945–53).[86] He said in an autobiographical dialogue that he never had "the feeling [he] was working for an imperialist power" because he simply "wasn't really conscious of it [U.S. imperialism]."[87] He was only, on his account, fulfilling a specific function, namely directing a department "within the American propaganda apparatus," without making the political decisions himself.[88] He was "not interested in posing as an ardent critic of American foreign policy."[89] The fact that VOA had "a special ideological warfare unit which develops master scripts to show how immediately current news items can be interpreted to the embarrassment of Communist doctrine" did not seem to bother him in the least.[90] Indeed, the director of VOA broadcasts since 1949, Foy Kohler, publicly celebrated the achievements of his propaganda agency for its contributions to the anticommunist psywar:

I think it is clear that the Voice of America can take a considerable share of the credit for fostering the growing strength and determination of the free world; for the votes in the United Nations strongly condemning Communist aggression in Korea; for the declining strength of Communism throughout the free world, and particularly in such vital countries as France and Italy.[91]

Löwenthal understood that he and his Frankfurt friends were contributing to this ideological world war, and he maintained that they were justified in doing so because they were on the right side of history:

---

86. See Gerald Sussman, *Branding Democracy: U.S. Regime Change in Post-Soviet Eastern Europe* (New York: Peter Lang Publishing, 2010), 42. On Löwenthal's work for VOA, see Leo Bogart, "In Memoriam: Leo Löwenthal, 1900–1993," *The Public Opinion Quarterly*, Vol. 57, No. 3 (Autumn, 1993): 377–79. Bogart claims that VOA, after being housed in the OWI, was integrated into the USIA.
87. Löwenthal, *An Unmastered Past*, 94, 95.
88. Ibid., 93.
89. Ibid.
90. Edward P. Lilly Papers, 1828–1992, Box 54, Folder "Doctrinal Programs 1953 (1)," Dwight D. Eisenhower Library, 14–15.
91. Foy Kohler, "The Effectiveness of the Voice of America," *The Quarterly of Film Radio and Television*, Vol. 6, No. 1 (Autumn 1951): 25.

DUBIEL: If you, Marcuse, Pollock, and Neumann had no scruples as intellectuals to work for the American government during the war, you were probably also motivated by the belief that this was also a war of ideologies.
LÖWENTHAL: Certainly.[92]

Although Dubiel here references their wartime activities, Löwenthal showed no signs of regret throughout the dialogue for his work in psychological warfare after the end of the Second World War. This included his service to empire during the Korean War in the early 1950s, to take but one example. The United States' allies in South Korea, bent on ridding the country of communists, carried out mass executions of "at least 300,000 people" in the first months of the war, and General Douglas MacArthur oversaw a ruthless bombing campaign that flattened North Korea, ordering "the use of incendiaries to burn to the ground every city, every village, and every factory."[93]

The Frankfurt School's alignment with the U.S. empire in the battle of ideas positioned it to be promoted as the source of some of the most innovative and cutting-edge forms of Marxism. What a novelty, and how remarkable, to develop a version of Marxism that would openly fight an ideological world war against communism, while fulfilling the academic and intelligence needs of the world's leading imperialist power. Here was, indeed, a Marxism that had overcome the supposed limitations of those old-school Marxists invested in breaking the chains of imperialism and building socialism. This new-fangled Marxism was radical enough to turn things around—via a doggerel version of dialectics—by accommodating capitalism, and even imperialism, while traducing communism. As a servant of empire, the Washington School developed a commodifiable, imperial version of Marxism that gained global prominence, in part because it was feted by the capitalist ruling class and supported by bourgeois states.

Were Critical Theorists Soviet Spies?

Psychological warfare is not propaganda. It is politics.
　　　　　　　　　　　　　　　　　　　　—FRANZ NEUMANN[94]

---

92. Löwenthal, *An Unmastered Past*, 158.
93. Stephen Gowans, *Patriots, Traitors and Empires: The Story of Korea's Struggle for Freedom* (Montreal: Baraka Books, 2018), 128, 130 (the first citation is a quote from Korean historian Hun Joon Kim).
94. Franz Neumann, *Behemoth: The Structure and Practice of National Socialism, 1933–*

The Washington School critical theorists were not all faithful to the agenda of the U.S. national security state. A few of them had connections to Soviet espionage networks and shared information with the USSR. Richard Sorge, to begin with, was an early research associate of the Institute.[95] He was also a Soviet military intelligence agent, and he connected Hede Massing to his networks.[96] Her husband, Paul Massing, was a sociologist who worked for the Institute for Social Research with Adorno and Horkheimer at Columbia University. The two most prominent intellectuals of the Frankfurt School even wrote a preface to Massing's book *Vorgeschichte des politischen Antisemitismus* (*Pre-history of Political Antisemitism*). Massing also became involved in working for Soviet intelligence, and he was the one who introduced Franz Neumann to a spy in his circles. Neumann, as we shall see, was apparently integrated into these networks and shared information with his handler, although some of the details regarding his involvement are at least partially shrouded in mystery.

Neumann was among the first émigrés to be recruited in Washington. He had supported the German revolution of 1918 and later worked as a lawyer for trade unions. However, an FBI investigation confirmed his political reliability and loyalty to the United States.[97] Efforts were even made to expedite his naturalization process. He was then hired by the government, and he rose through the ranks to become head of the Central European Section of the OSS's R&A, gaining access to secret information.

In the 1990s, select Soviet intelligence service archives became accessible, and the United States made its "Venona" project public, which was the massive operation run by the National Security Agency (NSA) aimed at intercepting and decrypting messages from Soviet intelligence. This fragmentary information allowed researchers to identify the person behind the code name "Ruff," who was mentioned in Venona telegrams: Franz Neumann.[98] According to Alexander Vassiliev and Allen Weinstein,

---

1944 (Chicago: Ivan R. Dee, 2009), xx.

95. See Wheatland, *The Frankfurt School in Exile*, 12.

96. See Hede Massing, *This Deception: The Story of a Woman Agent* (New York: Duell, Sloan and Pearce, 1951).

97. See the report on the Institute of [sic] Social Research, dated January 21, 1944, in Theodor Adorno's FBI file, obtained through a FOIA request.

98. See, for instance, John Earl Haynes and Harvey Klehr, *Venona: Decoding Soviet Espionage in America* (New Haven: Yale University Press, 1999), 194–95, 359. Also see the entry on "Franz Neumann" in *Spartacus Educational*: https://spartacus-educational.

Ruff was recommended to the Russian spy services by one of his good friends, "Mary," as well as by "Noah" and "Git."[99] They described him as pro-Soviet and leftist, with no affiliation with émigré organizations. He was contacted in 1942, and he apparently agreed to give all the information he had to Elizabeth "Vardo" Zarubina, a Russian secret agent he had met through his friends Paul and Hede Massing.[100]

Alexander Vasiliev, a former KGB officer turned journalist and historian, was granted access to KGB archives for a book project, and his notes on what he read there are publicly available. In them, there is a list of the secret information provided by Ruff, then an undated note that simply states: "R. [Ruff] does practically nothing. His excuse is that there isn't any important information. The other day, he became a U.S. citizen—bit of a coward."[101] Mary was given instructions to put pressure on him. Then there is a note dated September 1, 1943: "We have taken an interest in Herbert Marcuse in view of his work at 'Cabin' [OSS?]. A close friend of Ruff's. The exact nature of his work in the OSS is unknown. 'Noah' knows M. through Germany and thinks that although he did not belong to a party there, he was very close to the fellow countrymen."[102] It is not clear, however, whether the Soviet intelligence service decided to contact Marcuse. According to at least one source, Neumann did recommend his colleague Donald Wheeler to the KGB, describing him as "talented and progressive," and he later became probably "the KGB's most productive source in the OSS."[103]

According to a note from January 6, 1944, Ruff (i.e. Neumann) reaffirmed that he would pass on all really important information, explaining

com/Franz_Neumann.htm.

99. See Allen Weinstein and Alexander Vassiliev, *The Haunted Wood: Soviet Espionage in America—The Stalin Era* (New York: Random House, 1999) and Alexander Vassiliev, "Vassiliev White Notebook #3," 2009, Wilson Center Digital Archive, Alexander Vassiliev Papers, Manuscript Division, Library of Congress, https://digitalarchive.wilsoncenter.org/document/112566, 133–36.

100. See Weinstein and Vassiliev, *The Haunted Wood*, 250, and Müller, *Krieger und Gelehrte*, 69–73. Hedda Gumperz was known in the United States as Hede Massing, and Weinstein and Vassiliev use the former rather than the latter name, but they are referring to the same person. See the entry on "Hede Massing" in *Spartacus Educational*: https://spartacus-educational.com/Hede_Massing.htm.

101. Vassiliev, "Vassiliev White Notebook #3," 133.

102. Ibid., 135. "Cabin" appears to refer to the OSS.

103. John Earl Haynes, Harvey Klehr, Alexander Vassiliev, *Spies: The Rise and Fall of the KGB in America* (New Haven: Yale University Press, 2009), 305, 307.

that 90 percent of what he learned came out a few days later in the newspapers.[104] Then came the revelations of May and June 1944, when Neumann warned the Soviets that OSS operative Allen Dulles (who would later become the head of the CIA), was discussing with prominent Nazi military officials and businessmen the possibility of a peace deal with the West that would give the Nazis the "freedom to operate in the East in order to continue the war against the USSR."[105] The Kremlin did not fully trust Neumann, and it took time to verify this story by confirming it through other sources, concluding in a note dated April 4, 1945, that it was quite reliable.[106]

This is precisely what the Soviets feared, namely that their supposed allies were traitors who were ready to sign a peace agreement with the Nazis behind their backs. Hitler had made his intention of destroying the Soviet Union perfectly clear, and this had been the project of fourteen capitalist countries during their brutal—but ultimately unsuccessful—invasion of 1918–1920. Dulles, who was explicitly named by Neumann, was not a minor figure. He was running what some have described as the most important U.S. intelligence outpost in Europe. From the end of 1942, he received leaders of the Nazi regime to confer about the possibility of a peace agreement, which would allow Germany to intensify its war against the communists. In addition to the two Nazi contingents identified by Neumann—General Walther von Brauchitsch, Commander-in-Chief of the German Army for the first two years of the war, and a group with Colonel General Kurt Zeitzler, Chief of the Army General Staff for the *Wehrmacht*—Dulles met with Max von Hohenlohe, an envoy of Heinrich Himmler and Walter Schellenberg (the director of intelligence of the SS) to discuss a U.S.-German rapprochement. "Germany would inevitably become a 'factor of order and progress' in Europe following a settlement of the present conflict, Dulles indicated, and should be permitted to keep

---

104. Perhaps reacting to the pressure and seeking more information, Neumann sent a harsh letter to Crane Brinton in the OSS's London office on January 17, 1944, beseeching him to "communicate to us the views held by the London staff members and their British counterparts" regarding Germany, as well as "additional intelligence on the state of affairs in Germany," including information gleaned from interrogated prisoners of war. Franz Neumann, "Letter to Crane Brinton," January 17, 1944, Washington Operations and Service Records, RG 0226 Office of Strategic Services, Entry A1 146 Miscellaneous Washington Files: Budget, Box 84, National Archives, Washington, D.C.

105. Vassiliev, "Vassiliev White Notebook #3," 135.

106. See Haynes, Klehr, Vassiliev, *Spies*, 320.

Austria and several other territories that Hitler had already claimed."[107]
He added, "due to the inflamed state of public opinion in the Anglo-Saxon
countries," Hitler could not serve as the postwar leader of Germany, but
it might be possible to replace him with another powerful Nazi, such as
SS chief Himmler.[108] Allen Dulles and his brother John Foster Dulles, the
future Secretary of State, "became two of the more influential advocates
of separate peace tactics in elite U.S. circles."[109] Although this plan did not
materialize, the future Director of Central Intelligence maintained that
the Nazis shared the same fundamental values as the United States, and
they were therefore fighting the wrong enemy: the Nazis were—unlike
the godless communists—Christians, Aryans, and capitalists.

On the U.S. side, there were also fears of a peace agreement between
Germany and the Soviet Union. This was one of the reasons why
Colonel Carter Clarke, head of the U.S. Army's Special Branch, which
oversaw the Signal Intelligence Service (that would later become the
NSA), started the Venona Project to crack the secret codes used by the
Soviets. Although the project did not succeed before the end of the war,
the discoveries from 1946 did not reveal attempts to negotiate an independent peace with the Nazis. Rather, what Clarke and his team learned
was how successful the USSR had been in placing spies in almost every
department and agency of the U.S. government. The Venona Project,
which was able to decipher only a small portion of the messages, identified 349 individuals in the United States with secret links to Soviet intelligence (but almost 200 remained hidden behind their code names).
Among the spies discovered, there were a significant number of high-
ranking officials like Lauchlin Currie (a personal assistant of President
Roosevelt) and Maurice Halperin (the director of the research service
of the OSS). There was also the infiltration of the Manhattan Project by
Julius Rosenberg and others, which allowed the Soviet Union to develop
atomic weapons more quickly.

---

107. Christopher Simpson, *The Splendid Blond Beast: Money, Law and Genocide in the
Twentieth Century* (Monroe, ME: Common Courage Press, 1995), 123.

108. Ibid. "While Dulles was not blind to the possibilities of using the negotiations
simply as a means of sowing dissension in the SS," Simpson notes, "all of the available
telegrams indicate that he saw Hohenlohe's proposal as a realistic and desirable basis for
U.S. strategy in Europe" (124).

109. Ibid., 121.

IMPORTANT DOUBTS HAVE BEEN raised about Neumann's work as a double agent. First of all, Vassiliev's notes from the KGB archives were the result of a book deal with Crown Publishers (a subsidiary of Random House), which provided him and his co-author Weinstein with exclusive access to Soviet documentation.[110] More needs to be known about this agreement, which was part of a larger project—in the wake of the destruction of the USSR—of publishing five books based on Soviet archives, with obvious propaganda potential. Unfortunately, an independent verification of Vassiliev and Weinstein's findings has not been allowed. Permitting other researchers to read the files would obviously be necessary, not simply to verify the validity of their claims but also to explore alternative explanations for the rather fragmentary evidence that is available. According to Tim Müller, the Massings, who were purportedly responsible for connecting Neumann to Soviet intelligence, "had already broken away from the Soviet intelligence service networks in 1938 and sought cooperation with the FBI."[111] Is it possible, as he suggests, that Neumann was simply sharing information with the Massings as friends, who then perhaps reconnected with their former Soviet contacts to help an allied nation that was bearing the brunt of the war?

Moreover, Vassiliev and Weinstein's project has some complicated aspects to it that merit greater scrutiny. To begin with, Weinstein was a professor who had become deeply involved in anticommunist destabilization efforts at least since 1980, "when he joined Soviet dissidents in organizing a citizens' committee to monitor the Helsinki Accords on Human Rights."[112] He was one of the driving forces behind the Center for Democracy, which he ran from 1985 to 2003, when it was folded into the National Endowment for Democracy (NED) and he became its

---

110. See Alexander Vassiliev, "Introduction: How I Came to Write My Notebooks, Discover Alger Hiss, and Lose to His Lawyer," in John Earl Haynes, Harvey Klehr, and Alexander Vassiliev, *The Rise and Fall of the KGB in America* (New Haven: Yale University Press, 2009), xxvii–liii.

111. Müller, *Krieger und Gelehrte*, 71. Müller's position appears to be at least partially contradicted by Hede Massing's memoirs, in which she claims that her first contact with the FBI was in 1947, when she decided to cooperate and tell the Bureau her story (see Massing, *This Deception*, 313–14). It is noteworthy, moreover, that she does not make a single reference to Franz Neumann in *This Deception*. Was she covering for him since the Venona codes had not yet been cracked, or is there another explanation?

112. David Ignatius, "Innocence Abroad: The New World of Spyless Coups," *Washington Post*, September 22, 1991, C4.

co-director.[113] In describing the NED, he candidly explained, as we briefly saw above, that "a lot of what we do today was done covertly 25 years ago by the CIA."[114] Indeed, Weinstein was directly involved in supporting Boris Yeltsin's anti-Soviet coup d'état. He was, according to his co-author Vassiliev, friends with CIA director James Woolsey and "a suspected CIA agent" who some presumed was "allowing the agency to use the Center for Democracy as a cover for secret operations."[115] Vassiliev, a former agent in the KGB intelligence directorate, was fearful of the Communists coming back to power in 1996, so he remained in Britain after the British Foreign Office organized his second trip there in 1993.[116] All of this raises serious questions about the reliability of Weinstein and Vassiliev's co-authored book. Were they providing a faithful transcription of the archives, as well as a reliable framing of the facts? Or is it possible that they were trying to "bad-jacket" Neumann, disingenuously presenting him as an informant in order to discredit him—and thus one of the more Marxist scholars of the Frankfurt School—as a communist collaborator not to be trusted? This would not explain, however, why his name surfaced in the Venona telegrams. Unfortunately, more information is necessary in order to resolve these questions.

Müller draws the following conclusion, which appears to be the most prudent, given the extant state of research in the field (though more information could come to light requiring this to be revised):

> It seems certain that Hede Massing . . . and Paul Massing received OSS documents from Neumann in 1943. The Massings forwarded these documents to the NKGB and established a brief contact between Neumann and a Russian agent. Neumann provided the NKGB agent with information about secret negotiations of the German opposition with the Americans. He broke off contact in July 1944. Even Weinstein and Vassiliev cannot help but describe Neumann as a "problematic and ambivalent source" for the Soviets.[117]

---

113. See Rick Shenkman, "Allen Weinstein: The Overlooked Controversy in His Career," History News Network, https://www.historynewsnetwork.org/article/allen-weinstein-the-overlooked-controversy-in-his-.

114. Ignatius, "Innocence Abroad."

115. Vassiliev, "Introduction," in Haynes, Klehr, and Vassiliev, *The Rise and Fall of the KGB in America*, xlii, xxxv.

116. See ibid.

117. Müller, *Krieger und Gelehrte*, 70.

In spite of these qualifications, Müller nonetheless concludes: "It cannot be ruled out that Neumann was active as a Soviet 'spy' for a short time."[118]

Neumann died in a car accident in 1954, before history could catch up with him and shed light on his possible secret dealings. If anyone was aware of his activities, it would likely have been his wife, Inge Werner, who also worked for the OSS, or his close friend Herbert Marcuse.[119] The latter had moved in with the Neumanns and lived in a trio with them after his wife died in 1951. When Franz was killed three years later, Herbert married his widow, Inge, the following year. Nobody in their circles was more intimately connected than these three. I am unaware, however, of any time when Marcuse or his new wife publicly discussed Neumann's possible role as the Soviet agent known as Ruff. It is interesting to note, however, that some have attributed Marcuse's radicalization to his relationship with Inge: "Many of their friends have testified that it was . . . Inge who first pressured him to become more actively allied to the political movements taking shape in the 1960s."[120] Whatever the case may be, it is widely recognized that Marcuse moved further to the left, beginning around 1965. This is illustrated by publications like *An Essay on Liberation* (1969) and *Counter-Revolution and Revolt* (1972), as well as by his public support for the student, antiwar, ecological, feminist, and antiracist movements.

Can You Seriously Fight Fascism While Combating Communism?

In assessing the Frankfurt School's collaboration with the U.S. government, it is of the utmost importance to highlight different levels of complicity. The Frankfurt scholars needed employment. Like many intellectuals, their employers had questionable reputations, to put it mildly, but this must be contextualized and situated within an overall calculus of scholarly survival. The simple fact of working for a particular organization does not

---

118. Ibid., 72. Whatever the case may be, we do know that Marcuse and Neumann were working with other spies at the OSS, such as Hans Hirschfeld and Robert Soblen, as Müller explains. According to Marcuse's FBI file, he wrote letters and sent an affidavit regarding Soblen's activities in the OSS and that of his alleged accomplices (see Marcuse's FBI file, obtained through a FOIA request). Soblen's widow and fingered accomplice, according to the same document, "did not remember her husband ever having mentioned Marcuse." Marcuse's FBI file.

119. On Inge Werner and the OSS, see Katz, *Foreign Intelligence*, 26.

120. Barry Kätz, *Herbert Marcuse and the Art of Liberation: An Intellectual Biography* (London: Verso, 1982), 210.

automatically disqualify someone intellectually or politically. Within the OSS, for instance, there was a wide spectrum of political orientations, and some researchers were open to or even supportive of certain aspects of socialism. The agency itself was highly compartmentalized, with a clear distinction between the analytic and action arms (although the former fed into, and provided cover for, the latter). Moreover, some intellectuals made a significant portion of their career out of their government service, while others only served for a rather brief wartime stint. Several of them went on to produce important scholarship that was not simply an expression of the dominant ideology. Paul Baran, Arno Mayer, and Paul Sweezy are three such examples. A dialectical approach, which examines the social totality and all of the nuances of individual orientations within it—as well as how they changed over time—is necessary in order to avoid reductivist accounts.

Much of the academic debate on the Frankfurt School's involvement with the government has, unfortunately, been framed in terms of what historian Jacques Pauwels insightfully diagnosed as *The Myth of the Good War*.[121] The principal claim is that the members of this school were fighting fascism, and their valiant contributions to this cause are therefore beyond criticism. Marcuse intoned, in perfect harmony with this orientation: "If critics reproach me for that [working for the OSS], it only shows the complete ignorance of these people, who seem to have forgotten that the war then was a war against fascism and that, consequently, I haven't the slightest reason for being ashamed of having assisted in it."[122] There is some truth to this insofar as a number of the critical theorists, including Marcuse, provided important studies of Nazi Germany and lobbied for more serious forms of de-Nazification than were actually implemented. They were invested in anti-fascist politics within the confines of bourgeois democracies, which can be a laudable tactic, even though it is not a viable long-term strategy.

In any case, one cannot simply analyze this phenomenon at a subjective level by looking at the thoughts, motivations, and actions of individual scholars. These need to be situated within the objective system in which they participated. One of the principal interests that the U.S. national

---

121. See Jacques R. Pauwels, *The Myth of the Good War: America in the Second World War* (Toronto: James Lorimer & Company, 2015).

122. Herbert Marcuse and Karl Popper, *Revolution or Reform? A Confrontation*, ed. A.T. Ferguson, trans. Michael Aylward and A.T. Ferguson (Chicago: New University Press, 1985), 59.

security state had in hiring German researchers with some knowledge of Marxism was that it was beneficial to have people who knew the European left from the inside. Non-communist Marxists were particularly useful because their expertise in Marxism could be mobilized to understand and fight the enemy, while their anticommunism helped guarantee their ultimate fealty to the bourgeois state (although there are some exceptions). This was not only true in the case of the Frankfurt School but more generally, so much so that some scholars talk—with plenty of evidence to support this claim—of a Trotskyism-to-CIA pipeline. One of the objectives of the U.S. national security state was to wage a highly sophisticated intellectual world war on Marxism, driving a wedge between its supposedly authentic and respectable Western forms, on the one hand, and its purported perversions in the East, where it became a material reality instead of a pristine system of ideas. The Frankfurt School, like the dominant forms of Trotskyism in the imperial core, played an important role in this war.

Another key aspect of the U.S. national security state, and more specifically agencies like the OSS, needs to be highlighted: it was far from simply being antifascist. It is worth recalling that the country was racially segregated at the time, and lynchings were still taking place, as well as racist police terror. The Nazis had, in fact, diligently studied the United States prior to the war because they considered it to be at the vanguard of racial apartheid.[123] Moreover, Uncle Sam engaged in violent wars of imperial conquest and repeatedly refused—including during the Spanish Civil War—to fight the spread of fascism around the world. There was also ample fascist support on the home front, including by mainstream leaders and the media.

During the Palmer Raids of 1919–20, state forces arrested thousands and deported hundreds of suspected radicals with complete disregard, in most cases, for due process. In 1934, it was revealed that a group of powerful capitalists—including the Morgan, Du Pont, Rockefeller, Pew, and Mellon interests—had conspired to overthrow the New Deal government and establish a fascist dictatorship, although none of the conspirators were held accountable or punished for it.[124] The Smith Act of 1940

---

123. See James Q. Whitman, *Hitler's American Model: The United States and the Making of Nazi Race Law* (Princeton: Princeton University Press, 2018).

124. See Gabriel Rockhill, "Fascist Plots in the U.S.: Contemporary Lessons from the 1934 'Business Plot,'" *Liberation School*, June 6, 2021, https://www.liberationschool.org/fascist-plots-in-the-u-s-contemporary-lessons-from-the-1934-business-plot/.

made it a criminal offense to advocate for the (communist) overthrow of the government. The proposed Mundt-Nixon Bill of 1948 explicitly presented itself as an effort to combat communism by requiring members of the Communist Party to register with the Attorney General, and Senate liberals proposed establishing "concentration camps to intern potential troublemakers."[125] Although it did not ultimately pass, many of its provisions were integrated into the 1950 McCarran Act, which authorized the detention of any person suspected of being a potential threat to internal security. This is precisely what had been done to some 120,000 denizens of Japanese descent—the majority of whom were U.S. citizens—beginning in 1942 (German and Italian nationals were also interned in smaller numbers). They were forcibly relocated to what President Roosevelt and other officials openly called "concentration camps" at the time.[126] These were not death camps like in Germany, but they were prisons on a grand scale that indiscriminately trammeled the rights of a large number of people (they only came to be described as internment centers after a postwar propaganda effort to distinguish them from the Nazi camps).

All said and done, then, when the Frankfurt scholars were working as the Washington School, the United States was a racially segregated state with an established history of anticommunist fascistic practices at home and abroad, which had established concentration camps to detain perceived threats to national security. While it was obviously not an open fascist dictatorship, it is important to approach this issue dialectically in order to bring out all of the dimensions of governance, rather than being trapped within the metaphysical opposition between a supposedly pure state of bourgeois democracy, and another of outright fascism. As forms of capitalist political management that are intricate processes with different dimensions, bourgeois democracy and fascism often overlap,

---

125. Noam Chomsky, "Introduction," in Nelson Blackstock, *Cointelpro: The FBI's Secret War on Political Freedom* (New York: Pathfinder Press, 1988), 35.

126. See Edward Schumacher-Matos, "Euphemisms, Concentration Camps and the Japanese Internment," *National Public Radio*, February 10, 2012, https://www.npr.org/sections/publiceditor/2012/02/10/146691773/euphemisms-concentration-camps-and-the-japanese-internment; Aiko Herzig-Yoshinaga, "Words Can Lie or Clarify: Terminology of the World War II Incarceration of Japanese Americans," 2009, https://manzanarcommittee.org/wp-content/uploads/2010/03/wordscanlieorclarify-ahy.pdf; Roger Daniels, "Words Do Matter: A Note on Inappropriate Terminology and the Incarceration of the Japanese Americans," in *Nikkei in the Pacific Northwest: Japanese Americans and Japanese Canadians in the Twentieth Century*, ed. Louis Fiset and Gail Nomura (Seattle: University of Washington Press, 2005), 183–207.

intersect, coalesce, and mutually support one another in complex con-figurations that cannot be reduced to the simplistic opposition between two radically distinct forms of governance.

The day after the Nazis invaded the USSR in 1941, Harry Truman said: "If we see that Germany is winning, we ought to help Russia, and if Russia is winning, we ought to help Germany, and that way let them kill as many as possible, although I don't want to see Hitler victorious in any circumstances."[127] When the United States finally opened a second front in 1944, it was largely in reaction to the fact that the Red Army had been marching West, and the U.S. administration did not want to see Western Europe fall under the liberating influence of the communists. Moreover, on the Eastern front, the United States became the only country to use atomic weapons against a civilian population during war. This wanton act of destruction was not at all a military necessity, however. It was, instead, a gruesome message to the real enemy of the U.S. empire: the communists.

Even before the official end of hostilities during the Second World War, the same organization that many of the Frankfurt scholars worked for, the OSS, began recruiting fascists from around the world and integrat-ing them into a veritable fascist international for the so-called Cold War. Allen Dulles and James Angleton, who were working for the OSS and would later become leading figures in the CIA, were involved in white-washing and repurposing tens—if not hundreds—of thousands of fas-cists, including from Nazi Germany, Italy, and Japan.[128] In many cases, they were put right back in power, but sometimes blowback required that they be exfiltrated or redeployed in other ways. Over 10,000 Nazis were brought directly to the United States. In Europe, the CIA integrated them into fascist stay-behind armies that were later activated to commit acts of terrorism that were blamed on communists.[129] Many fascists were also sent to other places around the world, such as Latin America, to serve the interests of U.S. imperialism.

Much more could be said about this particular context, but the idea that the United States was simply an antifascist beacon of democracy is an

---

127. Cited in Blum, *Killing Hope*, 10.
128. See Gabriel Rockhill, "The U.S. Did Not Defeat Fascism in WWII, It Discretely Internationalized It," *CounterPunch*, October 16, 2020, https://www.counterpunch.org/2020/10/16/the-u-s-did-not-defeat-fascism-in-wwii-it-discretely-internationalized-it/.
129. See Ganser, *Nato's Secret Armies* and Francovich, *Gladio*.

ideological illusion, as is the assumption that the OSS was only invested in the noble cause of fighting fascism (the same is true of the State Department, of course, where some of the Frankfurt scholars worked as well). It is certainly the case that much of this information about the integration of fascists was not as readily available during the early Cold War as it is today. However, Marcuse candidly admitted in an interview that he knew that Nazi officials were being hired by the U.S. government while he was working there (given his close friendship with the other Frankfurt intellectuals, it is safe to assume that they must have known as well):

> Q: At the same time you were providing intelligence on the Nazis, weren't Nazi officials already working with the U.S. government against the communists?
>
> A: Not so much early on; they were lying low. But they came in gradually. There were two trends [within the OSS]. One was to disarm and destroy the German war potential completely. Two, there was a fear of the Soviet Union. That was until 1950. And then, more and more, the OSS worked on communism.[130]

Since the OSS was officially terminated in 1945, Marcuse must have been referring to the R&A where he worked, which was integrated into the State Department. He was employed there until 1953, becoming the State Department's "leading authority" on communism.[131] He therefore had plenty of time to see the Nazis trickle in gradually to fight communism alongside him.

What is more, it was in Frankfurt, the capital of the U.S. occupation zone, that former SS officer Hans Otto turned himself in and declared that he was serving in a secret fascist army, providing first-person testimony regarding its operations.[132] This was in 1952, and it led to widespread debate in the mainstream press in Frankfurt and around the world. It was revealed at the time that the Nazi terrorist network was trained, armed, and overseen by the CIA.[133] I am unaware of any public statement that the Frankfurt critical theorists made about these revelations regarding a Nazi militia in their hometown. Perhaps this is because, as we saw in the

---

130. Marcuse, *Marxism, Revolution and Utopia*, 430.

131. Müller, *Krieger und Gelehrte*, 119.

132. See, for instance, "Germany Rocked by Scandal of U.S. Arming Storm Troops," *Newsweek*, October 20, 1952, 42–47.

133. See Rockhill, "Critical and Revolutionary Theory."

last chapter, the Institute for Social Research was working with erstwhile Nazi scholars and integrated several of them into leadership positions, including as directors of the Institute. In any case, in contradistinction to the silence and complicity of the Frankfurt scholars, many communist intellectuals were fully aware of U.S. support for fascism at the time, which they spoke out against. When assessing the scientific validity of Marxism and critical theory, these historical facts should be at the center of the discussion since the Institute intellectuals did not fully grasp—or they conveniently ignored—fundamental aspects of the material reality in which they lived.

The communists, it is worth recalling, are the ones who deserve the most credit for routing fascism: some thirty-five million Soviets and twenty million Chinese died in the war against it (compared to approximately 400,000 U.S. soldiers). In openly embracing the anticommunist war waged by the United States, the Frankfurt scholars also contributed to the fight against the real antifascists (not the opportunist ones). This explains why the supporters of fascism saw them as natural partners, following the adage that "an enemy of my enemy is my ally." The fundamental distinction, at the end of the day, is not between bourgeois democracy and fascism, which are two forms of capitalist political management that often work in tandem with one another. The real opposition is between capitalism in whatever form—bourgeois democratic or fascist—and socialism. In positioning themselves in the former camp, the Washington school of critical theory was objectively contributing to pro-capitalist anticommunism.

This means, in conclusion, that even if they subjectively considered themselves to be antifascists and, more important, worked to uproot fascism through bourgeois democratic means (which, again, is a laudable tactic), they remained accommodationist toward the capitalist system, the seedbed of fascism, while fighting the truly antifascist communists. Their subjective ambitions—particularly the desire to fight fascism— were certainly praiseworthy, and some of them did make commendable contributions within the bourgeois democratic struggle against it. At the same time, their subjective understanding of the bourgeois democracy they worked for in this endeavor misconstrued its fundamental nature since, objectively speaking, it was complicit with maintaining, and even strengthening, certain fascist forms of political management. Moreover, in opposing actually existing socialism and directly contributing to the ideological war against communism, the Washington School intellectuals were, at an objective level, foreclosing the definitive strategic defeat of fascism and contributing to the maintenance of the very system (capitalism) that generates fascism. This more dialectically nuanced historical materialist assessment is necessary to avoid the facile assumption that they were beyond reproach because they were contributing to the U.S. state's supposed fight against fascism. It allows us to see that if the Frankfurt scholars in Washington were subjectively antifascist, in the sense that they were individually dedicated to fighting fascism as they understood it, they were, nonetheless, objectively speaking, accommodating—and sometimes supporting—the socioeconomic system driving fascism, while condemning the one that eliminates it.

CHAPTER 6

The Radical Piper of Western Marxism: Marcuse

Was Marcuse an Agent of Empire?

Herbert, tell us why are you getting paid by the CIA?

—DANIEL COHN-BENDIT[1]

This epigraph is from an animated exchange that purportedly took place between the *enfant terrible* of the 1968 student movement and the figure widely promoted as the so-called godfather of the New Left: Herbert Marcuse. It occurred in June 1969 during a student-led interruption of one of his lectures in Italy. "I have been accused of being paid," retorted the Frankfurt School scholar, "by the Kremlin, by Beijing, by capitalism, by Wall Street."[2] Marcuse's sarcasm was likely entertaining, perhaps even distracting, for some of those present, but shrewd observers surely registered the most important aspect of his witty reply: he did not actually deny the accusation.

---

1. Diego Giachetti, "Giugno 1969: I 'caldi' giorni Italiani di Herbert Marcuse," *Il Protagora: Rivista di filosofia e cultura*, Vol. 4 (July-December 2004): 168. Also see "Obszöne Welt," *Der Spiegel*, Vol. 27, June 30, 1969, 108–9 and Wolfgang Kraushaar, ed., *Frankfurter Schule und Studentenbewegung: Von der Flaschenpost zum Molotowcocktail 1946–1995*, Vol. I, *Chronik* (Hamburg: Rogner & Bernhard GmbH & Co. Verlags KG, 1998), 438–39. Cohn-Bendit later denied having said this. See Esther Leslie, "Introduction to Adorno/Marcuse Correspondence on the German Student Movement," *New Left Review*, Vol. 233 (January–February 1999): 122n12. In a letter to Leo Löwenthal on July 16, 1969, Marcuse wrote that "Cohn-Bendit accused me of being an agent of the bourgeoisie, while other extreme groups on the left denounced me as a CIA agent." Quoted in Tim B. Müller, *Krieger und Gelehrte: Herbert Marcuse und die Denksysteme im Kalten Krieg* (Hamburg: Hamburger Edition, 2011), 630n181.

2. Giachetti, "Giugno 1969," 168.

The allegations that Marcuse was a CIA agent "were first made in 1968 in the communist press, with the direct support of Moscow."[3] Highlighting his intelligence links, Yuri Zhukov denounced him in *Pravda* on May 30 as part of a counter-revolutionary offensive that was "attempting to undertake a 'de-communization of Marxism' to divide and bring internal quarreling to progressive forces, and thus carry out the quite explicit social imperatives of the enemies of the working movement."[4] Zhukov further emphasized that, in the bourgeois press, Marcuse was "advertised like a movie star, and his books just like the latest brand of toothpaste or razor blades."[5] In the following months and year, similar denunciations of this longtime intelligence operative being commercialized as a non-communist radical were published by the Italian Communist Giorgio Amendola, Gus Hall of the Communist Party USA, and the Progressive Labor faction of Students for a Democratic Society.[6] Hall decried, for instance, the "petty-bourgeois radicalism" and "anti-working class" orientation of Marcuse's New Left politics.[7] He even claimed that the author of *Soviet Marxism* was "part of a plot by the American government to drive young people to cultural radicalism and thus divert them from a political revolution."[8] Similar allegations continued to circulate widely in the coming years, and the tenor of the critiques is reflected in the titles of some of the articles, such as "Herbert Marcuse and His Philosophy of Copout," "Marcuse: Cop-Out or Cop?" and "Herbert Marcuse: The Ideologue as Paid Agent of U.S. Imperialism."[9]

L. L. Matthias likely went the furthest in accusing Marcuse of being a CIA agent involved in constructing an anti-Soviet spy center in Frankfurt that collaborated with the Gehlen Organization (the postwar

---

3. Müller, *Krieger und Gelehrte*, 630.
4. Yuri Zhukov, "The Three M's," in Klaus Mehnert, *Moscow and the New Left*, trans. Helmut Fischer (Berkeley and Los Angeles: University of California Press, 1975), 149.
5. Ibid., 145.
6. The 1968 statements by Amendola and Hall were reported in the *New York Times*, June 7, 11, and July 5, 14, respectively. Also see Barry Kātz, *Herbert Marcuse and the Art of Liberation: An Intellectual Biography* (London: Verso, 1982), 188.
7. See Will Lissner, "U.S. Reds Score New Left's Ideas: The Theories of Marcuse and Debray Called Bourgeois," *New York Times*, July 5, 1968, 14.
8. Müller, *Krieger und Gelehrte*, 629. Müller is paraphrasing Hall.
9. See Jared Israel and William Russel, "Herbert Marcuse and His Philosophy of Copout," *Progressive Labor*, Vol. 6 (October 1968): 59–72; N.A., "Marcuse: Cop-Out or Cop?," *Progressive Labor*, Vol. 6 (1969): 61–66; Eric Scheper, "Herbert Marcuse: The Ideologue as Paid Agent of U.S. Imperialism," *Literature & Ideology*, Vol. 7 (1970).

anticommunist intelligence agency established and overseen by the CIA and headed by the notorious Nazi general Reinhart Gehlen, who filled its ranks with fellow Nazis).[10] Matthias even asserted that Marcuse served as the principal intermediary between Gehlen and the CIA's Frank Wisner. He also relayed the *National Observer*'s claim that Marcuse had been the mastermind behind the 1968 riots, declaring that he "succeeded in splitting the revolutionary student movements from the workers' movement . . . and thus prevented a merger that was feared in Washington more than almost any other event."[11] Marcuse publicly rejected Matthias' assertions as "rubbish . . . spread by bankrupt persons and groups of the old left, who avoid argumentation," adding that they were aimed at discrediting the New Left, and particularly the student movement.[12] Matthias responded with the following:

> Marcuse had already been described or characterized as a CIA agent and agent provocateur by two American magazines in 1968. A man with a name to lose would have sued the two magazines for libel. Herbert Marcuse has not done so to this day. Moreover, my statements were confirmed in a letter by a former CIA agent, so a former colleague of Marcuse's, who now lives in Philadelphia and has read my article.[13]

Is it possible, then, that Marcuse was a CIA agent, and perhaps even the liaison officer that Reinhard Gehlen mysteriously referred to in his memoirs as "Colonel M—"?[14] Unless I am mistaken, he was never publicly known to have achieved the rank of colonel, nor was he overtly employed by the CIA. However, Jürgen Habermas revealed that Marcuse did return to Germany "as an officer of the US army," and in 1948 he moved up the ladder at the State Department, taking over responsibility for Europe from Stuart Hughes, who had been State's "top authority for Western, Central

---

10. See Gabriel Rockhill, "The U.S. Did Not Defeat Fascism in WWII, It Discreetly Internationalized It," *CounterPunch*, October 16, 2020.

11. L. L. Matthias, "Wer ist Herbert Marcuse?," *Bulletin des Fränkischen Kreises*, Vol. 121 (May 1969): 15. Also see L. L. Matthias, "Noch einmal: Herbert Marcuse," *Bulletin des Fränkischen Kreises*, Vol. 124 (August 1969): 19–20.

12. "Interview with Marcuse," *Australian Left Review* (December 1969): 46.

13. "Briefe," *Der Spiegel*, Vol. 29, July 13, 1969, https://www.spiegel.de/politik/linksband-a-7dc35f19-0002-0001-0000-000045549173.

14. Reinhard Gehlen, *The Service: The Memoirs of General Reinhard Gehlen*, trans. David Irving (New York: World Publishing, 1972), 143.

and Eastern Europe."[15] This was after having served, along with Otto Kirchheimer and Felix Gilbert, under Franz Neumann, who directed the German section of the Research & Analysis branch until 1947 (originally housed in the Office of Strategic Services, or OSS, R&A was transferred to the State Department after the war). Since Marcuse's mother tongue was German, and he was the State Department's "leading authority" in "intelligence regarding communism [*Kommunismusaufklärung*]"—not unlike Gehlen, who had directed Nazi intelligence against the Soviets before continuing his anticommunist espionage for the CIA—it seems unlikely that their paths would not have crossed, either in person or via intermediaries and overlapping projects.[16] In fact, in 1951, Gehlen was given a VIP tour of the United States to meet the leaders of the U.S. national security state and develop their plans for a common war on communism, which was one of Marcuse's fundamental tasks. Gehlen met William Donovan, the chief of the OSS and Marcuse's boss during the war, as well as three major figures in the CIA, two of whom had served in the OSS, whom Marcuse almost certainly knew in some capacity: Walter Bedell Smith, Allen Dulles, and Frank Wisner.[17] Marcuse himself, it is worth recalling, "had a clearance for the security level 'Top Secret.'"[18] More research clearly needs to be done in this area since there is no hard evidence—as far as I know—regarding connections between Marcuse and Gehlen, outside of Matthias's claim that a CIA agent confirmed his statements in this regard.

Many Western academics, particularly those who have a direct stake in the Critical Theory franchise, have ignored or rejected out of hand all of the allegations mentioned above, contending that they are little more than scurrilous slander unworthy of scholarly investigation. Marcuse, after all, is well known for being the most visibly radical theorist of the Frankfurt School. This became particularly apparent during the mobilizations of the late 1960s, when—to take but one example—the magazine *Konkret*

15. Herbert Marcuse, et al., "Theory and Politics: A Discussion with Herbert Marcuse, Jürgen Habermas, Heinz Lubasz and Telman Spengler," *Telos*, Vol. 38 (September 1978): 130, and Müller, *Krieger und Gelehrte*, 61.

16. Müller, *Krieger und Gelehrte*, 119. *Kommunismusaufklärung* also refers to "education in communism."

17. Among other sources, see Daniele Ganser, *NATO's Secret Armies: Operation Gladio and Terrorism in Western Europe* (London: Frank Cass, 2005), 191, and Christopher Simpson, *Blowback: America's Recruitment of Nazis and Its Effects on the Cold War* (New York: Weidenfeld & Nicolson, 1988), 40–51.

18. Müller, *Krieger und Gelehrte*, 119.

lauded Marcuse as "the only representative of the 'Frankfurt School' who supports those who wish to realize the claims of Critical Theory: the students, young workers, persecuted minorities in the metropolises, and the oppressed in the Third World."[19] The same year this article was published (1969), sixteen representatives of the New Left, including Rudi Dutschke and Oskar Negt, issued a public letter defending Marcuse against what they called the "the revival of Stalinist practices" and celebrating the New Left for "fighting the traditional party bureaucrats and the authoritarian social state."[20] In it they asserted: "Whoever describes Marcuse as an 'agent of the CIA' or as an 'agent of the bourgeoisie' and thereby attempts to silence him, has abandoned the terrain on which the New Left works politically."[21] More recently, Raffaele Laudani, in his introduction to *Secret Reports on Nazi Germany: The Frankfurt School Contribution to the War Effort*, flatly stated that the accusation that Marcuse was CIA was "inaccurate": "The German philosopher did not in fact have any collaborative relationship with the controversial American agency."[22] Laudani likely had in mind Marcuse's own response to these allegations. For instance, this is what he replied to Jürgen Habermas in an interview where the latter asked him to talk about his "return to Germany as an officer of the U.S. army":

MARCUSE: At first I was in the political division of the OSS and then in the Division of Research and Intelligence of the State Department. My main task was to identify groups in Germany with which one could work toward reconstruction after the war; and to identify groups which were to be taken to task as Nazis. There was a major denazification program at the time. Based on exact research, reports, newspaper reading, and whatever, lists were made up of those Nazis who were supposed to assume responsibility for their activity. Later it was said that I was a CIA agent.
HABERMAS: Yes, yes.
MARCUSE: Which is ridiculous, since the OSS wasn't even allowed near the CIA. They fought each other like enemies.[23]

---

19. Cited in Leslie, "Introduction to Adorno/Marcuse Correspondence."
20. Quoted in Marcuse, "Interview with Marcuse."
21. Ibid., 37.
22. Raffaele Laudani, "Introduction," in Franz Neumann, et al., *Secret Reports on Nazi Germany: The Frankfurt School Contribution to the War Effort*, ed. Raffaele Laudani, trans. Jason Francis Mc Gimsey (Princeton: Princeton University Press, 2013), 1.
23. Marcuse, "Theory and Politics," 130–31.

Are these simply specious allegations "spread by bankrupt figures and groups of old leftists who avoid argumentation," seeking instead to discredit Marcuse and the New Left through slander?[24] What are we to make, then, of the fact that the OSS was officially terminated in 1945, and the CIA was not established until 1947? How could they have "fought each other like enemies" if they never existed at the same time? Since Marcuse was a state operative for at least eleven years, if we count his first year of contract work, he surely knew this. So was he being disingenuous in making such a claim? Perhaps, to be fair, he just misspoke because he was thinking of the Research and Analysis Branch, where he worked, which moved from the OSS—the predecessor of the CIA—to the State Department when the former closed.[25] Was it the State Department and the CIA that were not allowed near one another, at least in the case of Marcuse's R&A?

If this is what he meant to say, he must not have read his job description very closely. According to the Register of the Department of State 1948, on the same page where Marcuse is listed as the Acting Chief of the Central European Branch, his agency is described as being:

> responsible for planning and implementing a program of positive-intelligence research pertaining to all of continental Europe . . . to meet the intelligence requirements of the Department [of State] in the formulation and execution of foreign policy and the intelligence requirements of the Central Intelligence Agency and other authorized agencies.[26]

Marcuse's branch was part of the Office of Intelligence Research (OIR), which was responsible for coordinating its work "with those of the other

---

24. Herbert Marcuse, et al., "Revolution aus Ekel: *Spiegel*-Gespräch mit dem Philosophen Herbert Marcuse," *Der Spiegel*, Vol. 31, July 28, 1969, 106.

25. Since this is not the only interview where Marcuse acts as if the OSS outlived its termination, it does seem safe to assume that he was talking about R&A. See Herbert Marcuse, *Marxism, Revolution and Utopia*, Vol. 6 of *Collected Papers of Herbert Marcuse*, ed. Douglas Kellner and Clayton Pierce (New York: Routledge, 2014), 430.

26. Department of State, *Register of the Department of State* (Washington, DC: U.S. Government Printing Office, 1948), 76, https://archive.org/details/registerofdepart 1948unit/page/n5/mode/2up. "Positive intelligence," according to the "Glossary of Intelligence Terms and Definitions," is "a term of convenience sometimes applied to foreign intelligence to distinguish it from foreign counterintelligence," June 15, 1978, the CIA FOIA Electronic Reading Room, https://www.cia.gov/readingroom/document/cia-rdp80m00596a000400010001-1.

Federal agencies so that the Department [of State] will be provided with the intelligence concerning foreign countries necessary for the formulation and execution of United States foreign policy, and so that the National Intelligence Authority and Central Intelligence Agency will be provided with studies pertinent to the national security."[27] Among the OIR's four functions, the second is that it "provides positive intelligence research in regional and functional fields of study, and prepares or participates in the preparation of intelligence studies and spot intelligence for authorized recipients in the Department, the Central Intelligence Agency, and other Federal agencies."[28] According to his job description, there can be no doubt: Marcuse collaborated with the CIA and other government agencies in producing intelligence reports that guided U.S. foreign policy.

To give Marcuse the benefit of the doubt, perhaps this was just a general description that did not adequately capture the specific nature of the work he was doing. However, this would not explain, to take but one example, why we have internal documents in which Marcuse demanded of his employees in the State Department that they pursue research into the ideological and political differences in the communist world with the highest degree of urgency because "the P sector and CIA" were absolutely dependent upon it (the P sector refers to propaganda agencies).[29] Tim Müller, whose 736-page book on intellectual cold warriors is based on one of the most extensive engagements with the extant archival record to date, explained the relationship as follows:

'R' [the Research & Analysis branch where Marcuse worked] was the link between the other American intelligence services and the State Department, the military agencies, as well as the new CIA. On behalf of the National Security Council (NSC), these intelligence agencies jointly produced the National Intelligence Estimates from 1950 onwards, the final editing of which was the responsibility of the CIA. Herbert Marcuse was also involved in this process.[30]

---

27. Department of State, *Register of the Department of State* (1948), 75.
28. Ibid.
29. Müller, *Krieger und Gelehrte*, 148. "'P sector' referred to the operational area of the Assistant Secretary of State for Public Affairs, which was responsible for the official information and propaganda activities of the United States, such as Voice of America" (ibid., 148n308).
30. Ibid., 61.

Someone, it seems, was being rather sly in his attempted self-exoneration.

Marcuse, the CIA, and Anticommunist Destabilization

> What is completely unknown is that Marcuse provided advice and
> assistance to the leadership of the intelligence apparatus and wrote
> National Intelligence Estimates for the United States of America.
>   —TIM MÜLLER[31]

In a 1954 internal State Department survey, Frankfurt School scholar Otto
Kirchheimer reported that he worked closely with the CIA, "to whom he
sometimes supplied templates for NIEs [National Intelligence Estimates],
which were strictly regulated by the CIA."[32] As Tim Müller explained,
"Marcuse's bureaucratic position was higher [than Kirchheimer's], his
position in the apparatus much more important."[33] Given Marcuse's disingenuous claims regarding his ties to the world's most infamous spy
agency, what does the archival record reveal concerning his relationship to the CIA and, more specifically, the anticommunist destabilization
efforts undertaken by the U.S. national security state?

As briefly mentioned, Marcuse had a "Top Secret" security clearance,
and he was, according to Müller, "the leading authority" on communism "in the State Department in 1951."[34] He served as the head of the
Committee on World Communism (CWC), which reported directly to
Allan Evans, the director of the Office of Intelligence Research (OIR).
When the OSS was disbanded in 1945, its Research and Analysis Branch
(R&A) was integrated into the State Department, and it was officially
renamed the OIR in 1947.[35] The State Department, we should recall, was
represented on all intelligence committees and worked with the other
agencies. The OIR's research, in addition to being shared with the leadership of the State Department and the Policy Planning Staff, had as its
"main customers" the "President's National Security Council (NSC),

---

31. Ibid., 169.
32. Ibid., 178n391.
33. Ibid., 119.
34. Ibid.
35. See ibid., 59. When first integrated into the State Department, R&A was named
the Interim Research and Intelligence Service (IRIS), then the Office of Research and
Intelligence (ORI), which soon became the Office of Intelligence Coordination and
Liaison (OCL), before finally being called the OIR.

the psychological warfare agencies (the Eisenhower administration had renamed the Psychological Strategy Board the Operations Coordinating Board), the military, and the CIA."[36] The OIR did not limit itself to scientific exchanges with the Office of National Estimates (ONE), the agency charged with developing National Intelligence Estimates (NIE) for the Director of Central Intelligence, which brought together intelligence professionals, military and political officials, and academics. As Müller explains: "'Operations support' for the CIA's Directorate of Plans was one of the tasks of the OIR. It provided the CIA with the knowledge it needed to carry out secret operations: local knowledge, for example, economic and biographical data or information about organizations and political movements."[37]

Marcuse's CWC, within the OIR, "was involved, like the other sectors of the state intelligence apparatus, in the planning of psychological warfare."[38] It amassed a treasure trove of information on the global communist movement, and "the most important 'customer' of this enormous knowledge storage and production site was demonstrably the CIA."[39] As the chairman of the CWC, Marcuse—and later his pupil and fellow professor Bernard Morris—reported to the director of the OIR, Allan Evans. He was thus only one administrative step away from Richard Bissell of the CIA, the Yale economics professor turned spy, who embodied the dark side of the Agency and oversaw some of its most sordid covert operations. Although these clandestine activities were compartmentalized and carried out on a "need-to-know" basis, "the OIR and, within it, Marcuse, was in permanent contact with the other side of the CIA during his time in the State Department anyway" (meaning the wing focused on research and analysis).[40] In fact, in 1951, the notorious master of the dark arts, longtime CIA chief of counterintelligence James Angleton, worked with Marcuse's boss, Evans, on developing more coordination between the OIR and the CIA.[41] Marcuse was, in the words of Müller, "Evans' right-hand man."[42]

---

36. Ibid., 126.

37. Ibid.

38. Ibid., 144.

39. Ibid., 137.

40. Ibid., 140.

41. Ibid., 142. On Angleton, see Jefferson Morley, *The Ghost: The Secret Life of CIA Spymaster James Jesus Angleton* (New York: St. Martin's Press, 2017).

42. Müller, *Krieger und Gelehrte*, 144.

The Psychological Strategy Board (PSB), the high-level inter-agency committee formed to centrally coordinate and plan psychological operations, "used the memoranda of . . . [Marcuse's] CWC as one of its most important sources of information."[43] The CIA's Office of Current Intelligence (OCI), which provides information on a daily basis, collaborated directly with the CWC and, at least in 1951, "was entirely dependent on Marcuse's CWC for its education and intelligence regarding communism [*Kommunismusaufklärung*]."[44] The same year, Marcuse and Morris founded a secret magazine, *Communist Monthly*, that provided the latest information on communism and how to fight it.[45] There was thus a common epistemic community where information was shared and different state agencies coordinated their work. Marcuse's activities were not limited to heading the CWC, which "worked directly with the CIA," since he was considered the State Department's resident expert on communism.[46] He provided intelligence leadership with advice and assistance, and he was even involved in drafting at least two National Intelligence Estimates (NIE) for the United States, in collaboration with the CIA.[47]

NIEs are classified documents that were produced by the Board of National Estimates and officially published by the CIA. According to former Agency officer Victor Marchetti, they "were considered the highest form of national intelligence."[48] They expressed the coordinated judgments of the U.S. intelligence community, bringing together "the assessments and forecasts of all intelligence services on central strategic issues into a uniform and binding form."[49] They assisted political leaders in making policy decisions, and they formed the intelligence basis that could serve covert operations.[50] For instance, when Professor Calvin Hoover

---

43. Ibid., 145.
44. Ibid., 155 (also see 154).
45. See ibid., 156.
46. Ibid., 145.
47. See ibid., 176–77.
48. Victor Marchetti and John D. Marks, *The CIA and the Cult of Intelligence* (Manchester, UK: Coronet Books, 1976), 344.
49. Müller, *Krieger und Gelehrte*, 125. According to Müller, "no producer of intelligence developed such a close form of cooperation with the ONE as the intelligence arm of the State Department" (ibid.).
50. Former CIA officer Victor Marchetti and John D. Marks explained what became of NIEs, citing a case when they were shared with the "40 Committee," which is "an interdepartmental panel responsible for overseeing the CIA's high-risk covert-action operations." Marchetti and Marks, *The CIA and the Cult of Intelligence*, 42.

described his work as a CIA consultant on a secret academic panel tasked with contributing to NIEs, he recognized that they could be used as background for clandestine activities and even referenced Iran's Mossadegh as an example, suggesting that NIEs played a part in the CIA's 1953 coup d'état.[51]

Marcuse began regularly attending the Estimates Group's meetings as a specialist on Soviet intentions and capabilities. Moreover, both Marcuse and Morris were involved in revising NSC-68, the top-secret National Security Council policy paper that the State Department's Office of the Historian refers to as "among the most influential documents composed by the U.S. Government during the Cold War."[52] Although Marcuse was a proponent of *détente*, as we will see, NSC-68 argued that, due to the pressing threat of the USSR's purported hostile designs, "the best course of action was to respond in kind with a massive buildup of the U.S. military and its weaponry."[53]

Thanks to Tim Müller's sedulous archival research, it has now been proven that Marcuse was a major State Department operative who regularly collaborated with the CIA and the larger U.S. intelligence community, playing a central role in the imperial war on communism. The fact that he later flagrantly misrepresented his past—a tendency continued by many of his followers—suggests that he knew full well that the history of his decade or so in Washington would discredit at least certain aspects of his work. If he had simply been involved in gathering intelligence to fight Nazism, why wouldn't he have told the truth about the extent of his work for the U.S. national security state?

Is There a Left Wing of the U.S. State Department?

If we synthesize the complex set of relations outlined above, a clear picture of Marcuse's collaboration with the U.S. government emerges. He worked for over a decade in the national security state, including as a top-secret intelligence operative who headed an important State Department committee involved in psychological warfare (the Committee on World

---

51. See Calvin Hoover, *Memoirs of Capitalism, Communism, and Nazism* (Durham, NC: Duke University Press, 1965), 1965, 270, and John Cavanagh, "Dulles Papers Reveal CIA Consulting Network," *Forerunner*, Vol. 5, No. 9 (April 29, 1980).
52. Office of the Historian, Department of State, "NSC-68, 1950," https://history.state.gov/milestones/1945-1952/NSC68.
53. Ibid.

Communism, or CWC), whose principal client was the CIA. He also served as the right-hand man to his boss (the head of the OIR), who closely collaborated with the Agency, which he did as well, notably by working directly with the CIA's Office of Current Intelligence (OCI). He contributed to drafting NIEs, which can serve as the basis for covert operations and are "the U.S. intelligence community's most authoritative and coordinated written assessment of a specific national-security issue."[54] The idea that he had no relationship to the CIA can now be put to rest as a disingenuous claim made by Marcuse and his followers in an obvious endeavor to whitewash his reputation.

This leads to the all-important question of the positions that Marcuse took and his recommendations to the U.S. government. He occupied what might be euphemistically referred to as the left wing of the State Department. It is important to note, in this regard, that he was not tightly controlled from above but rather was allowed to more or less freely articulate positions that differed from others in the same organization. His subjective contributions therefore need to be situated within the objective system of knowledge production, which permitted and even encouraged multiple vantage points. He primarily served as a form of left correction, in the sense of occupying a position that could adjust the system from the left, thereby allowing policymakers to see problems from different perspectives.[55] In this regard, he rejected the totalitarianism thesis and the forms of base anticommunism found, for instance, in McCarthyism. He also advocated for *détente* rather than an aggressive attack on the Soviet Union, and he argued for a subtler approach to destabilization. This consisted in fostering internal divisions and liberalization within the communist camp, as well as splits between Moscow and national parties. He encouraged a climate of defections and recommended that clandestine financial aid be provided to dissident communist groups.[56] He also supported non-alignment and neutralism as a way of minimizing Soviet influence. At the same time, given the broad appeal of Soviet social policies, he asserted the need to develop social democracy in the capitalist West, as a means of fostering hegemonic rule. He was a stalwart supporter of the Marshall Plan, which sought to integrate Western

---

54. Greg Bruno and Sharon Otterman, "National Intelligence Estimates," Council on Foreign Relations website, May 14, 2008, https://www.cfr.org/backgrounder/national-intelligence-estimates.

55. See Müller, *Krieger und Gelehrte*, 29 and 514.

56. See ibid., 152–53. On his support of dissident art, see ibid., 472.

Europe into the capitalist camp overseen by the United States. Finally, he supported decolonization in places like Vietnam, and he advocated for improving social and economic conditions in the Global South through massive development aid.

Overall, Marcuse understood the relationship between the capitalist West and the Soviet sphere to be one in which it was necessary to materially demonstrate the superiority of the former, while seeking to isolate and splinter the latter by baiting targeted groups into turning against communism. He thereby contributed—along with close allies like Philip Mosely, Isaiah Berlin, and Siegfried Landshut—to what is known as the Bohlen line of U.S. strategy: instead of seeing the Warsaw Pact countries as a totalitarian monolith that needed to be toppled from the outside, this orientation held that divisions within the system could be exploited to foster liberalization and revisionism, thereby cultivating an internal counter-revolution. "Marcuse thus pointed to a possibility of overthrowing the Soviet order from within by ideological means," Müller explains.[57] This was one of the objectives identified by the Special Ideological Warfare Panel of the PSB in 1952: "Our task is to deepen these ideological rifts within Communism, to strengthen the heretical forces."[58] Since this panel "consulted with outside authorities engaged in rebutting Communist philosophy," it is very possible that its members sought input from Marcuse.[59] In the long run, in any case, this is precisely one of the key strategies of the U.S. national security state that eventually bore fruit during the presidency of Ronald Reagan.[60] It encouraged anti-Stalinist alternatives, as well as a rapprochement with Eurocommunism and Western social democracy, and it lent strong support to anticommunist dissidents, among many other things. All of this helped foster a *Counter-Revolution from Above*, as David Kotz and Fred Weir demonstrated in their co-authored book with this title.[61]

Marcuse advocated for the promotion of the non-communist left, along with the demonization and isolation of the Soviets. In a strategy

---

57. Ibid., 460.
58. Memorandum re Special Ideological Warfare Panel in PSB, Edward P. Lilly: Papers, 1928–1992, Box 54, Folder Doctrinal Programs 1952, Dwight D. Eisenhower Library, 7.
59. Memorandum re Status of Ideological Warfare, June 5, 1952, Edward P. Lilly: Papers, 1928–1992, Box 54, Folder Doctrinal Programs 1952, Dwight D. Eisenhower Library, 1.
60. See Müller, *Krieger und Gelehrte*, 512–13.
61. See David Kotz and Fred Weir, *Revolution from Above: The Demise of the Soviet System* (London and New York: Routledge, 1998).

paper titled "Conditions Engendering Defections," which was "an official document requested by the CIA," Marcuse and his employees in the CWC explained that the goal was "to marginalize communism in Western Europe that was loyal to Moscow and to increase the independence of communists in the Third World from the Soviet Union."[62] At the core of this project was the endeavor to drive a wedge between social-democratic Marxism, which was "respectable," and Eastern communists influenced by Stalin and others of his ilk, who were cast as perversions of Marxism. This clever strategy was thus explicitly revisionist, and it consisted, among other things, in attempting to reclaim authentic Marxism for the West. The latter was presented as both free from ideological indoctrination and more faithful to the canonical texts, as Müller explained:

> To get to the heart of the core idea that Marcuse had reinforced . . . : What young Chilean or Indian academic would still look to Moscow if it were proven that Marxist research in the West was ideologically unhindered, philologically and historically more accurate, and was unsurpassed in its textual fidelity to the revolutionary thinkers? And if, at the same time, the poverty of Eastern philosophy, its stereotypical repetition of Marxist formulas, issued from the most recent political course, had become obvious?[63]

Marcuse was thus directly involved in the psychological warfare campaign that consisted in depicting Eastern Marxists as orthodox ideologues and Western Marxists as free thinkers and serious scholars, who were much more advanced than their indoctrinated counterparts.

The Robber Barons' Patronage of Western Marxism

> The bourgeoisie and the opportunists in the labor movement concur in this "revision" of Marxism. They omit, obliterate and distort the revolutionary side of its doctrine, its revolutionary soul. They push to the foreground and extol what is or seems acceptable to the bourgeoisie.
>
> —V. I. LENIN[64]

Through his work for the U.S. national security state, Marcuse also

---

62. Müller, *Krieger und Gelehrte*, 153, 152.

63. Ibid., 415.

64. V. I. Lenin, *Essential Works of Lenin: "What Is to Be Done?" and Other Writings*, ed. Henry M. Christman (New York: Dover Publications, 1987), 272.

became one of the major operatives in the soft-power anticommunist propaganda projects funded by the capitalist ruling class. The bourgeois state and the bourgeoisie were—and are—involved in the same war on communism, and Marcuse's dutiful service to the former made him a reliable investment for the latter. His contributions to the intellectual world war therefore need to be situated within the broader framework of the financial-state-intellectual complex.

The Rockefeller corporation, working hand in glove with the U.S. national security state, provided ample financial support for the development of the form of anticommunist Marxism that would later become widely known as Western Marxism. In the early 1950s, Rockefeller began funding the Program in Legal and Political Philosophy, which sought to "'recapture' the larger context of political thought" and usher in "a profound and long-term reshaping of the scientific landscape."[65] In the course of a decade, it invested $1.7 million in an overall project of transforming political and legal theory, which is the equivalent of some $20 million in 2024.[66] Its grant recipients included Marcuse, Kirchheimer, and Neumann, as well as figures like Hannah Arendt, Allan Bloom, Zbigniew Brzezinski, Henry Kissinger, and Leo Strauss.[67]

The Rockefeller interests also launched the Marxism-Leninism Project, whose roots can be traced back to a 1952 proposal made by Lebanese ambassador Charles Malik (who had studied with Heidegger) and Harvard philosophy professor John Wild.[68] They offered to rejuvenate academic philosophy by promoting existentialism and vitalism over and against Marxism, and they requested $1 million of the Rockefeller's stolen wealth to do so. Although the project was ultimately rejected, Wild was encouraged to take stock of Soviet philosophy, and the Rockefeller Foundation initiated a search for a "well-founded and comprehensible philosophical answer to dialectical materialism."[69] Wild did receive $2,000 for preparatory work on dialectical materialism.

The influential Rockefeller advisor Philip Mosely argued that Wild's project should be repurposed as a philosophical criticism of dialectical materialism, and he recommended that Marcuse be recruited to Harvard's Russian Research Center to accomplish this task. This is

---

65. Müller, *Krieger und Gelehrte*, 318.
66. See ibid., 341.
67. See ibid., 389, for information about Kirchheimer.
68. See ibid., 416.
69. Quoted in ibid., 417.

precisely what happened: "The entire international Marxism-Leninism Project, with its source editions, historical and sociological studies, and philosophical investigations as well, began in 1953/54 with a fact-finding mission to Harvard University."[70] In the summer of 1953, the Rockefeller Foundation also recruited Isaiah Berlin to collaborate with Marcuse on the project. Berlin had been working in the service of the British government since 1940.[71] He wrote weekly political reports that "reached the top of the Foreign and Information Ministries," and Winston Churchill himself read them zealously.[72] For much of the war, "he worked at the British Embassy in Washington D.C., where he carried out intelligence gathering for both the Ministry of Information and the Foreign Office."[73] Berlin shared the same basic tactical orientation and ideological horizons as Marcuse and their common capitalist benefactor: fanatical anticommunism was excessive and counter-productive; the best approach was to rescue Marx from the clutches of his Leninist and Stalinist descendants. According to Berlin, whose social chauvinist racism was on full display, the founder of Marxism was "too European" and too influenced by the liberal, humane Enlightenment tradition to accept—as Lenin and his followers purportedly did—the "brutal disregard for civilized morality" in the name of "coercion, violence, executions, the total suppression of individual differences, the rule of a small, virtually self-appointed minority."[74] Karl Marx "liked violence," Berlin opined, but he "did not advocate mass murder—this is a new idea in the West. The true author of this is Lenin. Under Lenin more innocent people were exterminated than in any previous revolution, many more than in 1789 or 1848 or 1870. This was real terror, not on the scale of Stalin, but real terror which hit out right and left, it was on this that Leninism was based."[75]

Rockefeller invested $165,200 in the Marxism-Leninism Project by

---

70. Ibid., 412.

71. On Berlin, see David Caute, *Isaac and Isaiah: The Covert Punishment of a Cold War Heretic* (New Haven: Yale University Press, 2015).

72. Müller, *Krieger und Gelehrte*, 425.

73. Louis Allday, "Isaiah Berlin of the FO," *London Review of Books*, July 27, 2017.

74. Isaiah Berlin, *Liberty*, ed. Henry Hardy (Oxford: Oxford University Press, 2002), 71.

75. Ramin Jahanbegloo, *Conversations with Berlin* (London: Halban Publishers, 1992), 130. Berlin was categorical, though he provided no evidence for his brazen accusations: "Communism is a total failure, and there are more terrible crimes on its conscience— if it exists—than on that of any other movement in history, even of the great religious persecutions" (ibid.). Also see chapter seven of Caute's *Isaac and Isaiah*.

1960 (the equivalent of approximately $1.7 million in 2024).[76] It established an international research group, funded nine global conferences between 1957 and 1964, supported scholarly exchanges and meetings, set up a research program in New York, supported dissertations, and funded numerous publication projects, one of whose goals was to make purportedly authentic versions of Marxist texts available that had not been perverted by Moscow's influence.[77] The scholars involved in this network received thousands of dollars for their research projects, and many of them were also provided with paid research assistants.[78] They included Werner Philipp in Berlin, A. J. C. Rüter in Amsterdam, Thomas Bottomore in London, Józef Bocheński in Switzerland, and Lucien Goldmann in Paris, among many others.[79] Rockefeller support led to the publication of a long list of monographs, unpublished manuscripts, new editions, bibliographies, journal issues, and articles.

The Rockefeller's Marxism-Leninism Project also set up a collaborative network between participating institutions across Europe, whose backbone was formed out of the Institute for East European Studies at the Free University in Berlin, the Amsterdam International Institute of Social History, and the University of Fribourg in Switzerland.[80] Importantly, the Sixth section of the École Pratique des Hautes Etudes (EPHP), a bastion of French structuralism, was also involved in this Rockefeller-funded anticommunist network, with Fernand Braudel and Clemens Heller playing leading roles.[81] As Rockefeller executive Edward F. D'Arms recounted in his diary, the CIA-connected organizational man at the center of the Marxism-Leninism Project (Philip Mosely) "is very favorably impressed

---

76. See Müller, *Krieger und Gelehrte*, 529.

77. See ibid., 504, as well as 531 for a partial list of the publications.

78. See, for instance, the 1957 budgets for $64,025 and $99,925 respectively, the former for book-related research and other expenses, and the latter for research assistants, scholarships, research stays, etc. RG 1.2, Series 717, Box 7, Folder 84, Rockefeller Center Archive.

79. Goldmann's name is sometimes misspelled "Goldman" in internal documents, but it is almost certainly the case that these are nonetheless references to Lucien Goldmann.

80. See Müller, *Krieger und Gelehrte*, 236.

81. See ibid., 493, 496, 501, as well as Ioana Popa, "International Construction of Area Studies in France during the Cold War: Insights from the École Pratique Des Hautes Études 6th Section," *History of the Human Sciences*, Vol. 29, No. 4–5 (2016): 125–50. Many internal documents at the Rockefeller Center Archive testify to this fact, as well as Brigitte Mazon's *Aux origines de l'École des Hautes Études en Sciences Sociales: Le rôle du mécénat américain (1920–1960)* (Paris: Éditions du Cerf, 1988).

by the leadership which F. Braudel has given to area studies in general
and Slavic studies in particular and would like to see continued support
and encouragement for the program."[82] Mosely, as other documents make
clear, oversaw the vetting of participants and "reviewed the backgrounds
and political orientation of the major leaders of the program" to guarantee their ideological alignment.[83] When the Institute for Social Research,
aka the Frankfurt School, was moved back to West Germany after the war
with the financial assistance of the U.S. government and the Rockefellers,
it also became part of this anticommunist institutional framework.[84]

For the Rockefeller robber barons, as Müller explains:

> The central idea of the war of ideas . . . [was] to wrest Marxism from the
> Soviets and to strengthen the socialists against the communists—which
> was both the line of the European specialists in the OIR and the policy of
> psychological warriors like Allen Dulles or the intention behind the CCF's
> support of left-wing intellectuals. One need not even refer, as far as the
> State Department connections were concerned, only to Marcuse's past or
> Mosely's contacts: the State Department was on board from the very begin-
> ning, even if it was not obvious to everyone. Mosely kept the intelligence
> department—Marcuse's OIR, which had been operating as the Bureau of
> Intelligence and Research (INR) since 1957—up to date. The INR took an
> interest in what was happening in the Marxism-Leninism Project.[85]

In fact, Marcuse's disciple in the INR, Bernard Morris, ran a parallel project as a continuation of Marcuse's CWC, demonstrating the continuity and
synergy between the psywar operations undertaken by the bourgeoisie

---

82. Excerpt from Edward F. D'Arms's Diary of Talk with Philip E. Mosely, October 30,
1956, RG 1.2, Series 717, Box 7, Folder 82, Rockefeller Archive Center. Two years later,
Mosely expressed his increased enthusiasm for the activities of the Sixth Section of the
EPHE, while also communicating his ongoing support for Marcuse as a knowledgeable
critic of Marxism. See Charles B. Fahs, Interview with Philip E. Mosely, September 11,
1957, RG 1.2, Series 717, Box 7, Folder 84.
83. Edward F. D'Arms, Interview with Philip E. Mosely, May 1, 1957, RG 1.2, Series 717,
Box 7, Folder 83, Rockefeller Archive Center.
84. The U.S. government contributed $103,695 in 1950, or the equivalent of just over 1.3
million dollars in 2024, and the Rockefellers only needed to make a modest contribution.
See Rolf Wiggershaus, *The Frankfurt School: Its History, Theories, and Political Significance*,
trans. Michael Robertson (Cambridge MA: MIT Press, 1995), 434.
85. Müller, *Krieger und Gelehrte*, 525, also see 459.

and those carried out by the bourgeois state.[86] Moreover, archival records demonstrate that Mosely continued to receive financial support from the OIR for research projects at Columbia University.[87]

Marcuse himself was a key player at the center of all these networks. He made a decisive contribution from the beginning, via the pilot project with Berlin, and he was regularly sought out as a collaborator who was trusted by the Rockefeller interests and the intelligence world.[88] The Russian historian Robert F. Byrnes, who had served in military intelligence and then the CIA, recommended Marcuse's writings as basic texts for international Marxist education within the Marxism-Leninism Project.[89] This made perfect sense since the "fundamental purpose" of the operation, according to one of the scholars involved, was to foster a "non-communist interpretation of Marx and Lenin," thereby promoting Western Marxism, as social-democratic and purportedly humanist, over and against what was condemned as its supposed dictatorial perversion in the East.[90]

If Marcuse was in many ways the intellectual godfather of the Marxism-Leninism Project, then Philip Mosely was "the Cold War's Organization Man" who managed much of the operation.[91] They were close personal friends, and their families got together frequently.[92] They were both scholars and State Department operatives, and Mosely was the founder (1946) and the director (1951–55) of the Russian Institute at Columbia University.[93] He also worked "for many years as a consultant to the CIA with a clearance for the security level 'Top Secret,'" and he "advised two

---

86. See ibid., 526.

87. In an interesting 66-page document that shows how the CIA kept tabs on governmental funding of social scientific research, which has been expansive, Mosely's name appears twice for grants in 1953 to support the indexing of Stalin's *Collected Works*. The fact that a CIA advisor received State Department funding via the OIR to index Stalin's work should raise some questions about the objectivity of this publication project. See "Federal Government Research Contracts and Grants Categorized according to Areas within the Social Sciences," June 30, 1953, the CIA FOIA Electronic Reading Room, https://www.cia.gov/readingroom/document/cia-rdp92b01090r000600010012-8.

88. See Müller, *Krieger und Gelehrte*, 536.

89. See ibid.

90. Quoted in ibid., 527.

91. See David C. Engerman, "The Cold War's Organization Man," *Humanities*, Vol. 30, No. 5 (September/October, 2009), https://www.neh.gov/humanities/2009/septemberoctober/feature/the-cold-war%E2%80%99s-organization-man.

92. See Müller, *Krieger und Gelehrte*, 538.

93. See Engerman, "The Cold War's Organization Man."

Army think tanks."[94] He served for years on an important secret board of
CIA academic consultants that met four times per annum at Princeton
with CIA director Allen Dulles and Sherman Kent to work on intelligence
assessments for the Agency's ONE.[95] Since the NIEs he was collaborating
on were the highest form of intelligence, potentially serving as the basis
for covert operations, this clandestine committee—described by Dulles
as "part of our organization on which I rely highly for all sorts of purposes"—constituted a major and central project of academic collaboration for the CIA.[96] Mosely served as well on the national security state
panel to study "Psychological Aspects of Future U.S. Strategy," which was
overseen by Nelson Rockefeller.[97] He also collaborated with the American
Committee for Liberation from Bolshevism (ACLB), a CIA front, and was
a foundations consultant and Research Director of the Council on Foreign
Relations (CFR).[98] In this capacity, he corresponded with Dulles, who was

---

94. Müller, *Krieger und Gelehrte*, 234.

95. See John Cavanagh, "Dulles Papers Reveal CIA Consulting Network," *Forerunner*,
Vol. 5, No. 9 (April 29, 1980): 4. Numerous internal documents attesting to Mosely's
participation in the "Princeton Consultants" group are available via the CIA FOIA
Electronic Reading Room: https://www.cia.gov/readingroom/search/site/Princeton%20
Consultants.

96. "Letter to William L. Langer from Allen W. Dulles," July 2, 1956, the CIA FOIA
Electronic Reading Room, https://www.cia.gov/readingroom/document/05963738. A
number of other internal documents concerning the "Princeton Consultants" are available
via the CIA FOIA Electronic Reading Room, which also includes press articles on this
group. See https://www.cia.gov/readingroom/search/site/Princeton%20Consultants.

97. See "Memorandum for the President," August 27, 1955, Dwight D. Eisenhower: Papers
as President of the United States, 1953–1961 (Ann Whitman file), Administration Series,
Box 30, Folder "Rockefeller, Nelson 1952–55 (3)," Dwight D. Eisenhower Library and
"Psychological Aspects of United States Strategy: Panel Report," November 1955, Dwight
D. Eisenhower: Records as President, White House Central Files (Confidential File),
1953-1961, Subject Series, Box 61, Folder Nelson Rockefeller (4), Dwight D. Eisenhower
Library. C. D. Jackson (*Time*), Henry Kissinger (Harvard), and Max Millikan (CENIS),
among others, also served on this panel. Also see the "Source Book of Individual Papers"
in Dwight D. Eisenhower: Records as President, White House Central Files (Confidential
File), 1953-1961, Subject Series, Box 61, Folder Nelson Rockefeller (5).

98. The ACLB, also known as the American Committee for the Liberation of the Peoples
of Russia, was part of CIA project QKACTIVE. See "Research Aid: Cryptonyms and
Terms in Declassified CIA Files," https://www.archives.gov/files/iwg/declassified-
records/rg-263-cia-records/second-release-lexicon.pdf. Howland H. Sargeant, president
of the ACLB, refers in his correspondence to meeting with Mosely, notably to discuss
their shared views on the anticommunist Chekhov Publishing House, which was jointly
funded by the Ford Foundation and the CIA. See "Letter to Miss Nancy Hanks, Assistant

kept informed and attended their meetings.[99] It was Mosely, moreover, who made Marcuse a member of the Honorable Foreign Policy Society of the CFR, which is yet another sign of how well ensconced Marcuse was in the power-knowledge networks of the imperial elite.[100]

According to Müller, "For Marcuse and his friends, the path from the State Department to academic fame passed through philanthropic foundations."[101] It was the financial backing of the capitalist ruling class that facilitated their transition from intelligence operatives to academics and, although their conditions changed, their actual work, collaborators, and backers remained nearly identical:

> The transition from the world of the intelligence services to the world of foundations and universities was a smooth one. The framework conditions changed, but the personnel remained the same. The foundations made it easier for some of the protagonists to enter or re-enter the academic world. The careers of these scholar-intellectuals rested on a solid material foundation.[102]

In summary, a high-level CIA advisor and longtime collaborator originally recommended Marcuse, the State Department's leading specialist on communism, for an anticommunist research pilot project lavishly funded by the capitalist ruling class. He was seconded in this endeavor by another intellectual—Isaiah Berlin—with an established history of serving an imperial state's intelligence services. This led to a long-term collaboration in a Rockefeller-funded intellectual world war on Marxism that sought to subtly break up the communist understanding of Marxism via immanent critique and promote—through well-funded knowledge networks—a

---

to Mr. Rockefeller," May 19, 1955, Dwight D. Eisenhower: Records as President, White House Central Files (Confidential File), 1953–1961, Subject Series, Box 14, Folder Chekhov Publishing House, Dwight D. Eisenhower Library.

99. Some of the correspondence between Mosely and Dulles is available via the CIA FOIA Electronic Reading Room: https://www.cia.gov/readingroom/search/site/Philip%20Mosely%20Allen%20Dulles. See in particular the letter in which Mosely refers to Dulles's "very helpful custom of attending as many as possible of the meetings." "Letter to Honorable Allen W. Dulles from Philip E. Mosely," September 26, 1958, the CIA FOIA Electronic Reading Room, https://www.cia.gov/readingroom/document/cia-rdp80b01676r004000060006-8.

100. See Müller, *Krieger und Gelehrte*, 513–14 and 236.

101. Ibid., 189.

102. Ibid.

version of revisionist, social-democratic Marxism that could be championed in the West, with no serious threat to the capitalist interests that
were funding and promoting it. When Marcuse finally left Washington
in 1952, after his close friend—CIA collaborator Mosely—recommended
that he be recruited to his institute at Columbia University, it was by no
means to do independent research in an ivory tower, disconnected from
his earlier work for the U.S. national security state.[103] On the contrary, it
was a continuation of the exact same research agenda, and his collaborators and supporters were largely identical.[104] He was simply pursuing his
intelligence work under academic cover. When he began his academic
career, he was actually still officially a member of the State Department
(his temporary leave from it only became permanent in September 1953).

The Dark Foundations of the Ivory Tower

Marcuse's transition from the bourgeois state to the bourgeois university,
far from being a radical break, constituted a shift from one nodal point
of the financial-state-intellectual complex to another. Since all three of
these are so deeply connected, and he had already been working with so
many academic subcontractors for the state and big capital, he continued
to collaborate with many of the same people on similar projects, and with
the same backers.

Marcuse claimed in his book of interviews with Karl Popper that he
remained in Washington so long because of his wife's illness.[105] When she
died in 1951, he took a position as a Senior Fellow at the Russian Institute
(RI) at Columbia University (1952–53) and then moved on to the Russian
Research Center (RRC) at Harvard (1953–54).[106] A Rockefeller grant supported his work at both of these prestigious institutions on his book *Soviet
Marxism: A Critical Analysis* (1958).[107] The acknowledgments in this book

---

103. See ibid., 423.
104. See ibid., 189.
105. See Herbert Marcuse and Karl Popper, *Revolution or Reform? A Confrontation*, ed.
A. T. Ferguson, trans. Michael Aylward and A.T. Ferguson (Chicago: New University
Press, 1985), 59.
106. See Müller, *Krieger und Gelehrte*, 239–40. Barry Kātz puts Marcuse at Columbia in
1952–1953 and Harvard in 1954–1955. See *Herbert Marcuse and the Art of Liberation: An
Intellectual Biography* (London: Verso, 1982), 145. Although Marcuse had several different
appointments and Rockefeller research grants, some of them overlapping, the Harvard
dates appear to be one year off since Marcuse began his career at Brandeis in 1954.
107. Kātz, *Herbert Marcuse and the Art of Liberation*, 145.

clearly situate it as a continuation of his research for the U.S. national security state. Marcuse emphasizes, in the first place, his great debt to William Langer, the director of the RRC, and the RRC's Deputy Director Marshall Shulman, who ceded the publication rights of the second part of his project to Columbia University Press. Langer had been Chief of R&A at the OSS from 1942 to 1945 and became Special Assistant to the Secretary of State in 1946. A proponent of clandestine operations since at least 1947, he organized, along with Sherman Kent, the CIA's ONE in 1950 and worked as its Assistant Director from 1950 to 1951 (ONE is a kind of R&A in the CIA).[108] He then became the director of the Russian Research Center at Harvard from 1954 to 1959 (and president of the American Historical Association in 1957). However, he continued to collaborate closely with the CIA and served on its "Princeton Consultants" group for years.[109] He was also on the Board Panel on Covert Action Operations, which oversaw black ops around the world, and he took leave from his "academic duties to work for the CIA."[110]

This powerful intelligence operative, along with Philip Mosely, was "Marcuse's most important supporter from the academic establishment."[111] To be clear, this means that Marcuse's two main academic promoters were major intelligence operatives, who cut their teeth in the OSS and the State

---

108. See Robin W. Winks, *Cloak and Gown: Scholars in the Secret War, 1939–1961* (New Haven: Yale University Press, 1987), 81 and *Müller, Krieger und Gelehrte*, 60.

109. See, for instance, CIA Director Allen Dulles' personal letter to Langer summarizing their collaborations and Langer's role in CIA recruitment, while pleading with him to limit his requested leave from the Agency to one academic year (Langer decided not to take a leave at all after receiving Dulles's letter). "Letter to William L. Langer from Allen W. Dulles," July 2, 1956, the CIA FOIA Electronic Reading Room, https://www.cia.gov/readingroom/document/05963738.

110. Cavanagh, "Dulles Papers Reveal CIA Consulting Network," 6. Also see White House, PFIAB, "Board Panel on Covert Action Operations," Top Secret Memo, September 10, 1963, National Archives, JFK Assassination Records, 2025 release, https://nsarchive.gwu.edu/document/32956-document-6-white-house-pfiab-board-panel-covert-action-operations-top-secret.

111. Müller, *Krieger und Gelehrte*, 236. It is interesting to note that Langer met with Leon Trotsky in Mexico and was responsible for arranging for his papers from his exile period in Mexico to be archived at Harvard. See Winks, *Cloak and Gown*, 73. On Trotsky's willingness to collaborate with the U.S. government (such as with the anticommunist Dies Committee), his dependance on U.S. funds and personnel, and his interest in going to the United States, see William Chase, "Trotsky in Mexico: Toward a History of His Informal Contacts with the U.S. Government, 1937–1940," published (in Slovak) in *Otechestvennaia istoriia*, Vol. 4 (July/August 1995): 76–102 (English version obtained directly from the author).

Department respectively, before becoming top-level CIA consultants and collaborators. They were not minor players but occupied major leadership positions and worked for years on NIEs, the highest form of intelligence for the U.S. government.[112] These activities were not restricted, moreover, to the war effort or the immediate postwar. Langer's CIA collaborations continued until the end of his life (1959), and Mosely's persisted at least into the 1960s.[113]

RRC Deputy Director Shulman, like Langer, spent his life between universities and Washington, working for the State Department from 1949 to 1953 and serving as Special Advisor on Soviet Affairs to the Secretary of State from 1977 to 1980. In the acknowledgments for *Soviet Marxism*, Marcuse also expressed his gratitude to his close friend Barrington Moore for reading and commenting on his manuscript. They had served together as researchers in the OSS, and Moore worked with leading figures in the CIA like Dulles and Richard Bissell on the "Soviet Vulnerabilities Project."[114] This was run as a collaboration between Columbia, Harvard, and MIT, and it brought together academics and intelligence operatives, following up on the work of Project Troy (a flagship academic-intelligence research project on psychological warfare involving Harvard, MIT, and the RAND Corporation).[115] In sum, of the six principal individuals thanked by Marcuse in his ostensibly academic publication, at least three were major CIA collaborators (and the others circulated in similar networks).[116]

Those familiar with this history might object that two of the CIA-connected individuals thanked by Marcuse were only acknowledged for

---

112. Numerous internal documents attesting to Langer and Mosely's participation in the "Princeton Consultants" group are available via the CIA FOIA Electronic Reading Room: https://www.cia.gov/readingroom/search/site/Princeton%20Consultants.

113. See Cavanagh, "Dulles Papers Reveal CIA Consulting Network," which is based on special, private access to the archive of Allen Dulles's papers. It thereby provides a rare glimpse into some of his secret relations with the academic world.

114. Müller, *Krieger und Gelehrte*, 439.

115. On Project Troy, see Allan A. Needell, "'Truth Is Our Weapon': Project Troy, Political Warfare, and Government-Academic Relations in the National Security State," *Diplomatic History*, Vol. 17, No. 3 (Summer 1993): 399–420. There is every indication, according to Müller, that Marcuse knew about Project Troy. See *Krieger und Gelehrte*, 119.

116. I am not counting the seventh person, Maud Hazeltine, who, as a graduate student at Brandeis University, prepared the index. See "Maud Hazeltine Will Be Married to Ansel Chaplin: Candidate for Ph.D. at Brandeis Engaged to a Law Student," *New York Times*, January 17, 1959, 11.

granting him publication rights. This is true, but it misses the bigger picture: when Marcuse moved from the U.S. national security state to the university, he largely continued to do the same job, with the same people, for the same bosses and financial supporters. His acknowledgments are thus just one tiny indication that he was working for an academic cut-out overseen by the CIA.

The CIA's predecessor organization, the OSS, had already begun, as early as the fall of 1942, to subcontract research projects to specialized institutes at various universities, including Stanford, Berkeley, Columbia, Princeton, and Yale.[117] Representatives of the Carnegie Foundation visited the OSS's R&A chief William Langer and "raised the question of whether some similar system might not be introduced in our universities."[118] Toward the end of the war, Langer established a committee on relations between the intelligence services and the university. One of its reports explained that scholars who often traveled abroad and spoke foreign languages could quietly but effectively transform their academic knowledge into intelligence.

The area studies programs at Columbia and Harvard, where Marcuse was relocated after Washington, were a joint project backed by the capitalist ruling class and the state. Funded by the Rockefeller, Carnegie, and Ford foundations, as well as by the government for more than twenty years through the National Defense Education Act of 1958, these programs aim to produce experts specializing in specific regions of the world.[119] They therefore offer an interdisciplinary education that ranges from geography and foreign languages to history, economics, religion, and sociology. Given their emphasis on holistic knowledge about specific locations, these programs are particularly well adapted to training future CIA officers and other governmental officials. Indeed, the model for these programs was the OSS according to McGeorge Bundy, who served as Army Intelligence Officer during the war and National Security Advisor in the postwar period (as well as president of the Ford Foundation). He explained that "the first great center of area studies in the United States was not located in any university, but in Washington . . . in the Office of

117. See Winks, *Cloak and Gown*, 79.
118. Barry M. Katz, *Foreign Intelligence: Research and Analysis in the Office of Strategic Services, 1942–1945* (Cambridge, MA: Harvard University Press, 1989), 159.
119. See Immanuel Wallerstein, "The Unintended Consequences of Cold War Area Studies," in Noam Chomsky, et al., *The Cold War & the University: Toward an Intellectual History of the Postwar Years*, ed. André Schiffrin (New York: New Press, 1997), 195–231.

Strategic Services."[120] "In very large measure," he added, "the area study programs developed in American universities in the years after the war were manned, directed, or stimulated by graduates of the OSS—a remarkable institution, half cops-and-robbers and half faculty meeting."[121] The "two most important area studies centers in the USA" set up after the war, and based on the model of the predecessor agency to the CIA, were the RI at Columbia and the RRC at Harvard.[122]

At Columbia's RI, "the war-related research department of the OSS and the foundation-financed academic world of the postwar period merged."[123] Geroid T. Robinson, who had served as the head of the USSR Division in the OSS's R&A, was the driving force behind the project and the Institute's first director. According to Bernard Katz, in 1945 "plans were secure to relocate the USSR Division in Morningside Heights," which is precisely what happened the following year with the official opening of the RI at Columbia.[124] The "continuity of personnel" and "the continuity of the epistemological premises" were remarkable, and it was Robinson who invited Marcuse to join his team.[125] The Rockefeller Foundation provided $250,000 to launch the United States' first center for Soviet Studies, and its contributions over the first fifteen years of its existence added up to $1.4 million (the equivalent of some $16 million in 2024).[126] "The Russian Institute can justifiably be described as the continuation of R&A by academic means," Müller concludes.[127] It served to train Soviet experts to work in the government, the military, intelligence agencies, the diplomatic corps, the university, and the media. Officers from all branches of the military were sent there, and the student body was often a combination of governmental employees and civilians. Many of the latter were recruited to agencies like the State Department.[128] In fact, Robinson wrote to CIA director Walter Bedell Smith in 1951 to suggest that "50 CIA, armed forces and foreign service officers enroll in a

---

120. Cited in Winks, *Cloak and Gown*, 115.
121. Ibid. (also see 114).
122. Popa, "International Construction of Area Studies in France During the Cold War,"
132. Also see Katz, *Foreign Intelligence*, 159–61.
123. Müller, *Krieger und Gelehrte*, 220.
124. Katz, *Foreign Intelligence*, 160.
125. Ibid., 160. Also see Müller, *Krieger und Gelehrte*, 239.
126. See Müller, *Krieger und Gelehrte*, 223, as well as 186.
127. Ibid., 223.
128. See ibid., 224.

one-year 'comprehensive training program.'"[129] Invited speakers to the RI included intelligence operatives like the director of the Psychological Strategy Board and the chief of Air Force intelligence.[130] The CIA and the State Department both drew on RI research, very much like they did with Marcuse's earlier work for the OIR.[131] Moreover, as CIA director Robert Gates noted in a 1986 speech at Harvard regarding academic research on the Soviet Union, the CIA's "cooperation for nearly 40 years has remained both close and constant."[132] In short, it is safe to say that Columbia's RI was founded as a government and intelligence cut-out funded by the capitalist ruling class as part of its intellectual war on communism.

The Russian Research Center (RRC) at Harvard, the second Soviet Studies institute established in the United States, was "even more closely interlinked with the state apparatus."[133] The initiative to found it came out of exchanges between the Carnegie Foundation, Harvard, and Washington. Indeed, the president of Harvard, James Conant, took part in discussions with the CIA and gave his consent to its involvement.[134] The Provost of Harvard at the time, Paul Buck, bluntly stated that the model for the RRC, as well as for the Harvard Social Relations Department, was the OSS.[135] The first Deputy Director of the RRC was none other than Marcuse's friend and collaborator in the OSS, as well as his former boss at the State Department, Stuart Hughes. In addition to the State Department, the RRC

129. Jim Schachter, "Documents Disclose CIA Research: Agency Financed Covert Studies in '50s and '60s," *Columbia Daily Spectator*, April 17, 1980, 1. The CIA responded indicating its interest, but no additional correspondence appears to exist. According to CIA assistant general counsel Lee Strickland, "It seems quite possible that some CIA employees attended the program in 1951–52 or thereafter." Cited in ibid.

130. See Müller, *Krieger und Gelehrte*, 224.

131. See ibid., 227.

132. Robert M. Gates, "CIA and the University," February 13, 1986, the CIA FOIA Electronic Reading Room, https://www.cia.gov/readingroom/document/cia-rdp90-00806r000100480004-4, 4. Multiple versions of this speech are available in the same database.

133. Müller, *Krieger und Gelehrte*, 434. As Walter Rodney insightfully explained: "Not only is Harvard a bastion of the ideological superstructure of the United States, but that particular Russian center has been exposed as a very active instrument of the American state." *The Russian Revolution: A View from the Third World* (London: Verso, 2018), 18.

134. See Sigmund Diamond, *Compromised Campus: The Collaboration of Universities with the Intelligence Community, 1945-1955* (Oxford: Oxford University Press, 1992), 109–10.

135. See ibid., 73.

had close ties with the military, CIA, and FBI.[136] A 1955 memorandum on the RRC reports that "six of the fifty-five persons who had worked at the center had gone into government service (including the CIA); 40 percent of the graduates of the Regional Studies Program had gone into government, and 40 percent continued graduate work."[137] The Regional Studies Program had "two people a year from the CIA for [the] last several years [and . . .] trained 8 Foreign Service Officers during 1950–51."[138] The RRC also regularly performed special services for the U.S. government, such as "a two-day conference with representatives from Harvard, MIT, and the American Committee for the Liberation from Bolshevism."[139]

The Carnegie Foundation provided the initial capital for the RRC by contributing $1.5 million in the first four years.[140] Carnegie was dominated by powerful men with close ties to the bourgeois state and the world of intelligence. Its presidents have included Nicholas Butler (president of Columbia University), John Foster Dulles (Secretary of State and brother of CIA director Allen Dulles), and Harvey Bundy (a Special Assistant to the Secretary of War and the father of McGeorge Bundy, the U.S. National Security Advisor, and William Bundy, a CIA chief). The same is true of the other major foundations. For instance, from 1952 to 1961, Dean Rusk was the president of the Rockefeller Foundation, after having served in the State Department, and before returning to Washington as the Secretary of State.

The FBI was also involved in the RRC and had very close ties with Harvard.[141] A June 29, 1950, memorandum from the Boston bureau to the director of the FBI confirms that an arrangement had been finalized to establish "the most cooperative and understanding association between the Bureau and Harvard."[142] Hoover's agency had informants like Charles Baroch and numerous contacts in the administration, faculty, and staff. As for the RRC, a Boston Special Agent memo dated December 12, 1947, states that it would be funded by the Carnegie Foundation to provide information to government agencies prior to release by the university.

---

136. See Müller, *Krieger und Gelehrte*, 435.
137. Diamond, *Compromised Campus*, 73.
138. Cited in ibid., 73.
139. Ibid.
140. See Müller, *Krieger und Gelehrte*, 434.
141. See all of the important archival documentation available in Diamond, *Compromised Campus*.
142. Cited in ibid., 40.

The Bureau, which compiled dossiers on student associations and professors, closely followed everything that happened at the RRC. It is likely that it opened files on all the people associated with it.[143]

The Ford Foundation, which has a long and dark history of working hand in glove with the CIA, was involved in funding both the RRC at Harvard and the RI at Columbia.[144] It notoriously collaborated with the Agency in funding the Congress for Cultural Freedom (CCF), which it continued to finance after it was publicly revealed that it was a CIA front organization. It also supported other knowledge networks infamous for their intelligence ties, including St. Antony's at Oxford, a well-known den of spies, and Harvard's Salzburg Seminar (the brainchild of predominantly wartime intelligence veterans intent on foiling "the communist bid for ideological hegemony").[145]

These two intelligence cut-outs at Columbia and Harvard, funded by the capitalist ruling-class' "Big Three" (Rockefeller, Carnegie, Ford), "trained the first generation of professional Sovietologists."[146] It is not an exaggeration to say, then, that at least postwar U.S. Sovietology was an intelligence product. *Pravda* was not overstating its case when it assailed the RI—and much the same could have been said about the RRC—as "a hotbed of American slanderers, spies, and diversionaries," headed by "arch reactionaries . . . who are systematically poisoning students' minds with slander about the Soviet Union."[147]

There is nothing extraordinary about this kind of collaboration, which is integral to the inner workings of the military-industrial-academic complex or, more generally, the financial-state-intellectual nexus. Consider,

---

143. See ibid.

144. On Ford's funding of the RI and the RRC, see Francis X. Sutton, "The Ford Foundation and Europe: Ambitions and Ambivalences," in *The Ford Foundation and Europe (1950's–1970's): Cross-Fertilization of Learning in Social Science and Management*, ed. Giuliana Gemelli (Brussels: European Interuniversity Press, 1998), 55–56. Regarding the Ford Foundation and the CIA more generally, see James Petras, "The Ford Foundation and the CIA: A Documented Case of Philanthropic Collaboration with the Secret Police," *The James Petras Website* (blog), December 15, 2001, https://petras.lahaine.org/the-ford-foundation-and-the-cia-a-documented-case-of-philanthropic-collaboration-with-the-secret-police/.

145. Hugh Wilford, *The Mighty Wurlitzer: How the CIA Played America* (Cambridge, MA: Harvard University Press, 2008), 129. Also see Sutton, "The Ford Foundation and Europe," 55–56.

146. Katz, *Foreign Intelligence*, 160.

147. Cited in ibid., 161.

for instance, another example. While a student, Henry Ass-Kissinger—as his classmates called him—established the Harvard International Summer School in 1950 with the help of his teacher William Elliott.[148] This grandee of the department of government at Harvard went once a week to Washington to see his friends in the CIA and the State Department, where he also worked, and he was the one who obtained funding from the Office of Policy Coordination (OPC) of the CIA for the Summer School, then a grant from the Ford Foundation in 1954 (the Rockefeller Foundation would contribute that same year to the launch of the journal *Confluence*, directed by Kissinger as an extension of the summer program).[149] According to a 1967 report in the *New York Times*, Harvard admitted to receiving $456,000 from the Agency between 1960 and 1966, including $135,000 allocated to this center for "spiritual resistance to communism" run by Kissinger (who also served as a government informant at Harvard, where he opened other people's mail).[150]

To take a different example, the professor of economics Max Millikan, who had worked as the Assistant Director of the CIA, returned to MIT in 1953 where he established a network of exchange of expertise between Agency researchers and scholars at the Center for International Studies (CENIS), which was funded by the CIA.[151] Similarly, the Woodrow Wilson International Center for Scholars at the Smithsonian Institution was directed by the CIA's James Billington (who had been a student of Isaiah Berlin). The Kennedy School of Government at Harvard regularly receives CIA officers, normally with university approval, and Daniel Golden identified six who were affiliated in 2017 with the Kennedy School's Belfer Center or its journal *International Security*.[152] This pattern can be seen

148. See Diamond, *Compromised Campus*, 138–50.

149. On Elliott's working relationship with the CIA and State Department, see Diamond, *Compromised Campus*, 145.

150. On Kissinger's work as a spy at Harvard, see Diamond, *Compromised Campus*, 138–50.

151. See Ronald Grigor Suny, *Red Flag Unfurled: History, Historians, and the Russian Revolution* (London: Verso, 2017), 83: "A team of researchers and writers at MIT's Center for International Studies (CENIS) worked in the modernization mode, developing analyses of the deviant Soviet road. CENIS, a conduit between the university community and the national government, had been established with CIA funding and was directed by Max Millikan, former assistant director of the intelligence agency."

152. Daniel Golden, *Spy Schools: How the CIA, FBI, and Foreign Intelligence Secretly Exploit America's Universities* (New York: Henry Holt and Co., 2017), 214.

internationally as well: the Institute for the Study of the USSR in Munich was founded in 1950, and it was "secretly funded by the CIA."[153]

The case of Marcuse, where an ostensible Marxist moved between the bourgeois state and the bourgeois university while performing the same basic function in both cases, with the same politico-financial supporters, should not, therefore, be understood as an anomaly. The revolving door, or rather the breezeway, between power politics in Washington and ideological production in the university is a general phenomenon characteristic of imperial knowledge production. If Marcuse stands out, in this regard, it is primarily because of his role as the radical pied piper of Western Marxism who played a central role in the intellectual world war on actual Marxism, meaning the Marxism invested in the practical project of developing socialism in the real world.

State Department Anticommunism Outsourced to the Academy

> To ascribe to an opponent an obviously stupid idea and then to refute it is a trick practiced by none too clever people.
>
> —V. I. LENIN[154]

The foundations of the bourgeoisie made Marcuse's move from the bourgeois state to the bourgeois academy as seamless as possible.[155] As a matter of fact, there was no clean break at all. He was put on the payroll of Columbia's RI in the fall of 1950 as a visiting professor, while he was still at the State Department.[156] When he left Washington in 1952, he was only on temporary leave, and he did not officially stop working for the State Department until September 1953 (even though he disingenuously claimed that he left government service in 1950).[157] Since the Russian think tanks at Columbia and Harvard were national security state cutouts, it is also important to note that "Marcuse, who was appointed to a professorship at Brandeis in 1954, continued to give guest lectures at the Russian Institute in New York until the early 1960s."[158] It was his close

---

153. Suny, *Red Flag Unfurled*, 72.
154. V. I. Lenin, *Collected Works*, Vol. 28 (Moscow: Progress Publishers, 1981), 288.
155. See Müller, *Krieger und Gelehrte*, 189.
156. See ibid., 231, 239.
157. See Marcuse, *Marxism, Revolution and Utopia*, 430.
158. Müller, *Krieger und Gelehrte*, 240.

personal friend, top-level CIA advisor and collaborator Philip Mosely, who kept inviting him.[159]

Müller has marshalled ample evidence to demonstrate that Marcuse's 1958 book "*Soviet Marxism* was a sophisticated adaptation and continuation of the research program that Marcuse had pursued as a communism expert in the State Department."[160] Effective psychological warfare, as he knew from his intelligence work, began with intimate knowledge of the enemy. This is what Clyde Kluckhohn, director of the RRC and a key Project Troy collaborator, described as "immanent critique": "It is crucial that we know the target from within [*aus sich selbst*] and do not create an image for ourselves that is a projection of our fears."[161] In writing *Soviet Marxism*, Marcuse was thus, in many ways, academically laundering State Department research and analysis, while in the pay of the capitalist class (the Rockefeller Foundation funded his work and partly that of an assistant at Harvard to the tune of $9,900).[162] The first part of the book was a result of his work at Columbia, when he was still officially an employee of the State Department, and his pilot study for the Rockefeller's Marxism-Leninism Project, completed at Harvard, formed the basis for the second part. The book was so bound up with the espionage and military community that the U.S. Air Force's intelligence service regarding communism (*Kommunismusaufklärung*)— which funded the RRC, the RAND Corporation, and other military-academic collaborations—actually received galley proofs in advance that it used to prepare classes.[163]

Peter Marcuse, Herbert's son, described *Soviet Marxism* as "a Marxist critique of a pseudo-Marxist theory and a pseudosocialist (later 'protosocialist') reality."[164] Indeed, its author framed the entire project in terms of an "immanent critique" that employed "the conceptual instruments of its object, namely, Marxism, in order to clarify the actual

---

159. See ibid., 538.

160. Ibid., 472, also see 239.

161. Cited in ibid., 115.

162. See ibid., 433.

163. See ibid., 488–89.

164. Peter Marcuse, "Marcuse on Real Existing Socialism: A Hindsight Look at Soviet Marxism," in *From the New Left to the Next Left*, ed. John Bokina and Timothy J. Lukes (Lawrence: University Press of Kansas, 1994), 59. Also see Douglas Kellner, "Introduction" to Herbert Marcuse, *Soviet Marxism: A Critical Analysis* (New York: Columbia University Press, 1985), 1–13.

function of Marxism in Soviet society and its historical direction."[165]
The key takeaway is that, if one aspires to be an authentic Marxist à la
Marcuse, it is imperative to reject Soviet Marxism as an aberration and
a perversion of Marxism's fundamental essence. Instead of establishing
a dictatorship of the proletariat, it imposed a "dictatorship . . . over the
proletariat and the peasantry."[166] The social organization of the productive forces served as "instruments of control rather than liberation."[167]
Whereas Marxism was supposed to free human beings from ideology, it
instead became "ideology" for the Soviets by entering "the superstructure
of an established system of domination" and indoctrinating people into
accepting repression.[168] Rather than abolishing classes, the USSR erected
a "bureaucracy" that constituted "a separate class which [controlled] the
underlying population."[169] Instead of "the negation of capitalism," Soviet
society partook, "in a decisive aspect, of the function of capitalism,"
and it followed a parallel tendency to the West in driving toward "total
industrialization."[170] In his preface to the 1961 Vintage edition, Marcuse
brought a number of these threads together by claiming that, in the
USSR, "the means of liberation and humanization operate for preserving domination and submission, and the theory that destroyed all ideology is used for the establishment of a new ideology."[171] In sum, Soviet
Marxism stood Marxism proper on its head by transforming a philosophy of liberation into a philosophy of subjugation, engendering a
society far worse than capitalist societies. "Compared with the Marxian
idea of socialism," Marcuse wrote in his 1954 epilogue to *Reason and
Revolution*, "Stalinist society was not less repressive than capitalist society—but much poorer."[172]

Devoid of any clear grasp of imperialism, the dialectics of socialism,
or a fine-grained materialist account of the arduous difficulties faced by
the world's first socialist state, Marcuse engaged in a puerile celebration

---

165. Herbert Marcuse, *Soviet Marxism: A Critical Analysis* (London: Forgotten Books,
2018), 1.
166. Ibid., 74.
167. Ibid., 83.
168. Ibid., 137, also see 89.
169. Ibid., 116, also see 149.
170. Ibid., 150, 195.
171. Herbert Marcuse, *Soviet Marxism: A Critical Analysis* (New York: Vintage Books,
1961), xiv.
172. Herbert Marcuse, *Reason and Revolution: Hegel and the Rise of Social Theory*
(London: Routledge & Kegan Paul, 1954).

of a utopian version of socialism in order to juxtapose it to the horrors of socialism in the real world. He clearly had not learned a lesson that Paul A. Baran, who had also served in the OSS, had tried to teach him in their personal correspondence as early as 1954:

> But if it is possible—and historically it has proven to be possible—for a socialist party to seize power a long way before the conditions for a socialist society have materialized, all that can be reasonably demanded is that this party should do the best it can in promoting the cause of socialism at home and abroad. NB: the best it can is not the best one could think of—there is no more room for utopianism here than before. If this test is applied, I would submit that the Russians have done extremely well, so well in fact as to surpass the most optimistic expectations.[173]

Ironically, Marcuse shamelessly boasted in the 1961 preface to his academically laundered intelligence propaganda, bankrolled by the imperialist ruling class, that he had "achieved a modicum of success in freeing [himself] from Cold War propaganda."[174] A more truthful statement would have been that he achieved a modicum of success in making his state capitalist Cold War propaganda look like a product of free thinking to its unsuspecting consumers. His work is, in fact, so lacking in a rigorous, historical materialist analysis of the USSR—which can be found in the scholarly research undertaken by Annie Lacroix-Riz, Domenico Losurdo, Ludo Martens, Michael Parenti, and many others—that he does not even avail himself of an important report made by his colleagues at the CIA, which would have corrected his false, repeated depiction of the Soviet Union as a "dictatorship."[175] In a document dated March 2, 1955, Marcuse's fellow intelligence operatives clearly stated: "Even in Stalin's time there was collective leadership. The Western idea of a dictator within the Communist setup is exaggerated. Misunderstandings on that subject are caused by lack of comprehension of the real nature and organization of the Communist power structure."[176]

---

173. John Bellamy Foster, ed., "The Baran-Marcuse Correspondence," *Monthly Review Online,* March 1, 2014, https://mronline.org/2014/03/01/baran-marcuse-correspondence/.

174. Marcuse, *Soviet Marxism* (1961), v.

175. See, for instance, Marcuse, *Soviet Marxism* (2018), 111, 145.

176. See "Comments on the Change in Soviet Leadership," March 2, 1955, the CIA FOIA Electronic Reading Room, https://www.cia.gov/readingroom/document/cia-rdp80-00810a006000360009-0. I would like to express my gratitude to Colin Bodayle for

As Marcuse was putting the finishing touches on *Soviet Marxism* in 1957, he was invited by Mosely to an international conference in Berlin funded by the Rockefeller Foundation. This was the next major step in the capitalist-funded Marxism-Leninism Project, the first of which had been Marcuse's pilot project with Isaiah Berlin. The goal of the conference was to reclaim Marxism from the Soviets, which perfectly aligned with Marcuse's Rockefeller-financed research agenda at the time. "The plan," Müller explains, "was to beat the opponent with their own ideological weapons in the battle of ideas."[177] Berlin was also invited, as was Fernand Braudel from the 6th Section of the École Pratique des Hautes Études (EPHE), though they both had to cancel, along with Marcuse. However, the latter actively participated in the conference planning and drew up a list of possible collaborators, which included theoretical Marxists and anticommunism mavens. He dutifully played the role of an international anticommunist gatekeeper, following "the rules of the game and vouch[ing] for the suitability of the Marxists" as an advisor to the ruling class' foundation.[178] This was very similar to what his co-collaborator in the Marxism-Leninism Project, Siegfried Landshut, did for the Science and Freedom committee of the CIA's CCF. He was tasked with recruiting "prominent natural scientists and humanities scholars who were suitable and could be instrumentalized for ideological 'front-line service' in the Cold War."[179] Landshut was present at the Berlin conference, along with figures like H. B. Acton, Clemens Heller, Hans-Joachim Lieber, and Otto Stammer.[180] Marcuse followed the conference with great interest and immediately requested Mosely's personal report on it.[181] As an aside, it is worth noting that the State Department, according to Pierre Grémion, was aware that the CCF was a CIA front, which suggests that Marcuse—given his leadership position and role in the State Department—was likely in on one of the biggest secrets of the Company's cultural Cold War.[182] In any case, he was doing parallel work himself and never, to my knowledge, spoke out against the CIA's war of ideas, including after the public revelations in 1966.

---

drawing my attention to this document.

177. Müller, *Krieger und Gelehrte*, 497.

178. Ibid.

179. Ibid., 509.

180. See ibid., 501.

181. See ibid.

182. See Pierre Grémion, *Intelligence de l'anticommunisme: Le Congrès pour la liberté de la culture à Paris 1950–1975* (Paris: Librairie Arthème Fayard, 1995), 453.

In 1958, at Mosely's request, the Rockefeller Foundation sent Marcuse to France for a long sojourn. Thanks to Hellers's intermediation, he was hosted at the 6th Section of the EPHE as an intellectual ambassador and visiting professor.[183] The 6th Section, the primary institutional home of the Annales school of historiography, had been established in 1947, under the guidance of Braudel's close friend Lucien Febvre and Charles Morazé, with funding from the Rockefeller Foundation and the French government.[184] Marcuse was keen on meeting Polish dissidents, and the EPHE had strong contacts. He was "entrusted with the mission of drawing the Marxists among France's intellectuals into the Western camp without them having to give up their Marxism."[185] The well-paid piper of Western Marxism was thereby engaged in a thoroughly international ideological war on communism, and he reported on his activities in Paris to his close friend Mosely, who was—it bears recalling—a high-level, longtime CIA collaborator.[186]

One-Dimensional Marcuse

The critical theory of society possesses no concepts which could bridge the gap between the present and its future; holding no promise and showing no success, it remains negative. Thus it wants to remain loyal to those who, without hope, have given and give their life to the Great Refusal.

—HERBERT MARCUSE[187]

One of Marcuse's most famous books, *One-Dimensional Man* (1964), was, as he explained to Raya Dunayevskaya, a "Western counterpart to *Soviet Marxism*."[188] In 1958, he had proposed a research project to the Rockefeller Foundation, titled "Cultural Changes in Contemporary Industrial Society," which can be recognized as a preliminary draft of

---

183. See Popa, "International Construction of Area Studies in France."

184. See ibid.

185. Müller, *Krieger und Gelehrte*, 523. Also see Popa, "International Construction of Area Studies in France," 141.

186. See Müller, *Krieger und Gelehrte*, 523–24.

187. Herbert Marcuse, *One-Dimensional Man: Studies in the Ideology of Advanced Industrial Society* (Boston: Beacon Press, 1968), 257.

188. Herbert Marcuse, *Collected Papers of Herbert Marcuse*, Vol. 2: *Towards a Critical Theory of Society* (New York: Routledge, 2001), 219.

the book.[189] Marcuse recommended two of his friends whom he had met doing intelligence work for the U.S. government, Barrington Moore and Philip Mosely, as references for the project (along with the theologian Paul Tillich).[190] Both of them spoke very highly of Marcuse and directly referenced his work for the U.S. national security state in their letters of recommendation.[191] After being informed by a Rockefeller manager that the foundation was more likely to fund his work if it was in continuity with his earlier writings, Marcuse himself described the project as "certainly the continuation (and perhaps even culmination . . . of my work)."[192] He received $6,250 for the project, the equivalent of 50 percent of his annual salary at Brandeis University, which allowed him to be released from half of his annual teaching and other duties.[193] It is not an exaggeration to say, then, that *One-Dimensional Man* was funded by the capitalist ruling class and vetted by current (Mosely) and former (Moore) intelligence operatives.

According to Müller, Marcuse "had reached the height of his influence in the liberal establishment" at the time, and "his cultural-critical perspective was met with approval there."[194] Mosely was inviting him on a yearly basis to the Russian Institute at Columbia, where he also held a Senior Fellowship, to give "a series of background lectures on Marxism and the origins of Leninism."[195] A statement of receipts and expenditures reveals that he was paid $600, the equivalent of $6,464 in 2024, for a single lecture at the RI in 1958 or 1959.[196] His work on *One-Dimensional Man* "was also carried out as a project of the Russian Research Center [at Harvard] under

---

189. See Marcuse's grant application, December 9, 1958, RG 1.2, Series 200, Box 481, Folder 4113, Rockefeller Archive Center.

190. Ibid.

191. See Moore to Thompson, December 27, 1958, and Mosely to Thompson, March 6, 1959, RG 1.2, Series 200, Box 481, Folder 4113, Rockefeller Archive Center.

192. Marcuse to Thompson, November 4, 1958, RG 1.2, Series 200, Box 481, Folder 4113, Rockefeller Archive Center. Also see Thompson to Marcuse, October 3, 1958, in the same folder.

193. Grant in Aid Summary, June 8, 1959, RG 1.2, Series 200, Box 481, Folder 4113, Rockefeller Archive Center.

194. Müller, *Krieger und Gelehrte*, 537.

195. Mosely to Thompson, March 6, 1959, RG 1.2, Series 200, Box 481, Folder 4113, Rockefeller Archive Center.

196. See File Summary of Chief Accountant, Columbia University, January 11, 1960, RG 1.2, Series 200, Box 481, Folder 4113, Rockefeller Archive Center (as well as Series 200 S, Columbia University, Russian Institute).

the title 'The Ideology of Advanced Industrial Civilization.'"[197] Indeed, he wrote to his fellow Frankfurt OSS friend Leo Löwenthal: "I am secretly beginning to think about a study on the ideology of late industrial society, which was suggested to me by the Harvard people."[198]

One of Marcuse's fundamental arguments in this book is that the bourgeoisie and the proletariat are no longer antagonists in developed capitalist society because they share "an overriding interest in the preservation and improvement of the institutional status quo."[199] Class struggle having been displaced, "advanced industrial society"—which includes the developed communist world—had proven itself "capable of containing qualitative change for the foreseeable future."[200] In this brave new world, into which underdeveloped societies are likely to be integrated in the future according to him, there emerged "a pattern of *one-dimensional thought and behavior* in which ideas, aspirations, and objectives that, by their content, transcend the established universe of discourse and action are either repelled or reduced to terms of this universe."[201] Human beings thus find themselves trapped in a world of total domination in which capitalist and communist societies tend toward assimilation and are both pitted against human freedom and imagination. "The fateful interdependence of the only two 'sovereign' social systems in the contemporary world," Marcuse writes, "is expressive of the fact that the conflict between progress and politics, between man and his masters has become total. . . . Both systems have these capabilities [of communist development or capitalist comforts] distorted beyond recognition and, in both cases, the reason is in the last analysis the same—the struggle against a form of life which would dissolve the basis for domination."[202]

Marcuse thereby replaces the international class struggle between imperialist capitalism and communism by what he perceives as a common front of totalitarian societies against human liberation. People can, at least in principle, break the repressive grip of these societies by negating their negation of humanity through what Marcuse refers to as the Great Refusal. This rejection of the status quo in favor of emancipation is perhaps most visible in his celebration of art—or, more precisely, the

---

197. Müller, *Krieger und Gelehrte*, 444.

198. Ibid., 446.

199. Marcuse, *One-Dimensional Man*, xiii.

200. Ibid., xv.

201. Ibid., 12. On the fate of less developed societies, also see, for instance, ibid., xvii, 47.

202. Ibid., 55.

bourgeois ideology of art—which purportedly transcends the status quo. However, this anarchist-inflected refusal of extant states in favor of a magical third way beyond capitalism and communism, whose path is lit by bourgeois ideology, is notoriously under-theorized in the book, which primarily focuses on the generalized inability to surpass the status quo in the direction of real, historical alternatives.[203]

The irony of this book's production history should not be lost on us. Renowned for its critique of a totalitarian world and so-called affluent society, it was—at least in its early stages—directly bankrolled by the capitalist class of the most affluent society, while being a direct outgrowth of its totalitarian system, neither of which were subjected to a Great Refusal but were instead objects of a Grand Embrace. Indeed, the book famously condemned the totalitarian control of society and culture without clearly disclosing the extent to which it emerged out of imperial financial-state-intellectual networks and was met with the approval of intellectual operators with strong ties to the U.S. national security state. Marcuse did note in the acknowledgments that he had received Rockefeller support and feedback from figures like Barrington Moore, Jr., Arno J. Mayer, and Hans Meyerhoff.[204] However, he neglected to mention that Moore was his friend from the OSS and a CIA collaborator, Mayer worked in army intelligence and was involved in Operation Paperclip (the secret U.S. intelligence program that brought some 1,600 Nazi scientists to the United States after the war), and Meyerhoff was employed—like him—by the OSS and then the State Department.[205]

Marcuse's capitalist and state backers were clearly pleased with the central thesis of the book, namely that class struggle had been overcome by economic and technological development, and the possibility of an alternative society was thereby foreclosed, or at least banished to the realm of the imagination. This begs the question: was Marcuse diagnosing

---

203. See ibid., xi.

204. See ibid., vi.

205. On Mayer, see his first-person testimony in Mor Loushy and Daniel Sivan, *Camp Confidential: America's Secret Nazis*, 2021, film, and his Princeton University obituary: Jamie Saxon, "Arno Mayer, Elie Wiesel Award Honoree and Eminent Historian of Modern Europe, Dies at 97," Princeton University website, January 24, 2024, https://www. princeton.edu/news/2024/01/24/arno-mayer-elie-wiesel-award-honoree-and-eminent-historian-modern-europe-dies-97. Regarding Meyerhoff, see his University of California obituary: Donald S Piatt, Herbert Morris, Leon Howard, "Hans Meyerhoff, Philosophy: Los Angeles," UC Libraries, 2011, https://oac.cdlib.org/view?docId=hb629006vt&doc. view=content&chunk.id=div00016&brand=calisphere&anchor.id=0.

one-dimensional man, or was he himself the prototype of the one-dimensional man in the sense of a bureaucrat, as well as a capitalist state propagandist, who—while in the pay of a system he openly described as totalitarian—sought to take the real alternative off the table?

The Propagandized Godfather of the New Left,
with the FBI on His Heels

Marcuse was radicalized by the movements of the 1960s. He strayed so far from the political center of gravity of the most prominent intellectuals of the Frankfurt School that he became a vocal supporter—as well as a highly mediatized spokesperson—of the New Left. In this capacity, he was a target of FBI surveillance, was publicly attacked by conservative forces, and received death threats from the Ku Klux Klan. In order to understand his evolution and dialectically situate it within the social totality, it is integral to elucidate the contradictory nature of the New Left for the U.S. empire. On the one hand, it was, at least to some degree and within certain parameters, understood as an anticommunist weapon that could be promoted to splinter the left in general and, most important, discredit and ideally destroy the so-called Old Left of the communists. On the other hand, however, its progressive orientation nonetheless remained a threat, and it is clear from the archival record that there was a massive campaign to destroy it. In this sense, the New Left—like Marcuse—was recognized as an enemy by certain elements of the U.S. national security state, but an enemy that could nonetheless be very useful for fighting the supposed Old Left.

Let us begin with Marcuse's relationship to the FBI. When the State Department came under fire in 1950 due to the rising wave of McCarthyism, Marcuse had to answer a Bureau questionnaire, but he only came under direct scrutiny when a former employee of the Institute, Karl Wittfogel, cast suspicion on him. Müller's summary of one of the Bureau's reports on Marcuse is worth citing in full:

> Investigations among his American colleagues, including avowed conservatives, revealed that Marcuse was a loyal public servant, a Marxist in theory, but in practical politics far removed from any subversive activity. He had always pursued American interests. The FBI also obtained an internal State Department review, which came to the clear conclusion that Marcuse was anticommunist and loyal to the United States. . . . His superiors praised Marcuse as a leading expert on Europe and international communism.

Marcuse was a loyal American citizen through and through and "definitely an anticommunist."[206]

The FBI, according to Stephen J. Whitfield, "repeatedly cleared Marcuse of any suspicions of disloyalty and formally ended systematic surveillance of his activities in 1952," although it continued to "monitor him during his teaching career at Brandeis."[207]

Judging from Marcuse's voluminous FBI file, this surveillance intensified considerably and once again became systematic in the 1960s and 1970s.[208] The Bureau kept detailed reports on his writings and activities, gathered information from numerous stool pigeons, tracked his movements, followed the press coverage of his work, and even had informants record at least one of his lectures.[209] He was placed on its Administrative Index or ADEX, which kept tabs on people considered a threat to national security, and the justification given in one secret report was the following: "Subject maintains his association with the radical left and acts as a public spokesman of the left."[210] He was removed from the ADEX, according to a document dated October 31, 1972, because he did not advocate violence or "the overthrow of our government through rebellion or insurrection," although another document from 1974 continues to list him as "potentially dangerous."[211]

Unlike his Frankfurt School colleagues Adorno, Horkheimer, and Habermas, Marcuse defended the student movement in the United States and Western Europe.[212] He also took a firm stance against the U.S. war in Vietnam and tried to convince other members of the Institute to join him in making critical theory relevant to the rebellions of the time. These included the feminist and Black liberation movements, memorably personified in the life and work of his student Angela Davis, as well as the antiwar movement and struggles for Third World liberation. Although he

---

206. Müller, *Krieger und Gelehrte*, 78.

207. Stephen J. Whitfield, "A Radical in Academe: Herbert Marcuse at Brandeis University," *Journal for the Study of Radicalism*, Vol. 9, No. 2 (Fall 2015): 95.

208. See Herbert Marcuse's FBI file (number 9-48255), obtained through a FOIA request.

209. See ibid.

210. Ibid.

211. Ibid.

212. Among the many sources, the most detailed overview is provided by Wolfgang Kraushaar, ed., *Frankfurter Schule und Studentenbewegung: Von der Flaschenpost zum Molotowcocktail 1946–1995*, 3 vols. (Hamburg: Rogner & Bernhard Verlags KG, 1998).

was loath to accept the title, he came to be promoted in the mainstream press as the godfather of the New Left.

In his correspondence with Adorno, Marcuse readily accepted that the ideas of the Frankfurt School had become "cruder and simpler" in his work, if only to bring out their hidden radical substance.[213] Adorno, recognizing that Marcuse, with his straightforward ideas, had become "a kind of sacred cow for rebellious students," asked him to come to Frankfurt in the late 1960s.[214] He wanted to save face and calm the mounting tensions between the Institute's leaders and the student movement. Marcuse arrived in Rome in the summer of 1969. He left behind a California under the jackboot of state repression: Governor Ronald Reagan had launched a brutal assault on the students (128 injured, 1 dead) and deployed 2,200 National Guard troops to occupy Berkeley. Having clearly shown his support for the students' antiwar struggle, notably by participating in numerous demonstrations, Marcuse was identified as a problem. In order to end his teaching career, the American Legion later attempted to buy out his contract at the University of California at San Diego.[215] Although it failed, the university administration eventually forced him out by modifying its rules regarding the age of professors.[216]

Because of his commitments, the FBI kept a close eye on him. When Marcuse left for Europe in June 1969, the Bureau obtained his entire itinerary from Pan American Airways and then followed his journey step by step through airport informers.[217] Having discreetly obtained a copy of *Essay on Liberation* (1969), one of his most radical publications, Hoover's agency prepared a report noting that its author advocated a revolution in the United States to eliminate poverty, and even labor. The report concluded that Marcuse was a powerful force in the New Left and that the young radicals who admired and were inspired by him did not really understand his philosophy. Nevertheless, the radical youth would continue to follow him, wrote the author of the report, as long as he advocated the overthrow of the system, without recognizing that Marcuse was

---

213. Theodor Adorno and Herbert Marcuse, "Correspondence on the German Student Movement," *New Left Review*, Vol. 1, No. 233 (January/February 1999): 134.

214. Quoted in Steven Müller-Doohm, *Adorno: A Biography*, trans. Rodney Livingstone (Cambridge: Polity Press, 2005), 606.

215. See the documentary film by Paul Alexander Juutilainen, *Herbert's Hippopotamus: Marcuse and Revolution in Paradise*, 1996, https://www.youtube.com/watch?v=gbzhmMDFcFQ.

216. See ibid.

217. See the FBI's file on Herbert Marcuse (9-48255), obtained through a FOIA request.

simply using young people as instruments to establish his "intellectual dictatorship."[218]

The scene described at the beginning of this chapter, when Marcuse was heckled by students in Rome and Daniel Cohn-Bendit accused him of being paid by the CIA (which he apparently denied ever doing), brings into focus the complexities and contradictions of Marcuse's later life. He was, on the one hand, a long-standing collaborator with U.S. intelligence agencies and the capitalist ruling class, having occupied a leading position in the intellectual world war on communism, both within the U.S. national security state and then as an academic subcontractor for the capitalist class with strong and persistent ties to intelligence agencies. On the other hand, he showed every sign of having been radicalized, to some degree, by the rebellious movements of the 1960s. Müller described him as a "disillusioned liberal" of a social-democratic persuasion, whose ideological orientation—initially shaped by the Second World War and the early Cold War—shifted due to his contact with students and other young activists (a trajectory shared by some of his fellow liberal collaborators in Washington).[219] By the time he arrived in Rome, he was an outspoken critic of the war in Vietnam and a vocal supporter of New Left radicalism (although he also had some criticisms). For a properly dialectical analysis, it is crucial to grasp these nuances and contradictions rather than paste over them with a unidimensional account of his life and work.

Marcuse had become such a visible intellectual spokesperson for the movements of the 1960s that he was not only monitored by the FBI, but the CIA as well, as attested to by numerous internal documents. For instance, Henry Kissinger's 1969 memo for the President summarizing the CIA's report on "Restless Youth" lists Marcuse as one of the "prophets" of the New Left.[220] Other documents refer to him as one of its "heroes" and provide overviews of his philosophy.[221] Putting this contradiction even more succinctly, he was at one and the same time a national security state collaborator—at least in the past—and a target of surveillance. This

218. C. D. Brennan, "Memorandum (to W. C. Sullivan)," September 11, 1969, Herbert Marcuse's FBI's file (9-48255), obtained through a FOIA request.

219. See "Marcuse and the U.S. National Security State: Cold War Discourse, with Tim Müller," interview by Gabriel Rockhill, Critical Theory Workshop, https://www.youtube.com/live/hnOCQC1TFvY?si=91DSJBSNxI-jvN9D.

220. "Summary of CIA Survey, 'Restless Youth,'" March 7, 1969, the CIA FOIA Electronic Reading Room, https://www.cia.gov/readingroom/document/loc-hak-1-2-21-4w.

221. See, for instance, "The New Left," August 2, 1968, the CIA FOIA Electronic Reading Room, https://www.cia.gov/readingroom/document/cia-rdp78-03061a000400030036-7.

was not as anomalous as it might sound. When the U.S. national security state collaborated with self-declared Marxists, even of the Western sort, it wanted to make sure that they were doing the kind of work that served its interests.[222] This had clearly been the case with Marcuse, who was considered a trusted ally by the Establishment, but his radicalization was cause for concern. At the same time, Kissinger noted in his memo that one of the New Left themes, central to Marcuse's work, was that "the revolution has not come because the capitalists have duped the workers with color televisions and Mustangs."[223] Kissinger concluded that its program was "nihilism."[224] If it was dangerous insofar as it asserted that "the system must be destroyed," its inability to articulate a real alternative was also registered.[225]

As briefly mentioned above, the New Left was often seen as a double-edged sword by imperialist intelligence agencies. On the one hand, it served as a weapon of ideological warfare against communism and the so-called Old Left, which could be demonized as class reductionist, authoritarian, bureaucratic, orthodox, and dismissive of all of the purportedly novel issues raised by the New Left (which were not actually new to the communist left): racism, misogyny, environmental degradation, etc. On the other hand, the New Left had some radical aspirations that were seen as a threat, particularly when it sought to call into question imperialism, the reign of capital, and the dominant socioeconomic order. It therefore needed to be contained and controlled, and ideally it would be eliminated along with the communist left. The U.S. national security state thereby often took a two-pronged approach, using what it could of the New Left as a weapon of war against the purported Old Left, while seeking overall to beat back any form of left politics. In other words, the New Left was an enemy, which is clear from the long and detailed history of the FBI's COINTELPRO (COunterINTELligence PROgram), which was officially run from the mid-1950s through the early 1970s and was designed to "disrupt and destabilize," "cripple," "destroy" or otherwise "neutralize" dissident political movements and organizations.[226] However, the New

---

222. The same was true, for instance, of New York University philosophy professors James Burnham and Sidney Hook, both of whom worked for the CIA while being surveilled by the FBI.
223. "Summary of CIA Survey, 'Restless Youth.'"
224. Ibid.
225. Ibid.
226. This vocabulary is found in many internal FBI documents and is also cited in Ward

Left was also sometimes recognized, particularly by agencies like the CIA, as a *useful* enemy.[227]

To appreciate the complexities of Marcuse's later life and work, it is imperative to be attentive to this contradiction, while also foregrounding the nuances of how his positions related to the broader class struggles of the time. As we will see in the next section, the precise form of radical politics embraced by Marcuse never went to the point of an identification with communism. Although he did continue to support Angela Davis after she joined the Communist Party USA, he remained an anticommunist radical.[228]

This helps to explain why the bourgeois press widely promoted him as the spokesperson of the New Left. Between 1968 and his death in 1979, more than 85 substantial articles in English appeared about him in major venues like the *New York Times* (28 articles), the *Los Angeles Times* (14), *Time* (10), the *Washington Post* (6), the *Boston Globe* (4), *New York Times Magazine* (2), and *Newsweek* (1).[229] He became so famous that his book *One-Dimensional Man* came in fifth in one of *Time*'s "Top of the Decade" lists.[230] Even *Playboy* magazine was in on the media blitz, offering Marcuse "a large sum of money" for an interview.[231] Although the discussion fell through, Hugh Hefner's publication did run a long exposé on his work.[232] Marcuse was also frequently interviewed on the radio and television, including an extended conversation with Bryan Magee for the BBC

Churchill and Jim Vander Wall, *The COINTELPRO Papers: Documents from the FBI's Secret Wars Against Dissent in the United States* (Boston: South End Press, 1990), 1.

227. See Churchill and Wall, *The COINTELPRO Papers*; Nelson Blackstock, *Cointelpro: The FBI's Secret War on Political Freedom* (New York: Pathfinder Press, 1988); Ward Churchill and Jim Vander Wall, *Agents of Repression: The FBI's Secret Wars Against the Black Panther Party and the American Indian Movement* (Boston: South End Press, 1990).

228. See Juutilainen, *Herbert's Hippopotamus*. According to his FBI file, Anthony Floyd Dumas, a former member of the Black Panther Party (BPP), reported that he made donations to the BPP (see Herbert Marcuse's FBI file, obtained through a FOIA request).

229. These are minimal calculations for substantive articles based on online databases, whose searches can generate different results based on their precise configurations. For instance, searching simply "Marcuse" on *Time*'s historical database generates 88 results: https://time.com/search/?q=Marcuse&page=4.

230. "Top of the Decade," *Time*, December 26, 1969.

231. See Juutilainen, *Herbert's Hippopotamus*. Also see Christopher Pollard, "The Philosopher Who Was Too Hot for *Playboy*," *The Conversation*, October 3, 2017, https://theconversation.com/the-philosopher-who-was-too-hot-for-playboy-85002.

232. See Michael G. Horowitz, "Portrait of the Marxist as an Old Trouper," *Playboy*, September 1970, https://www.marcuse.org/herbert/newsevents/1970/709PlayboyInt.htm.

and another with Helen Hawkins for PBS.[233] Not all of this coverage was positive, and some of the press focused on his problems at the University of California at San Diego, as well as the controversies surrounding his famous students Angela Davis and Abbie Hoffman. It is also true that he had already gained some public notoriety with *One-Dimensional Man* (1964), which had sold "more than 300,000 copies in its first edition."[234] Nevertheless, it is remarkable how much Marcuse was promoted as the intellectual leader of the radical movements of the long 1960s. Instead of perceiving him as a revolutionary who was a serious threat to the system, the bourgeois media and those behind it clearly considered that he was the optimal face of the movement. He had dutifully served the Establishment for many years, including as a radical recuperator for the capitalist class. Only a decade earlier, he was in the pay of the Rockefeller Foundation for a mission to domesticate radicals in France and bring them into the camp of the Western—that is, anticommunist—Marxists.

As we saw earlier in the discussion of the Mighty Wurlitzer, the bourgeois media is largely controlled and overseen by the U.S. national security state. This begs the question: was the promotion of Marcuse as the godfather of the New Left due, at least in some degree, to the bourgeois state's mobilization of its media assets? The *New York Times*, in many ways the leader of the press pack, had signed a secrecy agreement with the CIA, at least when it was under the leadership of Arthur Hays Sulzberger, "a good friend of [CIA director] Allen Dulles."[235] The author of one of the articles on Marcuse in its pages, as well as a letter to the editor, was Sidney Hook, a prominent philosophy professor at New York University. Hook was a major operator in the anticommunist intellectual world war, and a mover and shaker in the CIA's CCF, including its U.S. chapter (the ACCF). He negotiated directly with Allen Dulles for the ACCF's funding, and he also served as a consultant to the Director of Central Intelligence

233. Magee's interview is titled "Marcuse and the Frankfurt School," and it is archived here: https://www.youtube.com/watch?v=0KqC1lTAJx4. Hawkins' discussion was called simply "Dr. Herbert Marcuse," and it aired on the series *Viewpoints* on KPBS-TV/ Channel 15 on April 25, 1979: https://www.youtube.com/watch?v=XhzKyvLbY8M. For an archive of other interviews with Marcuse, see https://www.marcuse.org/ herbert/audio-video/#interviews.

234. Ronald Aronson, "Marcuse Today," *Boston Review*, November 17, 2014, https:// www.bostonreview.net/articles/ronald-aronson-herbert-marcuse-one-dimensional- man-today.

235. Wilford, *The Mighty Wurlitzer*, 227.

and to the PSB.[236] Hook's review of one of Marcuse's most radical books in the *New York Times, An Essay on Liberation*, was long and rather critical, but it took his work seriously and helped with its visibility. The famous daily, as well as the weekly *Time*—to take but these two examples—had extensive intelligence ties: "Like the *New York Times*, Henry Luce's weekly [*Time*] provided CIA officers with journalistic credentials ...; [CIA director] Dulles laid on regular dinners for *Time* foreign correspondents similar to those he gave for CBS, receiving in return post-assignment debriefings and favorable publicity."[237] It is difficult to ascertain, in these cases, whether the media's extensive coverage of Marcuse was the result of the Agency's direct mobilization of its press assets or instead the consequence of the bourgeois media's standard operating procedures, where managers and producers instinctively understand via their echo chamber what is to be promoted or demoted. In any case, the ultimate result was the same.

After the brouhaha in Rome involving Marcuse and Cohn-Bendit, an article emphasizing the splits between the septuagenarian and the student militants appeared simultaneously in the *Rome Daily American* and the *International Herald Tribune*, with a large photograph of the Frankfurt School scholar. This was obviously a lot of press coverage for a philosophy lecture. However, forty percent of the first newspaper's budget was funded by the CIA until the 1970s, and its general manager, as of 1964, Robert Cunningham, had just come off a twelve-year stint working for the CIA.[238] Moreover, Cunningham also owned a stake in the paper, which was at twenty-five percent in 1983.[239] The second newspaper continued the tradition of its predecessor, the *New York Herald Tribune*, by closely collaborating with the CIA.[240] In the case of these articles, Marcuse was

236. See, for instance, Saunders, *The Cultural Cold War*; Wilford, *The Mighty Wurlitzer*; Hugh Wilford, *The New York Intellectuals: From Vanguard to Institution* (Manchester, UK: Manchester University Press, 1995); and Peter Finn and Petra Couvée, *The Zhivago Affair: The Kremlin, the CIA, and the Battle Over a Forbidden Book* (New York: Pantheon Books, 2014), 132.

237. Wilford, *The Mighty Wurlitzer*, 231.

238. See Carl Bernstein, "The CIA and the Media," *Rolling Stone*, October 20, 1977, and Sidney Bedingfield, "Ex-CIA Agent Battles Thurmond," United Press International, April 17, 1984, https://www.upi.com/Archives/1984/04/17/Ex-CIA-agent-battles-Thurmond/9425054120006/.

239. See Reuters, "Paper for Americans in Rome Is Ordered to Reinstate Editor," *New York Times*, July 29, 1983, A2.

240. Philip Agee and Louis Wolf, eds., *Dirty Work: The CIA in Western Europe* (New York: Dorset Press, 1978), 186–87.

promoted as a major spokesperson of the New Left, while the newspapers were simultaneously seeking to foster splits within it.

There is an established history of CIA press assets promoting Marcuse, including a long review of *One-Dimensional Man* in *Encounter* magazine.[241] This same CIA and MI6-backed publication also showered praise on his *Soviet Marxism*, referring to its author as a Dante of ideology critique "who led his readers on a journey through the hell of the Soviet worldview."[242] The *Economist*, a magazine that had a "close relationship" to MI6 and the Information Research Department (IRD), also ran a laudatory review of Marcuse's critique of the USSR.[243] Although there is not sufficient evidence to draw a definitive conclusion, it is plausible that the U.S. national security state would have activated its Mighty Wurlitzer—its global network of media assets—to promote a longtime ally as the intellectual face of the New Left.

As mentioned above, it was Marcuse's work for—and contacts within— the U.S. national security state that helped him secure prestigious university appointments and lucrative research contracts, as well as develop his professional reputation as a scholar. Then, as Müller explained, "it was the Rockefeller Foundation-sponsored positions at the renowned universities of Columbia and Harvard that gave him a reputation that led to an appointment to a professorship in political theory at Brandeis University in May 1954 and the offer of a visiting professorship at Berkeley."[244] He was, in more ways than one, a ruling-class intellectual, and his public visibility grew directly out of his promotion within the imperial superstructure, including both its political and its cultural components. He continued to collaborate with the Rockefeller Foundation for years, "without any ideological clashes," as well as with his fellow intelligence analysts from the bourgeois state, who were the principal researchers providing feedback on his manuscripts.[245] All of the major books that he published in

---

241. See Julius Gould, "The Dialectics of Despair: On Herbert Marcuse," *Encounter*, September 1964, 68–73.

242. Cited in Müller, *Krieger und Gelehrte*, 490.

243. Paul Lashmar and James Oliver, *Britain's Secret Propaganda War* (Phoenix Mill, UK: Sutton Publishing, 1998), 117. On the following page, 118, the authors note that "many of *The Economist*'s staff were very close to the intelligence establishment." The review begins by pointing out that the book is a product of the RI and the RRC, noting that "like all the products of these institutions, this is a thoughtful, scholarly and interesting work." "Marxism in Russia," *The Economist*, February 21, 1959, 684.

244. Müller, *Krieger und Gelehrte*, 447.

245. Ibid.

English after his intelligence and Rockefeller connected *One-Dimensional Man* (1964), meaning those that were not collections of lectures or earlier essays, included acknowledgments that recognized the ongoing contributions of his fellow bourgeois-state analysts turned professors. After co-authoring a book with former CIA collaborator and OSS and DOJ operative Barrington Moore Jr. (*A Critique of Pure Tolerance*, 1965), Marcuse acknowledged the latter's feedback on *An Essay on Liberation* (1969). He also thanked OSS veterans Arno J. Mayer and Inge Marcuse for their comments on the book, as well as Leo Löwenthal, who had served for fourteen years as a professional propagandist for the OWI and VOA (and surely had important contacts in the media). This means that all four of the people who provided feedback on that book, renowned for being one of his most radical, shared Marcuse's history of working for the U.S. national security state and its propaganda agencies. The same is true of *Counter-Revolution and Revolt* (1972), since Mayer and Löwenthal were the principal reviewers of that manuscript. His last book, *The Aesthetic Dimension* (1978 in English), was less overtly political, and it was not vetted by Moore or Mayer, but the indefatigable propagandist Löwenthal read and commented on it. Marcuse obviously did not turn his back on his intelligence and public relations contacts later in life.[246]

Given all of these connections, it seems highly unlikely that the mainstream press was simply acting on its own in contributing to Marcuse's renown. Some of this could very well have been due to the inertia and interconnected symbiosis of the imperial superstructure, whose media and cultural apparatus tends to echo and support the intellectual apparatus and the work promoted by it, as well as the political apparatus. However, even if one assumes that the media was functioning autonomously or semi-autonomously, at least in some of its coverage, it would have most certainly been put back in its place if it had strayed too far from the political line of the propaganda agencies of the U.S. government.

Most important, Marcuse's status as the godfather of the New Left cannot be separated from the media and cultural apparatus that bequeathed this status on him. The imperial superstructure, of which this apparatus forms an integral part, provided uplift and public visibility to Marcuse because he was a non-threatening anticommunist radical rather than a revolutionary communist. The orientation of the bourgeois media, and

---

246. To be clear, having worked for an intelligence or propaganda agency does not necessarily discredit one's later scholarly work, particularly if it breaks with the ideological horizons of those agencies.

those behind it, was clearly that it was better to have one of their longtime anticommunist collaborators as the face of radical movements, instead of a revolutionary dedicated to making socialism a material reality. This should be obvious when one compares his fame and public visibility in the capitalist world to all the communist intellectuals who have been denigrated, sidelined, silenced, de-platformed, incarcerated, and even killed.

Although the comparison is far from perfect because of the discrepancies between their lives, the case of George Jackson provides a revealing contrast. He was, like Marcuse, a major intellectual and militant at the time, and there was only one degree of separation between them since Jackson maintained a correspondence with Marcuse's student Angela Davis. Jackson's prison letters, collected in *Soledad Brother* (1970), became a sensation, and the book sold over 400,000 copies. This inevitably led to some media coverage. However, as an incarcerated, Black communist from a poverty-stricken background, who lacked contacts in the intelligence, academic, and propaganda world, let alone the capitalist ruling class, the pages of the bourgeois press were not open to him in the same way as Marcuse for long interviews or articles on his work, not to mention platforms like the BBC or PBS. Instead of being promoted as the face of the radical movements of the time, Jackson was killed in prison before his thirtieth birthday. The fame and glory bestowed on the Western Marxist, who was upheld as a global spokesperson for radicalism, contrasted starkly with the repression and murder unleashed on the anti-imperialist Marxist.

Marcuse: An Anticommunist to the End?

> I do not question the right of the United States to fight communism in the Western hemisphere.
>
> —HERBERT MARCUSE
> (IMMEDIATELY AFTER THE BAY OF PIGS INVASION)[247]

Marcuse had the merit of recognizing that communism had a particular appeal for "the underprivileged people—still the great majority of the population of earth," and he knew that "the ascent of Communism is not entirely (and not even primarily) due to power and violence."[248] Yet he

---

247. Marcuse, *Marxism, Revolution and Utopia*, 153.
248. Herbert Marcuse, "Marcuse—The Problem of Political Debating," *The Justice*, May 14, 1957. Also see Müller, *Krieger und Gelehrte*, 405.

was crystal clear regarding where he stood: "The struggle against communism is the struggle against a hostile world-historical force, against a whole form of civilization, against a philosophy and political theory which has deep roots in Western civilization."[249]

He not only completely identified with this struggle against communism, but he wrote these words in a 1957 text where he openly opposed academic freedom for communists, recommending that they not be invited to university campuses.[250] It is a sad and bitter truth that the supposedly radical philosopher was taking the same position that the Association of American Universities (AAU) had taken in 1953, namely that membership in the Communist Party "extinguishes the right to a university position."[251] According to the twisted logic of anticommunist ideology, this was not, however, an attack on academic freedom, but rather its defense. In the words of the AAU: "If an instructor follows communistic practice by becoming a propagandist for one opinion, adopting a 'party line,' silencing criticism or impairing freedom of thought and expression in his classroom, he forfeits not only all university support but his right to membership in the university."[252] Marcuse repeated the AAU's "line" nearly verbatim, adding for rhetorical good measure that it is acceptable to exclude "murderers":

> We may regard the invited communists [meaning those invited to speak on university campuses] as a mere mouthpiece of the "apparatus," without any opinion and will of his own. In this case, there is no point in inviting him and talking with or against him—unless we discuss the "line" itself which he plugs. Or, we may regard the communist as a murderer who has to be accused but not to be argued with. But then, why invite a murderer to campus?[253]

---

249. Marcuse, "Marcuse—The Problem of Political Debating."
250. Ibid.
251. Association of American Universities, "The Rights and Responsibilities of Universities and Their Faculties: A Statement on Communism and the Colleges," *Engineering and Science* 16 (April 1953): 14. Howard Zinn recalls that "the Heads of Harvard, Yale, Columbia, Princeton, MIT, Chicago, Caltech, and thirty other institutions subscribed to that [AAU] statement." "The Politics of History in the Era of the Cold War: Repression and Resistance," in *The Cold War and the University: Toward an Intellectual History of the Postwar Years*, ed. André Schiffrin (New York, New Press, 1997), 42.
252. Association of American Universities, "The Rights and Responsibilities of Universities," 14.
253. Marcuse, "Marcuse—The Problem of Political Debating."

Although Marcuse was radicalized by what he sometimes described as the movements of marginals—students, women, racialized minorities, the Third World, etc.—his anticommunism, though perhaps tempered to some degree, did not significantly wane with the years.[254] He embraced radical insurgency and populism, as well as the search for a third way beyond capitalism and communism. It is true that he sometimes showed signs of being open to countries like China or Cuba, but this was generally insofar as they represented the possibility of breaking with Moscow, fragmenting the socialist world, and moving in a direction that was markedly different from the anti-imperialist project of national development. The following statement, from an interview in 1969, is a good example:

> I have always thought there was an alternative, and in my books I have not kept to the old Marxist ideology. Socialist societies as they are set up today do not seem to me what I call "qualitatively different" from other capitalist societies. They allow one type of domination to exist instead of another; that is all. True socialism is something else again. I am convinced that it is possible from now on to construct a truly socialist society without going through a Stalinist-type period. A socialist society must be founded on true solidarity, on true cooperation: the Cuban revolution seems to me to be moving in that direction.[255]

While he sometimes remained cautiously open, then, to the future possibility of the emergence of what he referred to as a free society distinct from the USSR, he also regularly expressed his view that other socialist experiments were not living up to his ideal of a "socialist society as a free society" that was qualitatively different from "the existing society."[256] For instance, in a 1978 interview where he asked himself if there were places where the foundations of a free and just society were being laid, he responded: "I would indeed mention China, probably also Cuba. However as far as both are concerned, especially China, it seems to me we see there

---

254. It is, of course, notable that Marcuse was an outspoken supporter of his former student, Angela Davis, who was a self-declared communist and member of the Communist Party USA. His ongoing opposition to communism primarily took the form of a rejection of actually existing socialist states, or at least a very high degree of skepticism regarding whether or not they were really socialist. On an interpersonal level, he was still willing to work with and even support some of those who disagreed with him on this point.
255. Herbert Marcuse, "Interview," conducted by Pierre Viansson-Ponte, *Le Monde*, June 1969, https://www.marxists.org/reference/archive/marcuse/works/1969/interview.htm.
256. Marcuse, *Marxism, Revolution and Utopia*, 253.

the same we have seen so many times, namely the priority of repressive modernization over liberating socialization: a technocratic authoritarian trend, at the expense of socialism."[257] Similarly, he opened *An Essay on Liberation* (1969) by celebrating how countries like China, Cuba, and Vietnam were purportedly eschewing "the bureaucratic administration of socialism," while maintaining that they did not represent, nor did other concrete movements, "the alternative" but rather "the limits of the established societies."[258] The task of critical theory was thus still to reexamine "the prospects for the emergence of a socialist society qualitatively different from existing societies, the task of redefining socialism and its preconditions."[259] Indeed, he elsewhere explicitly called into question the "Marxian concept of socialism."[260]

Similarly, he recognized in a 1967 lecture that the victory of the Vietnamese people would be "an immensely positive and constructive step," but he insisted that "this has nothing to do with the construction of a socialist society."[261] He condemned the infernal scarcity that persisted outside of advanced industrial societies, but he did not appear to register that the act of throwing off the chains of imperialism and capitalist underdevelopment in the name of a sovereign—and self-declared socialist—project of national development had something to do with socialism.[262] In the conclusion to *An Essay on Liberation*, he even condemned the idea that socialist countries need to develop their economy in order to overcome imperialist underdevelopment and finally catch up with or surpass the advanced capitalist countries. Apparently oblivious to imperialist power dynamics and the constant war on socialism, he described this as a "false policy" that perpetuates "the pattern of the unfree societies," rather than a requirement for socialist survival that has been imposed by the imperial powers.[263] For him, socialism as an anti-imperialist project of national development—meaning socialism in the real world—was an impediment to the emergence of socialism as an "aesthetic-erotic" endeavor of developing a society "in which work becomes play" and

---

257. Ibid., 366, also see 416 and 425.

258. Herbert Marcuse, *An Essay on Liberation* (Boston: Beacon Press, 1969), viii.

259. Ibid., ix.

260. Marcuse, *Marxism, Revolution and Utopia*, 249.

261. Herbert Marcuse, *Five Lectures: Psychoanalysis, Politics, and Utopia* (Boston: Beacon Press, 1970), 98.

262. See Domenico Losurdo, *Western Marxism: How It Was Born, How It Died, How It Can Be Reborn*, ed. Gabriel Rockhill (New York: Monthly Review Press, 2024), 125–26.

263. Marcuse, *An Essay on Liberation*, 87.

everyone is free (that is, socialism in la-la land).[264] In other words, he explicitly embraced utopian socialism à la Fourier (whom he celebrates in the passage just cited), over and against scientific socialism.

HIS ESSAY ON RUDOLF BAHRO, published the year after Marcuse's death, is an incredibly revealing document for understanding his overall political orientation late in life. Bahro was a Communist in the German Democratic Republic (GDR) who, as a mid-level cadre, was considered one of the most important dissidents of the time. In 1977, he published *The Alternative in Eastern Europe* in the Federal Republic of Germany (FRG), and he appeared on West German television to discuss his views.[265] He was subsequently arrested and accused of conspiring with Western intelligence agencies, becoming "the only East German dissident to be held on such grounds," according to a heavily redacted CIA document on dissidents.[266] In November of that year, an "International Congress on and for Rudolf Bahro" was organized in West Berlin to oppose his arrest, support his work, and call for his release.[267] Marcuse participated in it and then published his paper, along with the others from the conference, in the book *Rudolf Bahro: Critical Responses*.

The capitalist world's campaign to support Bahro and his "scathing criticism of the East German regime," in the words of the CIA, continued the following year.[268] Some of his most visible backers in the West co-signed a call for support in the intelligence-connected *Times* of London in 1978.[269] They included the writers Heinrich Böll, Graham Greene,

---

264. Marcuse, *Marxism, Revolution and Utopia*, 254.

265. See the biographical timeline for Rudolf Bahro available here: https://www.hdg.de/lemo/biografie/rudolf-bahro.html. Also see Alexander Amberger, *Dissident Marxism and Utopian Eco-Socialism in the German Democratic Republic: The Intellectual Legacies of Rudolf Bahro, Wolfgang Harich, and Robert Havemann*, trans. Carla Welch (Leiden: Brill, 2024).

266. "National Intelligence Bulletin," June 3, 1978, the CIA FOIA Electronic Reading Room, https://www.cia.gov/readingroom/document/cia-rdp79t00975a030700010038-9. Also see "Dissidence in Eastern Europe (A Research Paper)," September 1, 1978, the CIA FOIA Electronic Reading Room, https://www.cia.gov/readingroom/document/cia-rdp80t00634a000900110001-5.

267. See Rudolf Bahro, et al., *Rudolf Bahro: Critical Responses* (White Plains, NY: M.E. Sharpe, 1980).

268. "National Intelligence Bulletin," June 3, 1978, 9.

269. "Rudolf Bahro," *The Times*, February 1, 1978, 15.

Günter Grass, and Carola Stern. Böll, to begin with, was a former *Wehrmacht* soldier, a CCF member and thus a CIA collaborator, and he hosted the famous philo-fascist anticommunist Alexander Solzhenitsyn in his home when he defected to the imperial core in 1974 (Böll was the first person the infamous dissident wanted to meet in the West).[270] Böll also became, in 1971, the president of International PEN, the worldwide association of writers whose leadership, by the mid-1960s, had been deeply penetrated by the CIA.[271] Böll's publisher, Josef Caspar Witsch of Kiepenheuer & Witsch, was—in addition to being a former Nazi cultural functionary—"the secret head of the Congress [for Cultural Freedom] in Cologne," and he delivered Böll's reports on his visits to Eastern Europe to the Agency.[272]

The other major signatories of this public letter of support for Bahro had similar intelligence connections. Greene had served in MI6 along-side the master double agent Kim Philby, who defected to the USSR after having served as MI6's head of anti-Soviet espionage and the top British intelligence liaison with the CIA and FBI. Greene, after ostensibly leaving MI6, visited Philby four times in Moscow and reported back to the head of MI6 each time, most likely in unsuccessful attempts to convince Philby to turn against the Soviets.[273] Grass was a former Nazi who was promoted

---

270. See Hans-Rüdiger Minow, *Quand la CIA infiltrait la culture*, ARTE/ZDF, 2006, film, https://www.youtube.com/watch?v=58QTcf_mFag. Also see Wolf-Dieter Roth, "Deutsche Künstler und Journalisten als 'IM' der USA?," *Telepolis*, November 26, 2006, https://www.telepolis.de/features/Deutsche-Kuenstler-und-Journalisten-als-IM-der-USA-3408894.html and "Er hat sich nicht tiefer geduckt," *Taz*, https://taz.de/Biograf--Verleger-ueber-Joseph-C-Witsch/!5026717/.

271. See Robert C. Conard, *Understanding Heinrich Böll* (Columbia SC: University of South Carolina Press, 1992), 15, and Saunders, *The Cultural Cold War*, 359–68.

272. Minow, *Quand la CIA infiltrait la culture*. Also see the reference to Witsch and the CCF's "Cologne Circle" in François Bondy, "Reflexions by Someone Directly Concerned: What Is to Become of the 'Congress for Cultural Freedom' and Its Publications?," International Association for Cultural Freedom Records, Box 318, Folder 3, Central Intelligence Agency 1967, Hanna Holborn Gray Special Collections Research Center at the University of Chicago. Jorgen Schleimann references the CCF's "close collaboration with Kiepenheuer & Witsch" on publications in his March 9, 1959, letter to Walter Hasenclever of the CCF, International Association for Cultural Freedom Records, Box 145, Folder 1, Germany 1959, Hanna Holborn Gray Special Collections Research Center at the University of Chicago.

273. See Phillip Knightley, "Introduction," in Kim Philby, *My Silent War: The Autobiography of a Spy* (New York: Modern Library, 2002), xiii.

by the CIA's CCF networks.[274] Stern had been "an enthusiastic member of the Hitler Youth" before becoming a U.S. Counterintelligence Corps (CIC) agent involved in anticommunist subversion, and she worked for years for Kiepenheuer & Witsch and as a prominent journalist.[275] Witsch's publishing house, widely suspected of being financed by the CIA, featured anticommunist work, and Stern collaborated with Böll and Grass on founding the journal L'76 to provide "a platform for dissident Czecho Slovak [sic] emigres."[276] Archival documents reveal that the CCF, at least on one occasion, bought 300 copies of a Kiepenheuer & Witsch book, *Der Fall Imre Nagy*, and distributed it across its network.[277]

This was quite the web of cultural operators. It is hard to imagine that all of their intelligence ties as anticommunist cultural warriors had nothing to do with their vocal public support for a dissident celebrated by the intelligence agencies of the imperial core, who was himself accused of being one of their collaborators. It is even more difficult if one is familiar with the extensive history of the powerful promotional networks built up by intelligence services and their—witting or unwitting—cultural collaborators over the years.

It is improbable that Marcuse's fulsome public support for Bahro's book, whose German subtitle was *Toward the Critique of Real Existing Socialism* (*Zur Kritik des real existierenden Sozialismus*), was completely independent of his extensive and long-standing intelligence ties within the financial-state-intellectual complex. Whatever the case may be, the position he took perfectly aligned with the agenda of his former colleagues in the State Department and his friends who managed the soft-power investments of the capitalist ruling class. Claiming that Bahro's manuscript had "universal significance" well beyond the case of the GDR, he asserted that "his book is not merely a critique of 'actually existing socialism.'"[278] It was

---

274. See Gunter Grass, "How I Spent the War," *The New Yorker*, May 28, 2007, and Saunders, *The Cultural Cold War*, 352.

275. Paul Oestreicher, "Carola Stern: German Liberal Who Revealed a Double Life," *The Guardian*, February 16, 2006. Also see Thomas Schadt, *Carola Stern—Doppelleben*, 2004, television documentary.

276. Oestreicher, "Carola Stern."

277. See the correspondence between Charlotte Ehlers and Ivan Kats available in International Association for Cultural Freedom Records, Box 145, Folder 2, Germany A–K 1960, Hanna Holborn Gray Special Collections Research Center at the University of Chicago.

278. Herbert Marcuse, "Protosocialism and Late Capitalism: Toward a Theoretical Synthesis Based on Bahro's Analysis," *International Journal of Politics*, Vol. 10, No. 2/3

nothing short of "the most important contribution to Marxist theory and practice to appear in several decades."[279] This is quite the accolade for an anticommunist book published in the imperial West in 1977. The work of Mao Zedong, Ho Chi Minh, Ernesto Che Guevara, Walter Rodney, György Lukács, and so many others was inferior, at least for Marcuse, to Bahro's critique of socialism. Ernest Mandel, who would later celebrate the destruction of Soviet-style socialism, largely agreed with Marcuse, claiming that Bahro's book was "the most important theoretical work to come out of the 'post-capitalist societies' since Trotsky's *The Revolution Betrayed*."[280] New Left Books (later Verso) quickly translated and published it in English.

It is worth noting that Bahro was convicted for the betrayal of state secrets (*Geheimnisverrat*) in July 1978 for having collaborated with West Germany's intelligence services (though he was sentenced to eight years in prison, he was granted amnesty in 1979 and released to the West). The FRG's Federal Intelligence Service was established and overseen by the CIA. The Agency put the Nazi master spy Reinhard Gehlen in charge of the organization, and he then stocked it with his fellow Nazis.[281] Moreover, one of Bahro's inspirations for his manuscript was apparently Frankfurt scholar Karl Wittfogel's Rockefeller-funded book *Oriental Despotism*. Marcuse knew Wittfogel, of course, and, due to his leadership positions in the U.S. State Department and his frequent collaborations with the CIA, he also certainly knew something about West Germany's intelligence services. In fact, he probably knew quite a bit about the organizations that Bahro was accused of collaborating with because he was an expert on Germany, had served as the State Department's acting chief of central Europe, and was considered one of the U.S. government's leading experts on fighting communism.

Why did Marcuse ascribe such monumental importance to Bahro's book, which was apparently written with the support of a Nazi-stocked

---

(Summer-Fall 1980): 25.

279. Ibid.

280. Hugh Mosley, "The New Communist Opposition: Rudolf Bahro's Critique of the 'Really Existing Socialism,'" *New German Critique*, No. 15 (Autumn 1978): 25. Regarding Mandel's celebration of the destruction of socialism, see Ludo Martens, *L'URSS et la contre-révolution de velours* (Brussels: Éditions EPO, 1991).

281. See Simpson, *Blowback* and Kevin C. Ruffner, ed., *Forging an Intelligence Partnership: CIA and the Origins of the BND, 1945-49*, Vol. 1, Center for the Study of Intelligence, 1999, the CIA FOIA Electronic Reading Room, https://www.cia.gov/readingroom/document/519cd81a993294098d515f0a.

imperialist intelligence service under CIA tutelage and was promoted by writers with an established history of working for imperialist espionage agencies (just like Marcuse)? What he found in it was, in many ways, a summary of the major positions that he himself had taken over the years, and this is obviously why he subtitled his article "Toward a Theoretical Synthesis Based on Bahro's Analysis." As a matter of fact, Marcuse's free indirect writing style in his panegyric often makes it difficult to discern between his descriptions of Bahro and his own assertions. What he refers to as the German dissident's groundbreaking ideas segue so perfectly with his own work, that the essay reads—with a few notable exceptions—like a late-in-life recap of Marcuse's own philosophy. Summarizing its fundamental points, insofar as they are corroborated by Marcuse's other work, therefore provides a useful overview of his political orientation, as he synthesized it himself at the end of his life.[282]

First of all, Marcuse asserts that "today it is evident to what degree the Marxist-Leninist model for revolution has become historically obsolete."[283] This is because the armed seizure of power is "beyond the realm of real possibility," at least in the most developed countries, and "late capitalism has created a broad material basis for the integration of diverse interests within the dependent population."[284] The authenticity of Marxism, or what Marcuse calls "fidelity to Marxian theory," can however be maintained, precisely by severing it from Marxism-Leninism.[285] This position perfectly corresponds to one of Marcuse's main objectives in the State Department and in his work at the center of the Rockefeller Foundation's Marxism-Leninism Project: to discredit Marxism-Leninism and to shore up consensus in the imperial core through social-democratic class compromises that foster bourgeois hegemony, as well as via a return to purportedly authentic—that is, anticommunist—Marxism. Given the historical moment in which he was writing, at the end of the 1970s, it is unfortunate that Marcuse did not bother to explain how the obsolescence of Marxism-Leninism could be proven, given that it was so central to the successful anticolonial liberation struggles in countries like Guinea-Bissau and Cape Verde (1973), Angola (1975), Mozambique (1975), Nicaragua (1979), and Grenada (1979). Perhaps his caveat that Marxism-Leninism is irrelevant *in the most developed countries* is sup-

---

282. I am not considering here whether Marcuse's interpretation of Bahro is correct.
283. Marcuse, "Protosocialism and Late Capitalism," 36.
284. Ibid.
285. Ibid., 32.

posed to account for these examples, but, if so, it does not explain its ongoing relevance to much more developed societies like the Warsaw Pact countries. Moreover, why would one make the blanket statement that Marxism-Leninism is "historically obsolete" if it is still so relevant to the global South, unless the unstated premise behind one's—social chauvinist—conclusion is that developments outside of the imperial core are historically irrelevant?[286]

Second, class struggle between the bourgeoisie and the proletariat, Marcuse maintains, has been replaced by "a new *populism*," which is not founded on "class opposition" and does not seek state power, but is rather a rebelliousness that cuts across different classes.[287] The proletariat is not, therefore, a revolutionary class, even potentially, but has rather been absorbed into "the prevailing system of compensatory needs."[288] In fact, Marcuse advocates for revising what he interprets as "the traditional Marxian concept of class."[289] In lieu of class struggle, he claims there are "*catalyst* groups" that instigate rebellions: "the student movement, women's liberation, citizens' initiatives, concerned scientists, etc."[290] They engage in forms of local and regional revolt reminiscent of what Marcuse had referred to in his earlier work as the Great Refusal, which can target "the dictatorship of the political bureaucracy" (that is, socialism) as much as so-called affluent societies in the West.[291]

Third, Marcuse celebrates what he sees in Bahro's work as a displacement of objective in favor of subjective factors: "The focal point of the social dynamic is shifted from the objectivity of political economy to

---

286. Ibid., 36.

287. Ibid., 37. In discussing *"what is obsolete* in Marxian socialism," Marcuse claims that in reality (unlike in Marxian theory), there has been "no impoverishment of the laboring classes, no sharpening of class consciousness and class struggle, no bipolarization of society . . . no inevitable all-out conflicts among the capitalist powers." Marcuse, *Marxism, Revolution and Utopia*, 236.

288. Marcuse, "Protosocialism and Late Capitalism," 30, also see 32–33. It is equally worth consulting "Theses" in Herbert Marcuse, *Technology, War, and Fascism*, ed. Douglas Kellner (New York: Routledge, 1998), which Kellner aptly summed up in the following terms: "Marcuse anticipates many of the defining positions of *One-Dimensional Man*, including the integration of the proletariat, the stabilization of capitalism, the bureaucratization of socialism, the demise of the revolutionary left and the absence of genuine forces of progressive social change" (ibid. 32).

289. Marcuse, "Protosocialism and Late Capitalism," 37.

290. Ibid., 29.

291. Ibid., 36. On rebellionism and populism, see Losurdo, *Western Marxism*.

subjectivity, to consciousness as a potential material force for radical change."[292] The attention of the "catalyst groups" is concentrated on a "journey inwards," which is the purported precondition for objective changes.[293] Subjectivism is a hallmark of Marcuse's work in general. It is visible in his ill-fated attempts to merge Marxism with the subjectivist discourses of phenomenology and psychoanalysis.[294] It is also one of the guiding threads of books like *Counter-Revolution and Revolt*, where he affirmed that "no qualitative social change, no socialism, is possible without … a radical change in the individual agents of change," which means that "the emancipation of *consciousness*" is "the primary task."[295] "Libertarian idealism," oddly described as the *telos* of historical materialism in his text on Bahro, is situated at the very beginning of the emancipatory process.[296] Echoing *Eros and Civilization* (1955), Marcuse insists on linking subjective intellectual pursuits to "an emancipatory instinctual

---

292. Marcuse, "Protosocialism and Late Capitalism," 26.

293. Ibid., 34. Here is how he formulated this point in *An Essay on Liberation*: "A society constantly re-creates, this side of consciousness and ideology, patterns of behavior and aspiration as part of the 'nature' of its people, and unless the revolt reaches into this 'second' nature, into these ingrown patterns, social change will remain 'incomplete,' even self-defeating" (11, also see 25).

294. By "subjectivist," I do not mean that these discourses have nothing to say about objective social reality. It is rather that they situate the individual human subject at the very center of their theories and practice (in the case of psychoanalysis), taking it as a fundamental starting point, rather than beginning with the objective social totality and situating subjects within it. This is also the case for versions of phenomenology, like the one developed by Emmanuel Levinas, that place the Other at the core of their analyses, based on a reified and largely acontextual account of alterity. The deification of the Other does not displace subjectivism in favor of objective analysis; it sacralizes isolated points of subjectivity (renamed and retheorized as alterity) while shunning any rigorous, objective account of the social totality that produced them and that regulates their interaction.

295. Herbert Marcuse, *Counter-Revolution and Revolt* (Boston: Beacon Press, 1972), 48, 132.

296. Marcuse, "Protosocialism and Late Capitalism," 33. Also see Marcuse, *Counter-Revolution and Revolt*, 70–71: "This is the *idealistic core* of dialectical materialism: the transcendence of freedom beyond the given forms. In this sense too, Marxian theory is the historical heir of German Idealism. Freedom thus becomes a 'regulative concept of reason'. . . . Dialectical materialism understands freedom as historical, empirical transcendence, as a force of social change, transcending its immediate form also in a socialist society—not toward ever more production, not toward Heaven or Paradise, but toward an ever more peaceful, joyful struggle with the inexorable resistance of society and nature. This is the philosophical core of the theory of the permanent revolution."

structure" that drives them by making liberation into "a vital need."[297] Personal feelings, united with individual consciousness, are the purported drivers of rebellion, not class struggle conditioned—though not wholly determined—by objective material forces and class consciousness, as Marxist-Leninists would have it.

Fourth, "the relationship between base and superstructure is redefined": instead of economic forces and class struggle being the motors of social change, Marcuse sees intellectuals as playing a leading role.[298] Unlike the workers, who are bereft of time and adequate training, intellectuals have had the opportunity "to think freely, to learn, to understand the facts in their social context, and—to transmit this knowledge."[299] This remains beyond the reach of the working class, due precisely to its social conditions in relation to education: "The radical turn toward emancipatory interests lies beyond the reach of subaltern consciousness; it takes place as part of a process of 'internal emancipation,' as a condition for external emancipation. Given the social conditions of the class (alienating 'full-time' labor, exclusion from educational privilege, unemployment), only a minority can accomplish this rupture."[300] Since subjective thoughts and feelings are the real drivers of history, and the intelligentsia has time to indulge in them, intellectuals constitute the veritable vanguard of social change. Marcuse's idealism is here on full display.

Fifth, he openly advocates for "an antistate politics" that rejects centralization.[301] This is one of the points where he clearly diverges from Bahro, who spurns anarchism and maintains the importance of some form of party and state, even if it is an "anti-state."[302] Marcuse, by contrast, asserted in a 1971 lecture that he believed "that a strong element of anarchism should be incorporated into Marxism."[303] He also suggested that the "revolutionary mass party" is probably outdated.[304] Very much in line with this sentiment and his earlier work, he celebrates council democracy in

---

297. Marcuse, "Protosocialism and Late Capitalism," 45.

298. Ibid., 26.

299. Ibid., 40.

300. Ibid., 32–33.

301. Ibid., 39. In *An Essay on Liberation*, he championed the "new radicalism" of the 1960s that rejected "traditional forms of the political struggle" and militated "against the centralized bureaucratic communist . . . organization" (89).

302. Marcuse, "Protosocialism and Late Capitalism," 30.

303. Herbert Marcuse, "The Radical Movement: A Marxist Analysis," lecture, 1971, https://www.youtube.com/watch?v=lSJvMY0Yl68.

304. Marcuse, *Counter-Revolution and Revolt*, 42.

the article on Bahro and embraces a populist account of socialism, according to which it is understood first and foremost in superstructural terms as democratic rather than primarily in socioeconomic terms as a reconfiguration of the relations of production (the infrastructure).[305] Although these two poles are, of course, dialectically enmeshed within each other, Marcuse's primary focus is on socialism as anarchist workers' democracy, and he does not appear to grasp two important facts: 1) substantive democracy is only really possible when the relations of production have been transformed; and 2) control of state power has been the only way this has been materially possible on a grand scale. Furthermore, socialist revolutions securing state power have thus far only occurred in countries in the Global South that have been subjected to decades and usually centuries of capitalist underdevelopment, including cultural underdevelopment, and they have been the victims of the most heinous forms of imperialist hybrid warfare. The idea that such countries should immediately decentralize and dismantle their own state, while under imperialist attack, and that they also need to democratically empower the entire population—including the landlords, the capitalists, the comprador elite, the lackeys of empire, the fascists, etc.—is tantamount to insisting that they must create the objective conditions for being overthrown if they are to remain truly socialist. Such an argument is worthy of a U.S. State Department intellectual. It amounts to saying that the only real socialists are those who maintain the sanctity of a socialist creed that creates the necessary material conditions for socialism to fail in the real world.

Overall, Marcuse advocates for *actually non-existing socialism*, which is a form of socialism that coheres in the mind of intellectuals, as a utopian order distinct from the material existence of socialism. This is a version of what Engels incisively diagnosed as utopian socialism.[306] Marcuse's particular variant is an excellent example of what some Marxists refer to as magical third-way politics, which invents a stairway to socialist heaven that miraculously transcends—in the mind of the beholder—the material reality of class struggle between two rival socioeconomic orders (capitalism and actually existing socialism). Given the illusory basis of his politics, it is not surprising that Marcuse openly embraced "libertarian

---

305. See Marcuse, "Protosocialism and Late Capitalism," 31.
306. See Friedrich Engels, "Socialism: Utopian and Scientific," in *The Marx-Engels Reader*, ed. Robert C. Tucker (New York: W. W. Norton, 1978), 683–717.

idealism," "socialist idealism," and the need to freely invent abstract ideas unmoored from the realities of class struggle.[307]

All in all, Marcuse espoused in this late text a profoundly revisionist and utopian version of Marxism, or what might more appropriately be called anticommunist Marxianism, which reiterates many of the positions he had taken over the years, including during his phase of radicalization. He stalwartly rejected Marxism-Leninism in favor of Western or cultural Marxism. He sought to replace class struggle with populism, meaning that he generally maintained, on the one hand, that the antagonism between owners and workers had been superseded, and on the other, that popular insurgencies were to be celebrated as long as they avoided developing real institutionalized power through parties and socialist state-building projects. Lenin, it is worth recalling, had trenchantly criticized populism as an ideological position that celebrates the moral excellence of those who are oppressed and bereft of power without scientifically identifying the means to effectively struggle against this oppression. This perfectly applies to Marcuse (as well as many other Western Marxists, as Losurdo has insightfully argued).[308] In his particular version of populism, objective class analysis and an emphasis on the economic forces operative in society are displaced in favor of subjectivism and a preoccupation with individual consciousness. As a matter of fact, Marcuse went so far as to present himself as an open idealist (rather than a materialist). For him, workers were not the driving force behind revolutionary change, but rather intellectuals and cultured members of the middle stratum. Instead of the superstructure growing out of the infrastructure, in a dialectical manner with reciprocal effects, ideology was foundational and the primary battle was to be waged in the realm of ideas and culture. Finally, rather than organizing politically in parties aiming for state power, he advocated for an anarchist rejection of the state, which is of course perfectly in line with his populism.

These were not minor or subtle adjustments to the tradition of dialectical and historical materialism. They were rather an attack on its very foundation, in an attempt to replace anti-imperialist Marxism with cultural Marxianism, class struggle by petty-bourgeois radicalism, objective analysis of reality and its economic forces by subjectivism, materialism by

---

307. Marcuse, "Protosocialism and Late Capitalism," 33 and 43. Also see Herbert Marcuse, "Reason and Revolution Today," lecture, 1970, https://www.youtube.com/watch?v=W2ZBLWiaVnA&t=2682s.
308. See Losurdo, *Western Marxism*.

idealism, workers by intellectuals, the infrastructure by ideology, the party and state by anarchist rebellionism, etc.[309] In sum, Marcuse sought to turn Marxism on its head and then market it as the only true and authentic Marxism, which is precisely what he had been doing when he was in the direct pay of the capitalist ruling class and the bourgeois state. Instead of Western Marxism, the most appropriate expression for Marcuse's orientation would be imperial pseudo-Marxism.

Although his version of Marxism sought to displace class struggle, it is very much a symptom thereof. To begin with, it is a form that is palatable to the capitalists and their state. This, of course, is why they supported it. Its rejection of actually existing socialism, with very few exceptions, as well as its attempt to make Marxism into an academic tool of cultural interpretation rather than a weapon of revolutionary social transformation, clearly situate it on the compatible left. Moreover, the fact that Marcuse's criticisms of capitalism and imperialism are regularly tempered by stalwart condemnations of the socialist alternative ultimately makes his version of Western Marxism open to accommodating capitalism, as the lesser of two evils.

It is certainly true that Marcuse took stances that situated him to the left of colleagues like Adorno and Horkheimer, particularly during the student, antiwar, feminist, and Black liberation movements affiliated with the New Left. It is also the case that the FBI invested ample resources into keeping tabs on him, and that he was forced out of his teaching position in California for political reasons. What a dialectical approach allows us to bring into view, however, is that the same individual can occupy somewhat contradictory positions. Marcuse's embrace of populism and rebellionism, as radical as they might seem within a certain framework, went hand in hand with his persistent anticommunism. His tendency to fetishize revolt, and more specifically the freedom of subjectively acting out against systems of power, applied at least as much to anticommunist counter-revolutionaries as to rebels in the West. His radicalization did not, therefore, call into question the fundamental orientation that allowed him to dutifully serve the U.S. national security state and the capitalist ruling class in their intellectual world war: he remained an anticommunist until the end.

---

309. To be clear, these are general tendencies in Marcuse's work, not systematic axioms that were rigorously maintained across the board and in every instance.

Imperial versus Anti-Imperialist Marxism, or the Scourge of Western Marxism

Dialectics of Critique

If the designing of the future and the proclamation of ready-made solutions for all time is not our affair, then we realize all the more clearly what we have to accomplish in the present—I am speaking of a *ruthless criticism of everything existing*, ruthless in two senses: the criticism must not be afraid of its own conclusions, nor of conflict with the powers that be.

—KARL MARX[1]

The second part of this book has been highly critical of the Frankfurt School and Western Marxism more generally. The purpose of such a critique is not primarily destructive but rather constructive, or rather reconstructive. This is the case at multiple levels. To begin with, the argument is not that we should completely disregard everything that has been written by the Frankfurt School or Western Marxists. This book has primarily focused on its leaders and the most well-known figures: Adorno, Horkheimer, and Marcuse. It has not provided an exhaustive account, particularly of more marginal or left-leaning scholars. Moreover, even if we limit ourselves to these key thinkers, we should learn anything that we can from them, while being vigilant about the pernicious influence that they can have. This orientation is precisely the one found in Marx, Engels, Lenin, and so many others in this tradition, who insisted on

---

1. Karl Marx, "For a Ruthless Criticism of Everything Existing," in *The Marx-Engels Reader*, ed. Robert C. Tucker (New York: W. W. Norton, 1978), 13.

learning from thinkers with whom they did not agree politically, while also situating them in history and class struggle in order to shed light on their underlying presumptions. This process of learning is not restricted, then, to their internal arguments, but it also includes, crucially, how they function within the social totality.

The task of materialist contextualization has been at the core of this book insofar as it has examined the life and work of individual subjects but also the objective social world within which their theoretical practices developed. This is a unique feature of dialectical hermeneutics, which considers both subjective theoretical practices and objective socioeconomic conditions, as well as, most decisively, the relationship between the two. This is what has allowed us to cultivate a deeper understanding of the Frankfurt School, not simply as a group of individual thinkers or isolated texts, but as an intellectual tradition that took on specific forms within a precise sociohistorical conjuncture. In other words, the dialectics of critique is never satisfied with the decontextualized and reified analysis of theory (which is so widespread within the bourgeois humanities). Instead, it always situates people's ideas within the material realm of practice and the social totality. In the case of the Western Marxists, it is important to examine what they said and did, while situating their activities within the overall social relations of intellectual production and global class struggle, in order to elucidate the general practical impact of their contributions. From the point of view of the primacy of practice, this is the most important issue: Western Marxists have significantly contributed to shoring up the compatible left over and against the socialist alternative, thereby promoting a version of Marxism that is not at all incompatible with capitalism and imperialism.

As we have seen, the leading Frankfurt scholars focused on here are, in more ways than one, imperial Marxists. They are, to begin with, a product of the imperial core. They have been bolstered and supported by the imperial superstructure, including both the bourgeois state, where many of them worked for years, and the bourgeois cultural apparatus. They have also been directly funded and supported by the capitalist ruling class, and their extensive promotion has led to their work being widely consumed by the intellectual labor aristocracy and their comprador allies in the periphery. Situated at the apex of an international pyramid of knowledge production, their writings have been promoted around the globe as some of the most advanced and sophisticated. These objective realities are, in part, a result of their subjective orientations. With the partial and limited exception of Marcuse in his late phase of radicalization, they have tended to support, or at least accommodate, imperialism. They have also aggressively fought against the anti-imperialist Marxists and their practical projects of socialist state-building. Both objectively and subjectively, they are imperial Marxists. It is crucially important to recognize, moreover, that these two planes are dialectically enmeshed within one another: it is the imperial superstructure that encouraged and cultivated the types of theoretical practices willfully engaged in by the Frankfurt scholars. This is why they have earned a place in the bourgeois pantheon of great thinkers.

It is the anti-imperialist Marxist perspective that brings this into view and offers a dialectical and historical materialist account of Western Marxism and its principal function within the objective social world. This approach is more rigorously materialist and dialectical because it does not naively assume, for instance, that the Frankfurt School is simply an autonomous theoretical tradition whose ideas have evolved independently of material reality, or only within the naturalized parameters of bourgeois historical narratives. Instead, it is a product of the social totality of international class struggle, which needs to be understood to fully elucidate the history of the Institute for Social Research. Anti-imperialist Marxism—which is ultimately just Marxism in its universal form, at least as it manifests itself in our era—thereby has the distinct advantage of being able to situate the particularity of Western Marxism within the international world war on communism and the history of intellectual imperialism, thereby elucidating its fundamental contributions to the world historical struggle between capitalism and socialism.

Making an Imperial Commodity Out of Marxism

What is now happening to Marx's theory has, in the course of history, happened repeatedly to the theories of revolutionary thinkers and leaders of oppressed classes fighting for emancipation. . . . After their death, attempts are made to convert them into harmless icons, to canonize them, so to say, and to hallow their *names* to a certain extent for the "consolation" of the oppressed classes and with the object of duping the latter, while at the same time robbing the revolutionary theory of its *substance*, blunting its revolutionary edge and vulgarizing it.

—V. I. LENIN[2]

2. V. I. Lenin, *Collected Works*, vol. 25 (Moscow: Progress Publishers, 1964), 385.

The capitalist class and the imperial superstructure have contributed to the development of the commodified version of anticommunist Marxism known as Western or cultural Marxism. Severed for the most part from practical, progressive political struggles, it significantly alters some of the fundamental tenets of Marxism in becoming little more than a consumer product of the imperial theory industry, meaning an ideologically infused commodity for the professional managerial class stratum in the imperial core and their comprador collaborators in the periphery.

This is one of the most important features of Western or cultural Marxism, which includes but also far surpasses the Frankfurt School. By concretely abstracting from specific discourses in order to identify their overall ideological orientation, in spite of some partial exceptions, we can identify additional characteristics.[3] To begin with, as a theoretical practice, Western Marxism is founded on the primacy of theory, rather than practice, and it generally shuns organized progressive politics and repudiates socialist states in favor of engaging in theoretical debates and the analysis of bourgeois cultural products. The point, for the Western Marxists, is not to change the world, but to interpret it, or sometimes even just to interpret texts or other cultural products instead of having to deal with the real world. Their theoretical practice is oriented primarily toward exchange-value, not use-value, in the sense that they are engaged in the symbolic economy of the academic world and the so-called marketplace of ideas, not in a collective, practical project of social transformation. As a result, they are invested in brand management, and their discourses are replete with idiosyncratic conceptual vocabularies, extensive bourgeois cultural references, trendy rhetoric, theoretical obscurantism, and intellectual eclecticism.

Methodologically, Western Marxists are revisionists who attempt to transform some of the fundamental tenets of dialectical and historical materialism (DHM). They generally reject Marxist materialist ontology and the dialectics of nature, and they focus on cultural criticism at the expense of political economy. This severely limits the scope and depth of their analyses, and there is a widespread tendency to assume that culture and the world of ideas constitute the driving forces of history, not class struggle. This idealism often goes hand in hand with utopian—rather than scientific—socialism. In other words, if they actually defend

---

3. On this topic, also see John Bellamy Foster and Gabriel Rockhill, "Western Marxism and Imperialism: A Dialogue," *Monthly Review*, Vol. 76, No. 10 (March 2025).

revolutionary socialism in any form, it is almost exclusively socialism in theory, not in practice.[4]

The bourgeois idea that only art, culture, or theory can save us—not revolutionary class struggle—is one of the leitmotifs of their discourse. This over-inflation of the superstructural expresses a self-aggrandizing assessment of the role of professional intellectuals like themselves and reflects their petty-bourgeois class standing. Unsurprisingly, given the inability of art and culture to save us, they simultaneously insulate themselves against revolutionary social transformations that would shake the foundations of their class position within the imperial core. Instead of orienting their readers toward social change, then, they indulge in a self-fulfilling prophecy of defeatism, often accompanied by leftwing melancholia. When they do try to identify a political exit to the quagmire of consumer capitalism, which they bemoan and sometimes incisively criticize, they generally engage in third-way politics, meaning the classic petty-bourgeois belief that there is a magical third way beyond capitalism and actually existing socialism. This can come in the form of a new idea or a messianic opening of the heavens, on the one hand, or on the other, in more terrestrial form, a popular movement or jacquerie that rejects the status quo. However, they eschew the disciplined forms of hierarchical organization and strategic planning identified with communism. This helps guarantee that their defeatist convictions will be confirmed: you will never be able to change the world if you think this only requires a new-fangled theory or you are waiting on divine intervention, nor will you ever succeed politically if you assume that an unorganized popular revolt can magically win against extremely well-funded, highly organized, and militarized imperialist states with extensive expertise in counter-insurgency, as well as the most powerful propaganda network in the history of humanity to back them up.

The specific ideological coordinates of Western Marxism include, first and foremost, a rejection of actually existing socialism. Many Western Marxists are opposed to organized revolutionary politics across the board, which includes the party form and the very idea of seizing state power. If

---

4. Some Western Marxists support social democracy, usually without a full contextualization of the history of imperialism, the real-world socialist alternative, and the role of social-democratic class compromises in shoring up imperialism over and against socialism. Tactical support for social-democratic reforms within an overall strategy of socialist transformation can, of course, make perfect sense in certain cases, but this is not the same thing as embracing (capitalist and imperialist) social democracy as the strategic objective.

they are not simply liberals, they tend to be, in practical terms, very close to anarchists. They often fall back on simplistic moralizing approaches that naively advocate for horizontalist democracy and criticize all forms of domination, rather than thinking in politically strategic terms about how to structurally modify society over the long term in order to make democracy truly universal and substantive. They thus tend not to be strategic thinkers who recognize that the dialectics of socialism sometimes requires tactics that might appear to contradict the overall goal, but are the only way of advancing socialism in the real world. Finally, if given the choice between communism and capitalism, Western Marxists practically side with the latter over and against the former. Despite their criticisms of capitalism, some of which are well founded, they tend to be anticommunist capitalist accommodationists.

The overall effect of Western Marxism has been the global promotion of a petty-bourgeois cultural commodity with little use-value for practical struggles over and against the collective and innovative science of liberation known as DHM. Since the latter has proven its ability to practically transform the world by breaking the chains of imperialism, it is clearly, from the vantage point of the ruling class, the most dangerous theoretical weapon of class struggle. Because it has not been able to eradicate it outright, the bourgeoisie has worked with elements of the bourgeois state and the bourgeois cultural apparatus to cultivate a commodified version of Marxism that can spread the virus of anticommunism under the cover of a red-colored pill. This has produced an imperious industry of ineffective academic discourses that are promoted around the globe as the vanguard of Marxist theory, but which, practically speaking, serve to misdirect, confuse, or simply alienate those in search of a rigorous theoretical guide to understanding and transforming the world.

The primary purpose of undertaking an extensive dialectical critique of Western or cultural Marxism, thereby demonstrating that it is ultimately imperial Marxism, has been to provide people with the knowledge necessary for them to orient themselves in the intellectual world war, figure out what side they are on, and advance in the most coherent direction. Since this has been more of a subtext throughout the analysis, let us conclude, then, by indicating that direction by briefly outlining the principal features of anti-imperialist Marxism.

AIM: Anti-Imperialist Marxism

Anti-imperialist Marxism has not been promoted by the imperial theory industry, which has instead demoted and often demonized it, or at least repackaged it to try and make it look like something different. It is oriented, first and foremost, toward changing the world, instead of merely interpreting it. In this regard, it maintains what Lenin referred to as the "revolutionary core" of Marxism, which revisionists of various stripes have tried to gut. In this sense, anti-imperialist Marxism is Marxism *tout court*, or Marxism in the era of imperialism that is unaltered by those who have tried to eliminate its essence. It might also be said, more generally, that whereas Western Marxism is a particular cultural permutation or perversion, which would best be described as imperial Marxism (indicating both its source and its ideological orientation), the Marxism dedicated to anticolonial and anti-imperialist emancipation is universal Marxism.

DHM of this sort developed in opposition to the capitalist class and bourgeois states, through popular struggles and the fight from below. As Lenin insightfully argued, drawing on Marx, revolutionary politics requires that segments of the bourgeois intelligentsia commit class suicide and ally with the working class, thereby contributing developed forms of scientific analysis that require training and expertise beyond what the working class is generally given access to under capitalism. However, the class basis of DHM is in the working and oppressed peoples of the world, and particularly those that have been the most exploited in the colonial periphery, not the intellectual labor aristocracy à la imperial Marxism.

DHM is firmly grounded in the primacy of practice. It is an evolving, collective tradition of analyzing and intervening in the world, and it is therefore, of necessity, a practical process of learning. Rather than exchange-value, it is use-value that guides it insofar as it strives to provide the most rigorous, coherent, and systematic understanding of concrete reality and how to change it. What is often fetishized in imperial Marxism is theoretical innovation for its own sake, and practical Marxism is commonly denigrated for being reductivist, dogmatic, orthodox, and so forth. Although there have sometimes been elements of this sort operative in particular movements, many of which have been correctly criticized and practically overcome by anti-imperialist Marxists, the expansive international history of DHM has been one characterized by significant innovations, impressive levels of creativity, highly refined and dialectical analyses, extremely perceptive strategic and tactical calculations, savvy practical solutions, and, in general, a successful charting of uncharted territory.

This does not mean that there have not been major mistakes and setbacks, as well as conflicts and disagreements. The path to developing socialism in the real world has been tortuous and complicated, to say the least. However, this is the price one has to pay if you are not operating in the purportedly pristine world of pure ideas. When you are developing socialism in the real world, you are tasked with creating something that has never existed before, and you have to do it under conditions of constant imperialist aggression. There has never been a single instance where socialism has been allowed to develop on its own.[5] We have only known socialism under siege, as Michael Parenti emphasized, never socialism set free. This has meant that socialists have had to be extremely innovative and open to an ongoing process of practical readjustment, as well as, when necessary, honest and humble self-critique.

Let us cite a few examples, using the names of individuals with the full recognition that they are figures who embodied the collective struggle of the masses. Lenin is such a titan in the world socialist movement, not only because he led the first successful socialist revolution, but also because he situated the anti-imperialist struggle at the very heart of socialist state-building projects by recognizing that the class struggle, in an imperialist world, primarily takes the form of a national struggle of liberation from imperialism. Drawing on Lenin, Mao Zedong adapted this lesson and others to the specificities of underdeveloped, agrarian China, with its large peasant population. Ho Chi Minh incorporated Lenin's insights into the liberation struggle in Vietnam, which was woefully underdeveloped by colonialism and then became a major target of imperialist warfare for decades, bringing a whole series of additional problems that needed to be dealt with through a protracted people's war. Fidel Castro and Ernesto Che Guevara drew on these lessons and others to engage in guerrilla warfare, organize the peasantry, and bring socialism to the Western Hemisphere on an island just ninety miles from the U.S. empire. Thomas Sankara, operating in a very different context, organized radical elements of the military to coordinate a takeover of the state in Upper Volta, backed by a popular uprising. In all of these cases, and many more that could be cited, there was not a blueprint for revolution or an orthodox doctrine to be applied. Instead, there was a rich collective tradition that provided a holistic worldview and an archive of experience to draw on, but everything concrete needed to be invented in each case and adapted to new and changing situations. Innovation was of the essence, but not for its own

---

5. See William Blum, *Killing Hope: US Military and CIA Interventions since World War II* (London: Zed Books, 2014), esp. 7–20.

sake or in a theoretical vacuum, but rather to solve practical problems and chart new territory. This is the real task of DHM: to construct a new world out of the ruins of the old.

The practical orientation of DHM has led to a refined understanding of the relationship between tactics and strategy in what we can refer to as the dialectics of socialism.[6] Lenin provided one of the most succinct and insightful metaphors for understanding it. He described a scene in which a mountain climber, seeking to access a summit that had never before been attained, was "forced to turn back, descend, seek another path, longer, perhaps, but one that [would] . . . enable him to reach the summit."[7] At a safe distance, people below watched his movements through a telescope and maligned him for failing to attain his goal. Some gleefully celebrated his lack of success and denounced him as a lunatic, hoping he would fall, whereas others concealed their joy and feigned sorrow over the fact that the poor soul had not awaited the completion of their well-thought-out plan for scaling the mountain. They all agreed, however, that what they saw before their eyes was a clear case of failure.

The onlookers in this metaphor rely on sense-perception to arrive at their conclusion. What they saw was a mountain climber turning back from the summit and descending. What they lacked was understanding: since the climber could not advance on the chosen path, the only possible way of making it to the summit was to descend and find another way forward. This text was written eleven months after the promulgation of the New Economic Policy (NEP) in March 1921, which temporarily introduced "a free market and capitalism, both subject to state control."[8] As becomes clear in the final paragraph of Lenin's article, the climber he described was a metaphorical representation of the Soviets who had enacted the NEP, which Lenin described as "our retreat, our 'descent.'"[9] The leader of the Russian Revolution thereby provided us with a metaphorical depiction of the dialectics of socialism: what appears to sense-perception as a step backward is, at the level of the understanding, simply a necessary maneuver in order to successfully advance toward the overall objective.

---

6. The paragraphs that follow draw on Gabriel Rockhill, "Lenin and the Dialectics of Socialism," *World Marxist Review*, Vol. 4, No. 4 (2025).

7. V. I. Lenin, "Notes of a Publicist," in *Collected Works*, Vol. 33 (Moscow: Progress Publishers, 1966), 204.

8. V. I. Lenin, "The Role and Functions of the Trade Unions Under the New Economic Policy," in *Collected Works*, Vol. 33, 184.

9. V. I. Lenin, "Notes of a Publicist," 211.

Sense-perception is the lowest level of socialist consciousness. It simply consists in looking at the world and comparing it to a picture in one's mind, without necessarily understanding the nature of the world or the struggles at hand. This reductive approach is characteristic of imperial—and imperious—Marxists, and their analysis of socialism usually consists in comparing a preconceived image of socialism or communism to what they perceive in the world, which is powerfully mediated by the ideological propaganda that they consume via the bourgeois media and academic world. The dialectics of socialism requires that one moves to the higher level of understanding, which necessitates making a clear distinction between tactics and strategy. Tactics are the short-term maneuvers necessary to advance toward the strategy, or the ultimate goal. As Lenin made clear, tactics sometimes appear to contradict the strategy. After all, if someone sees a mountain climber descending, why would they assume that this is a tactic for attaining the summit? In the same manner, if someone perceives socialist countries that introduce market elements under state control in order to foster necessary development, why would they think that this is the path to communism?

The answer is to be found at a higher level of socialist consciousness than sense-perception. At this level, it becomes clear that the material nature of the world is such that certain tactics, which appear to amateur eyes to be forms of retreat, are actually necessary steps backward in order to make leaps forward. The faster socialist countries can establish their sovereignty and develop their productive forces, the quicker they are going to be able to—if they stay on the socialist path—move to the next level and work through these contradictions because they are no longer simply struggling for survival. This does not mean that one has to simply accept any and all tactics that wave the flag of socialism. It is important, in this regard, that social struggle continues under socialism, and that socialist projects have engaged in different tactics for dealing with imperialism and responding to the need to develop. We can, and should, critically assess the relative successes or failures of specific tactics, which is part of the ongoing, collective process of practical learning.

The apex of socialist consciousness is not understanding but applied practical reason or praxis, which goes hand in hand, of course, with the recognition that practice is the ultimate arbiter of truth. This is what will clarify what works or does not. In the case of the mountain climber, did his apparent descent lead to his practical success in scaling the mountain, or at least making it to the next plateau? In the case of socialism, have these apparent steps backward allowed socialist countries to advance toward the strategy over time, even if it takes decades? If not, what can be learned from this backtracking, and what other viable paths forward exist? There are no perfect blueprints for producing socialism; there is only an archive of experience and a practical process of learning that advances, in part, through trial and error. This is one of the reasons that it is so important for socialists to learn from their mistakes, or those of others, in order to collectively figure out how best to scale the mountain, thereby accomplishing practical tasks that have never been done before.

For such a gargantuan undertaking, the holistic, scientific, innovative, and practically oriented approach of DHM is necessary. By contrast, imperial Marxism has remained woefully underdeveloped. It lacks practical knowledge of how to build socialism, and it does not grasp the dialectics of development. Instead, it traffics in the most simplistic and reductivist accounts of actually existing socialism, and it dogmatically adheres to its own—ideologically conditioned—theoretical assumptions. It remains duped, moreover, by the propaganda pumped out by the imperial superstructure, to which it makes its own academic contributions. The choice between the two is stark because DHM leads to the difficult, collective project of building the preliminary forms of socialism out of the ruins of capitalism, whereas imperial Marxism seeks to reinforce these ruins—thereby consolidating the class standing of those intellectuals supported by them—while attacking those on the other path.

Class struggle in theory is so polarized because these two positions are ultimately grounded in two different practical orientations in a historical conjuncture where the stakes of class struggle are arguably higher than at any point in history. As discussed in the introduction to this book, imperialism has driven us to the age of exterminism, where it is now undeniable that its continuation will lead to the end of humanity, and possibly the entire biosphere. If human beings and life on Earth are to have a future, it is necessary to develop a socioeconomic system that breaks with the one that is leading to annihilation, which is the one that is ultimately supported by imperial Marxism.

There is no doubt that this is an extremely difficult task, one that requires heightened levels of creativity, intelligence, hard work, practical ingenuity, self-critique, sacrifice, humility, collaboration, strategic thinking, and much more. Everyone has their role to play, wherever they are in the world, and whatever contribution they might be able to make, regardless of how small or large. It is the greatest struggle of our times, for it is the fight for our collective future. We are all situated in it, whether we choose to be or not, and we need to bring as many people over to our side as possible if we are going to win. The intellectual world war is but one of the skirmishes in this overall class struggle for the future of the world and for the path of humanity's development—or not—on planet Earth. Nevertheless, it is extremely important because its outcome determines the horizons of people's consciousness and how they orient themselves in the world. If one conclusion can be drawn from this book, it is that, in relationship to the commodified forms of Marxism promoted by the imperial superstructure, we have nothing but our intellectual chains to lose, and we have a world to win!

APPENDIX

INTRODUCTION

This appendix provides a small yet revealing sample of the extensive historical documentation that underpins this study, offering the reader a window into
the archival records that were consulted. These include thousands of pages of
unpublished documents obtained through scores of Freedom of Information
Act (FOIA) requests, as well as documentation available through numerous digital archives and the following archival collections:

- National Archives and Records Administration in Washingto, D.C.
- Dwight D. Eisenhower Presidential Library in Abilene, Kansas
- Rockefeller Archive Center in Sleepy Hollow, New York
- Hanna Holborn Gray Special Collections Research Center at the University
  of Chicago (location of the International Association for Cultural Freedom
  Records, including those of the Congress for Cultural Freedom)
- Tamiment Library at New York University (location of the American
  Committee for Cultural Freedom Papers)

The appendix also includes a collection of photographs, primarily from
archives, which allows the reader to identify some of the key actors involved in
the intellectual world war, while also providing a sense of the nature and scope
of their activities.

DOCUMENTS

1. *"Ideological Warfare,"* May 16, 1952, the CIA FOIA Electronic Reading Room,
   *https://www.cia.gov/readingroom/document/cia-rdp80-01065a0001000
   10006-0.*

The United States Psychological Strategy Board (PSB) was established in
1951 to oversee and coordinate the psychological warfare operations of the
State Department, the Central Intelligence Agency (CIA), military services,
and other government agencies. Although it was short-lived, it laid the foundations for many aspects of the international psywar on communism. This
memorandum is of particular interest for at least two reasons. First, it insists
on the importance of producing and promoting "attacks against Communist
ideology developed *in Marxist terms,"* including assaults on "basic premises"
like materialism and dialectics, as well as attacks on "the Stalinist deteriora-
tion of Marx, *again in Marxian terms, but on the assumption that the basic
premises are correct."* Similarly, it advocates for a "defense of Western society *in Marxist terms"* that targets "intellectuals everywhere" who have been
infected by a Marxist worldview (my emphases). The objective was clearly
to allow intellectuals influenced by Marxism—a widespread phenomenon at
the time—to retain their Marxism through a process of transmogrification
that would ultimately make it compatible with anticommunism and capitalist accommodation (at a minimum). Second, this memo sheds light on the
importance of having the state directly but covertly involved in subsidizing the production and distribution of publications along these lines. These
strategies help explain the bourgeois state's financial support for anticommunist Marxist discourses that accommodate capitalism and sometimes
openly support imperialism, which is a key feature of Western Marxism,
and much of the Frankfurt School more specifically.

[DOCUMENTS REPRODUCED ON PAGES 345–48]

16 May 1952

25X1A

MEMORANDUM FOR: LT. COL. ███████████
                         PSYCHOLOGICAL STRATEGY BOARD

SUBJECT   : Ideological Warfare

1. The following remarks are addressed toward a further
focusing on the problem of how to proceed with the development
of an ideological offensive.

2. First, a few comments on the Kennedy paper. I found
it very stimulating and comprehensive. In fact, I found it to
cover a large area of the cold war — only a portion of it seems
to be directed to the specific subject of ideological warfare.
The heart of the matter is, to quote Kennedy, that "we cannot
expect to subvert the enemy if we cannot even speak his language."
This point is substantiated later on where it is indicated that
in order to promote splits within the Party, "we must employ
Marxian terms of reference." It is interesting to observe in
connection with our particular problem that most of the specific
comments in this excellent paper do not adhere to this basic
premise. I think it would be helpful in defining the problem
to comment on this point. A psychoanalysis description of
Stalin, explaining his actions on the base of his subconscious
hate of the father image, might have very effective results in
the United States, perhaps elsewhere in Western Europe, but
probably have very little impact within the USSR where the very
subject of psychology, especially Freudian psychology, is
verboten. Similarly, the analogy between the USSR and a prison
is a very apt one and can be put to good use in the psychological
offensive, but does not represent a form of ideological attack.

3. I labor these points only to show how difficult it is
for even politically sophisticated Americans to think in terms
of Communist ideology with any facility.

4. For the purpose of this problem I suggest we adopt a
rather narrow definition of terms. If for these purposes
ideology is defined as "the basic beliefs motivating a social

system," our

system," our ideological warfare should have this basic content:

    a.   Attacks against Communist ideology developed in Marxist terms. This attack would have two main divisions: (1) attacks against the basic premises of the system, i.e. materialism, dialectics, etc.; and (2) attacks against the Stalinist deterioration of Marx, again in Marxian terms, but on the assumption that the basic premises are correct. This type of attack is a universal one in that it would reach members of international Communist movements everywhere.

    b.   Attacks against the existing Communist system, both its fundamental premises and acts of ideological practices in colloquial terms for every area in which the Communist movement has any importance. The aim of this attack would be to immunize potential converts who have not received any Marxist indoctrination from Communist propaganda. (The exposure literature against Communism which has appeared in this country since 1945 represents an effective example of this type of ideological counter-attack. It has been remarkably successful.)

    c.   Defense of Western society in Marxist terms. This defense would be addressed to intellectuals everywhere who have been so indoctrinated in Marxist terms that their whole political and sociological language is to a large degree Marxist. To illustrate this type of ideological task, we might consider a booklet recently published by the U. S. Chamber of Commerce entitled "Profits." This booklet attempts to set out in lay language that anyone can understand the "hows" and "whys" of the profit system. A Marxist defense of the American system, on the other hand, would show how the surplus values of our productive system have been progressively distributed in ever greater amounts to the workers rather than concentrated in the hands of a few grasping capitalists. This would be a much more effective eye-opener abroad than anything published by the U. S. Chamber of Commerce.

    d.   A defense of Western society, written in the vernacular to act as an antidote in overseas areas where the Communists are attacking the basic system.

    e.   As an example of type content of the ideological attack written in Marxist terms, see Tab A.

               5.   Production of ideological

SECRET

SECURITY INFORMATION

5. Production of ideological ammunition. One of the first
tasks to be accomplished is to survey the existing field of books
that have already been written that could fit into one of these
four categories. Souvarine's "Stalin" comes to mind as one such
book, but there are many others. We should find out what circulation such works have received, and as part of the problem of
distributing, see that these books are revised, popularized and
given intensive distribution.

6. The next thing we must do is to shape up in some detail
the type of additional books that should be written in the United
States, but primarily abroad to cover as many aspects as possible
of the problem. The next task is to survey the field of potential
authors of appropriate books, pamphlets, articles, etc. It is the
consensus of most people that this enterprise will be worthwhile
only if the books (articles, etc.) themselves have high sponsorship
and are superbly done. We have it within our means to stimulate
the production of such books by competent foreign authors.

7. Distribution. It is the general consensus that insofar
as possible, normal existing outlets should be used for this purpose.
There is much greater authenticity and credence in a book having the
stamp of an internationally known publishing house than in those
published by new or relatively unknown concerns. It is believed
that most of these books, if well written, can find a publisher on
their own. It may be, however, that the actual writing of them
may have to be subsidized in certain cases. It is generally
believed that the distribution of any large quantities of these books
— and our aim should be to get them into every library and every
discussion center of every critical area — may have to be supported.
The USIS has, of course, done very useful work in this field, but its
selection of titles may not have been made with this purpose in
mind.

8. The subject of distribution should, of course, involve
more than books. Consideration might be given to the publication
of a journal sponsored by one of the more prominent anti-Communist
international organizations. Such a journal would, of course, not
be controlled by any government. But its editorial and news contents could emphasize ideological factors and be slanted to defend
the Western cause. There is also the problem of stimulating the
writing of substantial articles on various facets of the ideological
struggle in existing publications.

9. The distribution problems are not insoluble, but they
will require a carefully worked out plan.

10. Procedure

-3-

Approved For Release 1999/09/27 : CIA-RDP80-01065A000100010006-0
SECURITY INFORMATION

      10. Procedure. What the Psychological Strategy Board can
do with regard to this effort is (1) to give its official seal of
approval to the necessity for waging an ideological offensive,
(2) help delineate the substance and boundaries of such an offensive, and (3) charge the appropriate agencies with certain missions
with regard to this offensive. In connection with the question of
developing various aspects of this problem, I am attaching at
Tab B a memorandum prepared for you by Mr. ████████ with 25X1A
reference to the problem of procedure.

                             25X1A ████████

Attached:
  Tab A
  Tab B

2. *Psychological Strategy Board, Report on U.S. Doctrinal Program, June 29,
    1953, Edward P. Lilly Papers, Box 54, Folder Doctrinal Programs 1953 (3),
    Dwight D. Eisenhower Library, 1–2.*

The opening pages of this report lay out the fundamental objectives of the
U.S. Doctrinal Program, which sought to weaken and ideally destroy communist "doctrine," meaning its overall ideological worldview, while shoring up support for the doctrine of the so-called Free World. This document
is notable for its insistence on fomenting schisms, doubts, and confusion
among Communists, while promoting the idea that the Free World embraces
a diversity of opinions. It also specifically foregrounds the need for material
support for the production and distribution of theoretical materials among
"intellectuals, including scholars and opinion-forming groups."

[DOCUMENTS REPRODUCED ON PAGES 349–50]

PSB D-33
Jun 29, 1953

U. S. DOCTRINAL PROGRAM

1. Psychological Objectives for a U. S. Doctrinal Program

(a) The U.S. Doctrinal Program (as defined in Annex "A") will seek, by providing permanent literature and by fostering long-term intellectual movements, which will appeal to intellectuals, including scholars and opinion-forming groups, to:

  (1) break down world-wide doctrinaire thought patterns which have provided an intellectual basis for Communism and other doctrines hostile to American and Free World objectives.

  (2) foster a world-wide understanding and sympathetic acceptance of the traditions and viewpoints of America and the Free World.

(b) The U.S. Doctrinal Program (as defined in Annex "A") will seek to achieve the following results:

  (1) increase among target groups a realistic understanding of the Communist threat.

  (2) further general understanding and encourage acceptance for the traditions and viewpoints of the U. S. and the Free World.

  (3) pave the way for deviations from, and schisms in, totalitarian thought patterns by stimulating intellectual curiosity and free thought on political, scientific and economic subjects.

  (4) create confusion, doubts and loss of confidence in the accepted thought patterns of convinced Communists, captive careerists, including the managerial and military groups, and others under Communist influence susceptible to doctrinal appeals.

PSB D-33

Jun 29, 1953

(5) weaken objectively the intellectual appeal of other doctrines which may be hostile or inimical to American objectives, e.g., extreme nationalism in some areas, dangerous neutralism in others, or rampant racialism, and to
foster among such adherents a basic understanding of the
traditions of America and the Free World.

2. Basic Principles

(a) A fundamental characteristic of America and the Free World is
the diversity of its doctrines and philosophies. The U. S. Doctrinal
Program does not envisage an attempt to channel these diversities into
one particular doctrine, but the Program is an effort to develop a means
to make better known to the specific target groups the traditions and
viewpoints of America and the Free World.

(b) To be effective, this U.S. Doctrinal Program requires the interdepartmental development of:

(1) long-range plans for the production and distribution of
intellectual materials and for the direction of activities aimed separately and concurrently at appealing to
intellectuals, including scholars and opinion-forming
groups.

(2) provocative and stimulating doctrinal materials which critically and effectively analyze Communist doctrines, as well
as those objectively setting forth the viewpoints of
America and the Free World.

(3) improve distribution mechanisms for permanent literature,
not only American, but also foreign materials.

(c) Government control over the production of most overt material
will be kept to the minimum. Control over the production of other materials must be flexible and not restrictive.

of 3 pages

3. *Congress for Cultural Freedom brochure published in Paris in 1963, International Association for Cultural Freedom, Box 319, Folder 4, Hanna Holborn Gray Special Collections Research Center at the University of Chicago, excerpts.*

The Congress for Cultural Freedom (CCF), an international organization headquartered in Paris and explicitly dedicated to promoting the supposed liberties of the West, was "one of the most important artistic patrons in world history, sponsoring an unprecedented range of cultural activities" (Hugh Wilford, *The Mighty Wurlitzer: How the CIA Played America*, Cambridge, MA: Harvard University Press, 2008, 101–2). Almost every intellectual and cultural producer in Western Europe was affected by it in some way, according to Frances Stonor Saunders, and many were directly involved in its activities, including figures like Theodor Adorno, Hannah Arendt, Raymond Aron, and Max Horkheimer (see Frances Stonor Saunders, *The Cultural Cold War: The CIA and the World of Arts and Letters*, New York: New Press, 2000, 2). Far from being a free organization celebrating intellectual and cultural liberty, as its manifesto maintains, the CCF was a psychological warfare operation run by the CIA, with funding from the capitalist ruling class through the Ford, Rockefeller, and other foundations. This brochure gives a sense of the breadth and intensity of its activities, some of the intellectuals involved, as well as the extensive coverage they received in the bourgeois media.

[DOCUMENTS REPRODUCED ON PAGES 352–60]

ERNST   REUTER.   1889-1953
Mayor of West Berlin, 1947-1953
Chairman, Founding Committee,
Congress for Cultural Freedom

JACQUES MARITAIN

JAYAPRAKASH NARAYAN

SALVADOR DE MADARIAGA

HONORARY

PRESIDENTS

KARL JASPERS

REINHOLD NIEBUHR

LÉOPOLD S. SENGHOR

THEODOR HEUSS

Major Conferences and Seminars

1950	June	BERLIN	Founding Conference
—	November	BRUSSELS	International Conference
1951	March	BOMBAY	First Asian Conference on Cultural Freedom
1952	May	PARIS	Masterpieces of the XXth Century
1953	July	HAMBURG	Science and Freedom (Co-sponsored by University of Hamburg)
1954	April	ROME	Music of the XXth Century (Co-sponsored by European Cultural Centre and Italian Radio)
1955	February	RANGOON	Second Asian Conference on Cultural Freedom (Co-sponsored by the Society for the Extension of Democratic Ideals)
—	September	MILAN	The Future of Freedom
1956	September	MEXICO CITY	Inter-American Conference on Cultural Freedom
1957	April	TOKYO	Problems of Economic Growth
—	June	OXFORD	Changes in Soviet Society (Co-sponsored by St. Antony's College, Oxford)
1958	September	VIENNA	Workers' Participation in Management (Co-sponsored by the Austrian College, Austrian Productivity Centre, Austrian Council for Economy and the College for World Trade)
—	October	RHODES	Representative Government and Public Liberties in the New States
1959	January	CALCUTTA	Belief and Literature (Sponsored by Quest Magazine)
—	Jan.-Feb.	KARACHI	Islam in the Modern World
—	March	IBADAN	Representative Government and National Progress (Co-sponsored by the University College, Ibadan)
—	April	TUNIS	Freedom and Responsibility—The Role of the Scholar in Society (Sponsored by the Committee on Science and Freedom and the Free University of Tunis)
—	September	BASLE	Industrial Society and the Western Political Dialogue
1960	February	BEIRUT	The Traditional Legal Systems in the Arab World and their Interaction with Modern Change
—	June	BERLIN	Progress in Freedom; A Discussion of Human Ideals in Modern Society
—	August	CANBERRA	Constitutionalism in Asia (Co-sponsored by the International Commission of Jurists)
—	September	COPENHAGEN	The Writer and the Welfare State (Sponsored by Perspektiv Magazine)
—	November	MANILA	Drama in the Philippines (Co-sponsored by the Philippine Normal College)
—	December	CAIRO	The New Metropolis in the Arab World (Co-sponsored by the Egyptian Society of Engineers)
1961	January	KHARTOUM	Tradition and Change—Problems of Progress (Co-sponsored by the University of Khartoum)
—	January	POONA	Paths to Economic Growth (Co-sponsored by Gokhale Institute of Politics and Economics)
—	February	NEW DELHI	South and South-East Asia Have a Second Look at Democracy (Co-sponsored by the Indian Institute of Public Administration)
—	April-May	TOKYO	East-West Music Encounter (Co-sponsored by the Tokyo Metropolitan Government and the Society for International Culture Exchange)

18

1961	June	DACCA	The Writer and his Social Responsibilty (Co-sponsored by the Pakistan P.E.N.)
—	July	GENEVA	Contemporary History in the Soviet Mirror (Sponsored by Survey Magazine and the Institut Universitaire de Hautes Etudes Internationales)
—	October	ROME	The Arab Writer and the Modern World (Co-sponsored by Tempo Presente and the Istituto per l'Oriente)
—	December	FREETOWN	Inter-University Cooperation (Co-sponsored by Fourah Bay College)
1962	June	KAMPALA	All-African Writers Conference (Sponsored by Mbari Writers and Artists Club and Makerere University College)

Among Participants in Congress Activities :

ALGERIA
Mouloud Mammarie
Kateb Yacine

ARGENTINA
Jorge Luis Borges
Americo Ghioldi
Roberto Giusti
Victoria Ocampo
Francisco Romero
Juan Antonio Solari

AUSTRALIA
Sir John Latham

AUSTRIA
Benedikt Kautsky
Lise Meitner
Hans Thirring

BELGIUM
Henri Janne

BRAZIL
Gilberto Freyre
Afranio Coutinho
Erico Verissimo

BURMA
Chan Htoon
Kyaw Nyein

CAMEROUN
Mongo Betti
Abel Eyinga
Bernard Fonlon

CEYLON
Gamani Corea
C. R. Hensman
E. R. Sarathchandra
S. Soedjatmoko

CHILE
Jaime Castillo
Amanda Labarca
Alejandro Magnet

COLOMBIA
German Arciniegas
Eduardo Santos

CONGO (BRAZZAVILLE)
Patrice Lhoni
Jean Malonga

CONGO (LEOPOLDVILLE)
Cyrille Adoula
Emmanuel Kimbimbi
Patrice Lumumba

CUBA
Pedro Vicente Aja
Mario Llerena
Jorge Manach

DAHOMEY
Alexandre Adande
Ignacio Pinto

DENMARK
T. Nyboe Andersen
Karl Bjarnhof
Frode Jakobsen
Steen Eiler Rasmussen

ETHIOPIA
Yawand-Wossen Mangasha

FINLAND
Bo Carpelan
Kai Laitinen
Heikki Waris

FRANCE
Raymond Aron
Gaston Berger
Robert Buron
Jean Cassou
Jean Cocteau
Jean-Maire Domenach
Pierre Emmanuel
Georges Friedmann
Bertrand de Jouvenel
André Malraux
André Philip
David Rousset
Manès Sperber
Germaine Tillion

GERMANY
Willy Brandt
Otto Hahn
Theodor Heuss
Max Horkheimer
Eugen Kogon
Max von Laue
Wolfgang Leonhard
Theodor Litt
Helmuth Plessner
Ernst Reuter
Carlo Schmid

Bruno Snell
J. Ch. Witsch

GHANA
K.A. Busia
Seth Cudjoe
Modjaben Dowuona
K.A.B. Jones-Quartey

GREECE
Gregory Cassimatis
C.A. Doxiadis

ICELAND
Bjarni Benediktsson
Gunnar Gunnarsson

INDIA
Buddhadeva Bose
Sudhin Datta
C.D. Deshmukh
D.R. Gadgil
A.D. Gorwala
Acharya Kripalani
Daya Krishna
Raj Krishna
Minoo Masani
Asoka Mehta
Lakshmi Menon
A.K. Mukerji
Jayaprakash Narayar.
N.A. Nikam
Raja Rao
Dr. Sampurnanand
Frank Thakurdas
Burra Venkatappian

INDONESIA
Takdir Alisjahbana
Mochtar Lubis
Sutan Sjahrir

IRAK
Badr Al-Sayab
Jabra Ibrahim Jabra

IRAN
Davoud Rassai
S.R. Shafaq
B. Tabatabei

ISRAEL
Nathan ben-Nathan
S.N. Eisenstadt
J.L. Talmon

19

ITALY
Carlo Antoni
Nicola Chiaromonte
Virgilio Ferrari
Gianfrancesco Malipiero
Adriano Olivetti
Ernesto Rossi
Ignazio Silone
Altiero Spinelli
Lionello Venturi

IVORY COAST
Bernard Dadié

JAPAN
Sadao Bekku
Kentaro Hayashi
Taiko Hirabayashi
Masmaichi Inoki
Michiaki Kawakita
Takeyasu Kimura
Tomoo Odaka
Zengo Ohira
Yoshihiko Seki
Michio Takeyama
Kenzo Takayanagi

JORDAN
Ahmed M. Dakhgan
Issa El Naoury

KOREA
Cho Ji-hoon
Kwon Nyong-dae
Lee Hye-ku
Oh Chong-shik
Suh Suk-soon

LEBANON
Jamil Jabre
Kamal Jumblat
Ahmad Makki
Khalil Sarkis

LIBERIA
Henry Cole

MEXICO
Salvador Azuela
Mauricio Magdaleno
Alfonso Reyes

MOROCCO
Mohammed Lahbabi
Mohammed El Fassi

NETHERLANDS
J.H. Bavinck
Hendryk Brugmans

NIGERIA
S.L. Akintola
Sabiru Biobaku
Ayo Ogunsheye
Wole Soyinka
Jaja Wachuku

NORWAY
Haakon Lie

PAKISTAN
Hatim Alavi
Syed Ali Ahsan
Moinuddin Baqai
A.K. Brohi
Mahmud Hussain

Javid Iqbal
M.L. Qureshi

PERU
Victor Raul Haya de la Torre
Luis-Alberto Sanchez

PHILIPPINES
Raul Manglapus

POLAND
Josef Czapski
Czeslaw Milosz
Waclaw Ostrowski

PUERTO RICO
Jaime Benitez

SENEGAL
Gabriel d'Arboussier
Thomas Diop
Simon Kiba

SIERRA LEONE
John Akar
Davidson Nicol

SOUTH AFRICA
Dan Jacobson
Colin Legum
Ezekiel Mphahlele
Ronald Segal

SPAIN
J.L. Aranguren
Pedro Lain Entralgo
Salvador de Madariaga
Alberto de Onaindia
Dionisio Ridruejo

SUDAN
Jamal Ahmad
Moh. Sayed Ahmad Mahgoub

SWEDEN
Ingemar Hedenius
Eyvind Johnson
Gunnar Myrdal

SWITZERLAND
Jacques Freymond
Jeanne Hersch
Walter Höfer
Herbert Lüthy
Hans Oprecht
Denis de Rougemont

SYRIA
Jamil Saliba

THAILAND
Kukrit Pramoj

TOGO
F.N. Agblemagnon
François Amorin

TUNISIA
Mahjoub Ben Milad
Lamine Chabbi
Cecil Hourani
Mhammed Mzali

TURKEY
Orhan Karaveli
Sabri Siyavusgil

U.A.R.
Bint Al-Shati'
Halim Aref
Ibrahim Madkour
Abdel Rahman
Mohammed Tewfik Ramzi

UNITED KINGDOM
Sir Eric Ashby
Kingsley Amis
W.H. Auden
A.J. Ayer
Max Beloff
Sir Isaiah Berlin
Colin Clark
C.A.R. Crosland
R.H.S. Crossman
Cyril Darlington
Hugh Gaitskell
Stuart Hampshire
Sir William Hayter
Max Hayward
Denis Healey
Richard Hoggart
Arthur Koestler
Malcolm Muggeridge
Iris Murdoch
Sir Herbert Read
Leonard Schapiro
Hugh Seton-Watson
Stephen Spender
John Strachey
H.R. Trevor-Roper

UNITED STATES
Hannah Arendt
Alfred H. Barr
Daniel Bell
Arthur H. Compton
John Dos Passos
Merle Fainsod
Julilus Fleischmann
William Faulkner
James Franck
John K. Galbraith
Sidney Hook
Robert Hutchins
George F. Kennan
Grayson Kirk
Hans Kohn
Mary McCarthy
Yehudi Menuhin
H.J. Müller
J. Robert Oppenheimer
Eugene Rostow
Arthur Schlesinger, Jr.
Edward Shils
Igor Stravinsky
Norman Thomas
Virgil Thomson
Bertram D. Wolfe

UPER VOLTA
Joseph Ki Zerbo

URUGUAY
F. Ferrandiz Alborz
Emilio Frugoni

VENEZUELA
Romulo Gallegos
Mariano Picon Salas

WEST INDIES
W. Arthur Lewis

YUGOSLAVIA
Rudolf Bicanic
Aser Deleon
Dragutin Gostuski

20

Magazines Associated with the Congress

ENCOUNTER: published monthly in England
Editors: Stephen Spender and Melvin J. Lasky
25 Haymarket
London S.W.1.

PREUVES: published monthly in France
Editors: François Bondy, Jacques Carat, Jean-Bloch Michel
18, avenue de l'Opéra
Paris 1er

CUADERNOS: published monthly in France, in Spanish
Editor : German Arciniegas
18, avenue de l'Opéra
Paris 1er

THE CHINA QUARTERLY: published in England
Editor: Roderick MacFarquhar
1-2 Langham Place
London W.1.

SURVEY: A JOURNAL OF SOVIET AND EAST EUROPEAN STUDIES: published bi-monthly in England
Editor: Walter Z. Laqueur
1-2 Langham Place
London W.1.

FORUM: published monthly in Austria
Editors: Friedrich Abendroth, Alexander Lernet-Holenia, Günther Nenning, Friedrich Torberg
Museumstrasse 5
Vienna 7

MINERVA: A REVIEW OF SCIENCE, LEARNING AND POLICY
Editor: Edward Shils
Ilford House
133-135 Oxford St.
London W.1.

DER MONAT: published monthly in Germany
Editors: Hellmut Jaesrich and F.R. Allemann
Schorlemer Allee 28
Berlin-Dahlem

TEMPO PRESENTE: published monthly in Italy
Editors: Ignazio Silone and Nicola Chiaromonte
7, Via Gregoriana
Rome

QUEST: published quarterly in India
Editors: Abu Sayeed Ayyub and Amlan Datta
5, Pearl Road
Calcutta 17

QUADRANT: published quarterly in Australia
Editor: James McAuley
Box 4714
Sydney NSW

CADERNOS BRASILEIROS: published quarterly in Brazil.
Editor: Afranio Coutinho.
Rua Paul Redfern 41
Ipanema
Rio de Janeiro

FREEDOM-JIYU:published monthly in Japan
Editor: Michio Takeyama
Bunka Jiyu Kan
11, Shin Ryudo-cho
Azabu Minato-ku
TOKYO

COMMENT: published quarterly in the Philippines
Editor: Francisco Sionil Jose
1729 J.P. Laurel, Sr..
Manila

HIWAR: published bi-monthly in Lebanon
Editor: Tawfiq Sayigh
B.P. 4737
Beirut

BLACK ORPHEUS: published quarterly in Nigeria
Editors : Ezekiel Mphahlele, Wole Soyinka, Ulli Beier
NW/48X Onireke St.
Ibadan

SASANGGE: published monthly in Korea
Editor: Kim Jun-yop
100 Chongro 2nd St.
Chongro-ku
Seoul

TRANSITION: published bi-monthly in Uganda
Editor : Rajat Neogy
Box 20026
Kampala

Books Sponsored By Congress Include:

Clegg, Hugh, A NEW APPROACH TO INDUSTRIAL DEMOCRACY, Basil Blackwell, Oxford, 1960 (Based on Vienna Seminar on "Workers' Participation in Management")

COLLOQUES DE RHEINFELDEN, Calmann-Lévy, Paris 1960 (Proceedings of Basle-Rheinfelden Seminar on "Industrial Society and the Western Political Dialogue")

LA DÉMOCRATIE A L'ÉPREUVE DU XXe SIÈCLE, Calmann-Lévy, Paris, 1960 (Proceedings of Study Group on "Political Progress", General Conference, Berlin, 1960)

Jelenski, K.A., ed., HISTORY AND HOPE, Routledge and Kegan Paul, London (Preager, New York), 1962 (Proceedings of Study Group on "Progress of Ideas", General Conference, Berlin, 1960)

Japan Cultural Forum, ed., MODERN ART OF ASIA: Toto Shuppan Co., Tokyo, 1961

Labedz, Leopold, ed., REVISIONISM: ESSAYS ON THE HISTORY OF MARXIST IDEAS; Allen and Unwin, London, 1962 (first volume in the Library of International Studies, published under the auspices of the Congress)

Lasky, Melvin J., ed., THE HUNGARIAN REVOLUTION: A WHITE BOOK, Secker and Warburg, London (Praeger, New York), 1957

MacFarquhar Roderick, ed., THE HUNDRED FLOWERS, Stevens and Sons, Ltd., London, 1960.

SCIENCE AND FREEDOM, Secker and Warburg, London, 1955 (Proceedings of Hamburg Conference)

Many books and pamphlets have also been published by Congress offices in India ("Basic Books"), Pakistan, Japan, the United States, Italy ("Problemi del Nostro Tempo"), Argentina ("Biblioteca de la Libertad"), Chile, Denmark, France, Germany and other countries.

and West confer at Rhodes

The End of the Ideol
By Prof. Edward Shils

THE CONGRESS AND THE PRESS

STER GUARDIAN

Herald NEW YOR
European Edition

AL CONGRESSO DI RHEINFELDEN

IL DIVORZIO DEL MONDO SCIENTIFICO
DA QUELLO DELLA COMUNE CULTURA

CORRIERE DELLA SERA

I più inquietanti problemi morali dell'era atomica acutamente
prospettati in un discorso del celebre fisico Oppenheimer

Il tempo libero

clansroll eröffnet:

La Cooperación de los Paises
Americanos en Defensa de la
Libertad de la Cultura
Por EDUARDO SANTOS

enschaft und Freiheit
nale Kundgebung im großen Festsaal des Rathauses

EXCELSIOR
EL PERIODICO DE LA VIDA NACIONAL

DIE WELT

افتتاح مؤتمر الثقافة العالمية

THE STA

تونس

REUNIS AU SÉMINAIRE D'IBADAN

Africains d'expression anglaise et française s'interrogen
sur l'opportunité d'instaurer
la démocratie dans les nouveaux Etats
De notre envoyé spécial PHILIPPE DECRAINE

Worker's Hand
in Management
By Anthony Crosland

Music: Gallant Players
80-Piece Philharmonia
Hungarica Bows

onismes

ée du Louvre

Le Monde

THE OBSERVER

SITY UNDER ISLAM

The New York Times.

Over 70 Invited t
In East-West Mus

Der Islam in unserer Zeit
Zu einer internationalen Konferenz in Karachi

TIMES

UCATIONAL SUPPLEMENT

Neue Zürcher Zeitung

Poetry In Ph
D. N. Chaudhur

IBAT

اقتصاد   فـن   ادب   الاقتصاد

The Times

تدريب موظفي الدولة

Frankfurter Allgemeine

Kunsten skranter men den overgiver sig

Berlingske Afte

PROBLEMS OF CULTUR
LIBERTY

200 DISTINGUISHED PEOPLE
MEET IN BERLIN

Verpflichtung zur Freiheit

LA PRENSA

Reaniose en Berlin
El Congreso por la
Libertad Cultural

Neue Zürcher Zeitung

'MBARI'
IBADAN'S
ARTS
CLUB

New social centre
where writers
and artists can meet

THE STATESMA

TIMES

olis in the Arab World

Urban Experts Discuss
Creation of New Cities

The 106th Encounter

Review

WEST AFRICAN

The Yorkshire Po

n Times

To Discover
ew Heritage

R ON LITERATURE AND
AL CONSCIOUSNESS

NOIR, BLANC
ET COULEURS

Découverte d'un
cinéma insolite

race au Cercle pour la liberté de la culture
avec Jean Cayrol et Claude Durand

LE PROGRES

The welfare
state and
the writer

by Anthony Hartley

Evolution Of Democracy
In South-East Asia

DISCUSSION AT DELHI SEMINAR

"The Times of India" News Service

Twain Meet in Music Fe

Works of East and
West Presented in
Tokyo Concert

News

African University Problems

The Times of India

THE GUARDIAN

The New York

The Economist

Congress Associates Around the World

REGIONAL OFFICES

ASIA
Congress for Cultural Freedom
Office for Asian Affairs
5 Hailey Road
New Delhi 1

SCANDINAVIA
Congress for Cultural Freedom
Office for Scandinavian Affairs
Vestervoldgade 10
Copenhagen V

LATIN AMERICA

Oficina Interamericana, Congreso por la Libertad de la Cultura
Casilla 1410, Montevideo

ARGENTINA
Asociación Argentina por la Libertad
de la Cultura
Libertad 1258
Buenos Aires

AUSTRALIA
Australian Association for Cultural
Freedom
G.P.O. Box 4714
Sydney

BRAZIL
Associaçao Brasileira do Congresso
pela Liberdade da Cultura
Rua Mexico, 90
Grupo 507
Rio de Janeiro

CHILE
Congreso por la Libertad de la Cultura
Comité de Chile
Casilla 9639
Santiago de Chile

CONGO
Institut d'Etudes Congolaises
Boite Postale 730
Brazzaville

FRANCE
Cercles pour la Liberté de la Culture
104, Boulevard Haussmann
Paris 8ᵉ

GERMANY
Kongress für Kulturelle Freiheit
Hamburger Büro
Nonnenstieg 1-a
Hamburg 13

Kongress für Kulturelle Freiheit
Kölner Büro
Goldsteinstrasse 185
Cologne-Bayenthal

ICELAND
Frjáls Menning
Tjarnargata 16
Reykjavik

INDIA
Indian Committee for Cultural
Freedom
Army and Navy Building
148 Mahatma Gandhi Road
Bombay 1

Calcutta Centre
Indian Committee
for Cultural Freedom
211 Park Street
Calcutta 17

ITALY
Associazione Italiana per la Libertà
della Cultura
Via Giuseppe Pisanelli 2
Rome

JAPAN
Japan Committee,
Congress for Cultural Freedom
Bunka Jiyu Kan
11, Shin Ryudo-cho
Azabu Minato-ku
Tokyo

NIGERIA
Mbari Writers and Artists Club
NW/48X Onireke Street
Ibadan

PAKISTAN
Pakistan Committee,
Congress for Cultural Freedom
94 Agamasi Lane
Dacca 2

Pakistan Committee
Congress for Cultural Freedom
II A/4-4, Nazimabad
Karachi 18

SOUTH KOREA
Chunchu-hoi—Korean
Committee for Cultural Freedom
Kwangwhamun
P.O. Box 342
Seoul

UNITED KINGDOM
Committee on Science and Freedom
Ilford House
133-135 Oxford St.
London W.1

UNITED STATES
American Committee for Cultural
Freedom
22 E. 17th St.
New York 3, N.Y.

The Congress has correspondents in Athens, Beirut, Cairo, Helsinki, Khartoum, Lima, Manila and Mexico City.

24

Members of International Council of Congress for Cultural Freedom

JAMAL MOHAMED AHMAD (*Sudan*)
GABRIEL D'ARBOUSSIER (*Senegal*)
GERMAN ARCINIEGAS (*Colombia*)
RAYMOND ARON (*France*)
A.K. BROHI (*Pakistan*)
NICOLA CHIAROMONTE (*Italy*)
C.A.R. CROSLAND (*Britain*)
PIERRE EMMANUEL (*France*)
JEANNE HERSCH (*Switzerland*)
SIDNEY HOOK (*U.S.*)
FRODE JAKOBSEN (*Denmark*)
W. ARTHUR LEWIS (*West Indies*)
MINOO MASANI (*India*)
ASOKA MEHTA (*India*)
DAVIDSON NICOL (*Sierra Leone*)
AYO OGUNSHEYE (*Nigeria*)
J. ROBERT OPPENHEIMER (*U.S.*)
MARIANO PICON-SALAS (*Venezuela*)
DENIS DE ROUGEMONT (*Switzerland*)

LUIS ALBERTO SANCHEZ (*Peru*)
ARTHUR SCHLESINGER, JR. (*U.S.*)
CARLO SCHMID (*Germany*)
YOSHIHIKO SEKI (*Japan*)
HUGH SETON-WATSON (*Britain*)
IGNAZIO SILONE (*Italy*)
SABRI ESAT SIYAVUSGIL (*Turkey*)
BRUNO SNELL (*Germany*)
STEPHEN SPENDER (*Britain*)
MANÈS SPERBER (*France*)
MICHIO TAKEYAMA (*Japan*)
GERMAINE TILLION (*France*)
J. CH. WITSCH (*Germany*)

Ex Officio

JULIUS FLEISCHMANN (*U.S.*)
MICHAEL POLANYI (*Britain*)
EDWARD SHILS (*U.S.*)
NICOLAS NABOKOV
(Congress Secretary-General)

We should like to take this opportunity to express our deeply felt gratitude to all those who have extended financial assistance to the Congress. Without the generous aid of these individuals and organisations, none of the activities outlined in the foregoing pages would have been possible.

Among the philanthropic foundations and other organisations which have made grants to the Congress during its first twelve years are the following:

Catherwood Foundation, Bryn Mawr

The Charles E. Merrill Trust, Ithaca, New York

Comité Suisse d'Aide aux Patriotes Hongrois, Zurich

The Council on Economic and Cultural Affairs, Inc., New York

Deutscher Künstlerbund, Berlin

Farfield Foundation, Inc., New York

The Ford Foundation, New York

Hoblitzelle Foundation, Dallas

Holmes Foundation, Inc., New York

International Rescue Committee, New York

The Miami District Fund, Cincinnati

The Rockefeller Foundation, New York

CONGRESS FOR CULTURAL FREEDOM   PUBLISHED IN PARIS 1963
104, Boulevard Haussmann
PARIS VIII

4. *Senate Select Committee to Study Governmental Operations with Respect to Intelligence Activities, Final Report, Book 1, Foreign and Military Intelligence (Washington, DC: U.S. Government Printing Office, 1976), https://www.intelligence.senate.gov/sites/default/files/94755_I.pdf, 189-191, excerpt.*

This short excerpt from the Church Committee report confirms that the CIA had "extensive" relationships with the academic community and was in contact with "many thousands of United States academics at hundreds of U.S. academic institutions." Prepared by William B. Bader, who was a former member of the same Agency he was tasked with evaluating, this report is nonetheless limited in its purview and does not reflect the full extent of Bader's findings. Indeed, the document mentions, as if to vaguely acknowledge this, that "the CIA considers these operational relationships with the United States academic community as perhaps its most sensitive domestic area." William Corson, who was an unofficial adviser to the Church Committee, wrote in 1977 that "Today, the original band of OSS academics has been expanded tenfold, producing a situation in which some 5,000 American academics are doing the bidding of the CIA" (*The Armies of Ignorance: The Rise of the American Intelligence Empire*, New York: Dial Press, 1977, 312).

[DOCUMENTS REPRODUCED ON PAGES 362–64]

189

The CIA relationships with the academic community are extensive and serve many purposes, including providing leads and making introductions for intelligence purposes, collaboration in research and analysis, intelligence collection abroad, and preparation of books and other propaganda materials.

The Select Committee's concentration has been on the area of clandestine relationships untouched by the Katzenbach Committee—individuals.

7. Covert Relations with Individuals in the Academic Community

As already noted, from the first days of the Katzenbach Committee, the CIA proceeded on the operating assumption that the inquiry was directed squarely at institutional relationships—not individuals in or affiliated with those private institutions. After the Katzenbach report, the Agency issued a basic instruction entitled "Restrictions on Operational Use of Certain Categories of Individuals." This instruction remains in force today. The instruction states that the "basic rule" for the use of human agents by the Operations Directorate is that "any consenting adult" may be used.

While all members of the American academic community, including students, certainly qualify as "consenting adults," the CIA since 1967 has been particularly sensitive to the risks associated with their use. In order to control and confine contacts with American academics, the handling of relationships with individuals associated with universities is largely confined to two CIA divisions of the Directorate of Operations—the Domestic Collection Division and the Foreign Resources Division. The Domestic Collection Division is the point of contact with large numbers of American academics who travel abroad or who are otherwise consulted on the subject of their expertise. The Foreign Resources Division, on the other hand, is the purely operational arm of the CIA in dealing with American academics. Altogether, DCD and FRD are currently in contact—ranging from the occasional debriefing to a continuing operational relationship—with many thousands of United States academics at hundreds of U.S. academic institutions.

It is imperative to underline that the majority of these relationships are purely for the purpose of asking an academic about his travels abroad or open informal consulting on subjects of the academic's expertise. The Committee sees no danger to the integrity of American private institutions in continuing such contacts; indeed, there are benefits to both the government and the universities in such contacts.

The CIA's Office of Personnel also maintains relationships with university administrators, sometimes in the placement office. These relationships, which are usually contractual, enable the CIA to approach suitable United States students for CIA employment.

The "operational use" of academics is another matter. It raises troubling questions as to preservation of the integrity of American academic institutions.

8. Covert Use of the U.S. Academic Community

The Central Intelligence Agency is now using several hundred American academics [11], who in addition to providing leads and, on

[11] "Academics" includes administrators, faculty members and graduate students engaged in teaching.

190

*occasion, making introductions for intelligence purposes, occasionally
write books and other material to be used for propaganda purposes
abroad. Beyond these, an additional few score are used in an unwitting
manner for minor activities.*

*These academics are located in over 100 American colleges, univer-
sities, and related institutes. At the majority of institutions, no one
other than the individual concerned is aware of the CIA link. At
the others, at least one university official is aware of the operational use
made of academics on his campus. In addition, there are several American academics abroad who serve operational purposes, primarily the
collection of intelligence.*[12]

The CIA considers these operational relationships with the United
States academic community as perhaps its most sensitive domestic area
and has strict controls governing these operations. According to the
Agency's internal directives, the following distinctions govern the
operational use of individuals: the CIA's directives prohibit the operational use of individuals who are receiving support under the Mutual
Education and Cultural Exchange Act of 1961, commonly known as
the Fulbright-Hays Act. Falling under this particular prohibition are
teachers, research scholars, lecturers, and students who have been
selected to receive scholarships or grants by the Board of Foreign
Scholarships. This prohibition specifically does not apply to the several
other categories of grantees supported by other provisions of the Fulbright-Hays Act, such as artists, athletes, leaders, specialists, or participants in international trade fairs or expositions, who do not come
under the aegis of the President's Board of Foreign Scholarships. As
far as the three major foundations—Ford, Rockefeller and Carnegie—
are concerned, the prohibition extends to "persons actively participating in programs which are wholly sponsored and controlled by any of
these foundations. Additionally, there will be no operational use made
of the officials or employees of these organizations." (These large foundations were cited by a CIA official in 1966 before the 303 Committee
as "a trouble area in New York City—reluctant to cooperate on joint
ventures.")

*9. Covert Relationships with Academeic and Voluntary Organizations:
    Conclusions*

With respect to CIA covert relationships with private institutions
and voluntary organizations, the Committee concludes:

(1) The CIA has adhered to the 1967 Katzenbach guidelines governing relationships with domestic private and voluntary institutions. The
guidelines are so narrowly focused, however, that the covert use of
American individuals from these institutions has continued.

(2) American academics are now being used for such operational
purposes *as making introductions for intelligence purposes* [12a] and
working for the Agency abroad. Although the numbers are not as great
today as in 1966, there are no prohibitions to prevent an increase in the
operational use of academics. The size of these operations is determined
by the CIA.

(3) With the exception of those teachers, scholars and students
who receive scholarships or grants from the Board of Foreign Scholar-

---

[12] For explanation of italics, see footnote, p. 179.
[12a] *Ibid.*

191

ships, the CIA is not prohibited from the operational use of all other categories of grantee support under the Fulbright-Hays Act (artists, athletes, leaders, specialists, etc.). Nor is there any prohibition on the operational use of individuals participating in any other exchange program funded by the United States Government.

In addressing the issues of the CIA's relationship to the American academic community the Committee is keenly aware that if the CIA is to serve the intelligence needs of the nation, it must have unfettered access to the best advice and judgment our universities can produce. But this advice and expertise can and should be openly sought—and openly given. Suspicion that such openness of intellectual encounter and exchange is complemented by covert operational exploitation of academics and students can only prejudice, if not destroy, the possibility of a full and fruitful exchange between the nation's best minds and the nation's most critical intelligence needs. To put these intellects in the service of the nation, trust and confidence must be maintained between our intelligence agencies and the academic community.

The Committee is disturbed both by the present practice of operationally using American academics and by the awareness that the restraints on expanding this practice are primarily those of sensitivity to the risks of disclosure and *not* an appreciation of dangers to the integrity of individuals and institutions. Nevertheless, the Committee does not recommend a legislative prohibition on the operational exploitation of individuals in private institutions by the intelligence agencies. The Committee views such legislation as both unenforceable and in itself an intrusion on the privacy and integrity of the American academic community. The Committee believes that it is the responsibility of private institutions and particularly the American academic community to set the professional and ethical standards of its members. This report on the nature and extent of covert individual relations with the CIA is intended to alert these institutions that there is a problem.

At the same time, the Committee recommends that the CIA amend its internal directives to require that individual academics used for operational purposes by the CIA, together with the President or equivalent official of the relevant academic institutions, be informed of the clandestine CIA relationship.

The Committee also feels strongly that there should be no operational use made of professors, lecturers, students, artists, and the like who are funded under United States Government-sponsored programs. The prohibition on the operational use of Fulbright grantees must be extended to other government-sponsored programs; and in this case the prohibition should be confirmed by law, given the direct responsibility of the Congress for these programs. It is unacceptable that Americans would go overseas under a cultural or academic exchange program funded openly by the United States Congress and at the same time serve an operational purpose directed by the Central Intelligence Agency.

B. COVERT RELATIONSHIPS WITH THE UNITED STATES MEDIA

In pursuing its foreign intelligence mission the Central Intelligence Agency has used the U.S. media for both the collection of intelligence

5. *Task Force on Greater CIA Openness, "Memorandum for Director of Public Affairs," November 18, 1991, http://www.takeoverworld.info/cia-openness. html, excerpt.*

This 1991 Gates memo provides an overview of the CIA's relationship to the media, academia, the business world, the government, and the private sector. This excerpt explains that "the Agency has a wide range of contacts with academics through recruiting, professional societies, contractual arrangements and OTE [Office of Training and Education]." It claims that the Agency's Public Affairs Office (PAO) "maintains a mailing list of 700 academicians who receive unclassified Agency publications four times a year." The PAO also sponsors the DCI Program for Deans that exposes "administrators of academic institutions to senior Agency officials."

[DOCUMENTS REPRODUCED ON PAGES 366-69]

20 December 1991

MEMORANDUM FOR: Director of Central Intelligence
FROM: Task Force on Greater CIA Openness
SUBJECT: Task Force Report on Greater CIA Openness
REFERENCE: Memo for D/PAO fr DCI, dtd 18 Nov, Subj: Greater CIA Openness (Tab A)

A. MEDIA
    1) Current Program:
        a) **PAO** *(Public Affairs Office)* **now has relationships with reporters from every major wire service, newspaper, news weekly, and television network in the nation. This has helped us turn some "intelligence failure" stories into "intelligence success" stories, and it has contributed to the accuracy of countless others. In many instances, we have persuaded reporters to postpone, change, hold, or even scrap stories that could have adversely affected national security interests or jeopardized sources and methods.**

        b) PAO spokespersons build and maintain these professional relationships with reporters by responding to daily inquiries from them over the telephone (3369 in 1991), by providing unclassified background briefings to them at Headquarters (174 in 1991), and by arranging for them to interview the DCI, DDCI and other senior Agency officials (164 in 1991).

        c. PAO responds to numerous requests from authors, researchers, filmmakers, and others seeking information, guidance, or cooperation from the Agency in their endeavours. Some responses can be handled in a one-shot telephone call. Others, such as Life Magazine's proposed photo essay, BBC's six-part series, Ron Kessler's requests for information for his Agency book, and the need for an Agency focal point in the Rochester Institute of Technology controversy drew heavily on PAO resources.

        d. PAO has also reviewed some film scripts about the Agency, documentary and fictional, at the request of filmmakers seeking guidance on accuracy and authenticity. In a few instances,

Document 2, p.7

        we facilitated the filming of a few scenes on Agency premises. Responding positively to these requests in a limited way has provided PAO with the opportunity to help others depict the Agency and its activities accurately and without negative distortions. Except for responding to such requests, we do not seek to play a role in filmmaking ventures about the Agency which come to our attention. For example, although we knew that Oliver Stone's movie on JFK was in the works for some time, **we did not contact him** *to volunteer an Agency viewpoint.*
        e. PAO coordinates the preparation of detailed background materials, usually in Q&A format, on major news issues for the DCI and DDCI for their appearances

before media groups, world affairs councils, universities, and business and professional groups. PAO also prepares verbatim transcripts of their interviews with reporters and their appearances before media groups.

B. ACADEMIA

1) Current Program

a. The Agency has a wide range of contacts with academics through recruiting, professional societies, contractual arrangements and OTE. PAO has recently been designated the focal point for all information about CIA's relations with the academic community. As such, PAO is building a database of information about Agency contacts with academia -- conferences and seminars, recruiting, officers and scholars-in-residence, contracts, teaching -- and serves as the clearinghouse of such information for Agency employees.

b. PAO officers also speak to approximately 250 academic audiences a year. Subject areas vary, but most focus on the structure and functions of the CIA, its role in the intelligence community, the intelligence process, and congressional oversight. PAO has developed a speakers' package for Agency officers and retirees who speak in public, including an annually updated Q&A package to aid the speaker in answering a broad array of questions.

c. PAO maintains a mailing list of 700 academicians who receive unclassified Agency publications four times a year. Recipients write to praise the quality of the products and to claim that these mailings are one of the most effective ways of reaching out.

d. PAO sponsors the DCI Program for Deans twice a year. This program seeks to expose administrators of academic institutions to senior Agency officials -- the DCI, the DDCI, all the DDs, and heads of independent offices -- and to give them a sense of what the Agency does, how it operates, and how it fits in and relates to American society.

[3] The recent Denison University Alumni Magazine feature on Martha Kessler is a good example. (See Tab C)

Document 2, p.9

2) Recommendations:

a. The Officer-in-Residence (OIR) program is seen by many as an excellent means of providing a window into CIA for the academic community. The program (currently 13 participants) could be enhanced with dedicated slots and resources, under central management. At present, individual offices provide the positions and about $100,000 per officer. Such enhancement would ensure that selection of schools and officers meets our needs.

_____Approve   _____Disapprove

b. PAO should work with OTE and OP to develop a program for CIA employees involved in recruiting to ensure that they are conversant on all issues affecting the CIA with emphasis on the intelligence process and multicultural sensitivities. Provide for periodic update for recruiters on long-term assignment.

_____Approve   _____Disapprove

c. PAO's Coordinator for Academic Affairs should take steps to see that CIA becomes an institutional member of relevant scientific and professional societies. Agency employees should participate openly in such meetings as CIA officers. Procedures for individuals to present papers in such fora need to be updated.

_____Approve   _____Disapprove

d. Sponsor either unilaterally or in cooperation with academic institutions or other government agencies conferences on the history and craft of intelligence, as well as on other areas of common interest. PAO will work with OTE's Center for the Study of Intelligence on these programs.[4]

_____Approve   _____Disapprove

[4] For example, PAO is currently talking with the Truman Library about a conference in late 1992 or 1993 on the origins of the Intelligence Community. A similar conference with the Wilson Center is being considered to mark the 30th anniversary of the Cuban Missile Crisis next fall.
Document 2, p.10

e. Conduct more academic conferences here at Langley. Take the successful DI model of substantive conferences with the academic community and explore how it could be valuable to S&T and DA.

_____Approve   _____Disapprove

f. PAO, CPAS and FBIS should examine ways to continue or enhance the program to disseminate unclassified publications (highly valued by all we talked to) to ensure that the Agency is receiving maximum benefit for its efforts.

_____Approve   _____Disapprove

g. Encourage the establishment of intelligence studies programs at academic institutions.

_____Approve   _____Disapprove

C. GOVERNMENT

1) Current Program:

a. **The Agency has a broad range of contacts throughout government and provides product, briefings, and exchanges to both Executive and Legislative Branches.** *PAO is an active participant in briefing the military and other government agencies on the CIA, its mission and functions. This year, PAO provided more than 70 briefings to groups from the*

National Security Agency, Foreign Service, Pentagon, Defense Intelligence College, and the United States Information Agency.

D. BUSINESS

    1) Current Program:

        *a. **The Agency currently has three types of basic relationships with the US business sector.** First, business is an important source of intelligence information via NR collection activities. Second, **the US corporate sector is involved in the vast bulk of the Agency's contracting efforts.** Finally, business receives selected briefings by the Agency -- talks on the counterintelligence challenge, counterterrorism and other presentations at business-oriented conferences organized by groups such as SASA. Given the emphasis on economic security for the United States in the '90s, the business sector is looking to the potential contributions the Intelligence community can make in this area.*

[5] Hill staffers rely heavily on OTA and CRS products. Moreover, active interaction with these congressional support organizations can provide invaluable insights into issues that key House and Senate committees and individual members believe are important, as well as what legislation is under consideration or in the conceptual state. Some Hill staffers have suggested that CIA assign officers to act as liaison through OCA for relevant OTA projects, as the military services do. For example, OTA is now focusing on two projects of particular interest to several congressional committees, proliferation and economic analyses of other nations as they relate to U.S. industrial competitiveness.

Document 2, p.12

        b. This past year, PAO provided remarks and support for the DCI and DDCI for some 40 appearances before outside audiences -- including a wide range of groups from the business, legal and civic communities. Most of these appearances were covered by the media giving even more visibility to our leaders' comments.

        c. PAO participates in providing briefings on the CIA to participants in AFCEA's biannual "Intelligence Community" course, attended by nearly 200 industry and government representatives.

E. PRIVATE SECTOR

    1) Current Program:

        a. PAO officers this year made presentations about the CIA to members of more than 60 civic and service clubs. Rotary and Kiwanis Clubs in particular have been the recipients of this service. PAO took steps to establish a speakers' bureau last sprint to increase the number of presentations that the Agency could provide.

Document 2, p.13

        b. PAO responds to nearly 4000 pieces of correspondence a year from the public. Queries range from the ridiculous to the scholarly request for information. PAO also answers some 6000 telephone queries from the public annually.

6.   *Theodor Adorno's FBI file (file number 62-60527), obtained through a FOIA request, is available here: https://vault.fbi.gov/theodor-adorno/theodor-adorno-part-01-of-01/view, excerpt.*

This 1955 FBI memorandum in Adorno's file shows that the Bureau used informants to gather information on him and other members of the Frankfurt School, due in part to some early concerns that the Institute for Social Research might be a communist front. The Bureau found little to no evidence of suspicious behavior in its investigations, and this memo describes Adorno as politically inactive, loyal, attached to his U.S. American citizenship, and inclined to see similarities between communism and Nazism. This latter tendency is also highlighted in a 1950 memorandum in Adorno's FBI file that indicates that an informant reported that the critical theorists of the Frankfurt School "believe there is no difference between Hitler and Stalin as to purpose and tactics."

[DOCUMENTS REPRODUCED ON PAGES 371-72]

~~CONFIDENTIAL~~

March 3, 1955

DOCTOR THEODOR ADORNO
Also known as: DOCTOR THEODOR WIESENGRUND
Born: September 11, 1903
Frankfurt/Main, Germany

No investigation has been conducted by the FBI concerning the captioned individual. However, a review of this Bureau's files reflects the following information which may pertain to the subject of your present request.

This Bureau's files reflect the receipt of information from a confidential source of known reliability advising that on September 15, 1944, the names of one Theodore W. Adorno, Hans Eisler, and others, appeared as on a committee to discuss music under Fascism. The Committee was reportedly sponsored by the University of California music department, and the "Musicians Congress." The informant, on September 10, 1944, advised that the "Musicians Congress" was mostly populated by Communist members, and that programs sponsored by this committee were an outlet for Communist propaganda.

It is noted that the Hans Eisler referred to above is the brother of Gerhart Eisler, the well-known Communist functionary.

In 1951, a source who has furnished reliable information in the past advised that Theodore Adorno was born Theodore Wiesengrund, but that he prefers to use the name Adorno. This source advised the following concerning Adorno.

"He is a philosopher, but belongs to those ingenious scholars who are pretty much at home in a good many fields. Adorno has written rather extensively on music, is a composer in his own rights, has done research in the field of psychology and sociology, and is quite familiar with European and American history.

Orig. to USIA
Reg Rec'd: 2-11-55   b7C

RECORDED - 40
INDEXED - 40

EXII MAR 4 1955

~~CONFIDENTIAL~~

To the best of my knowledge, Adorno never was politically active and during the years I have known him he was very clear in his appraisal of Communism and was interested in analyzing similarities of the national socialists and Soviet systems with regard to the treatment of the individual. I know that Adorno was a friend of Hans Eisler, a brother of Gerhart Eisler, and the two families, Eisler, and Adorno, met while they both were living in Santa Monica, California. Furthermore, Adorno and Eisler together worked on a study of film music. I have reason to believe that most of it, if not all, was written by Adorno. When the book was about to be published, the Gerhart Eisler story broke and Adorno decided not to have his name associated with that of Hans Eisler. The study, therefore, was published with Hans Eisler as the sole author."

The informant advised that "the mutual interest and friendship, as long as it lasted, between Eisler and Adorno must be explained on the basis of a common experience; both have been pupils of the outstanding modern composer Arnold Schoenberg and both were deeply interested in the theoretical problems of modern composing."   b2
     b7D

100-106126-30)

The informant further advised that the impressions and the factual knowledge which he had of Adorno with regard to his loyalty might be summed up as follows:

"As far as I know, he was neither in Europe nor in the United States politically active with the Communist Party or any of its affiliates. I have never heard of him being connected with any front organization in this country. I have no reason to believe that he is not loyal to this country, and I know that he cherishes his American citizenship."

The foregoing information is furnished to you as the result of a request for an FBI file check and is not to be construed as a clearance or a nonclearance of the individual involved. This information is furnished for your use and should not be disseminated outside of your agency.

7. *Theodor Adorno, letter to Melvin J. Lasky, December 6, 1949, published in Theodor Adorno and Max Horkheimer, Correspondance: 1927–1969, vol. 3, ed. Christoph Gödde and Henri Lonitz, trans. Didier Renault (Paris: Klincksieck, 2016), 347–49.*

This letter is an excerpt from Adorno's correspondence with Melvin Lasky, a witting CIA agent who was arguably the leading figure in the German anticommunist *Kulturkampf*. An employee of the U.S. military government in West Germany, Lasky was the founder and chief editor of *Der Monat* and a member of the original steering committee for the CIA's CCF. Adorno did not show signs of knowing he was a CIA agent. However, in a letter to Horkheimer and Gretel Adorno dated December 8, 1949, he explained that Lasky had just spent the entire afternoon at his home, writing: "He's a man just like Elliot Cohen [the founder and editor of *Commentary*]; it's just like the atmosphere of *Commentary*, which they are moreover very close to." (*Commentary* was another CIA journal, so Adorno had a keen sense of the ambiance and orientation.) *Der Monat* was officially operated by the U.S. military occupation government, and many intellectuals fully understood which country's government had ample funds for anticommunist cultural projects in war-torn Europe. Adorno, for his part, hosted Lasky in his home and, as this letter attests, collaborated with this CIA agent on publication projects. The Frankfurt scholar clearly identified with Lasky's camp in the cultural and intellectual war on communism. What is more, Adorno continued to work with the CCF after it was revealed that it was a CIA front organization.

(N.B.: this letter was translated from French rather than German because, as far as I know, it has not been published in German.)

[DOCUMENT REPRODUCED ON PAGE 374]

Frankfurt, December 6, 1949

T.W. Adorno
c/o Irmer
Liebigstraße
Frankfurt/Main

M. Melvin J. Lasky
Frankfurt/Main Berlin-Dalhem
Saargemünderstraße 25

Dear Mr. Lasky,

I must apologize for the delay in replying to your kind letter, and in sending you Horkheimer's texts and my own. This delay is due in part to my trip from Los Angeles to Frankfurt, during which I had to stay several days in New York and Paris, and to the impressive mass of academic work with which I was burdened immediately after my arrival here. The main reason, however, is purely technical: *Merkur* had sent the only corrected and updated version of the "Spengler" [article] to Los Angeles by regular mail, and I only received it last week.

Please find enclosed:

1. Horkheimer's *Eclipse of Reason*
2. His article on authoritarianism and the family, written for the recent Nanda Anshen conference.
3. The German version of my Spengler [article]
4. My article on "Huxley and Utopia."

None of these studies have appeared in German, and we'd be delighted if *Der Monat* could publish them. As for the *Eclipse*, the idea would be to choose a chapter (I'm thinking of the chapter on the individual, or the last one, but these are just suggestions). We would of course like to see the German translation of the English texts before publication. If this would speed up publication considerably, we could even have them translated ourselves; if not, we'd prefer your team to do it for us.

It's very important to us that at least one of Horkheimer's texts and one of my own studies should appear *together*, in the same issue, in order to highlight the total unity of our work. As soon as I hear from you, I'll send you a note to underline this unity, and possibly some of the political aspects of our endeavor. We'd be grateful if you could arrange for publication *in the near future*. Finally, it is important that our articles appear without any changes or cuts, strictly in our own version. Should you consider that modifications are absolutely indispensable, please be kind enough to inform us in advance so that we can take care of them in good time. Thank you in advance.

I sincerely hope to see you soon and to be able to discuss a certain number of questions with you. As I'm currently very busy with university work, the period immediately after Christmas would be the most convenient for me. Is there any chance of you coming to Frankfurt? My phone number is 75676.

With the assurance of my consideration.

Sincerely yours,

8. *Rockefeller Grant to the Institute for Social Research, December 28, 1951, RG 1.2, Series 717, Box 15, Folder 155, Rockefeller Archive Center.*

This grant for the equivalent in 2024 of a little over $60,000 was recommended by the high-level longtime CIA collaborator Philip Mosely, who was the director of Columbia University's Russian Institute and one of the Frankfurt School's major academic supporters. It provides a summary of some of the Institute's contributions to the anticommunist world war: a pilot study on the impacts of U.S. propaganda platforms like Voice of America and the intelligence-connected BBC (as well as the principal Russian broadcasting station), which had obvious psychological warfare implications; the dissemination of U.S. American research methods in Germany and their adaptation to German conditions; and the effort to bring scholars from the United States to Germany, thereby contributing to the further incorporation of the West German intelligentsia into the ideological horizons of U.S. intellectual culture. The Institute was already receiving financial support from the U.S. occupational force in West Germany, known as the High Commission for Occupied Germany (HICOG), so this grant was to support non-German scholars from the United States collaborating with the Frankfurt School, which was outside the purview of HICOG funding.

[DOCUMENT REPRODUCED ON PAGE 376]

GA SS 51103

GRANT IN AID to the Institute for Social Research, University of Frankfurt, Germany,
toward the cost of securing the assistance of non-German scholars in
its research and training program.

AMOUNT: $5,000   **ACCOUNT:** To be charged to RF 51183
leaving a balance of $ 17,600

JAN -3 1952

PREVIOUS INTEREST: None.

ADDITIONAL INFORMATION: The recently-established Institute for Social Research has
been quite successful thus far in building up a program of training and research
in social psychology. Projects under way or planned include a study of political
attitudes in Germany; a pilot study of reactions to the Voice of America, BBC, and
the principal Russian broadcasting station; a summarization and translation of the
California prejudice studies. Under the direction of Professor Max Horkheimer,
with the assistance of Professor T.W. Adorno, the Institute is attempting to adapt
American research methods to German conditions and to train German students in
these adapted methods. The lack of German personnel already trained in modern research methods necessitates the employment of scholars from abroad to assume the
functions for which trained Germans are not yet available and to assist in the
training program. A condition recently attached to HICOG grants makes it impossible
to use HICOG funds for this purpose, and financing from other sources is limited.

The Institute's most pressing need is for funds to employ Dr. Ernst von Schenck,
a Swiss citizen, who is to undertake the integration and editing of the Studies in
Prejudice translated as a part of last year's training program. The Institute is
also anxious to secure Dr. Erich Franzen, an American citizen and Professor of
Sociology at the University of Illinois who is now in Germany for a limited time,
to take over a substantial part of the evaluation of the material gathered for the
attitude study; his work would be devoted primarily to analysis of group dynamics
in the formation of public opinion. The Institute has requested a grant to enable
it to engage urgently-needed non-German collaborators, with the understanding that
the funds would not be used to bring scholars from the United States to Germany.
This grant is recommended on the advice of Drs. Mosely, DeVinney, and Lane, as one
useful way of developing technical competence in the Institute.

A grant of $5,000, or as much thereof as may be necessary, to the Institute

for Social Research, University of Frankfurt, toward the cost of securing the assist-

ance of non-German scholars, is hereby approved; this sum to be available during the

period ending December 31, 1953.

_____
Assistant Director for the Social Sciences

_____
Comptroller

_____
Vice-President

APPROVED: DEC 2 8 1951 _____

9. *Department of State, Register of the Department of State (Washington, DC: U.S. Government Printing Office, 1948), https://archive.org/details/register-ofdepart1948unit/page/n5/mode/2up, 76.*

Directly contradicting Herbert Marcuse's repeated claims to the contrary, this document clearly states that his role as the Acting Chief of the Central Branch of the State Department's research and analysis division included satisfying "the intelligence requirements of the Central Intelligence Agency." The Frankfurt School scholar Otto Kirchheimer is also listed on this document as the Acting Chief of the German Section.

[DOCUMENT REPRODUCED BELOW]

---

76   REGISTER OF THE DEPARTMENT OF STATE 1948

DIVISION OF RESEARCH FOR EUROPE (DRE)

Is responsible for planning and implementing a program of positive-intelligence research pertaining to all of continental Europe (except European Turkey and Greece), Union of Soviet Socialist Republics, Great Britain, Ireland, Australia, Canada, New Zealand, Union of South Africa, Iceland, Greenland, Algeria, European dependencies in South America and the Caribbean, and secondary interests, in collaboration with the appropriate research divisions, in countries which are closely related to the area of primary responsibility, to meet the intelligence requirements of the Department in the formulation and execution of foreign policy and the intelligence requirements of the Central Intelligence Agency and other authorized agencies. It maintains continuous, close, and informal relationships with officials of the Office of European Affairs and of other offices in the Department, to encourage the exchange of information and provide them with immediate and timely intelligence for their operations.

Philip J. Conley, *Acting Chief*
Marian C. Conroy, *Administrative Officer*

Isabel G. Blackstock	May I. Ferrari	Mary F. Hembry

CENTRAL EUROPEAN BRANCH

Herbert Marcuse, *Acting Chief*

GERMAN SECTION

Otto Kirchheimer, *Acting Chief*

Robert Eisenberg	John H. Herz
Manfred Halpern	Arnold H. Price

AUSTRIA-CZECHOSLOVAKIA SECTION

Hans Meyerhoff	Paul E. Zinner

ECONOMIC SECTION

Fred H. Sanderson, *Chief*

M. June Boeckman	Arthur L. Horniker	Murray Ryss
Albert G. Capet	William N. Parker	Erwin Strauss

EASTERN EUROPEAN BRANCH

William B. Ballis, *Chief*
Vladimir Kalmykow

POLITICAL SECTION

———— ————, *Chief*

Rudolf O. Altroggen	Pearl Joseph	Vladimir Prokofieff
John C. Guthrie	Boris H. Klosson	Stanley Wilcox

ECONOMIC SECTION

Herbert Block, *Acting Chief*

William Giloane	Elizabeth N. Landeau	George J. Rothwell
Stanley Graze	Paul A. Lifantieff-Lee	M. Gordon Tiger
Vladimir B. Grinioff	Helen J. A. Lincoln	Leon S. Wellstone
Samuel Hassman	Eugene Rapaport	Howard M. Wiedemann
Jacob Horak	Ruth T. Reitman	

10. *Alexander Vassiliev, "Vassiliev White Notebook #3," 2009, Wilson Center Digital Archive, Alexander Vassiliev Papers, Manuscript Division, Library of Congress, https://digitalarchive.wilsoncenter.org/document/112566, 133–136.*

Vassiliev's notes from KGB archival files report how Franz Neumann, aka "Ruff," was apparently working as a double agent for the Soviets, and there was some interest in trying to recruit Herbert Marcuse. According to these notes, "Ruff" shared information about OSS operative—and future CIA director—Allen Dulles' secret negotiations with high-ranking Nazis for a peace deal that would give the Third Reich the "freedom to operate in the East in order to continue the war against the U.S.S.R."

[DOCUMENTS REPRODUCED ON PAGES 379-82]

White Notebook #3

File 28734 v. 1 "Ruff" Franz Neumann

p.7   Report.
"Ruff" – Franz Neumann, b. 1900 in Germany, U.S. citizen. Lived in Germany till 1933, was a left social dem., and worked as a lawyer for trade unions. In 1933, he emigrated to England, where he graduated from an econ. inst. (The London School of Economics – p.28). He came to the USA in 1936.
Prior to Feb. 1942, Ruff worked as a teacher, engaged in scientific work, and, in addition, worked as a consultant for the German division of the Board of Economic Warfare. He simultaneously wrote a book on Germany's econ. questions, which was published in the USA. In Feb. 1942, R. was transferred to Cabin, where he began work as a consultant in the foreign division.
Ruff – Mary's lead; he is a good friend of his.[74] Mary, Noah, and Git give Ruff a positive reference, describing him as pro-Soviet, with left views, and unaffiliated with any emigrant organizations.
In 1942, R. was contracted with Mary's help. At the initial meeting, R. promised to pass us all the information that came his way. According to him, numerous copies of telegrams from Amer. ambassadors to Bank are sent to him; in addition, he has access to materials on Germany in Cabin.

p.8   Report by "Mary," dating from August 1942. (translated from German)
Neumann said that he has seen three reports devoted to the Caucasus: from the Board of Econ. Warfare, the Euro. Division of the Board of Military Info., and the OSS. The first two are not of interest. The report from the OSS contains a lot of valuable material and is excellently written. The author – Robinson, is Chief of the Russian Division at the OSS. The report is 124 pages long and contains very detailed facts and figures about the Caucasus: railroads, stations, warehouses, workshops, the number of trains passing through in a particular year, etc. Neumann says that Robinson has an unfriendly attitude toward the USSR but is highly competent in matters pertaining to the USSR.

p.13   1.2.43 Neumann's recruitment approved.

p.14   Letter NY – Moscow No. 4 from 1943
"'Ruff' was contracted by us with 'Mary's' help and will be handled primarily by him. Ruff is here once a week, and he usually stays at 'Mary's' place.
In conversation with 'Vardo,' whom Ruff knows as a Soviet by the cover name 'Helen', R. said that he will give us all the info. to which he has access."

p.15   NY – C c/t dated 3.4.1943
"'Vardo' met with R. for the first time; the latter promised to give us all the information that comes his way. According to R., he receives numerous copies of reports by Amer. ambassadors to 'Bank'; moreover, he has access to materials on Germany in Cabin.

White Notebook #3

p.15   The info. received this time from R. amounts to the following:
1. The Amer. ambassador to Spain, Hayes, informed "Bank" that he spoke with the Duke of Alba, who recently returned from Germany and Italy. In both these countries, Alba—as he himself put it—met with generals and industrialists who said they were willing to overthrow Hitler and Mussolini and make a deal with the Allies.
R. says that Hayes is a sworn enemy of the Sov. Union.
2. Spellman traveled to the Vatican with the intention of recruiting the Pope on the Allied side. The latter declared that the Allies must stop bombing civilian populations. The USA does not object to this, but England turned down the Pope's suggestion, which Sp-n seconded as well. Based on all the information that was obtained by R., it can be concluded that Sp-n's trip did not meet its goal.
3. "Bank" received a report from Standley stating that he had informed Comrade Molotov about the upcoming meeting of Allied countries to discuss issuing provisions and proposed that the Sov. gov't send a delegate to this meeting. In response, Comrade Molotov supposedly expressed a wish that in the future, questions of conducting this or that meeting be discussed with the Soviet gov't as well.
According to Standley's report, the Poles had told him that the Soviet gov't was not addressing their complaints about the supposedly compulsory adoption of Soviet citizenship for Poles living in the USSR, on pain of expulsion.
According to R., not one of the reports by Standley he had read betray any hint of anti-Soviet prejudice.
4. For now, Americans are not hiring any German immigrants. At the same time, however, Cabin has been asked to thoroughly study who could be hired. Thus, a certain Walter Dorn, Chief of the Division of Foreign Nationalities Groups at Cabin, was sent to Mexico to study the question of German emigrants (including CP members).
5. According to the Polish ambassador to the USA, Ciechanowski, the politics and claims of the Polish people are not supported by "Radio Station" supposedly because the people working there are for the most part Jews (both local and immigrant). C. intends to conduct a campaign against "Radio Station" if it does not rethink its line of conduct.
R. explained that Radio Station has instructions not to respond to the "Poles' complaints" in its propaganda work.

p.16   (Undated.)
R. does practically nothing. His excuse is that there isn't any important information. The other day, he became a U.S. citizen ➔ bit of a coward. Working in the *Foreign Nationalities' Branch*" of the OSS. "Vardo" herself is unable to see him often. "Mary" has instructions to pressure R. and force him to work.
We have not yet given R. any specific assignments, having indicated only that we are interested in information about Germany and its allies.

p.17   Mailing NY – M 1.9.43.
[We have taken an interest in Herbert Marcuse in view of his work at "Cabin." A close friend of Ruff's. The exact nature of his work

White Notebook #3

in the OSS is unknown. 'Noah' knows M. through Germany and thinks that although he did
not belong to any party there, he was very close to the fellowcountrymen.

p.20   Information based on a report by "Mary" from 6.1.44
"When Mary last saw Ruff, he asked him outright about the reasons for his inefficiency.
'Mary' wanted to find out if R. had changed his mind about working for us, or if there was
some oth. reason. R. answered the following:
'I have not changed my mind. If anything truly important comes up, I will tell you without
hesitation.
He then gave the usual explanation that he did not have anything worth telling us about, that
90% of everything he learns appears in the newspapers a few days later, and that precautions
had been taken recently to safeguard info. in connection with massive war preparations.
During the same meeting, R. told 'Mary' some information about Germany, the views of Gen.
Marshall, Roosevelt, and Churchill on the second front, etc. Based on an assessment by
station chief Maxim, this information is of merely informational interest."

p.27   R. reported that in the Mid. East, contingents of the Yugoslav army have begun crossing over
to the side of the partisans. Opinions differ among English military representatives under
Mihailovic: senior officer Armstrong supports the full backing of Mihailovic; jr. officer
McLean supports the partisans [Tito].

p.22   INFO 1st derect. of the NKGB gave a low assessment of R's information (on Yugoslavia)
(Apr. '44)

p.23   Maxim delivered from Wash. on 13.6.44 "Mary's" report.
On 10 June 1944, R. informed Mary that a Cabin representative at the Amer. embassy in
Bern (Switzerland), Dulles whom we know, telegraphed the following info. to Bank:
Supposedly, General von Brauchitsch came to him personally from Germany, and said that on
behalf of a group of servicemen, he was offering peace on the following terms:
1. This group of military men would overthrow Hitler.
2. A military gov't would be established, which would agree to unconditional surrender.
3. Sov. forces should not take part in occupying any German territory.
To this message, the director of Bank replied to Dulles that without the involvement of its
allies, the Americans would not conduct any peace negotiations with Germany.
Around the 25th-26th of May, R. reported the following to Mary:
Dulles informed Bank that he had been approached by a representative of a German group.
This group is made up of prominent military men, including Zeitzler, industrialists, and right-
wing socialist democrats who had remained in Ger. The group offered to conduct peace
negotiations on terms that occupied territories in W. Europe would be cleared of German
forces and they would have freedom to operate in the East in order to continue the war against
the USSR.
The dir. of Bank supposedly informed Gromyko of this offer. The bureau is checking this
information through oth. sources.

White Notebook #3

The bureau adds that in spite of the fact that R. gives little information, all of his previous reports have been corroborated by reports from oth. probationers at "Cabin."

p.24   Report (17.7.44)
         "All the information that came from R. – superficial; the report that Robinson (chief of the Russian Division of Cabin) has a report on the Caucasus is worthy of attention. We suspect that the latest reports are dis.[75] "

p.27   Report dated 4.4.45.
         [R's report on Dulles' negotiations in Bern is of great interest.]
         "At one time, this info. was labeled disinformation by the operational department. However, subsequent agent materials have confirmed that Amer. intelligence had conducted negotiations with representatives from the German opposition in Bern at that time."
         [Report on the back: "In view of 'Vardo's' departure from the USA in July 1944, the connection with 'Ruff' was broken off. Contact with 'Ruff' can only be established through 'Vacek'."]

p.28   Report by "Noah" from 8.8.45.
         Left for London. On General Jackson's staff. Works on questions regarding war criminals.

---

11. *Rockefeller Grant to Brandeis University for Herbert Marcuse, June 8, 1959, RG 1.2, Series 200, Box 481, Folder 4113, Rockefeller Archive Center.*

This grant for a little over $67,000 in 2024 dollars was for a research project that was obviously a preliminary draft of *One-Dimensional Man*. Two of Marcuse's friends, whom he had met through his intelligence work, Barrington Moore and Philip Mosely, wrote letters of recommendation for his grant proposal (both of them mentioned his intelligence connections in their letters). What is arguably Marcuse's most famous book was thus funded by the capitalist ruling class and vetted by a current (Mosely) and a former (Moore) intelligence operative. This grant was, moreover, part of the Rockefeller's broader Program in Legal and Political Philosophy, which sought to ideologically reshape political thought in ways beneficial to its interests. The Rockefeller Foundation had contributed the equivalent of $726,000 in 2024 dollars to these efforts at the date of this grant, but this number would grow to the current equivalent of $20 million over the course of a decade.

[DOCUMENT REPRODUCED ON PAGE 383]

GA 53 5967

FILES

Brandeis Univ

Marcuse

GRANT IN AID to Brandeis University to enable Dr. Herbert Marcuse, Professor of Politics and Philosophy, to undertake research on cultural changes in contemporary industrial society and their interrelation with political trends.

AMOUNT: $6,250   JUN 12 1959   ACCOUNT: To be charged to RF 58209-SS leaving a balance of $ 170,860.

PREVIOUS INTEREST: Since 1957, The Rockefeller Foundation has contributed a total of $22,000 to Brandeis University for research in the social sciences. In 1954, when on the Faculty of the Russian Research Center at Harvard University, Dr. Marcuse received a grant in aid of $9,900 under the Humanities Program for a preliminary critique of Soviet social philosophy. The grant herein recommended is the fourteenth in the Foundation's 1959 program in Legal and Political Philosophy, under which to date a total of $67,395 has been expended.

GENERAL DESCRIPTION: Professor Marcuse is the author of major works such as Reason and Revolution: Hegel and the Rise of Social Theory, Eros and Civilisation (a study of Freud's theories), and Soviet Marxism. His present project calls for an appraisal of the intellectual climate of modern industrial civilization. This study will enable Professor Marcuse to deal directly with the problems of contemporary society rather than indirectly through his analysis of earlier writers. He will assess the interrelation between culture and political trends, including new systems of political values and shifts in political philosophy and political behavior. He will investigate whether western society is undergoing a cultural and political transformation of a system which predates industrial society itself, and will test out in case studies the degree to which humanitarian and liberal values of western civilization have been supplanted.

Brandeis University has released Professor Marcuse from his teaching and other duties for approximately half-time during the academic year 1959-60 and will continue to pay his salary for half the year. The proposed grant of $6,250, which was recommended by the Foundation's Advisory Committee in Legal and Political Philosophy at its meeting in February, 1959, is intended to cover the other half of Professor Marcuse's salary for the academic year while he is engaged in research.

A grant of $6,250, or as much thereof as may be necessary, to Brandeis University to enable Dr. Herbert Marcuse, Professor of Politics and Philosophy, to undertake research on cultural changes in contemporary industrial society and their interrelation with political trends, is hereby approved; this sum to be available for one year beginning approximately September 1, 1959.

_____
Associate Director for Social Sciences

ASS'T. Comptroller _____

_____
Executive Vice-President

APPROVED: JUN 8 1959 _____

12. *Herbert Marcuse's FBI file (number 9-48255), obtained through a Freedom of Information Act (FOIA) request, excerpts.*

This 1969 report on Marcuse, from his 607-page FBI file, includes a biographical sketch that mentions his time in the State Department. It is followed by a long review of his 1969 book, *An Essay on Liberation*. Noting that Marcuse was a powerful force in the New Left, it claims that "he advocates eliminating poverty and work but offers no formula for achieving this goal." It also states that the majority of young radicals probably do not understand his philosophy and "remain oblivious to the fact that he is using them as tools in an attempt to gain an intellectual dictatorship." The 1971 memorandum on Marcuse's attendance at the annual convention of the American Philosophical Association reveals how closely the FBI was following Marcuse toward the end of his life. It obtained his travel itineraries and interviewed informants in the academic world (the political philosopher Frank Strauss Meyer is named in other documents as one of the FBI's snitches). The Bureau also recorded at least one of Marcuse's lectures and circulated the recording among its staff, as other documents reveal.

[DOCUMENTS REPRODUCED ON PAGES 385–89]

UNITED STATES GOVERNMENT

Memorandum

1 – Mr. DeLoach
1 – Mr. Sullivan
1 – Mr. C. D. Brennan

TO   :   Mr. W. C. Sullivan

DATE: September 11, 1969

FROM   :   C. D. Brennan

1 – Miss Butler
1 – Mr. Shackelford
1 – Miss Muir

SUBJECT :   BOOK REVIEW
"AN ESSAY ON LIBERATION"
BY HERBERT MARCUSE
INTERNAL SECURITY – NEW LEFT MATTER

This memorandum presents a review of captioned book, which is being retained in the Communist Infiltrated and New Left Groups Unit, Internal Security Section, Domestic Intelligence Division.

SYNOPSIS: Marcuse, a professor in the Philosophy Department of the University of California at San Diego, has been described as the philosopher of the New Left. Captioned book reiterates Marcuse's oft repeated advocacy of the need for a revolution in the United States. Recognizing that the workers in America have done so well under the free enterprise system that they want no part of any Marxian revolution, Marcuse turns to active minorities "mainly among the young, middle-class intelligentsia and the ghetto population," to carry the revolution, guided, of course, by the intellectuals. The goal of Marcuse's revolution is the creation of a "society in which the abolition of poverty and toil terminates in a universe where the sensuous, the playful, the calm and the beautiful become forms of existence." He advocates eliminating poverty and work but offers no formula for achieving this goal except to say this will involve the elimination of private property and the institution of economic central planning. He states that a precondition of his revolution is a weakening of the moral fiber and undermining faith in accepted values. Marcuse is a powerful force in the New Left movement today. It is doubtful that the majority of the young radicals really understand his philosophy, but so long as he advocates overthrow of the present system by, in their terminology, simply "doing their thing," they remain oblivious to the fact that he is using them as tools in an attempt to gain an intellectual dictatorship. The FBI is not mentioned in the book.

REC-20

ACTION: None. For information.

LM/lm
(8)
100-445771
1 – 62-46855 (Book Review file)

DETAILS – Page Two

55

56 SEP 24 1969

Memorandum for Mr. W. C. Sullivan
RE: BOOK REVIEW
      "AN ESSAY ON LIBERATION"
      BY HERBERT MARCUSE
100-445771

DETAILS:

The Author

        Herbert Marcuse (pronounced Markooza) has been
described as the foremost literary symbol and philosopher of
the New Left, as well as "the idol of the student rebels."
He was born in 1898 in Berlin, Germany, immigrated to this
country in 1934, and was naturalized in 1940. He was in the
State Department from 1945 to 1950. Subsequently, he was
affiliated with Harvard and Columbia Universities, and served
as Professor of Politics and Philosophy at Brandeis University
from 1954 to 1965. He is presently a professor in the Philosophy
Department at the University of California at San Diego. Marcuse
has been influenced by the writings of philosopher George Hegel,
psychoanalyst Sigmund Freud, and by Karl Marx. He admits he
is a Marxist but feels Marxism must be updated.

FBI Not Mentioned

        There are no references to the FBI in captioned book.

Book Review

        Captioned book, dedicated by Marcuse to "young
militants," was published in 1969 and reiterates Marcuse's oft
repeated advocacy of the need for a revolution in the United
States.

        Marcuse expresses a hatred of all liberal democracies
and their economic systems based on free enterprise, which, by
their success in improving the standard of living of the masses,
have made one of Marcuse's heroes, Karl Marx, appear ridiculous.
Marx predicted that the capitalist system would produce increasing
misery for the workers and that this would eventually cause its
collapse. Marcuse finds himself in the position of being forced
to reject Marx's cherished working class as the instrument of
revolutionary change because he recognizes that the workers have
done so well under the free enterprise system that they want no
part of any Marxian revolution. He says this would be "against

                        - 2 -   CONTINUED - OVER

51

Memorandum for Mr. W. C. Sullivan
RE: BOOK REVIEW
      "AN ESSAY ON LIBERATION"
      BY HERBERT MARCUSE
100-445771

the will and against the interest of the majority of people."

Who, then, will be the carriers of the revolution?
It can be done, according to Marcuse, only by "a new type of man
....a type of man with a different sensitivity as well as
consciousness; men who would speak a different language, have
different gestures, follow different impulses; men who have
developed an instinctual barrier against cruelty, brutality,
and ugliness." Marcuse finds his last hope for a truly free
society in active minorities, "mainly among the young, middle-
class intelligentsia and the ghetto population." These minor
will be guided by the intellectuals, who, Marcuse is convinced,
know what is best for mankind. It is difficult to fit the young
militants of the New Left into the roles of supermen envisioned
by Marcuse, although when he says they must be a group of people
who will reject conventional morality, who will 'break with the
familiar, the routine ways of seeing, hearing, feeling, understanding things," it is clear he looks hopefully toward the young
dissidents who have demonstrated their break with conventional
values by experimenting with drugs, sex, and riots.

The goal of Marcuse's planned revolution is the creation
of a "society in which the abolition of poverty and toil terminate
in a universe where the sensuous, the playful, the calm and the
beautiful become forms of existence." He advocates eliminating
poverty and work but offers no formula for achieving this goal,
except to say this will involve the elimination of private
property and the institution of economic central planning. He
states that a precondition of his revolution is a weakening of
the moral fiber and undermining faith in accepted values.

Marcuse, who has been publicly described as the "godfather of the student revolt" and the "idol of the student
rebels," is a powerful force in the New Left movement today.
It is doubtful that the majority of the young radicals really
understand his philosophy, but so long as he advocates overthrow
of the present system by, in their terminology, simply "doing
their thing," they remain oblivious to the fact that he is
using them as tools in an attempt to gain an intellectual
dictatorship.

BEST COPY AVAILABLE

GTA FPMR (41 CFR) 101-11.6

UNITED STATES GOVERNMENT

Memorandum

TO   : DIRECTOR, FBI ▓▓▓▓▓▓▓ *b7C*

                                              DATE: 4/3/71

FROM   : SAC, LOS ANGELES ▓▓▓▓▓▓▓ *b7C*

SUBJECT: ▓▓▓▓▓▓▓▓▓▓ *b7C*
         SM-ANA (EXTREMIST)(KEY ACTIVIST)
         OO:SAN FRANCISCO

    ReSeattle tel to Bureau, Los Angeles, Newark, New
York, San Francisco and WFO, 4/1/71, captioned as above,
indicating subject departed San Francisco on 3/25/71 to
attend convention of the American Philosophical Association
at the Beverly Hilton Hotel, and was to return the following
day.

▓▓
▓▓
Philosophical Association (APA) held its convention at that
hotel over the three day period from March 25-27, 1971.

▓▓▓▓▓▓▓▓▓▓▓▓▓▓▓▓▓ did have a printed program of some
scheduled speakers. An examination of this latter program
failed to reflect the name of ▓▓▓▓▓▓▓ as one of the scheduled
speakers. ▓▓▓▓▓▓▓ pointed out that this was merely a partial
listing. It was noted that Dr. HERBERT MARCUSE was listed
as one of the featured speakers and panelists at the convention. According to ▓▓▓▓▓▓▓, MARCUSE appeared as scheduled.
The Association for Symbolic Logic (ASL) participated in this
convention with the APA.

    Because of the information contained herein regarding
HERBERT MARCUSE, a copy of this letter is being furnished the
San Diego Division for its information.

    3 - Bureau (RM)
        1 - Bufile 100-445771(HERBERT MARCUSE)
    2 - Newark (RM)
    2 - New York (RM)
    2 - San Diego (RM)
        1 - 100-13701 (HERBERT MARCUSE)
    2 - San Francisco(RM)
    3 - Seattle
        1 - 176-66 ▓▓▓▓▓▓▓▓ *b7C*
    2 - Los Angeles ▓▓▓▓▓▓▓▓ *b7C*
        1 - 100-68462(HERBERT MARCUSE)

LA 100-76453

67c
67d

No further investigation in this matter is being undertaken in the Los Angeles Division at this time and this
matter is considered RUC.

ALL INDIVIDUALS INVOLVED IN NEW LEFT EXTREMIST

ACTIVITY SHOULD BE CONSIDERED DANGEROUS BECAUSE

OF THEIR KNOWN ADVOCACY AND USE OF EXPLOSIVES,

REPORTED ACQUISITION OF FIREARMS AND INCENDIARY

DEVICES, AND KNOWN PROPENSITY FOR VIOLENCE.

- 2 * -

PHOTOS

Administrative Secretary of the Congress for Cultural Freedom (CCF) and undercover CIA officer Michael Josselson (looking at camera), flanked by what appear to be Gerald Stern on the left and W. H. Auden and René Tavernier on the right, at a CCF anniversary party between 1952 and 1954 (the precise date is not specified). *Source*: International Association for Cultural Freedom Records, Box 658, Folder 4, Hanna Holborn Gray Special Collections Research Center at the University of Chicago.

Michael Josselson and dissident Polish poet Czesław Miłosz (left to right) at a CCF anniversary party between 1952 and 1954 (the precise date is not specified). *Source*: International Association for Cultural Freedom Records, Box 658, Folder 4, Special Collections Research Center at the University of Chicago.

Four major CCF operators at the 1950 Berlin conference: Arthur Koestler, Irving Brown, James Burnham, and Melvin Lasky (left to right). Koestler was a prominent anticommunist activist and writer who worked for the Information Research Department and helped found the CCF. Brown, who worked for CIA agent Jay Lovestone, was one of the chief union activists who worked hand-in-glove with the Agency to try to destroy communist unions around the world (while also serving on the CCF's steering committee). Burnham was a CCF intellectual and a philosophy professor at New York University who moonlighted for the CIA. Lasky, the editor of *Der Monat*, was a witting CIA agent and a member of the CCF's original steering committee, as well as the leader of the CIA's cultural and intellectual war in Germany (in this capacity, he corresponded and collaborated with the Frankfurt School, primarily via Theodor Adorno). *Source*: International Association for Cultural Freedom Records, Box 538, Folder 3, Hanna Holborn Gray Special Collections Research Center at the University of Chicago.

Aerial photograph of the 1950 CCF conference in Berlin, which reveals the massive scale of the event. 4,000 people were in attendance, and the delegates from outside of the Western sector of Berlin were all brought in on military aircraft in what Koestler would later refer to as an "intellectual airlift" (Saunders, *The Cultural Cold War*, 74). *Source*: International Association for Cultural Freedom Records, Box 538, Folder 4, Hanna Holborn Gray Special Collections Research Center at the University of Chicago.

Closing session of the 1950 CCF conference in Berlin, with Heinrich Böll at the podium, Sidney Hook in the foreground, and CIA agent Melvin Lasky on Hook's right. Böll was an anticommunist writer with multiple ties to CIA activities. Hook was a philosophy professor at New York University, as well as a CIA consultant and collaborator deeply involved in the anticommunist psywar. *Source*: International Association for Cultural Freedom Records, Box 538, Folder 4, Hanna Holborn Gray Special Collections Research Center at the University of Chicago.

Cartoon in the June 25, 1950, edition of the *Tägliche Rundschau*, a newspaper published by the Soviet Army in East Germany. It depicts the financing of the "Kongress für kulturelle Freiheit" (CCF) by the U.S. government, and more specifically what appears to be a reference to the Central Investigation Command (CIC), a parent organization to the CIA. This Soviet news outlet thereby captured—in simplified form—what is most essential to know about the CCF: far from being a free organization, it was funded and controlled from behind the scenes by the world's leading imperialist state. *Source*: Petra Schrott, ed., *Eine Kulturmetropole wird geteilt: Literarisches Leben in Berlin (West) 1945 bis 1961* (Berlin: Kulturamt Schöneberg, 1987), 41, https://www.bpb.de/themen/deutschlandarchiv/132953/eklat-beim-ersten-gesamt-deutschen-schriftstellerkongress-in-ost-berlin/?type=galerie&show=image&k=2.

François Bondy, Robert Oppenheimer, George Kennan, and Melvin Lasky (left to right) at a CCF event in Rheinfelden, Germany, 1959. Bondy was a member of the CCF Secretariat and the editor of its magazine *Preuves*. Oppenheimer, the well-known physicist and director of the Manhattan Project's Los Alamos laboratory, was a CCF collaborator. Kennan was a major U.S. State Department operative most known for advocating a policy of containment of the Soviet Union, as well as a CCF collaborator. His presence at CCF events should have been a clear indication of its orientation (regardless of CIA funding). *Source*: International Association for Cultural Freedom Records, Box 540, Folder 2, Hanna Holborn Gray Special Collections Research Center at the University of Chicago.

Michael Polanyi, George Kennan, Carlo Schmid, Nicolas Nabokov, Salvador de Madariaga, Seth Cudjoe, and Denis de Rougemont (left to right) at the 1960 CCF conference in Berlin. Polanyi was a member of the CCF's Executive Committee. Schmid was a leader in the Social Democratic Party of Germany. Nabokov was the secretary general of the CCF, and de Madariaga was one of its honorary presidents. Cudjoe was a physician and artist, and de Rougement was the president of the CCF's Executive Committee. *Source*: International Association for Cultural Freedom Records, Box 540, Folder 7, Hanna Holborn Gray Special Collections Research Center at the University of Chicago.

Willy Brandt, Nicolas Nabokov, and Robert Oppenheimer (left to right) at the 1960 CCF conference in Berlin. Brandt was a German politician and, from 1964 to 1987, leader of the Social Democratic Party of Germany. *Source*: International Association for Cultural Freedom Records, Box 540, Folder 7, Hanna Holborn Gray Special Collections Research Center at the University of Chicago.

Theodor Heuss, Sidney Hook, Raymond Aron, and Nicolas Nabokov (four men with visible faces, left to right) at the 1960 CCF conference in Berlin. Heuss was the first president of West Germany and one of the CCF's honorary presidents. Aron was the CCF's philosophic front man in France and a member of its inner circle. *Source*: International Association for Cultural Freedom Records, Box 540, Folder 9, Hanna Holborn Gray Special Collections Research Center at the University of Chicago.

This photograph of Theodor Adorno is included in a folder in the CCF archive titled "Berlin, 1960," presumably because Adorno was one of the recognized CCF collaborators in Germany at the time. *Source*: International Association for Cultural Freedom Records, Box 540, Folder 4, Hanna Holborn Gray Special Collections Research Center at the University of Chicago.

European Seminar with CIA agent Melvin Lasky at the center flanked by CCF operatives Denis de Rougemont on his right and François Bondy (second from his left), Munich, Germany, 1966. *Source*: International Association for Cultural Freedom Records, Box 543, Folder 9, Hanna Holborn Gray Special Collections Research Center at the University of Chicago.

Shepard Stone at an International Association for Cultural Freedom (IACF) event, Columbia University, 1972. Stone had a background in military intelligence and served as the Director of International Affairs at the Ford Foundation, where he worked closely with the CIA on funding cultural projects around the world. *Source*: International Association for Cultural Freedom Records, Box 543, Folder 12, Hanna Holborn Gray Special Collections Research Center at the University of Chicago.

G. C. McGhee, John J. McCloy, and J. H. Morse (left to right) at an IACF event, Columbia University, 1972. McGhee was a U.S. American oilman and diplomat with a background in naval air intelligence. McCloy was known as the "Chairman of the American Establishment" and was a major operator in the U.S. government and in the most powerful institutions of the corporatocracy. Scant biographical information is available regarding Morse. *Source*: International Association for Cultural Freedom Records, Box 543, Folder 12, Hanna Holborn Gray Special Collections Research Center at the University of Chicago.

Herbert Marcuse circa 1937 in his office at Columbia University, a few years before he began working for the U.S. national security state. Source: Nachlass Herbert Marcuse, Na 1, 1292, Goethe Universität, Frankfurt: https://hessenbox-a10.rz.uni-frankfurt.de/getlink/fi17RERpvD8Q9GpK2PT6to/.

Max Horkheimer and Theodor Adorno (left to right) in 1964 (Jürgen Habermas is on the far right). *Source*: Jeremy J. Shapiro/Creative Commons.

Geroid Tanquary Robinson (left) and Philip E. Mosely (top center), late 1940s. Robinson was the head of the USSR Division in the OSS, helped found the Russian Institute (RI) at Columbia University that continued the work of the OSS's USSR Division, and invited Marcuse to join his team. Mosely was a major psywarrior who was at the center of the Rockefeller Foundation's Marxism-Leninism Project, worked as a consultant for major foundations, directed the RI at Columbia, served as a high-level and long-standing CIA collaborator, and was—along with OSS operative and CIA collaborator William Langer—"Marcuse's most important supporter from the academic establishment" (Tim B. Müller, *Krieger und Gelehrte: Herbert Marcuse und die Denksysteme im Kalten Krieg*, Hamburg: Hamburger Edition, 2011, 236). Mosely was also close personal friends with Marcuse, and their families regularly met. He promoted Marcuse's work in his powerful networks, helped him secure major grants from the ruling class, regularly invited him to the RI, and made him a member of the Honorable Foreign Policy Society of the Council on Foreign Relations. It was at Mosely's request that the Rockefeller Foundation funded Marcuse's long sojourn in Paris, where he was "entrusted with the mission of drawing the Marxists among France's intellectuals into the Western camp without them having to give up their Marxism" (ibid., 523). *Source*: Rockefeller Archive Center, Sleepy Hollow, NY, https://harriman.columbia.edu/harriman-at-75-exhibit/people-books-and-archives-1903-2021-part-ii/.

INDEX